## DATE DUE

| | | | |
|---|---|---|---|
| DE 3 '96 | | | |
| NV 6 '98 | | | |
| AP 20 '99 | | | |
| NY 17 '99 | | | |
| 66 9 '00 | | | |
| DE 8 '99 | | | |
| JE 10 '00 | | | |
| DE 1 8 '00 | | | |
| NV 15 '03 | | | |
| OC 21 '04 | | | |
| NO 11 '04 | | | |
| NO 30 '05 | | | |
| JE 1 0 '09 | | | |
| JE - 9 '10 | | | |
| | | | |
| | | | |

# Taking SIDES

## Clashing Views on Controversial Psychological Issues

### Eighth Edition

**Edited, Selected, and with Introductions by**

**Brent Slife**
*Baylor University*

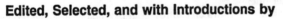

**The Dushkin Publishing Group, Inc.**

*Conor, Nathan, and Jacob*

Taking sides. Clashing view
on controversial

ledgments

Steiner/DPG
Part 2   Rebecca Holland/DPG
Part 3   UN Photo 154234/John Isaac
Part 4   UN Photo 152619/Bedrich Grunzweig
Part 5   Cheryl Greenleaf/DPG
Part 6   Lisa Holmes Doebrick/DPG
Part 7   Courtesy of the Yerkes Primate Research Center/Emory University

### Cover Art Acknowledgment

Charles Vitelli

Manufactured in the United States of America

Eighth Edition, Third Printing

### Library of Congress Cataloging-in-Publication Data

Main entry under title:
   Taking sides: clashing views on controversial psychological issues/edited, selected, and
with introductions by Brent Slife.—8th ed.
   Includes bibliographical references and index.
   1. Psychology. 2. Psychotherapy. I. Slife, Brent, *comp.*
     BF149.T34                                            150—dc20
     ISBN: 1–56134–294–7                                  93–48692

 Printed on Recycled Paper

DPG

*The Dushkin Publishing Group, Inc.*

# PREFACE

Critical thinking skills are a significant component of a meaningful education, and this book is specifically designed to stimulate critical thinking and initiate lively and informed dialogue on psychological issues. In this book I present 38 selections, arranged in pro and con pairs, that address a total of 19 different controversial issues in psychology. The opposing views demonstrate that even experts can derive conflicting conclusions and opinions from the same body of information.

A dialogue approach to learning is certainly not new. The ancient Greek philosopher Socrates engaged in it with his students some 2,400 years ago. His point-counterpoint procedure was termed a *dialectic*. Although Socrates and his companions hoped eventually to know the "truth" by this method, they did not see the dialectic as having a predetermined end. There were no right answers to know or facts to memorize. The emphasis in this learning method is on how to evaluate information—on developing reasoning skills.

It is in this dialectical spirit that *Taking Sides: Clashing Views on Controversial Psychological Issues* was originally compiled, and it has guided me through this eighth edition as well. To encourage and stimulate discussion and to focus the debates in this volume, each issue is expressed in terms of a single question and answered with two points of view. But certainly the reader should not feel confined to adopt only one or the other of the positions presented. There are positions that fall between the views expressed, or totally outside them, and I encourage you to fashion your own conclusions.

Some of the questions raised in this volume go to the very heart of what psychology as a discipline is all about and the methods and manner in which psychologists work. Others address newly emerging concerns. In choosing readings I was guided by the following criteria: the readings had to be understandable to newcomers to psychology; they had to have academic substance; and they had to express markedly different points of view.

**Plan of the book**  Each issue in this volume has an issue *introduction*, which defines each author's position and sets the stage for debate. Also provided is a set of point-counterpoint statements that pertain to the issue—they should help get the dialogue off the ground. Each issue concludes with *challenge questions* to provoke further examination of the issue. The introduction and challenge questions are designed to assist the reader in achieving a critical and informed view on important psychological issues. At the back of the book is a listing of all the *contributors to this volume*, which gives information on the psychologists, psychiatrists, philosophers, professors, and social critics whose views are debated here.

**Changes to this edition**   This new edition has been significantly updated. There are 14 completely new issues: *Are Gender Differences Rooted in the Brain?* (Issue 1); *Does Body Chemistry Govern Eating Behavior?* (Issue 2); *Are Memories of Sexual Abuse Always Real?* (Issue 4); *Is Subliminal Advertising Effective?* (Issue 5); *Is Television Harmful to Children?* (Issue 7); *Should Formal Schooling Begin at an Earlier Age?* (Issue 8); *Can Sex Be an Addiction?* (Issue 10); *Is Alcoholism a Disease?* (Issue 11); *Does Abortion Have Severe Psychological Effects?* (Issue 12); *Are Self-Help Groups Helpful?* (Issue 13); *Is Abstinence the Best Treatment for Drug Addiction?* (Issue 14); *Is Pornography Harmful?* (Issue 16); *Is Marriage Psychologically Beneficial?* (Issue 17); and *Is Parapsychology a Credible Science?* (Issue 19). In addition, the NO article has been changed in the issue on mental attitude and health (Issue 3) in order to bring a fresh perspective to the debate. The issues that were dropped from the previous edition were done so on the recommendation of professors who let me know what worked and what could be improved. In all, there are 29 new selections.

**A word to the instructor**   An *Instructor's Manual With Test Questions* (multiple-choice and essay) is available through the publisher for the instructor using *Taking Sides* in the classroom. A general guidebook, *Using Taking Sides in the Classroom*, which discusses methods and techniques for integrating the pro-con approach into any classroom setting, is also available.

**Acknowledgments**   In working on this revision I received useful suggestions from many of the users of the previous edition, and I was able to incorporate many of their recommendations for new issues and new readings. I particularly wish to thank the following professors:

William T. Bailey
Eastern Illinois University

Marvin Brodsky
University of Manitoba

Joseph R. Coble
Clark Atlanta University

Paul F. Cunningham
Rivier College

Evan G. DeRenzo
Marymount University

Isabella Harty-Hugues
Miami-Dade Community College

Barbara J. Hermann
Gainesville College

Harold Herzog
Western Carolina University

Michael Hughmanick
West Valley College

Marita Rosch Inglehart
University of Michigan

Mary Inman
Trinity University

Miriam LeGare
California State University,
   Sacramento

Louis Marchand
Chesapeake College

Robert J. Moore
University of Regina

Jacqueline Muir-Broaddus
Southwestern University

Linda Musun-Miller
University of Arkansas at Little
    Rock

Elizabeth Ozorak
Allegheny College

Marc Riess
Middlebury College

Bruce C. Stockin
Westmont College

Carl Thompson
Wabash College

Deb Vandervoort
University of Hawaii at Hilo

In addition, special thanks go to Mimi Egan, program manager of the Taking Sides series at The Dushkin Publishing Group, for her perspicacity.

Brent Slife
Baylor University

# CONTENTS IN BRIEF

# CONTENTS

Doreen Kimura argues that research has led to the discovery of the neurological and hormonal processes that lead to differences between men and women. Carol Tavris asserts that neurological explanations of gender differences are the result of scientific biases.

Hara Estroff Marano asserts that eating behavior is profoundly affected by neurochemicals in the brain. Peter Herman and Janet Polivy contend that eating is a psychological issue, influenced by an individual's thinking and beliefs about food.

Bernard Dixon proposes that a positive mental attitude can prevent illness because it reduces psychological stress, which can impair functioning of the immune system. Marcia Angell argues that maintaining a positive attitude will not ward off disease.

groups because they give everyone the status of victim and they have great potential for abuse.

---

Ray Hoskins supports abstinance for all individuals who are recovering from addictions, especially alcohol addiction. Michael S. Levy argues that abstinence may not be the best treatment for all addicts and that treatment for addiction is best tailored to each individual's specific needs.

---

Raymond R. Crowe argues that not only is ECT safe and effective, but it also acts quickly after many other treatments have failed. Leonard Roy Frank asserts that ECT only seems effective because of the brain damage it causes and that many practitioners of ECT underestimate its risks.

---

Victor Cline argues that pornography poses a great harm to viewers because it degrades women and desensitizes males to sexual violence. F. M. Christensen contends that there is little evidence that pornography is harmful and that pornography is only a scapegoat for other societal problems.

# INTRODUCTION

## Ways of Looking at Psychological Issues

Brent Slife

In a sense, all of life may be viewed as a trial. We are all members of the jury called upon to participate in decisions that will affect the lives of friends, neighbors, family, and ourselves. Somewhere along the line, even though we cannot be certain about what is "true," we must make a decision that calls for some sort of action. We must take a side.

People who are alert to social issues frequently ask specific questions to help them in their search for evidence. After gathering evidence from various points of view, they deliberate and make decisions. But, as any involved citizen is keenly aware, knowing the "facts" often is not enough to make useful decisions. It is seeing relationships after examining evidence from all sides and the development of personal insights that makes it worthwhile to gather "facts."

### YOUR LIFE IS IN YOUR HANDS—IF YOU CHOOSE

The issues that stimulate heated controversy usually do so because they touch our lives and because there is no final proof or fully objective answer. Although it may not always be obvious how they do it, issues have the potential to command our personal destinies, as people who wish to have a say in their future are well aware.

The process of our personal deliberation about these questions and attempts to find answers constitutes, in large measure, our role in the world in which we live. If we choose *not* to explore, we are placing major decisions about our lives in the hands of parents, teachers, salespeople, government officials, and others in our local community, state, and nation. On the other hand, a concern for exploring these issues can be a prelude to active community involvement and to taking a vital part in fashioning our future.

How some of the psychological issues in this anthology affect you, especially if you have no prior knowledge of them, may not be immediately apparent. However, coming to grips with questions such as *Can Mental Attitude Affect Biological Disease?* (Issue 3) is very likely to provide personal direction in your own life.

# DISTINGUISHING TYPES OF INFORMATION

In the exploration of public issues, there are certain skills that lead to constructive resolutions. Chief among these is the ability to distinguish among the various types of information we all use to arrive at conclusions. We become lost in a discussion when we cannot distinguish between fact and opinion or between evidence based on data and evidence based on values. When we can sort out types of information, we are prepared for an orderly discussion based on a combination of objective evidence and personal values. In the process, we frequently find out more about ourselves and what we really consider important in life.

In order to help you develop the ability to make these distinctions, several types of information are described below. A definition for each term is in italics.

## Hypothesis

*A statement of how at least two events or conditions may be related.* Hypotheses are stated as though they are answers to questions, but they are actually guesses. The reason for stating a hypothesis is to make clear what events or conditions must be investigated. The definitions for the terms in a hypothesis are very often at the heart of the problem being discussed. Participants in a discussion may be arguing without getting anywhere simply because they each have a different meaning for the same term and do not realize it. A research investigation is done in order to determine whether a hypothesis should be accepted or rejected.

## Data

*The recorded observations and measurements collected in a research study.* The data in some cases may be simply a collection of numbers. They indicate what the results of the study are *before* any conclusions are made.

## Evidence

*The application of data to confirm or reject a hypothesis that has been previously stated.* This involves a use of the data to make conclusions.

## Conclusions

*The final inferences concerning what the evidence allows us to assume.*

## Fact

*Information that we take to be true because it is widely accepted.* Facts are the trickiest kinds of information. In a court of law, the jury's responsibility is to decide what the "facts" are. The court's responsibility is to decide what is meant by the law. It is common in science for new facts to change old facts. In some cases, it can be done by a simple vote. Mental disorders, or "abnormalities," are officially designated and classified by a committee of the American Psychiatric Association. Trustees of the association vote to approve or disapprove of the committee's classifications. Since these experts agree that schizophrenia is abnormal, it is therefore a "fact."

### Opinion
*A judgment made by an individual who interprets the data in terms of what makes personal sense.* Opinions are often confused with objective evidence.

### Values
*Ideas held by an individual or a group about the way things ought to be.* Values are extremely important determinants of how we live our lives and make decisions. We all have values, but we are often not clear about them until we think about them or discuss issues with other people.

## FREE WILL AND DETERMINISM

Underlying many public issues dealing with the scientific study of humans is a fundamental question that philosophers have asked for centuries: Do people have *free will* to exert control over their own destinies, or are their destinies completely *determined* by forces outside their control?

If you are a strong believer in *free will,* then while reading the issues here, you may take the position that we are always free to make a decision that will change the future.

If you are an advocate of *determinism,* then you will believe that what we are is already locked up in our genetic structures and that how we behave is fully determined by a combination of our past experiences and our environmental circumstances.

When scanning the questions in the table of contents, you will note that some of them are specifically concerned with the extent to which certain characteristics, such as intelligence, are inherited. Others are concerned with the value of using psychological knowledge to control the behavior of other people.

To find out why people are as they are, psychologists assume that there are reasons for people being as they are. In other words, our biology determines what we are, and conditions and events determine how we will behave.

One scientific strategy accepted by many psychologists in their search for causes assumes that human nature is lawful and ordered by conditions and events. We attempt to predict the fate of humans by studying the forces acting upon them and within them. The responsibility of a scientist is to find as many cause-and-effect relationships and explanations as possible.

The idea that things cause us to be what we are has been quite fruitful. It has helped us discover some highly predictable relationships. For example, if certain areas of the brain are destroyed, a person will not be able to remember events that happen after the brain injury. But what are the limitations of predictability? Would knowing everything about the brain enable us to predict everything about the person? This scientific strategy assumes that there are *no* limitations to predictability. According to this notion, *everything* is caused by *something*.

This is primarily the premise of determinism. It keeps psychologists looking for causes that determine human affairs. It is not necessarily a "fact" or a "truth." In discussing these issues, you will soon begin to appreciate the difference between making assumptions about truth and making assumptions for strategic reasons.

Although psychologists may appear to take the strict determinist position in the search for causes, they are, nevertheless, very likely to take the free will position that we must accept personal responsibility for our conduct.

## PSYCHOLOGICAL APPROACHES

In making sense of information, we all use a framework to put it all together. As individuals, we are not always aware of our own frameworks. They are hard to recognize because we may change our way of looking at information from time to time. You may view the same information in a variety of ways, depending upon whether it comes from your boyfriend or girlfriend, your mother or father, your teacher, or today's newspaper.

The more we engage in specific attempts to put information together, the more likely we are to achieve personal insights and to believe that we know who we are and what we are like. This development of a sense of personal identity is a part of the excitement of discussing issues.

Just as we personally develop frameworks for putting information together, so do specialists in human behavior. In the brief history of psychology, specialists have developed a variety of scientific approaches. Several modern perspectives have evolved from these and are easily recognizable today. They may be roughly categorized as follows.

### Biological
In its extreme form, this point of view suggests that if we fully understood all there is to know about the human body and how all of its parts operate, we would understand all we wish to know about our emotions, creative urges, and social behavior. In this extreme form, we are just mechanisms. Prediction and control of human behavior may be achieved by fine technicians just as prediction and control of automobile performance may be achieved by fine engineers and mechanics.

If we knew enough, according to this view, we could eliminate fighting by cutting it out of the brain, or we could combat the blues by swallowing pills to change our personal chemistry.

### Psychodynamic
This point of view emphasizes that the behavior we are aware of in ourselves and in others stems from forces within us that we are not normally aware

of—that we are born with an inventory of drives and instincts that respond to life's experiences. These hidden inner forces are considered responsible for the way we feel, think, and behave. To understand these forces is to understand human nature, according to this school of thought.

## Behavioral

This perspective contends that we need only observe how a person responds to stimuli in the environment; all that we would ever want to know about a person can be described in terms of the individual's behavior. If we achieve control over the environment, we achieve control over the individual.

You may have noticed how obvious the deterministic assumption is in these frameworks. Humans are acted upon by their inherited nature, by the environment, or by a combination of both. The following two frameworks lean more toward the direction of free will, with humans taking an active role in decision-making.

## Cognitive

Human beings receive information about the world in which they live, and then they do something with it. From the cognitive viewpoint, we are active agents in choosing which information we will receive. After receiving information, we process it in some personally meaningful way and then either use it or put it away in the form of memories for later use. Here, consideration for the active selection and personal processing of information implies that we are not merely passive responders.

## Humanistic

This point of view grew specifically out of a reaction against other psychological perspectives that emphasize the forces determining human destiny. The humanistic orientation places emphasis on our *human* nature, rather than our mechanistic nature. It emphasizes how we see and think about ourselves, rather than what we do. It is a concern for our striving to become more than we are at this moment, a striving to fill our potentials.

There is yet another orientation: the *eclectic* one. An eclectic orientation chooses whatever seems to work best from any of the many existing frameworks for understanding human nature. An eclectic psychologist may take a biological point of view when researching and theorizing, a psychodynamic point of view when trying to understand his children, a behavioral point of view when training his experimental subjects to perform certain tasks, a cognitive point of view when teaching, and a humanistic point of view in his general way of dealing with people. You may best understand this if you think about the different ways you might answer the question, "What have you been doing lately?" when asked by your best friend, your kid sister, your mother, or your chemistry professor.

## IN CONCLUSION

As the editor of this volume, I respect all these points of view. I see the fruitfulness of scientific strategies that seek the determining causes of behavior. In that sense, I appreciate a deterministic orientation. Nevertheless, I am unwilling to ask you to sit back and take a passive role in these issues. I firmly believe that your active involvement in these issues will help you develop the skills that will give you increasing control over your own destiny. In that sense, I emphasize your freedom of will.

In order to have an impact on your world, you must learn, deliberate, discuss, decide, and act. To do this effectively, you should know the difference between what the objective evidence tells you and what your values tell you. And you should be able to distinguish between "truth" and "strategy" when you take sides.

# PART 1

# Biology and Behavior

*No behavioral or mental activity can take place without biology. Biological processes are fundamental to all mental functions, including emotion, perception, and mental health. Does this mean that differences in behavior are essentially the result of biological differences? Are differences between males and females or between thin people and fat people primarily biological? Are biological problems, such as cancer, solely affected by biological intervention? Or can they be influenced by psychological factors, such as attitude and self-esteem?*

- Are Gender Differences Rooted in the Brain?

- Does Body Chemistry Govern Eating Behavior?

- Can Mental Attitude Affect Biological Disease?

# ISSUE 1

## Are Gender Differences Rooted in the Brain?

**YES: Doreen Kimura,** from "Sex Differences in the Brain," *Scientific American* (September 1992)

**NO: Carol Tavris,** from *The Mismeasure of Woman* (Simon & Schuster, 1992)

**ISSUE SUMMARY**

**YES:** Doreen Kimura, a neuropsychologist, argues that research has led to the discovery of the neurological and hormonal processes that lead to differences between men and women.

**NO:** Social psychologist Carol Tavris asserts that neurological explanations of gender differences are the result of scientific biases and that there are many more similarities between men and women than there are differences.

A new spirit of equality has emerged in this country. Although men have traditionally held positions of economic and political power, women have made great strides toward gender equality in recent years. However, these strides toward equality do not negate other basic differences between men and women. There are, of course, obvious differences in biology, but many researchers also point out some basic differences in mental abilities. Although overall levels of intelligence are comparable, women and men seem to differ on some specific abilities. Men, for example, appear to have better spatial abilities, while women seem to have superior verbal abilities.

If there are such differences, the question arises: What is their cause? Questions such as this have traditionally been answered in psychology with one of two possible concepts: *nature* and *nurture*. Those who argue from nature would contend that gender differences are the result of natural differences in biological or genetic constitution. Those who support the nurture point of view, on the other hand, would rely upon differences in nurturance or the learning of various cultural norms to explain gender differences. Most psychologists these days support a view that combines both nature and nurture. Still, as the authors of the following articles show, there are usually leanings in one direction or the other.

Doreen Kimura clearly leans in the direction of nature. Although she does not dismiss the idea that gender differences in our culture are taught, she believes that gender differences in hormonal processes occur so early in life that biology is the dominant influence. From the start, she argues, "the environment is acting on differently wired brains in girls and boys." Kimura cites a number of studies—including some of her own research—that she feels reveals the physiological processes leading to brain differences between males and females. She also describes differences between brain organizations, which, together with hormonal processes, easily account for gender differences in mental ability and behavior.

Carol Tavris disagrees not only with Kimura's biological explanation of gender differences but also with the contention that differences even exist. She feels that most of the research findings that indicate the existence of physiological differences are biased. Tavris argues that scientific experimentation has traditionally been biased toward proving male superiority and that modern theories identifying the brain as the root of gender differences have arisen from the erroneous findings of such research. Tavris then questions whether there are any real differences to explain. The original differences in specific mental abilities between males and females—if there really were any to begin with—seem to be fading with time. Could this mean that as our culture approaches gender equality, gender differences will evaporate?

| POINT | COUNTERPOINT |
|---|---|
| • Research indicates major gender differences in patterns of mental abilities. | • This research is biased by a tradition of gender discrimination. |
| • Gender differences exist across a wide spectrum of mental and behavioral attributes. | • If gender differences do exist, they seem to be fading with time. |
| • Males and females have dramatically different brain organizations. | • Males and females differ in many irrelevant biological respects that can explain brain organization. |
| • All mental abilities and behaviors are ultimately based in one's biology. | • Biological processes cannot account for the enormous complexity of everyday actions. |

# YES

Doreen Kimura

# SEX DIFFERENCES IN THE BRAIN

Women and men differ not only in physical attributes and reproductive function but also in the way in which they solve intellectual problems. It has been fashionable to insist that these differences are minimal, the consequence of variations in experience during development. The bulk of the evidence suggests, however, that the effects of sex hormones on brain organization occur so early in life that from the start the environment is acting on differently wired brains in girls and boys. Such differences make it almost impossible to evaluate the effects of experience independent of physiological predisposition.

Behavioral, neurological and endocrinologic studies have elucidated the processes giving rise to sex differences in the brain. As a result, aspects of the physiological basis for these variations have in recent years become clearer. In addition, studies of the effects of hormones on brain function throughout life suggest that the evolutionary pressures directing differences nevertheless allow for a degree of flexibility in cognitive ability between the sexes.

\* \* \*

Major sex differences in intellectual function seem to lie in patterns of ability rather than in overall level of intelligence (IQ). We are all aware that people have different intellectual strengths. Some are especially good with words, others at using objects—for instance, at constructing or fixing things. In the same fashion, two individuals may have the same overall intelligence but have varying patterns of ability.

Men, on average, perform better than women on certain spatial tasks. In particular, men have an advantage in tests that require the subject to imagine rotating an object or manipulating it in some other way. They outperform women in mathematical reasoning tests and in navigating their way through a route. Further, men are more accurate in tests of target-directed motor skills—that is, in guiding or intercepting projectiles.

Women tend to be better than men at rapidly identifying matching items, a skill called perceptual speed. They have greater verbal fluency, including the ability to find words that begin with a specific letter or fulfill some other constraint. Women also outperform men in arithmetic calculation and in recalling landmarks from a route. Moreover, women are faster at certain precision manual tasks, such as placing pegs in designated holes on a board.

Although some investigators have reported that sex differences in problem solving do not appear until after puberty, Diane Lunn, working in my laboratory at the University of Western Ontario, and I have found three-year-old boys to be better at targeting than girls of the same age. Moreover, Neil V. Watson, when in my laboratory, showed that the extent of experience playing sports does not account for the sex difference in targeting found in young adults. Kimberly A. Kerns, working with Sheri A. Berenbaum of the University of Chicago, has found that sex differences in spatial rotation performance are present before puberty.

Differences in route learning have been systematically studied in adults in laboratory situations. For instance, Liisa Galea in my department studied undergraduates who followed a route on a tabletop map. Men learned the route in fewer trials and made fewer errors than did women. But once learning was complete, women remembered more of the landmarks than did men. These results, and those of other researchers, raise the possibility that women tend to use landmarks as a strategy to orient themselves in everyday life. The prevailing strategies used by males have not yet been clearly established, although they must relate to spatial ability.

Marion Eals and Irwin Silverman of York University studied another function that may be related to landmark memory. The researchers tested the ability of individuals to recall objects and their locations within a confined space—such as in a room or on a tabletop. Women were better able to remember whether an item had been displaced or not. In addition, in my laboratory, we measured the accuracy of object location: subjects were shown an array of objects and were later asked to replace them in their exact positions. Women did so more accurately than did men.

It is important to place the differences described above in context: some are slight, some are quite large. Because men and women overlap enormously on many cognitive tests that show average sex differences, researchers use variations within each group as a tool to gauge the differences between groups. Imagine, for instance, that on one test the average score is 105 for women and 100 for men. If the scores for women ranged from 100 to 110 and for men from 95 to 105, the difference would be more impressive than if the women's scores ranged from 50 to 150 and the men's from 45 to 145. In the latter case, the overlap in scores would be much greater.

One measure of the variation of scores within a group is the standard deviation. To compare the magnitude of a sex difference across several distinct tasks, the difference between groups is divided by the standard deviation. The resulting number is called the effect size. Effect sizes below 0.5 are generally considered small. Based on my data, for instance, there are typically no differences between the sexes on tests of vocabulary (effect size 0.02), nonverbal reasoning (0.03) and verbal reasoning (0.17).

On tests in which subjects match pictures, find words that begin with similar letters or show ideational fluency—such as naming objects that are white or red—the effect sizes are somewhat larger: 0.25, 0.22 and 0.38, respectively. As discussed above, women tend to outperform men on these tasks. Researchers have reported the largest effect sizes for certain tests measuring spatial rotation (effect size 0.7) and targeting accuracy (0.75). The large effect size in these tests means there are many more men at the high end of the score distribution.

* * *

Since, with the exception of the sex chromosomes, men and women share genetic material, how do such differences come about? Differing patterns of ability between men and women most probably reflect different hormonal influences on their developing brains. Early in life the action of estrogens and androgens (male hormones chief of which is testosterone) establishes sexual differentiation. In mammals, including humans, the organism has the potential to be male or female. If a Y chromosome is present, testes or male gonads form. This development is the critical first step toward becoming a male. If the gonads do not produce male hormones or if for some reason the hormones cannot act on the tissue, the default form of the organism is female.

Once testes are formed, they produce two substances that bring about the development of a male. Testosterone causes masculinization by promoting the male, or Wolffian, set of ducts and, indirectly through conversion to dihydrotestosterone, the external appearance of scrotum and penis. The Müllerian regression factor causes the female, or Müllerian, set of ducts to regress. If anything goes wrong at any stage of the process, the individual may be incompletely masculinized.

Not only do sex hormones achieve the transformation of the genitals into male organs, but they also organize corresponding male behaviors early in life. Since we cannot manipulate the hormonal environment in humans, we owe much of what we know about the details of behavioral determination to studies in other animals. Again, the intrinsic tendency, according to studies by Robert W. Goy of the University of Wisconsin, is to develop the female pattern that occurs in the absence of masculinizing hormonal influence.

If a rodent with functional male genitals is deprived of androgens immediately after birth (either by castration or by the administration of a compound that blocks androgens), male sexual behavior, such as mounting, will be reduced. Instead female sexual behavior, such as lordosis (arching of the back), will be enhanced in adulthood. Similarly, if androgens are administered to a female directly after birth, she displays more male sexual behavior and less female behavior in adulthood.

Bruce S. McEwen and his co-workers at the Rockefeller University have shown that, in the rat, the two processes of defeminization and masculinization require somewhat different biochemical changes. These events also occur at somewhat different times. Testosterone can be converted to either estrogen (usually considered a female hormone) or dihydrotestosterone. Defeminization takes place primarily after birth in rats and is mediated by estrogen, whereas masculinization involves both dihydrotestosterone and estrogen and occurs for the most part before birth rather than after, according to studies by McEwen. A substance called alpha-fetoprotein may protect female brains from the masculinizing effects of their estrogen.

The area in the brain that organizes female and male reproductive behavior is the hypothalamus. This tiny structure at the base of the brain connects to the pituitary, the master endocrine gland. Roger A. Gorski and his colleagues at the University of California at Los Angeles have shown that a region of the pre-optic area of the hypothalamus is visibly larger in male rats than in females. The size increment in males is promoted by the presence of androgens in the immediate postnatal, and to some extent prenatal, period. Laura S. Allen in Gorski's laboratory has found a similar sex difference in the human brain.

Other preliminary but intriguing studies suggest that sexual behavior may reflect further anatomic differences. In 1991 Simon LeVay of the Salk Institute for Biological Studies in San Diego reported that one of the brain regions that is usually larger in human males than in females—an interstitial nucleus of the anterior hypothalamus—is smaller in homosexual than in heterosexual men. LeVay points out that this finding supports suggestions that sexual preference has a biological substrate.

Homosexual and heterosexual men may also perform differently on cognitive tests. Brian A. Gladue of North Dakota State University and Geoff D. Sanders of City of London Polytechnic report that homosexual men perform less well on several spatial tasks than do heterosexual men. In a recent study in my laboratory, Jeff Hall found that homosexual men had lower scores on targeting tasks than did heterosexual men; however, they were superior in ideational fluency—listing things that were a particular color.

This exciting field of research is just starting, and it is crucial that investigators consider the degree to which differences in life-style contribute to group differences. One should also keep in mind that results concerning group differences constitute a general statistical statement; they establish a mean from which any individual may differ. Such studies are potentially a rich source of information on the physiological basis for cognitive patterns.

\* \* \*

The lifelong effects of early exposure to sex hormones are characterized as organizational, because they appear to alter brain function permanently during a critical period. Administering the same hormones at later stages has no such effect. The hormonal effects are not limited to sexual or reproductive behaviors: they appear to extend to all known behaviors in which males and females differ. They seem to govern problem solving, aggression and the tendency to engage in rough-and-tumble play—the boisterous body contact that young males of some mammalian species display. For example, Michael J. Meaney of McGill University finds that dihydrotestosterone, working through a structure called the amygdala rather than through the hypothalamus, gives rise to the play-fighting behavior of juvenile male rodents.

Male and female rats have also been found to solve problems differently. Christina L. Williams of Barnard College has shown that female rats have a greater tendency to use landmarks in spatial learning tasks—as it appears women do. In Williams's experiment, female rats used landmark cues, such as pictures on the wall, in preference to geometric cues, such as angles and the shape of the room. If no landmarks were available, however, females used geometric cues. In contrast, males did not use landmarks at all, preferring geometric cues almost exclusively.

Interestingly, hormonal manipulation during the critical period can alter these behaviors. Depriving newborn males of testosterone by castrating them or administering estrogen to newborn females results in a complete reversal of sex-typed behaviors in the adult animals. (As mentioned above, estrogen can have a masculinizing effect during brain development.) Treated females behave like males, and treated males behave like females.

Natural selection for reproductive advantage could account for the evolution of such navigational differences. Steven J. C. Gaulin and Randall W. FitzGerald of the University of Pittsburgh have suggested that in species of voles in which a male mates with several females rather than with just one, the range he must traverse is greater. Therefore, navigational ability seems critical to reproductive success. Indeed, Gaulin and FitzGerald found sex differences in laboratory maze learning only in voles that were polygynous, such as the meadow vole, not in monogamous species, such as the prairie vole.

Again, behavioral differences may parallel structural ones. Lucia F. Jacobs in Gaulin's laboratory has discovered that the hippocampus—a region thought to be involved in spatial learning in both birds and mammals—is larger in male polygynous voles than in females. At present, there are no data on possible sex differences in hippocampal size in human subjects.

Evidence of the influence of sex hormones on adult behavior is less direct in humans than in other animals. Researchers are instead guided by what may be parallels in other species and by spontaneously occurring exceptions to the norm in humans.

One of the most compelling areas of evidence comes from studies of girls exposed to excess androgens in the prenatal or neonatal stage. The production of abnormally large quantities of adrenal androgens can occur because of a genetic defect called congenital adrenal hyperplasia (CAH). Before the 1970s, a similar condition also unexpectedly appeared when pregnant women took various synthetic steroids. Although the consequent masculinization of the genitals can be corrected early in life and drug therapy can stop the overproduction of androgens, effects of prenatal exposure on the brain cannot be reversed.

Studies by researchers such as Anke A. Ehrhardt of Columbia University and June M. Reinisch of the Kinsey Institute have found that girls with excess exposure to androgens grow up to be more tomboyish and aggressive than their unaffected sisters. This conclusion was based sometimes on interviews with subjects and mothers, on teachers' ratings and on questionnaires administered to the girls themselves. When ratings are used in such studies, it can be difficult to rule out the influence of expectation either on the part of an adult who knows the girls' history or on the part of the girls themselves.

Therefore, the objective observations of Berenbaum are important and convincing. She and Melissa Hines of the University of California at Los Angeles observed the play behavior of CAH-affected girls and compared it with that of their male and female siblings. Given a choice of transportation and construction toys, dolls and kitchen supplies or books and board games, the CAH girls preferred the more typically masculine toys—for example, they played with cars for the same amount of time that normal boys did. Both the CAH girls and the boys differed from unaffected girls in their patterns of choice. Because there is every reason to think that parents would be at least as likely to encourage feminine preferences in their CAH daughters as in their unaffected daughters, these findings suggest that the toy preferences were actually altered in some way by the early hormonal environment.

Spatial abilities that are typically better in males are also enhanced in CAH girls. Susan M. Resnick, now at the National Institute on Aging, and Berenbaum and their colleagues reported that affected girls were superior to their unaffected sisters in a spatial manipulation test, two spatial rotation tests and a disembedding test—that is, the discovery of a simple figure hidden within a more complex one. All these tasks are usually done better by males. No differences existed between the two groups on other perceptual or verbal tasks or on a reasoning task.

*  *  *

Studies such as these suggest that the higher the androgen levels, the better the spatial performance. But this does not seem to be the case. In 1983 Valerie J. Shute, when at the University of California at Santa Barbara, suggested that the relation between levels of androgens and some spatial capabilities might be nonlinear. In other words, spatial ability might not increase as the amount of androgen increases. Shute measured androgens in blood taken from male and female students and divided each into high- and low-androgen groups. All fell within the normal range for each sex (androgens are present in females but in very low levels). She found that in women, the high-androgen subjects were better at the

spatial tests. In men the reverse was true: low-androgen men performed better.

Catherine Couchie and I recently conducted a study along similar lines by measuring testosterone in saliva. We added tests for two other kinds of abilities: mathematical reasoning and perceptual speed. Our results on the spatial tests were very similar to Shute's: low-testosterone men were superior to high-testosterone men, but high-testosterone women surpassed low-testosterone women. Such findings suggest some optimum level of androgen for maximal spatial ability. This level may fall in the low male range.

No correlation was found between testosterone levels and performance on perceptual speed tests. On mathematical reasoning, however, the results were similar to those of spatial ability tests for men: low-androgen men tested higher, but there was no obvious relation in women.

Such findings are consistent with the suggestion by Camilla P. Benbow of Iowa State University that high mathematical ability has a significant biological determinant. Benbow and her colleagues have reported consistent sex differences in mathematical reasoning ability favoring males. These differences are especially sharp at the upper end of the distribution, where males outnumber females 13 to one. Benbow argues that these differences are not readily explained by socialization.

It is important to keep in mind that the relation between natural hormonal levels and problem solving is based on correlational data. Some form of connection between the two measures exists, but how this association is determined or what its causal basis may be is unknown. Little is currently understood about the relation between adult levels of hormones and those in early life, when abilities appear to be organized in the nervous system. We have a lot to learn about the precise mechanisms underlying cognitive patterns in people.

Another approach to probing differences between male and female brains is to examine and compare the functions of particular brain systems. One noninvasive way to accomplish this goal is to study people who have experienced damage to a specific brain region. Such studies indicate that the left half of the brain in most people is critical for speech, the right for certain perceptual and spatial functions.

It is widely assumed by many researchers studying sex differences that the two hemispheres are more asymmetrically organized for speech and spatial functions in men than in women. This idea comes from several sources. Parts of the corpus callosum, a major neural system connecting the two hemispheres, may be more extensive in women; perceptual techniques that probe brain asymmetry in normal-functioning people sometimes show smaller asymmetries in women than in men, and damage to one brain hemisphere sometimes has a lesser effect in women than the comparable injury has in men.

In 1982 Marie-Christine de Lacoste, now at the Yale University School of Medicine, and Ralph L. Holloway of Columbia University reported that the back part of the corpus callosum, an area called the splenium, was larger in women than in men. This finding has subsequently been both refuted and confirmed. Variations in the shape of the corpus callosum that may occur as an individual ages as well as different methods of measurement may pro-

duce some of the disagreements. Most recently, Allen and Gorski found the same sex-related size difference in the splenium.

The interest in the corpus callosum arises from the assumption that its size may indicate the number of fibers connecting the two hemispheres. If more connecting fibers existed in one sex, the implication would be that in that sex the hemispheres communicate more fully. Although sex hormones can alter callosal size in rats, as Victor H. Denenberg and his associates at the University of Connecticut have demonstrated, it is unclear whether the actual number of fibers differs between the sexes. Moreover, sex differences in cognitive function have yet to be related to a difference in callosal size. New ways of imaging the brain in living humans will undoubtedly increase knowledge in this respect.

The view that a male brain is functionally more asymmetric than a female brain is long-standing. Albert M. Galaburda of Beth Israel Hospital in Boston and the late Norman Geschwind of Harvard Medical School proposed that androgens increased the functional potency of the right hemisphere. In 1981 Marian C. Diamond of the University of California at Berkeley found that the right cortex is thicker than the left in male rats but not in females. Jane Stewart of Concordia University in Montreal, working with Bryan E. Kolb of the University of Lethbridge in Alberta, recently pinpointed early hormonal influences on this asymmetry: androgens appear to suppress left cortex growth.

Last year de Lacoste and her colleagues reported a similar pattern in human fetuses. They found the right cortex was thicker than the left in males. Thus, there appear to be some anatomic reasons for believing that the two hemispheres might not be equally asymmetric in men and women.

Despite this expectation, the evidence in favor of it is meager and conflicting, which suggests that the most striking sex differences in brain organization may not be related to asymmetry. For example, if overall differences between men and women in spatial ability were related to differing right hemispheric dependence for such functions, then damage to the right hemisphere would perhaps have a more devastating effect on spatial performance in men.

My laboratory has recently studied the ability of patients with damage to one hemisphere of the brain to rotate certain objects mentally. In one test, a series of line drawings of either a left or a right gloved hand is presented in various orientations. The patient indicates the hand being depicted by simply pointing to one of two stuffed gloves that are constantly present.

The second test uses two three-dimensional blocklike figures that are mirror images of one another. Both figures are present throughout the test. The patient is given a series of photographs of these objects in various orientations, and he or she must place each picture in front of the object it depicts (These nonverbal procedures are employed so that patients with speech disorders can be tested.)

As expected, damage to the right hemisphere resulted in lower scores for both sexes on these tests than did damage to the left hemisphere. Also as anticipated, women did less well than men on the block spatial rotation test. Surprisingly, however, damage to the right hemisphere had no greater effect in men than in women. Women were at least as affected as men by damage to the right hemisphere. This result suggests that the normal differences between men and women on such rotational tests are not the result of differential dependence on the right hemisphere. Some other brain systems must be mediating the higher performance by men.

Parallel suggestions of greater asymmetry in men regarding speech have rested on the fact that the incidence of aphasias, or speech disorders, are higher in men than in women after damage to the left hemisphere. Therefore, some researchers have found it reasonable to conclude that speech must be more bilaterally organized in women. There is, however, a problem with this conclusion. During my 20 years of experience with patients, aphasia has not been disproportionately present in women with right hemispheric damage.

\* \* \*

In searching for an explanation, I discovered another striking difference between men and women in brain organization for speech and related motor function. Women are more likely than men to suffer aphasia when the front part of the brain is damaged. Because restricted damage within a hemisphere more frequently affects the posterior than the anterior area in both men and women, this differential dependence may explain why women incur aphasia less often than do men. Speech functions are thus less likely to be affected in women not because speech is more bilaterally organized in women but because the critical area is less often affected.

A similar pattern emerges in studies of the control of hand movements, which are programmed by the left hemisphere. Apraxia, or difficulty in selecting appropriate hand movements, is very common after left hemispheric damage. It is also strongly associated with difficulty in organizing speech. In fact, the critical functions that depend on the left hemisphere may relate not to language per se but to organization of the complex oral and manual movements on which human communication systems depend. Studies of patients with left hemispheric damage have revealed that such motor selection relies on anterior systems in women but on posterior systems in men.

The synaptic proximity of women's anterior motor selection system (or "praxis system") to the motor cortex directly behind it may enhance fine-motor skills. In contrast, men's motor skills appear to emphasize targeting or directing movements toward external space—some distance away from the self. There may be advantages to such motor skills when they are closely meshed with visual input to the brain, which lies in the posterior region.

Women's dependence on the anterior region is detectable even when tests involve using visual guidance—for instance, when subjects must build patterns with blocks by following a visual model. In studying such a complex task, it is possible to compare the effects of damage to the anterior and posterior regions of both hemispheres because performance is affected by damage to either hemisphere. Again, women prove more affected by damage to the anterior region of the right hemisphere than by posterior damage. Men tend to display the reverse pattern.

Although I have not found evidence of sex differences in functional brain asymmetry with regard to basic speech, motor selection or spatial rotation ability, I have found slight differences in more abstract verbal tasks. Scores on a vocabulary test, for instance, were affected by damage to either hemisphere in women, but such scores were affected only by left-sided injury in men. This finding suggests that in reviewing the meanings of words, women use the hemispheres more equally than do men.

In contrast, the incidence of non-right-handedness, which is presumably related to lesser left hemispheric dependence, is higher in men than in women. Even among the right-handers, Marion Annett, now at the University of Leicester in the U.K., has reported that women are more right-handed than men—that is, they favor their right hand even more than do right-handed men. It may well be, then, that sex differences in asymmetry vary with the particular function being studied and that it is not always the same sex that is more asymmetric.

Taken altogether, the evidence suggests that men's and women's brains are organized along different lines from very early in life. During development, sex hormones direct such differentiation. Similar mechanisms probably operate to produce variation within sexes, since there is a relation between levels of certain hormones and cognitive makeup in adulthood.

\* \* \*

One of the most intriguing findings is that cognitive patterns may remain sensitive to hormonal fluctuations throughout life. Elizabeth Hampson of the University of Western Ontario showed that the performance of women on certain tasks changed throughout the menstrual cycle as levels of estrogen went up or down. High levels of the hormone were associated not only with relatively depressed spatial ability but also with enhanced articulatory and motor capability.

In addition, I have observed seasonal fluctuations in spatial ability in men. Their performance is improved in the spring when testosterone levels are lower. Whether these intellectual fluctuations are of any adaptive significance or merely represent ripples on a stable baseline remains to be determined.

To understand human intellectual functions, including how groups may differ in such functions, we need to look beyond the demands of modern life. We did not undergo natural selection for reading or for operating computers. It seems clear that the sex differences in cognitive patterns arose because they proved evolutionarily advantageous. And their adaptive significance probably rests in the distant past. The organization of the human brain was determined over many generations by natural selection. As studies of fossil skulls have shown, our brains are essentially like those of our ancestors of 50,000 or more years ago.

For the thousands of years during which our brain characteristics evolved, humans lived in relatively small groups of hunter-gatherers. The division of labor between the sexes in such a society probably was quite marked, as it is in existing hunter-gatherer societies. Men were responsible for hunting large game, which often required long-distance travel. They were also responsible for defending the group against predators and enemies and for the shaping and use of weapons. Women most probably gathered food near the camp, tended the home, prepared food and clothing and cared for children.

Such specializations would put different selection pressures on men and women. Men would require long-distance route-finding ability so they could recognize a geographic array from varying orientations. They would also need targeting skills. Women would require short-range navigation, perhaps using landmarks, fine-motor capabilities carried on within a circumscribed space, and perceptual discrimination sensitive to small changes in the environment or in children's appearance or behavior.

The finding of consistent and, in some cases, quite substantial sex differences suggests that men and women may have different occupational interests and capabilities, independent of societal influences. I would not expect, for example, that men and women would necessarily be equally represented in activities or professions that emphasize spatial or math skills, such as engineering or physics. But I might expect more women in medical diagnostic fields where perceptual skills are important. So that even though any one individual might have the capacity to be in a "nontypical" field, the sex proportions as a whole may vary.

# NO

Carol Tavris

## MEASURING UP

### BRAIN: DISSECTING THE DIFFERENCES

In recent years the sexiest body part, far and away, has become the brain. Magazines with cover stories on the brain fly off the newsstands, and countless seminars, tapes, books, and classes teach people how to use "all" of their brains. New technologies, such as PET scans, produce gorgeous photographs of the brain at work and play. Weekly we hear new discoveries about this miraculous organ, and it seems that scientists will soon be able to pinpoint the very neuron, the very neurotransmitter, responsible for joy, sadness, rage, and suffering. At last we will know the reasons for all the differences between women and men that fascinate and infuriate, such as why men won't stop to ask directions and why women won't stop asking men what they are feeling.

In all this excitement, it seems curmudgeonly to sound words of caution, but the history of brain research does not exactly reveal a noble and impartial quest for truth, particularly on sensitive matters such as sex and race differences. Typically, when scientists haven't found the differences they were seeking, they haven't abandoned the goal or their belief that such differences exist; they just moved to another part of the anatomy or a different corner of the brain.

A century ago, for example, scientists tried to prove that women had smaller brains than men did, which accounted for women's alleged intellectual failings and emotional weaknesses. Dozens of studies purported to show that men had larger brains, making them smarter than women. When scientists realized that men's greater height and weight offset their brain-size advantage, however, they dropped this line of research like a shot. The scientists next tried to argue that women had smaller frontal lobes and larger parietal lobes than men did, another brain pattern thought to account for women's intellectual inferiority. Then it was reported that the parietal lobes might be associated with intellect. Panic in the labs—until anatomists suddenly found that women's parietal lobes were *smaller* than they had originally believed. Wherever they looked, scientists conveniently found evidence of female inferiority, as Gustave Le Bon, a Parisian, wrote in 1879:

In the most intelligent races, as among the Parisians, there are a large number of women whose brains are closer in size to those of gorillas than to the most developed male brains. This inferiority is so obvious that no one can contest it for a moment; only its degree is worth discussion.

We look back with amusement at the obvious biases of research a century ago, research designed to prove the obvious inferiority of women and minorities (and non-Parisians). Today, many researchers are splitting brains instead of weighing them, but they are no less determined to find sex differences. Nevertheless, skeptical neuroscientists are showing that biases and values are just as embedded in current research—old prejudices in new technologies.

The brain, like a walnut, consists of two hemispheres of equal size, connected by a bundle of fibers called the corpus callosum. The left hemisphere has been associated with verbal and reasoning ability, whereas the right hemisphere is associated with spatial reasoning and artistic ability. Yet by the time these findings reached the public, they had been vastly oversimplified and diluted. Even the great neuroscientist Roger Sperry, the grandfather of hemispheric research, felt obliged to warn that the "left-right dichotomy... is an idea with which it is very easy to run wild." And many people have run wild with it: Stores are filled with manuals, cassettes, and handbooks that promise to help people become fluent in "whole-brain thinking," to beef up the unused part of their right brain, and to learn to use the intuitive right brain for business, painting, and inventing.

The fact that the brain consists of two hemispheres, each characterized by different specialties, provides a neat analogy to the fact that human beings consist of two genders, each characterized by different specialties. The analogy is so tempting that scientists keep trying to show that it is grounded in physical reality. Modern theories of gender and the brain are based on the idea that the left and right hemispheres develop differently in boys and girls, as does the corpus callosum that links the halves of the brain.

According to one major theory, the male brain is more "lateralized," that is, its hemispheres are specialized in their abilities, whereas females use both hemispheres more symmetrically because their corpus callosum is allegedly larger and contains more fibers. Two eminent scientists, Norman Geschwind and Peter Behan, maintained that this sex difference begins in the womb, when the male fetus begins to secrete testosterone—the hormone that will further its physical development as a male. Geschwind and Behan argued that testosterone in male fetuses washes over the brain, selectively attacking parts of the left hemisphere, briefly slowing its development, and producing right-hemisphere dominance in men. Geschwind speculated that the effects of testosterone on the prenatal brain produce "superior right hemisphere talents, such as artistic, musical, or mathematical talent."

Right-hemisphere dominance is also thought to explain men's excellence in some tests of "visual-spatial ability"—the ability to imagine objects in three-dimensional space (the skill you need for mastering geometry, concocting football formations, and reading maps). This is apparently the reason that some men won't stop and ask directions when they are lost; they prefer to rely on their right brains, whereas women prefer to rely on a local informant. It is also supposed to be the reason that men can't talk about their feelings and would rather watch television or wax the car. Women have interconnected hemispheres, which explains why they excel in talk, feelings, intuition, and quick judgments. Geschwind and Behan's theory had tremendous scientific appeal, and it is cited frequently in research papers and textbooks. *Science* hailed it with the headline "Math Genius May Have Hormonal Basis."

The theory also has had enormous popular appeal. It fits snugly, for example, with the Christian fundamentalist belief that men and women are innately different and thus innately designed for different roles. For his radio show "Focus on the Family," James Dobson interviewed Donald Joy, a professor of "human development in Christian education" at Asbury Theological Seminary, who explained Geschwind and Behan's theory this way:

JOY: ... this marvelous female brain, is a brain that's not damaged during fetal development as the male brain is, but the damage gives a specialization to the male brain which we don't get in the female.

DOBSON: I want to pick up on that concept of us brain-damaged males. [laughter, chuckling]

JOY: ... It's giving a chemical bath to the left hemisphere and this connecting link between the two hemispheres that reduced the size and number of transmission passages that exist here ... So males simply can't talk to themselves across the hemispheres in a way that a woman does.

DOBSON: So some of the sex differences that we see in personality can be tracked back to that moment.

JOY: Oh, absolutely. And when we're talking about this now, we're talking about a glorious phenomenon because these are intrinsic sex differences... this is glorious because we are fearfully and wonderfully differentiated from each other.

DOBSON: Let's look at 'em, name 'em.

JOY: We're, we're mutually interdependent. Every household needs both a male brain and a female brain, for example. The woman's brain works much like a computer ... lateral transmission in her brain allows her to consult all of her past experience and give you an instant response. She can make a judgment more quickly than a male can.... [but how she arrives at it is] hidden even from her, because it is like a computer, all it gives is the answer, it doesn't give you the process.

The male brain, Joy added, is more like an "adding machine," in which facts are totaled and a logical solution presents itself. So males are good at logical reasoning, and females at intuitive judgments, because of the prenatal "chemical bath" that affects the male brain....

Now it may be true that men and women, on the average, differ in the physiology of their brains. It may even be true that this difference explains why James Dobson's wife Shirley can sum up a person's character right away, while he, with his slower, adding-machine brain, takes weeks or months to come to the same impressions. But given the disgraceful history of bias and sloppy research designed more to confirm prejudices than to enlighten humanity, I think we would all do well to be suspicious and to evaluate the evidence for these assertions closely.

This is difficult for those of us who are not expert in physiology, neuroanatomy, or medicine. We are easily dazzled by words like "lateralization" and "corpus callosum." Besides, physiology seems so *solid*; if one study finds a difference between three male brains and three female brains, that must apply to all men and women. How do I know what my corpus callosum looks like? Is it bigger than a man's? Should I care?

For some answers, I turned to researchers in biology and neuroscience who have critically examined the research and the assumptions underlying theories of sex differences in the brain. The first discovery of note was that, just like the nineteenth-century researchers who kept changing their minds about which *lobe* of the brain accounted for male superiority, twentieth-century researchers keep changing their minds about which *hemisphere* of the brain accounts for male superiority. Originally, the left hemisphere was considered the repository of intellect and reason. The right hemisphere was the sick, bad, crazy side, the side of passion, instincts, criminality, and irrationality. Guess which sex was thought to have left-brain intellectual superiority? (Answer: males.) In the 1960s and 1970s, however, the right brain was resuscitated and brought into the limelight. Scientists began to suspect that it was the source of genius and inspiration, creativity and imagination, mysticism and mathematical brilliance. Guess which sex was now thought to have right-brain specialization? (Answer: males.)

It's all very confusing. Today we hear arguments that men have greater left-brain specialization (which explains their intellectual advantage) *and* that they have greater right-brain specialization (which explains their mathematical and artistic advantage). *Newsweek* recently asserted as fact, for instance, that

"Women's language and other skills are more evenly divided between left and right hemisphere; in men, such functions are concentrated in the left brain." But [in their book *The Language of Love*, Christian fundamentalists Gary Smalley and John Trent] asserted that

> most women spend the majority of their days and nights camped out on the right side of the brain [which] harbors the center for feelings, as well as the primary relational, language, and communication skills . . . and makes an afternoon devoted to art and fine music actually enjoyable.

You can hear the chuckling from men who regard art museums and concert halls as something akin to medieval torture chambers, but I'm sure that the many men who enjoy art and fine music, indeed who create art and fine music, would not find that last remark so funny. Geschwind and Behan, of course, had argued that male specialization of the right hemisphere explained why men *excel* in art and fine music. But since Smalley and Trent apparently do not share these prissy female interests, they relegate them to women—to women's brains.

The two hemispheres of the brain do have different specialties, but it is far too simple-minded (so to speak) to assume that human abilities clump up in opposing bunches. Most brain researchers today believe that the two hemispheres complement one another, to the extent that one side can sometimes take over the functions of a side that has been damaged. Moreover, specific skills often involve components from both hemispheres: one side has the ability to tell a joke, and the other has the ability to laugh at one. Math abilities include both visual-spatial skills and reasoning skills. The right hemisphere is involved in creating art, but the left hemisphere is involved in appreciating and analyzing art. As neuropsychologist Jerre Levy once said, "Could the eons of human evolution have left half of the brain witless? Could a bird whose existence is dependent on flying have evolved only a single wing?"

These qualifications about the interdependence of brain hemispheres have not, however, deterred those who believe that there are basic psychological differences between the sexes that can be accounted for in the brain. So let's consider their argument more closely.

The neuroscientist Ruth Bleier . . . carefully examined Geschwind and Behan's data, going back to many of their original references. In one such study of 507 fetal brains of 10 to 44 weeks gestation, the researchers had actually stated that they found *no significant sex differences* in these brains. If testosterone had an effect on the developing brain, it would surely have been apparent in this large sample. Yet Geschwind and Behan cited this study for other purposes and utterly ignored its findings of no sex differences.

Instead, Geschwind and Behan cited as evidence for their hypothesis a study of *rats'* brains. The authors of the rat study reported that in male rats, two areas of the cortex that are believed to be involved in processing visual information were 3 percent thicker on the right side than on the left. In one of the better examples of academic gobbledygook yet to reach the printed page, the researchers interpreted their findings to mean that "in the male rat it is necessary to have greater spatial orientation to interact with a female rat during estrus and to integrate that input into a meaningful output." Translation: When having sex with a female, the male needs to be able to look around in case a dangerous predator, such as her husband, walks in on them.

Bleier found more holes in this argument than in a screen door. No one knows, she said, what the slightly greater thickness in the male rat's cortex means for the rat, let alone what it means for human beings. There is at present no evidence that spatial orientation is related to asymmetry of the cortex, or that female rats have a lesser or deficient ability in this regard. And although Geschwind and Behan unabashedly used their limited findings to account for male "superiority" in math and art, they did not specifically study the incidence of genius, talent, or even modest giftedness in their sample, nor did they demonstrate a difference between the brains of geniuses and the brains of average people.

Bleier wrote to *Science*, offering a scholarly paper detailing these criticisms. *Science* did not publish it, on the grounds, as one reviewer put it, that Bleier "tends to err in the opposite direction from the researchers whose results and conclusions she criticizes" and because "she argues very strongly for the predominant role of environmental influences." Apparently, said Bleier, one is allowed to err in only one direction if one wants to be published in *Science*. The journal did not even publish her critical Letter to the Editor.

At about the same time, however, *Science* saw fit to publish a study by two researchers who claimed to have found solid evidence of gender differences in the splenium (posterior end) of the corpus callosum. In particular, they said, the splenium was larger and more bulbous in the five female brains than in the nine male brains they examined, which had been obtained at autopsy. The researchers speculated that "the female brain is less well lateralized—that is, manifests less hemispheric specialization—than the male brain for visuospatial functions." Notice the language: The female brain is *less specialized* than, and by implication inferior to, the male brain. They did not say, as they might have, that the female brain was *more integrated* than the male's. The male brain is the norm, and specialization, in the brain as in academia, is considered a good thing. Generalists in any business are out of favor these days.

This article, which also met professional acclaim, had a number of major flaws that, had they been part of any other research paper, would have been fatal to its publication. The study was based on a small sample of only fourteen brains. The researchers did not describe their methods of selecting the brains in that sample, so it is possible that some of the brains were diseased or otherwise abnormal. The article contained numerous unsupported assumptions and leaps of faith. For example, there is at present absolutely no evidence that the number of fibers in the corpus callosum is even related to hemispheric specialization. Indeed, no one knows what role, if any, the callosum plays in determining a person's mental abilities. Most damaging of all, the sex differences that the researchers claimed to have found in the size of the corpus callosum were not statistically significant, according to the scientific conventions for accepting an article for publication.

Bleier again wrote to *Science*, delineating these criticisms and also citing four subsequent studies, by her and by others, that independently failed to find gender differences of any kind in the corpus callosum. *Science* failed to publish this criticism, as it has failed to publish all studies that find no gender differences in the brain.

Ultimately, the most damning blow to all of these brain-hemisphere theories is that the formerly significant sex differences that brain theories are attempting to account for—in verbal, spatial, and math abilities—are fading rapidly. Let's start with the famed female superiority in verbal ability. Janet Hyde, a professor of psychology at the University of Wisconsin, and her colleague Marcia Linn reviewed 165 studies of verbal ability (including skills in vocabulary, writing, anagrams, and reading comprehension), which represented tests of 1,418,899 people. Hyde and Linn reported that at present in America, there simply are no gender differences in these verbal skills. They noted: "Thus our research pulls out one of the two wobbly legs on which the brain lateralization theories have rested."

Hyde recently went on to kick the other leg, the assumption of overall male superiority in mathematics and spatial ability. No one disputes that males do surpass females at the highly gifted end of the math spectrum. But when Hyde and her colleagues analyzed 100 studies of mathematics performance, representing the testing of 3,985,682 students, they found that gender differences were smallest and favored *females* in samples of the general population, and grew larger, favoring males, only in selected samples of precocious individuals.

What about spatial abilities, another area thought to reveal a continuing male superiority? When psychologists put the dozens of existing studies on spatial ability into a giant hopper and looked at the overall results, this was what they reported: Many studies show no sex differences. Of the studies that do report sex differences, the magnitude of the difference is often small. And finally, there is greater variation *within* each sex than *between* them. As one psychologist who reviewed these studies summarized: "The observed differences are very small, the overlap [between men and women] large, and abundant biological theories are supported with very slender or no evidence."

Sometimes scientists and science writers put themselves through contortions in order to reconcile the slim evidence with their belief in sex differences in the brain. The authors of a popular textbook on sexuality, published in 1990, acknowledge that "sex differences in cognitive skills have declined significantly in recent years." Then they add: "Notwithstanding this finding, theories continue to debate why these differences exist." Pardon? Notwithstanding the fact that there are few differences of any magnitude, let's discuss why there are differences? Even more mysteriously, they conclude: "If Geschwind's theory is ultimately supported by further research, we will have hard evidence of a biological basis for alleged sex differences in verbal and spatial skills." "Hard evidence" for *alleged* sex differences—the ones that don't exist!

It is sobering to read, over and over and over again in scholarly papers, the conclusions of eminent scientists who have cautioned their colleagues against generalizing about sex differences from poor data. One leader in brain-hemisphere research, Marcel Kinsbourne, observing that the evidence for sex differences "fails to convince on logical, methodological, and empirical grounds," then asked:

Why then do reputable investigators persist in ignoring [this evidence]? Because the study of sex differences is not like the

rest of psychology. Under pressure from the gathering momentum of feminism, and perhaps in backlash to it, many investigators seem determined to discover that men and women "really" are different. It seems that if sex differences (e.g., in lateralization) do not exist, then they have to be invented.

These warnings have, for the most part, gone unheeded. Poor research continues to be published in reputable journals, and from there it is disseminated to the public. Many scientists and science writers continue to rely on weak data to support their speculations, like using pebbles as foundation for a castle. Because these speculations fit the dominant beliefs about gender, however, they receive far more attention and credibility than they warrant. Worse, the far better evidence that fails to conform to the dominant beliefs about gender is overlooked, disparaged, or, as in Bleier's experience, remains unpublished.

As a result, ideas enter the common vocabulary as proven facts when they should be encumbered with "maybes," "sometimes," and "we-don't-know-yets." Scientist Hugh Fairweather, reviewing the history of sex differences research in cognition, concluded: "What had before been a possibility at best slenderly evidenced, was widely taken for a fact; and 'fact' hardened into a 'biological' dogma."

Now, it is possible that reliable sex differences in the brain will eventually be discovered. Will it then be all right for Dobson to go on the air to celebrate how delightfully but innately different men and women are? Should we then all make sure we have a male brain and a female brain in every household? Should we then worry about the abnormality of households like mine, in which the male is better at intuitive judgments and the female has the adding-machine mentality?

The answers are no, for three reasons. First, theories of sex differences in the brain cannot account for the complexities of people's everyday behavior. They cannot explain, for instance, why, if women are better than men in verbal ability, so few women are auctioneers or diplomats, or why, if women have the advantage in making rapid judgments, so few women are air-traffic controllers or umpires. Nor can brain theories explain why abilities and ambitions change when people are given opportunities previously denied to them. Two decades ago, theorists postulated biological limitations that were keeping women out of men's work like medicine and bartending. When the external barriers to these professions fell, the speed with which women entered them was dizzying. Did everybody's brain change? Today we would be amused to think that women have a brain-lateralization deficiency that is keeping them out of law school. But we continue to hear about the biological reasons that keep women out of science, math, and politics. For sex differences in cognitive abilities to wax and wane so rapidly, they must be largely a result of education, motivation, and opportunity, not of innate differences between male and female brains.

Second, the meanings of terms like "verbal ability" and "spatial reasoning" keep changing too, depending on who is using them and for what purpose. For example, when conservatives like Dobson speak of women's verbal abilities, they usually mean women's interest in and willingness to talk about relationships and feelings. But in studies of total talking time in the workplace, men far exceed women in the talk department. In everyday life, men interrupt women more than vice versa, dominate the conversation, and are more successful at introducing new topics and having their comments remembered in group discussions. What does this mean for judgments of which sex has the better "verbal ability"?

Third, the major key problem with biological theories of sex differences is that they deflect attention from the far more substantial evidence for sex similarity. The finding that men and women are more alike in their abilities and brains than different almost never makes the news. Researchers and the public commit the error of focusing on the small differences—usually of the magnitude of a few percentage points—rather than on the fact that the majority of women and men overlap. For example, this is what the author of a scientific paper that has been widely quoted as *supporting* sex differences in brain hemispheres actually concluded:

Thus, one must not overlook perhaps the most obvious conclusion, which is that basic patterns of male and female brain asymmetry seem to be more similar than they are different.

Everyone, nevertheless, promptly overlooked it.

The habit of seeing women and men as two opposite categories also leads us to avoid the practical question: How much ability does it take to do well in a particular career? When people hear that men are better than women in spatial ability, many are quick to conclude that perhaps women, with their deficient brains, should not try to become architects or engineers. This reaction is not merely unfortunate; it is cruel to the women who *do* excel in architectural or engineering ability. The fields of math and science are losing countless capable women because girls keep hearing that women aren't as good as men in these fields.

None of this means that biology is irrelevant to human behavior. But whenever the news trumpets some version of "biology affects behavior," it obscures the fact that biology and behavior form a two-way street. Hormones affect sexual drive, for instance, but sexual activity affects hormone levels. An active brain seeks a stimulating environment, but living in a stimulating environment literally changes and enriches the brain. Fatigue and boredom cause poor performance on the job, but stultifying job conditions produce fatigue and boredom. Scientists and writers who reduce our personalities, problems, and abilities to biology thereby tell only half the story, and miss half the miracle of how human biology works.

Ruth Bleier, ... a neuroscientist, put the whole matter in perspective this way:

> Such efforts directed at the callosum (or any other particular structure in the brain, for that matter) are today's equivalent of 19th-century craniology: if you can find a bigger bump here or a smaller one there on a person's skull, if you can find a more bulbous splenium here or a more slender one there... you will know something significant about their intelligence, their personality, their aspirations, their astrological sign, their gender and race, and their status in society. We are still mired in the naive hope that we can find something that we can *see* and *measure* and it will explain everything. It is silly science and it serves us badly.

# CHALLENGE QUESTIONS
## Are Gender Differences Rooted in the Brain?

1. If gender differences are indeed rooted in the brain, what does this suggest about their modifiability (that is, the possibility that they may be changed)? What political implications might this have for our nation's striving toward gender equality?

2. Take either Kimura's or Tavris's side of this issue and explain what the author's arguments would mean to the parenting of girls and boys.

3. Could gender differences in mental abilities be a factor in marital problems? Provide reasons for your answer.

4. If gender differences were a factor in marital problems, how would you help a couple experiencing them?

# ISSUE 2

## Does Body Chemistry Govern Eating Behavior?

**YES: Hara Estroff Marano,** from "Chemistry and Craving," *Psychology Today* (January/February 1993)

**NO: Peter Herman and Janet Polivy,** from "Fat Is a Psychological Issue," *New Scientist* (November 16, 1991)

### ISSUE SUMMARY

**YES:** Drawing upon the research of behavioral neurobiologist Sarah Leibowitz, Hara Estroff Marano, executive editor for *Psychology Today,* asserts that our eating behavior is profoundly affected by neurochemicals in the brain.

**NO:** Professors of psychology Peter Herman and Janet Polivy contend that eating is a psychological issue, influenced by individuals' thinking and beliefs about food.

Body size has become a national obsession. Our society values thinness not only because most people feel it looks attractive but also because it reduces the risk of heart disease and other health-related problems. As a result, many people strive constantly to be thin, some with success and others with disappointment and more serious consequences, such as eating disorders. Why is it that some people find it easy to lose weight while others struggle? Is this tied to our biological makeup, or is it tied to our psychological beliefs?

Psychologists occupy an influential position in this struggle for thinness. Many people seek psychological help for eating disorders such as bulimia (characterized by a cycle of binge eating and purging, which involves self-induced vomiting or laxative abuse), anorexia nervosa (characterized by self-imposed starvation), and compulsive overeating. Difficulties in eating and appetite often accompany other psychological difficulties, such as stress or relationship problems. Therefore, conclusions about the nature of appetite and eating behavior can have a powerful influence on the practice of psychotherapy.

In the following selections, Hara Estroff Marano presents the research of Sarah Leibowitz, who has concluded that what we eat is affected by neurochemicals produced in the hypothalamus of the brain. Leibowitz's theory is that when two neurochemicals—neuropeptide Y (NPY) and galanin—are released, they influence our desire for carbohydrates and fat, respectively.

In effect, these chemicals tell us what to eat. Preference for one type of food or another, which is affected by these chemicals, varies among individuals. However, Marano asserts that these chemicals are intimately involved in all eating behavior (and, hence, all eating disorders) and can be present from birth.

In contrast, Peter Herman and Janet Polivy contend that eating behavior is not just physiologically determined. They emphasize the differences between the thoughts and beliefs of dieters and nondieters. Herman and Polivy believe that dieters stop responding to normal physiological controls for eating (hunger cues) and instead employ deliberate mental controls. Unfortunately, this produces changes in the thoughts and logic of dieters and increases obsessive thinking about food. Mental controls also increase the stress of dieters. Thus, Herman and Polivy conclude that thoughts and beliefs are at the heart of eating behavior and weight management.

| POINT | COUNTERPOINT |
|---|---|
| • Eating behavior is greatly determined by physiological factors. | • Eating behavior is influenced by an individual's thinking and beliefs regarding eating. |
| • Neurochemicals are at the root of food preference. | • Reliance on physiological factors for food preference is not sufficient. |
| • Eating disorders can result from disruption in the body's normal chemical rhythm. | • Eating disorders can be caused by faulty thinking and logic that results from dieting. |
| • Identifying an infant's neurochemically based food preferences will one day prevent weight management problems. | • Healthy weight management is best facilitated by remaining responsive to normal bodily controls. |

# YES

Hara Estroff Marano

# CHEMISTRY AND CRAVING

Some revolutions are waged with guns. Others are waged with words. But perhaps the major American revolt of the past two decades has been waged primarily with knife and fork. With butter banished, red meat in retreat, and humble grains advancing on our plates, we've toppled the old dietary regime on the grounds that you are what you eat.

Still, decisive victories in the battle of the bulge, the war on heart disease, and just plain healthy appetites elude us. And so we begin each year with solemn vows to tackle anew our waistlines and our arteries. But if a behavioral scientist in New York is right, a winning strategy can come only from a simple turn of the tables—we eat what we are.

In meticulous studies over the last 10 years, Sarah F. Leibowitz, Ph.D., of The Rockefeller University, has discovered that what we put in our mouths and when we do it is profoundly influenced by a brew of neurochemicals based in a specific part of our brain. They not only guide our selection of morsels at breakfast, lunch, and dinner—and even the need for high tea— they are probably the power behind individual differences in appetite and weight gain. They appear to determine whether we are sitting ducks for the eating disorders that now afflict 30 percent of Americans.

Unless we take into account the physiological function of these brain chemicals in dictating natural patterns of food intake and metabolism, we will never get closer than annual avowals in regulating our eating behavior, whatever our reason for doing so. The only plausible way to control body weight is by working *with* the neurochemical systems that control appetite—and re-tuning them.

Leibowitz' studies point far beyond our forks. They challenge the deeply held belief that we are strictly self-determining individuals acting, at least at the table, by unfettered choice—whim, if the moon is right. Sooner or later, in one context or another, we will have to overhaul our view of human behavior to acknowledge that there are a variety of physiological signals guiding what we now believe to be free will.

Leibowitz, however, has little taste for the philosophical soup. In classic meat-and-potatoes neuroscience, she has located the epicenter of eating behavior. It is a dense cluster of nerve cells, the neurochemicals they produce, and the receptors through which they act and are acted upon. They make up the paraventricular nucleus, deep in the brain's hypothalamus, a structure toward the base of the brain already known to control sexuality and reproduction.

## A MATTER OF ENERGY

The neurons that affect eating are part of the body's elaborate mechanism for regulating energy balance, the power ensuring that we take in sufficient fuel, in the form of food, to meet internal and external energy demands to survive from day to day. This is perhaps the body's most fundamental need.

Given so crucial a need, the location of the nerve cells of appetite in the hypothalamus is no accident of nature. They are the neurons next door to those that orchestrate sexual behavior. Leibowitz has found that we have clear-cut cycles of preference for high-carbohydrate and fat-rich foods, and they are closely linked to reproductive needs—that is, the ability of humans to survive from generation to generation. After all, the power to reproduce requires that we maintain a sufficient amount of body fat. The group of cells that tangle with sex and the cells that fancy our forks are in constant communication—like the sometimes overprotective mother she is, nature is constantly seeking reassurance that we have enough body fat for the survival of the species.

There are, in truth, many other brain areas that influence appetite. But from the lower brain stem up to the thalamus, which controls sensory processes such as taste, and on up to the forebrain and the cortex, where pleasure, affect, and cognitive aspects come into play, everything converges on the hypothalamus. The hypothalamus integrates all of the information affecting appetite. Its neurochemical signals coordinate our behavior with our physiology.

Through a daunting system of chemical and neural feedback, the brain monitors the energy needs of all body systems moment to moment And it makes very emphatic suggestions to the stomach as to what we should ingest.

On the menu are the standard nutritional war-horses: carbohydrate for immediate fuel, fat for longer-term energy reserves—it is particularly essential for reproduction—and protein for growth and muscle maintenance. Directives from the brain to the belly are issued by way of neurochemical messengers and hormones. These directives, Leibowitz finds, have their own physiological logic, their own sets of rhythms, and are highly nutrient-specific. There's one thing we now know for sure—the stomach definitely has a brain.

## A TASTE FOR CARBO

In the dietary drama unfolding in Leibowitz' ground-floor laboratory, there are two star players. One is Neuropeptide Y (NPY), a neurochemical that dictates the taste for carbohydrate. Produced by neurons in the paraventricular nucleus (PVN), it literally turns on and off our desire for carbohydrate-rich foods.

In animal studies the researcher has conducted, the amount of Neuropeptide Y produced by cells in the PVN correlates directly, positively, with carbohydrate intake. The more Neuropeptide Y we produce, the more we eat carbohydrate.

## "THESE CELLS TELL US TO EAT"

"We can see these neurons and analyze the neuropeptides in them," says Leibowitz. "We know that these cells tell us to eat carbohydrate. In studies, we either give injections of a known amount of Neuropeptide Y, or measure the amount of Neuropeptide Y that's naturally there. Then we correlate it to what the animal ate in carbohydrate." Neuropeptide Y increases both the size and duration of carbohydrate-rich meals.

If production of Neuropeptide Y turns on the taste for carbohydrate, what sets production of Neuropeptide Y spinning? Probably signals from the burning of carbohydrates as fuel are the routine appetite stimulants. But Leibowitz has found that cortisol, a hormone produced by the body during stress, has a particular propensity to turn on the taste for carbohydrate by revving up production of Neuropeptide Y. High levels of Neuropeptide Y lead to weight gain by prompting overeating of carbohydrate.

### FAT'S CHANCE

The body also has a built-in appetite system for fat, the most concentrated form of energy, and it marches to a different neurochemical drumbeat, a neuropeptide called galanin, also produced in the paraventricular nucleus of the hypothalamus. Galanin is the second star player in Leibowitz' studies.

These have shown that the amount of galanin an animal produces correlates positively with what the animal eats in fat. And that correlates with what the animal's body weight will become. The more galanin produced, the heavier the animal will become later on. To add insult to injury, galanin not only turns on the taste for fat, it affects other hormones in such away as to ensure that fat consumed is turned into stored fat.

What turns on the taste for galanin? When the body burns stored fats as fuel, the resulting metabolic byproducts signal the paraventricular nucleus for more fat—a case of nature safeguarding our energy storage. But hormones also turn galanin production on. To be specific, the sexual hormone estrogen activates galanin.

"Estrogen just increases the production of galanin and it makes us want to eat. It makes us want to deposit fat," says Leibowiz. The influence of estrogen on our taste for fat "is important in the menstrual cycle and in the developmental cycle, when we hit puberty."

### OF TIME AND THE NIBBLER

The two neurohormones of nibbling are not uniformly active throughout the day. Each has its own built-in cycle of activity.

Neuropeptide Y has its greatest effect on appetite at the start of the feeding cycle—morning, when we're just waking up. It starts up the entire feeding cycle. After overnight fasting, we have an immediate need for energy intake. Neuropeptide Y is also switched on after any environmentally imposed period of food deprivation—such as dieting. And by stress. "If you have lots of Neuropeptide Y in the system at breakfast," says Leibowitz, "you're going to be doing lots of eating."

Necessary as a quick-energy start is to get going, man cannot live by carbohydrate alone. After carbohydrate turns on our engines, the desire for this nutrient begins a slow decline over the rest of the daily cycle.

Around lunchtime, we begin looking for a little more sustenance. An afternoon of sustained energy expenditure stretches before us; we can afford to take in the other major nutrients—fat to refill our fat cells and protein to rebuild muscle. Both of these are converted more slowly to fuel. Our interest in protein rises gradually toward midday, holds its own at lunch, and keeps a more or less steady course during the rest of the day.

## A CLOCKWORK ORANGE

After lunch, the taste for fat begins rising, supported by increasing sensitivity to galanin and increasing galanin production; it peaks with our heaviest meal, at the end of the daily cycle. That's when the body is looking to store energy in anticipation of overnight fasting.

Take a late-afternoon coffee—or tea—break and you're virtually programmed to dive for energy-rich pastry, as appetite, spearheaded by the drive for fat, is gaining. We might, however, be better off appeasing the chemicals of consumption with a banana, or an orange.

Leibowitz believes that circadian cycles of neurochemical activity play a major role in eating problems. A late-afternoon fat snack, for example, could prime us neurochemically to consume more fat later into the night. Galanin activity late in the day gives fat consumed at dinner a head start, as it were, on our thighs.

## SILENT SIGNALS

What drives us from a carbohydrate-rich breakfast to a more nutrient-mixed lunch? The carbohydrate we take in at breakfast has a direct impact on more widely distributed neurotransmitters such as serotonin. Active in many systems of the brain, including learning and memory, serotonin is believed to play a general role of modulator; it is essentially an inhibitor of activity.

Eating carbohydrate leads straightaway to synthesis of serotonin. Under normal conditions, rising levels of serotonin are the feedback signals to the paraventricular nucleus to shut off production of Neuropeptide Y and put a stop to the desire for carbohydrate.

## BEHIND THE BINGE

Leibowitz now thinks that this serotonin signal is directly related to the bingeing behavior that is the *sine qua non* of bulimia. "Bulimics have a deficit in brain serotonin. The mechanism for stopping carbohydrate intake doesn't seem to be there."

Every meal, then, and the appetite for it, is differently regulated and presided over by a separate cocktail of neurochemicals. The neurochemically correct breakfast is a quick blast of carbohydrate right after awakening. Say, a glass of orange juice for speedy transport of sugar into the bloodstream to restore glycogen. Then a piece or two of toast, a more complex carbohydrate to deliver a more sustained supply of glucose over the morning.

For those who don't do it regularly, a breakfast of, say, eggs benedict—rich in protein and fat as well as carbohydrate—will send your neurochemicals spinning, throw off their normal rhythm of production, and affect many other neurotransmitters in the bargain. Ever wonder why you're just not sharp enough after an unusually rich breakfast?

## THE BIG SWITCH

Not only are the neurochemicals of appetite active at different times over the course of a day, they are differently active over the course of development. Before puberty, Leibowitz finds, animals have no interest in eating fat. Children, too, have little appetite for fat, preferring carbohydrates for energy and protein for tissue growth. But that, like their bodies, changes.

In girls, the arrival of the first menstrual period is a milestone for appetite as well as for sexual maturation. It stimulates the first desire for fat in foods....

"We hit puberty and that turns galanin on." The female hormone estrogen primes the neurochemical pump for galanin.

There are other sex-based differences in nutrient preference. In studies of animals, young females tend to have higher levels of Neuropeptide Y and favor carbohydrates. Their preference for carbohydrates peaks at puberty. Males favor protein to build large muscles.

When puberty strikes up the taste for fats, males are inclined to mix theirs with protein—that sizzling porterhouse steak. Women, their already high levels of Neuropeptide Y joined by galanin, are set to crave high-calorie sweets—chocolate cake, say, or ice cream. It's bread-and-butter nutritional knowledge that carbohydrate makes fat palatable in the first place.

This neurochemical combo particularly sets women up for late-afternoon snacking, possibly bingeing. Late afternoon may be the time when those who skip breakfast are particularly likely to pay for it, and there in turn with exaggerated increases in their Neuropeptide Y levels leading them into late-day gorging.

## PATTERNS OF PREFERENCE

When Leibowitz allows animals to choose what they eat, they show marked individual preferences for nutrients. These nutrient preferences, in turn, create specific differences in feeding patterns. In this animals are just like people, and fall into one of three general categories.

In about 50 percent of the population, carbohydrate is the nutrient of choice. Such people naturally choose a diet in which about 60 percent of calories are derived from carbohydrate, and up to 30 percent come from fat. They are neurochemically in line with what nutritionists today are recommending as a healthy diet. High-carbohydrate animals consume smaller and more frequent meals, and they weigh significantly less, than other animals.

## SOME LIKE IT FAT

A small number of people and animals are dedicated to protein. But 30 percent of us have a predilection for fat. And those who do take in 60 to 70 percent of their calories in straight fat, as opposed to the 30 percent considered appropriate to a lifestyle that's more sedentary than our ancestors'.

Not only is this not likely to sit well with arteries, but such preferences also correlate highly with body weight in animals. Those constituted to favor fat consume the most calories and weigh the most. And they seem to be particularly predisposed to food cravings late in the day.

## EARLY INDICATORS

What is perhaps most intriguing in all of this to Leibowitz is that individual taste preferences first show themselves when animals are very young, notably at the time of weaning, even before their neurochemical profiles are fully elaborated. The same is true of people. "We know early in family life what we are going to become," she contends.

The New York researcher believes that by sampling infants' tastes, it will be possible to predict eating and weight-control problems long before they occur. And, of course, if we choose, do something to prevent them from ever occurring.

## MORE THAN METABOLISM

At the time of weaning—21 days in rat pups, 1 1/2 to 2 years in human infants—taste preferences largely reflect differences in genetic makeup. And in those animals that prefer sucrose or fat— "you put it on an infant's tongue and watch how they react to it, whether they become active or not"—their appetite is strongly predictive of how much weight they will gain later on in life. And their neurochemical make-up.

"We believe there is strong appetitive component to pre-ordained weight gain," Leibowitz says. "We think there's more to it than just metabolism. We are on the verge of linking that early taste with later eating behavior and weight gain."

## THE WAGES OF STRESS

These ground-breaking studies of nutrient preferences show that inborn patterns are one way we can be set up for eating problems or weight gain we might prefer not to have. They also implicate another—stress. Stress potentially wreaks havoc with our eating patterns by altering us internally.

When we feel under stress, the body increases production of the hormone cortisol, from the adrenal gland. The purpose of this chemical messenger of alarm is to marshall forces of energy for immediate use—to prepare us, as it were, for fight or flight. It puts our whole system on alert, and makes us hyper-vigilant.

As it enters the bloodstream from the adrenal gland and circulates throughout the body, cortisol sees that carbohydrate, stored in muscles and liver as glycogen, is swiftly turned into glucose for fuel. If we are not burning up glucose, we have no energy. One reason cortisol is elevated in the morning is because the food deprivation of overnight fasting is a kind of stress to the body, destabilizing the system.

Cortisol, however, is also critical in the regulation of the neurochemicals that control eating behavior. "It up-regulates the neuropeptides when you don't want it to," says Leibowitz. Cortisol specifically stimulates production of Neuropeptide Y, which turns on the appetite—for more carbohydrate. "Stress is very much related to turning on Neuropeptide Y," reports Leibowitz. "It doesn't appear to increase galanin."

What's particularly tricky is that the effect of stress on eating is not uniform throughout the day. A bout of stress at the right time in the morning may keep Neuropeptide Y turned on all day. "We know that some people under stress get fat and others do not overeat. It depends on when the stress is occurring. Wouldn't it be nice to get your stress at a time when you are not so vulnerable?" Now if only she knew when that was.

## WHY WE OVEREAT

What she does know is that if there is no muscular activity to use up the carbohydrate stress sets us up to eat, the carbohydrate is put directly into storage as fat. But wait—there are other consequences. It is an axiom of neuroscience that the same chemical messenger has different effects at different sites.

Through neurochemical cross talk in the hypothalamus, the increase in Neuropeptide Y activity affects the master switch for sexual and reproductive behavior in the cluster of cells next door. In this back-and-forth signaling between cell groups, high levels of Neuropeptide Y, hell-bent on carbohydrate intake, turn off the gonadal hormones, which are far more interested in fat. The upshot is a dampening of sexual interest and activity. This effect turns out to be critically important in anorexia.

Eating carbohydrate under stress, however, has something going for it. It chases away the stress-induced changes in neurochemistry. The hormonal alarm signals dissipate. "After we eat a carbohydrate-rich meal, the world actually seems better," explains Leibowitz. We feel less edgy. "That's why we overeat."

## DIETING—BAD FOR THE BRAIN

Many studies have shown that curbing body weight by food restriction—dieting—makes no sense metabolically; in fact it's counterproductive. Leibowitz finds it also makes no sense to the biochemistry of our brains, either. "All dieting does is disturb the system." she says emphatically. "It puts you in a psychological altered state. You're a different person. You respond differently."

Erratically skipping meals upsets the natural daily rhythm of neurochemicals; "that's important because the body works on routines. If you disturb the routine, you're going to be a different person at lunch than if you didn't skip breakfast." What's more, "the chemicals that regulate appetite also directly affect moods and state of mind, our physical energy, the quality of our sex lives," says Leibowitz.

Fasting—restricting, in the parlance of those who study eating behavior—is particularly counterproductive to appetite. It simply turns on the neurochemical switches. "It's got to come out somehow," says Leibowitz. It specifically drives up levels of Neuropeptide Y and cortisol. Then, when the next meal rolls around, it turns it into a high-carbohydrate binge. "Neuropeptide Y is truly the neurochemical of food deprivation." Fasting or dieting drives the body to seek more carbohydrate. Her studies show that animals that love carbohydrate have higher levels of Neuropeptide Y in the paraventricular nucleus.

## THE WAY WE WERE

How, then, to lose weight? Certainly not diet pills. One reason they don't work is that they don't even aspire to cope with the array of neurochemicals setting the table for appetite. Assuming such an approach to be possible or even desirable, it would, in fact, take assorted concoctions of chemicals at different times of the day, since each meal is regulated differently.

Nevertheless, the way to control appetite and body weight, Leibowitz believes, is by working *with* the neurochemical systems—and re-tuning them.

"We need to help people understand what they are and what their appetite is, and how to work with the body the way it is. Some people are more sensitive." This may be a far gentler approach than skipping lunch, but in the long run, it may be the only workable one, the only one that can possibly do away with the preoccupation with dieting that now consumes 50 to 70 percent of all women.

However deterministic biochemistry at first appears, that is not, within broad bounds, the case with behavior. We are not wholly slaves of neurochemistry. "Neurons are plastic. They change. We can therefore educate the neurons," explains Leibowitz. "You can say that God dictated this biochemical pattern. But we are here to mold ourselves and train ourselves."

The secret to modifying neurons is to introduce a very gradual shift in their sensitivity to the neurochemicals of appetite—to down-regulate them s-l-o-w-l-y.

Given the plasticity of neurons, early experience is heavily weighted in shaping the behavior of brain cells for life. Early exposure to a certain nutrient—say, a high-fat diet—will bias neurochemistry. It will up-regulate sensitivity to galanin and prompt production of greater amounts of it, aiding and abetting the appetite for fat. "Your training, your habits, all have an effect," says Leibowitz. "We don't know how much is permanent and how much is reversible. It may be like the case with fat cells in the body; if you overeat when young and get fat cells, you may not be able to get rid of them." The bottom line is, we may be remarkably adaptable but not infinitely malleable.

## TASTE TESTS FOR ALL?

The ideal, then, is to start the neurochemicals of appetite out on the right foot, "to modulate them before an eating disorder sets in, or any disturbance in dieting. It's got to be preventative. What you eat is going to affect production of these peptides." At some point in the future, it may be possible to determine the right calorie and nutrient mix even to dampen the genetically outlined production of the appetite hormones.

Leibowitz would bypass the dismal enterprise of dieting altogether with a taste test at age two. "We're aiming for the goal of trying to characterize people at a very early age, just as we can now do with animals. We can predict adult height at two years of age. We may also want to predict adult eating behavior and weight gain."

Then, with nutrition and planning and behavioral therapy she would set out to educate the appetite. "I'm not thinking drugs, but there could be drugs. If we could do this ahead of time, we could prevent the development of eating disorders," disorders that now affect, by her calculation, 30 percent of the population.

"The question is, can we find some specific dietary situation, different foods at different times, that might help us to reduce neuropeptide activity without depriving ourselves. The whole point is, we can't deprive ourselves. But if we know that what we eat and when we eat it affect the production of neuropeptides, we can modulate what we eat and work the appetite so that we can get a new routine in."

Gastronomy may never be the same again.

# NO      Peter Herman and Janet Polivy

# FAT IS A PSYCHOLOGICAL ISSUE

Near the top of just about every Westerner's wish list is a slimmer figure. Exercise is a possibility, but the pain-to-gain (or pain-to-loss) ratio is uncomfortably high. Surgery is another approach, but it is not easily accessible, or even particularly reliable. That leaves dieting, the most widely adopted strategy. More people nowadays are watching their weight than ever before, and the benefits to health, appearance and self-esteem seem so obvious that one wonders why there is anyone who doesn't diet.

Of course, everyone is familiar with the difficulties of dieting. Every worthwhile diet demands sacrifices, and sacrifice is not something that comes naturally to most people. And then there is the well-known fact that most diets, while initially successful, quickly run out of steam. A few months later, dieters are likely to be back where they started. These are the problems of diet failure.

Just as important are the problems that plague even the successful dieter. We have found that dieters, whether successful or not, display pathologies of eating; their normal regulatory mechanisms are undermined. Indeed, the fact that their normal regulatory processes are compromised turns out to contribute to the overeating to which most dieters are prone, and which makes the eventual failure of the diet so likely. The demerits of dieting are not confined to eating behaviour, however. We have noted aberrations in the realms of emotion and cognition—broadly, how we feel and think about the world and ourselves—and these aberrations suggest that the dieter is under substantial stress. This stress, along with the weight fluctuations that accompany the typical alternation of extended abstinence and ruinous overeating, even threatens the dieter's physical health. All in all, we regard dieting more as a problem than as a solution, and recommend extreme caution before embarking on what may well prove to be a counterproductive enterprise.

Our jaundiced view of dieting arises from a series of experiments that we have conducted on mostly female undergraduates in and around Chicago and Toronto. Initially, we were interested in the question of how people regulate their calorie intake; that is, how well people compensate for a particular "preload" provided by the experimenter. In our first experiment the preload was either one 7.5 ounce (210 gram) milk shake, two such milk shakes, or none. Immediately following this preload, our subjects were given three different flavours of ice cream to eat.

We presented the experiment as a study of taste perception. The subjects thought that they were merely sampling the ice cream—although while doing so they could eat as much of it as they wanted—and that we were interested in how the ice cream tasted to them after they had drunk a milk shake of a particular flavour. The purpose of this deception was to convince subjects that we were not interested in how much ice cream they ate. For that reason, we secretly weighed the ice cream bowls before and after the students had eaten, to calculate their intake. We also made sure that these bowls contained ample ice cream, so that the students would not become self-conscious about consuming a great deal of it if they chose to. We also ensured that the subjects ate in absolute privacy.

At the end of the experiment, subjects completed a questionnaire that allowed us to divide them roughly in half into dieters and nondieters. The nondieters we tested behaved in a straightforward fashion: they ate less ice cream following one milk shake than following none, and still less following two milk shakes. This pattern should not surprise anyone. It simply indicates that people compensate for their prior consumption.

There is some dispute about whether this compensation is based on physiological feedback or on cognitive calculations of how much to eat. The physiological argument is that the caloric impact of the milk shake is registered in the bloodstream or hypothalamus, which in turn dictates less eating if recent intake has been high. Others, however, have argued that there is insufficient time in a study

such as this for physiological feedback to be effective, so people compensate on the basis of their beliefs regarding how much they can or ought to eat. Whichever is true, nondieters do compensate.

For the dieters we tested, the results were surprising. Instead of compensating for the milk shake preloads, the dieters actually ate more ice cream following one or two milk shakes than after none at all. We labelled this phenomenon "counter-regulation," because it runs counter to normal regulation. This surprising pattern has been replicated a number of times in our laboratory as well as elsewhere. But what does it signify?

One possibility is that dieters have a contrary physiology. Perhaps the effect of the milk shake is to make them paradoxically hungrier and thus more likely to eat. People with such a physiology would almost certainly have to become dieters. We and others have been able to eliminate this possibility by producing the effect in studies in which all the subjects receive the same preload (such as pudding), but half of them are led to believe that the preload is high in calories, while the other half are told that the preload is low calorie. Dieters eat more after the preload that they believe is high in calories, even if it is not. By contrast, nondieters eat slightly more after the preload labelled "low calorie", incidentally lending some support to the notion that the compensation they show is at least partially based on their thoughts and beliefs.

Why then do dieters counter-regulate? We believe that this bizarre response arises from the nature of dieting itself. A formal definition of dieting is that it is an intentional inhibition of caloric intake in the pursuit of a slimmer physique. This inhibition, however straightforward it may appear, produces a number of unintended and even counterproductive consequences. First, it demands that one's eating comes under deliberate control; no longer can one eat whenever one is hungry and the available food is tasty. The natural controls of physiological feedback combined with learnt regulatory strategies that govern nondieters' eating are dangerous for the dieter. After all, these natural controls have produced a physique that the dieter is evidently dissatisfied with—hence the diet. The alternative is to gain deliberate control over one's eating. Dieters decide how much, and when, and what, they will eat, irrespective of their natural inclinations.

After extended practice in neglecting one's physiology in favour of one's conscious caloric agenda, the normal controls on eating eventually atrophy. We do not mean to suggest that food deprivation no longer produces a "hunger" reaction in the bloodstream, but simply that this reaction no longer calls forth corrective measures at the behavioural level, that is, eating. In effect, the dieter stops responding to hunger cues. For instance, when dieters start off without a milk shake, they then eat very little ice cream. Their diet is intact, and the fact that they might be hungry is no reason to eat. In the experimental condition in which subjects receive no milk shake, dieters eat considerably less ice cream than do nondieters.

But why do dieters overeat after consuming a milk shake? Doesn't that overeating directly conflict with their dietary resolve? Certainly it does, but our research indicates that the effect of the milk shake—and here perhaps is the paradox—undermines the dieters' resolve, temporarily releasing them from their vows of abstinence. After the milk shake, instead of doing penance for the caloric sin, the dieter persists in sinful indulgence. After all, if staying on one's diet is no longer possible, then why not make the most of the situation?

The psychology of dieting hinges on the fact that dieters' ultimate goals of achieving or maintaining a slim physique are long term, but their dieters' behaviour-control strategies are about as short-sighted as could be. Virtually all diets involve caloric allowances over short periods of time. Instead of allowing ourselves 730 000 calories over the course of the year, we allow ourselves 2000 calories a day (or more likely, 1500). Even this short-term allowance is usually broken down into more immediate units, such as 350 calories for breakfast, or 650 calories for dinner.

This segmentation of the diet has the advantage of making it clear what one can or cannot eat at any particular time, but it has the tremendous disadvantage of inflexibility. If the units of a diet are calories per meal, and those allowances are relatively ungenerous, it becomes all too easy to find oneself violating the diet. For instance, what if you are in an experiment in which you are virtually forced to consume 7.5 ounces or even 15 ounces of milk shake? Such an event effectively blows the diet, and in response most dieters give up. Having failed to maintain their caloric virtue, they lapse into a state of perdition, in which ice cream represents a temptation to which they might as well yield, as the damage has already been done.

The psychology underlying this phenomenon is made clear by the fact that one need not actually exceed one's caloric quota in order to give up the diet and overindulge; one need only think that one has blown one's diet, as is clear from the study in which dieters who were told that the milk shake was fattening went on to overeat, whereas those who thought that it was low calorie maintained their customary rejection of ice cream. To further emphasise the psychological nature of diet-breaking, researchers have demonstrated that merely anticipating having to consume a high calorie milk shake will make dieters abandon their diet.

We believe this research accurately reflects the dynamics of real life. Much of our lives involves eating, and often this social eating involves being induced to "just try" this or "have some more" of that. We eat because others around us are eating, as research in our own laboratory and elsewhere has amply demonstrated. If we don't, we are often subjected to more explicit pressure to eat. Our hosts will be disappointed, if not insulted. The food will go to waste. Restaurant and dinner party meals are often larger than necessary. Our dining companions want us to join them (and not just watch them) eating. All these elements conspire to induce dieters to eat when they know that they shouldn't; and once they have, the floodgates are open, and they tend to stay that way for some time.

Researchers have not yet looked systematically at how dieters regain control of themselves. The standard assumption—derived from dieters' own rationalisations—is that they will begin their diet again tomorrow morning, or perhaps on Monday; in any event, not tonight. The diet unit is most often the day—say, 1500 calories a day—so it "makes sense" to rededicate one's diet when self-control and a concern for the future, intensified by remorse over one's past, greet the dawn.

On the night before the morning after, however, dieters' overindulgences may reach legendary proportions. The seeming inability of dieters to stop once they have truly started stems from the Faustian bargain that they made when they exchanged normal, physiologically based controls on eating for deliberate cognitive controls. As was noted above, those normal controls tend to atrophy; included in the wastage are the processes normally involved in registering satiety. Dieters do not eat interminably once their diets are broken, but they often eat much more than nondieters ever do.

Although exceeding one's caloric quota is a good way to break one's diet, there are many other routes to dietary breakdown. Just as dieters may be misled into thinking that a particular amount of milk shake is too rich and therefore calorically excessive, so dieters, displaying the convoluted "logic" for which they are notable, may convince themselves that one particular type of calorie is more of a threat to their diet than some other type. For instance, in one study, dieters overate ice cream following a milk shake, but dieters given a mixture of cottage cheese and fruit salad equivalent in calories to the milk shake did not overeat. In the mind of the dieter, a bowl of cottage cheese and fruit salad does not violate a diet, no matter how many calories it may contain, whereas certain foods—such as milk shakes—will break a diet even in quite small quantities.

This sort of "magical thinking" is fostered by many popular diets that confer special powers on certain foods: they are said to promote weight loss by virtue of nutritional mechanisms that operate independently of their caloric content. Salads are diet foods, while forbidden food, such as milk shakes, cakes, sweets and sometimes even bread can demolish a diet even in minute amounts. If this sort of diet logic escapes you, remember that these same dieters also believe that once your diet is blown, 2000 calories of overindulgence is not much worse than 500, and that the slate will be clean in the morning.

The threats to one's dietary virtue considered so far involve caloric overindulgence that breeds on itself. But there are other reasons for abandoning a diet. There is now a considerable literature which shows that dieters tend to overeat when they are distressed. Nondieters tend to respond to distress by eating less, owing to the physiological concomitants of distress, such as the activation of the autonomic nervous system, which in turn elevates blood sugar levels and decreases hunger.

When people are distressed, one of the first things that goes is their commitment to long-term goals. They tend to shorten their sights, and lose control of their behaviour to powerful stimuli in the immediate environment. Customary inhibitions are loosened. Dieters, as we have seen, are largely oblivious to hunger as a guide for eating; instead, they rely on their dietary resolve. With their resolve weakened, dieters faced with attractive food will eat it.

Many clinicians have interpreted as functional the overeating by fat people and other dieters when they are distressed: food or eating, they claim, serves to combat distress. Considerable research has failed to unearth any evidence for this; on the contrary, most dieters admit to feeling even worse once they acknowledge that they have added caloric insult to the original injury. Admittedly, it remains difficult to determine with any precision exactly how dieters are feeling while they are in the middle of a binge. Overeating may temporarily take their minds off their troubles, and asking them how they feel may serve merely to remind them that they have plenty to be upset about. Our preference, however, is to view distress-induced overeating not as a source of emotional comfort but as a result of a shift in the control of behaviour. The unperturbed dieter adheres to a long-term agenda of restraint, whereas agitated dieters cannot see beyond the irresistible temptations before them.

The same sort of process may well apply to anybody who chronically attempts to inhibit any sort of behaviour. Distress may make it difficult to say no to smoking, taking drugs or engaging in acts of aggression. All these behaviours are ordinarily under control, but people who are upset and no longer focused on the long-term consequences of their actions may find them irresistible. We believe that intoxicants such as alcohol similarly tend to undermine dieters' resolve by reducing their attention to long-term consequences, leaving them prey to immediate temptations.

The psychology of dieting is a struggle for control. Dieting demands self-control, but the world conspires to interfere, with the result that dieting has come to be known as a "losing battle". Dieters more often than not end up yo-yoing: weight fluctuates as periods of successful abstinence are cancelled out by bouts of capitulation to forbidden food. Indeed, there is mounting evidence that the periods of indulgence may more than compensate for the periods of abstinence.

Dieters' bodies may even actively defend the weight that so troubles the dieter. As weight is lost, various alterations occur that make it more difficult to lose more weight, and much easier to put weight on again. Most people are familiar with the sad fact that weight loss triggers a slowing of metabolic rate so that it takes fewer calories to support normal activities. Weight loss proceeds reasonably well at first on most diets, but eventually grinds to a frustrating halt. This is largely due to the fact that our bodies adjust to a lower weight by shifting to a thrifty metabolism that in effect squeezes more energy out of each calorie consumed.

At the same time other defensive adjustments make continued weight loss difficult or impossible. Significant weight loss breeds lethargy, which in its way contributes to the body's effort to restore its weight to a higher level. Weight loss alters our reaction to food as well. Michel Cabanac has documented a phenomenon he calls "negative alliesthesia", a decrease in the pleasantness of sweets following a meal or caloric load. Ordinarily, we all exhibit negative alliesthesia; after a rich meal, our preference for sweets is less than it was before the meal. But people who have lost weight do not show the negative alliesthesia reaction; their sweet preference remains high. In one study, Cabanac and two of his colleagues each lost about 10 per cent of their body weight to prove the point. Cabanac interprets this sweet tooth reaction as defensive in nature: the body is trying to seduce its owner into excessive indulgence—of sweet, calorically dense foods—so that the lost weight may be restored.

Finally, there is a wealth of evidence that dieters' attempts to resist food produce a countervailing pressure in the form of obsessive thinking about food. The most notable study in this regard involved a number of conscientious objectors during the Second World War who voluntarily lost almost a quarter of their body weight. Their minds, as a consequence, came to be monopolised by thoughts of food, including fantasies of gourmet meals past and to come, and plans for their future career as chefs. These obsessions are considered to be the mental equivalent of the physiological and perceptual defences trying to make the underweight individual eat if possible. Note that the food thoughts produced by hunger are about the sensual attractions of food, and not about food's caloric threat to the waistline.

All the foregoing reactions have been interpreted as natural defences, designed to promote eating in people who are eating less than they should. Of course, some people who are eating less than they should may have no alternative: our world contains many more genuinely starving people than dieters. If a starving person's metabolism slows down, that may prolong life. And starving people are likely to lower their threshold of acceptability for particular foods, occasionally eating substances that we would not normally consider edible.

But starving people do not usually need convincing; they are more than ready to comply with the nutritional demands of their bodies, if only food were to become available. Dieters, by contrast, are intent on resisting food, and resisting the weight-restoring defences erected by their bodies. They are engaged in a conflict that is opposite to that of the starving person: the dieter wants to eat less than the environment provides.

This conflict at the heart of dieting is a source of continual stress. As well as making it difficult to maintain control over eating, this stress has other, more remote effects. Dieters regularly score higher than nondieters on measures of emotional agitation; in the laboratory, they tend to overreact to emotional provocation. Also, dieters are more easily distracted when performing certain mental tasks, such as proofreading, and are more likely to show impairment of mental performance when they are observed by others. All these effects are consistent with the argument that dieters are in a chronically stressed state.

We have become so accustomed to dieting that the notion of deliberate undereating no longer seems to require explanation. But when we observe the defensive reactions with which our physiology combats deliberate undereating, and when we consider the evolutionary heritage that makes undereating a threat to our wellbeing, then perhaps we are entitled to question the wisdom of dieting. Let us begin by examining the reasons that people offer for undertaking dieting in the first place.

Until recently, the major problem facing people was how to obtain enough food. Just a century ago, our great grandparents' only concern was that their children be sufficiently stout. The dramatic extension of people's lifespan over the past century has had the ironic effect of bringing to the fore diseases that most people in earlier times did not live long enough to die from.

Heart disease and other diseases thought to be associated with being overweight must in this sense be considered luxury diseases. The actuaries who work in the insurance industry have provided us with "ideal weights" which allegedly minimise the risks of disease and death. You can now be too fat: a report published in 1985 from the US National Institutes of Health decreed that in general Americans were too fat for their own good. Even as little as five excess pounds may pose a serious health risk, the report suggested. No wonder dieting has become a national preoccupation in the US.

The case against being overweight, however, is not as clear as one might imagine. Many of the alleged health consequences of excess weight are merely correlations; they have not been shown to be caused by excess weight per se. More interestingly, recent evidence suggests that dieting itself may impair one's health, especially if dieting results in wide weight swings, which is the typical pattern. Thus, when fat people are judged actuarially to be at greater risk, we must ask whether the dieting that often accompanies their obesity contributes significantly to that risk.

Of course, health concerns are not the only reason for dieting. Many dieters—perhaps most—are at least equally concerned about their appearance, and strenuous dieting is still the main method for losing those unsightly bulges. But why is slimness considered more attractive than fatness? When we ask this question of our friends and relatives, we are usually met with a look of incredulity that seems specially designed for academics who persist in their obtuseness. It is evident to almost everyone that the overweight are aesthetically unappealing; beauty and ugliness require no explanation beyond their manifestation.

We remain uncertain as to the source of the aesthetic derogation of fatness, and the corresponding idealisation of slimness. We are not short of suggestions. Perhaps we value what is rare; nowadays, slimness is increasingly in short supply, whereas in the days of Rubens's well-endowed nudes a little extra flesh had a rare and special allure. Perhaps one's manifest physique is an index of prestige: whereas in feudal times only the lords could afford to feast, now it is only the well-off who can afford a week at a health farm.

Beyond health and attractiveness, dieters often gain a sense of personal satisfaction from dieting—often from just deciding to diet—because dieting represents an explicit commitment to self-improvement and confers a feeling that one has taken control over at least one facet of one's life. One is reminded of the Protestant ethic—and, perversely, of Ambrose Bierce's definition of an abstainer as "a weak person who yields to the temptation of denying himself a pleasure".

All the reasons that impel individuals to diet are reinforced socially. The medical profession is strongly and vocally committed to decrying the perils of overweight, and doctors are often inclined to blame various ills on excess weight itself—and then blame the overweight person for being overweight. The fashion and entertainment industries likewise have little use for the overweight. Media stars are notable for their idealised physical appearance; whatever else women have liberated themselves from, they remain subject to the tyranny of looking good—and that means slim. Our culture generally displays widespread prejudice against the wide-spread. "Fat" jokes are tolerated where jokes regarding other individual characteristics or disabilities would not be. One of the first epithets learned in the school playground is "fat", and school children in one study showed a stronger aversion to being obese than to being blind or physically crippled.

Recent years have seen attempts to combat prejudice against overweight people. The National Association to Advance Fat Acceptance in the US publishes a newsletter, holds conventions, monitors the media and assists in legal proceedings intended to overcome prejudice. Magazines directed to fat women are marketed. But like most liberation movements, fat liberation has had to reconcile two contradictory impulses: fat people's desires to be accepted as they are, and fat people's desire to become slim, or at least not fat. Some headway has been made in raising consciousness about the damage that prejudicial attitudes cause, but the battle has barely begun, and fat people remain socially stigmatised.

From the psychological point of view, perhaps the most interesting feature of dieting—one that helps to explain both society's aversion to fat and the tremendous difficulty fat people have in losing weight—is the ambiguity of weight control. The diet industry, worth tens of billions of dollars a year, has as its premise the notion that people can lose weight. It also adds its voice to the chorus suggesting that people should lose weight, but that chorus hardly needs additional support.

Much of the research on dieting and dieters, however, suggests that the attempt to lose weight is likely to fail, that deliberate restriction of one's food intake is, while obviously possible, nevertheless a precarious endeavour. As we have already seen, dietary restraint is subject to all sorts of disruptions. The allure of food is constantly threatening to break through and take control. Abstinence can all too quickly become unrestrained gorging, and the effect of these high calorie lapses is exacerbated by physiological defences that incline the body toward weight gain.

Although the past two decades have seen increasing media attention to the biological basis of weight, to the idea that the weight that we naturally attain may be a reflection of our underlying physiology, perhaps even our genetics, there is still insufficient attention paid to the difficulties and costs of weight reduction. Admittedly, weight reduction is possible; this evident fact makes it difficult to argue for a simple-minded interpretation of obesity in which weight is simply fixed by our genes.

Weight is not fixed, but it is apparently defended, and dieters who attempt to overcome those defences are going to have to pay a price. Substituting a diet for normal physiological controls on eating leads ultimately to counter-regulation and disinhibition. Even those who do succeed in losing some weight find that the struggle intensifies as their weight declines. Dieters' battle is with their own bodies; and to this point, matter has the upper hand on mind.

For many years, overweight has been regarded as a problem to which dieting is the solution. Now it is clear that being "overweight" cannot necessarily be viewed as a disorder; it may well be a perfectly natural state for some people. Dieting, in fact, may be more of an insult to nature. Certainly nature takes its revenge physiologically and psychologically on most dieters.

This argument is not equivalent to an endorsement of the notion that nothing must be restricted. But at the same time, we must remember that the ideal is by definition neither too much nor too little. Diet consciousness—with its paroxysms of logic, its attempt to subject the body to the whims of fashion, and its persistent stress and frustrations—continues to cause at least as many problems as it solves.

It is no accident that the major eating disorders—anorexia nervosa and bulimia nervosa—are invariably preceded by strenuous dieting. The normal psychology of dieting is simply a template for the abnormal psychology of eating disorders. And the symptoms of eating disorders—alternating abstinence and bingeing, emotional volatility, magical and disoriented thinking, low self-esteem and the pervasive pursuit of slimness—are all writ small in everyday dieting.

# CHALLENGE QUESTIONS

## Does Body Chemistry Govern Eating Behavior?

1. Is dieting dangerous? From what evidence do you draw your conclusion?

2. If you were experiencing a weight problem, from whom would you seek help: a medical doctor or a psychologist? Why?

3. How do you think eating disorders should be treated? Why would such a treatment be effective?

4. Herman and Polivy state that dieters "counter-regulate." What implications does this have for the treatment of chronic dieters?

# ISSUE 3

## Can Mental Attitude Affect Biological Disease?

**YES: Bernard Dixon,** from "Dangerous Thoughts," *Science86 Magazine,* a publication of the American Association for the Advancement of Science (April 1986)

**NO: Marcia Angell,** from "Disease as a Reflection of the Psyche," *The New England Journal of Medicine* (June 13, 1985)

### ISSUE SUMMARY

**YES:** Bernard Dixon, an editor and writer who specializes in science and health issues, proposes that a positive mental attitude can prevent illness because it reduces psychological stress, which can impair functioning of the immune system.

**NO:** After reviewing the available research, Marcia Angell, a physician and the executive editor of the *New England Journal of Medicine,* concludes that maintaining a positive attitude will not ward off disease.

Does our mood and self-esteem influence our physical health? Many scientists, from medical professionals to psychologists, are attempting to answer this provocative question. Proponents of holistic medicine believe in relying to some degree on oneself and one's own mood and attitude for physical health. This is the basis on which support groups for people who are battling diseases are developed. These groups are intended to empower members and improve their attitudes toward themselves and toward their disease and thus improve their health. Are these groups effective in promoting health? If so, what elements of the groups might be responsible?

The fields of health psychology and behavioral medicine attempt to answer questions such as these. Health psychologists study how psychological factors might influence the health and well-being of people, while professionals who study behavioral medicine are concerned with the "behaviors" of health, illness, and related dysfunctions. Persons in these fields consult with medical professionals regarding the effect of illness on a patient's psychological state and vice versa. Psychologists also involve themselves in support groups, bringing to these groups their knowledge of the relation between attitude and physical health. How is the *psyche* (mind) and *soma* (body) connected? Does a mind-body connection help explain recovery from disease?

In the selections that follow, Bernard Dixon presents some human and animal research indicating that psychological stressors (such as anxiety or bereavement) have a negative impact on the immune system, which is a crucial part of the body's defense against illness and disease. Additionally, he argues that mood disorders, such as depression, also negatively affect the immune system.

Marcia Angell criticizes the available research on the connection between mental state and disease. She states that most of this research is anecdotal or methodologically flawed, the biggest flaws being design problems and interpretive bias. Angell also describes research indicating that there is no effect of psychosocial factors on certain illnesses (such as cancer). Although she concedes that a *belief* that attitude can affect disease may have both negative and positive effects, she maintains that individuals should not be made to feel responsible for developing diseases.

| POINT | COUNTERPOINT |
|---|---|
| • In addition to organic components, illness has strong psychological components. | • Illness is governed by physiological processes almost exclusively. |
| • Research shows that mental state can profoundly affect physical health and illness. | • Research indicating that mental state can cause or cure illnesses is flawed. |
| • Improving mood and attitude can improve recovery from and future avoidance of physical illness. | • The belief that mental state determines physical health can be harmful. |

# YES

### Bernard Dixon

# DANGEROUS THOUGHTS

### HOW WE THINK AND FEEL CAN MAKE US SICK

Until recently, Ellen hadn't seen a physician in years. When other people got a bug, she was the one who invariably stayed healthy. But then her luck seemed to change. First she caught a bad cold in January, then had a bout of flu in February, followed by a nasty cough that still lingers. What an infuriating coincidence that these ailments hit as her career was faltering—months of unemployment following companywide layoffs.

But is it a coincidence? Intuition may suggest that we have fewer colds when we are content with our lives, more when we are under stress. That the mind can influence the body's vulnerability to infection in an insidious but potent way is a perennial theme of folklore and literature. Now even scientists are beginning to take that idea seriously. An alliance of psychiatrists, immunologists, neuroscientists, and microbiologists, specialists who rarely look beyond their own disciplines, are beginning to work together in a field so new that it goes under a variety of names, including behavioral immunology, psychoimmunology, and neuroimmunomodulation. Behind these polysyllables lies the challenge of understanding the chemical and anatomical connections between mind and body and eventually, perhaps, even preventing psychosomatic illness.

Just 10 years ago, most specialists in communicable disease would have scoffed at any suggestion that the mind can influence the body in this way. Textbooks portrayed infection as the simple, predictable outcome whenever a disease causing microbe encountered a susceptible host. Various factors such as old age, malnutrition, and overwork could make a disease more severe. But there was no place for the fanciful notion that elation, depression, contentment, or stress could affect the course of disease.

Today, that once-conventional wisdom is being revised by scientists around the world. Playing a major role in these investigations are researchers at England's Medical Research Council Common Cold Unit near Salisbury. Their work shows that even this relatively trivial infection is affected by the psyche. And the lessons learned may apply to more serious diseases, including cancer.

For nearly four decades now, volunteers at the Common Cold Unit have helped test the efficacy of new antiviral drugs and have proven that colds are caused by rhinoviruses and a few related viruses. In 1975 psychologist Richard Totman at Nuffield College, Oxford, and Wallace Craig and Sylvia Reed of the Common Cold Unit conducted the first psychological experiments. The scientists infected 48 healthy volunteers by dribbling down their nostrils drops containing two common cold viruses. The researchers then offered 23 of their subjects the chance to take a new "drug," actually a placebo, that would presumably prevent colds. The investigators warned these subjects that if they accepted this treatment, they would have to have their gastric juices sampled with a stomach tube. The scientists had no intention of doing this; the warning was simply a ruse to put the volunteers under stress. The other half of the group was neither offered the drug nor cautioned about the stomach tube. Totman and his colleagues theorized that the 23 offered the placebo would experience either mild anxiety or regret, depending on the decision they made. This might cause them to allay their state of mind by justifying to themselves their decision—as a theory called cognitive dissonance predicts—which would result in greater bodily resistance and milder colds.

The experts were wrong. When an independent physician assessed the volunteers' symptoms, he found that the 23 offered the choice had cold symptoms that were significantly more severe than those given no option. Apparently anxiety generated by contemplating some-thing unpleasant or refusing to help a worthy cause had a tangible influence on the course of the illness.

Totman's group also made some intriguing observations about the way stress affects people outside the laboratory. Volunteers were interviewed by a psychologist, received rhinoviruses, caught colds, and were monitored. Individuals who during the previous six months had experienced a stressful event, such as death of a loved one, divorce, or a layoff, developed worse colds than the others, and introverts had more severe colds than extroverts. Not only were the introverts' symptoms worse than those of their peers, their nasal secretions contained more rhinovirus, confirming that their illnesses were worse.

The Common Cold Unit is now trying to find out how stress affects people with strong social networks compared with their more introverted colleagues.

But how could an individual's mental state encourage or thwart the development of a cold? Research at several centers in the United States supports the most plausible explanation—that psychological stress impairs the effectiveness of the immune system, which has the dual role of recognizing and eliminating microbes from outside the body as well as cancer cells originating within.

The first line of defense of the immune system is the white blood cells called lymphocytes. These include B cells, which manufacture antibodies against microbes; helper T cells, which aid the B cells in making the right kind of antibodies; and killer T cells, which wipe out invading organisms if they have been exposed to them before. Another kind of lymphocyte, the natural killer cell, has received a lot of attention lately for its ability to detect and destroy harmful cells, including malignant ones, even if it hasn't encountered the invaders previously. Together with scavenging white blood cells that gobble up dead cells and debris, the various types of lymphocytes work in complex, coordinated ways to police the body's tissues.

Researchers can measure the efficiency of the immune system by measuring how well a patient's lymphocytes respond to foreign substances. For instance, they can grow the patient's lymphocytes in glassware and expose them to substances called mitogens, which mimic the behavior of microorganisms by stimulating the white cells to divide. Since a rapid increase in the number of white cells is a crucial early stage in the defense against invasion, patients whose white cells don't proliferate may have malfunctioning immune systems.

But most researchers are cautious about generalizing from the results obtained from a single technique of this sort, since the immune system has complicated backups to keep us healthy even when our lymphocytes aren't proliferating. Nevertheless, reports of stress reducing the efficiency of the immune system have been accumulating on such a scale—and with such variety—that it is becoming difficult to resist the conclusion that anxiety increases our vulnerability to disease.

In one landmark study, for example, Steven Schleifer and his colleagues at Mt. Sinai School of Medicine in New York sought help from spouses of women with advanced breast cancer. They persuaded 15 men to give blood samples every six to eight weeks during their wives' illnesses and for up to 14 months after the women died. While none of the men showed depressed lymphocyte response while their wives were ill, their white cell response was significantly lowered as early as two weeks after their wives died and for up to 14 months later. Schleifer believes he has shown, contrary to earlier studies, that it was bereavement, not the experience of the spouses' illness, that lowered immunity.

Prompted by his observations of the bereaved widowers, Schleifer wondered if serious, debilitating depression would also show up as weakened immunity. When he took blood samples from 18 depressed patients at Mt. Sinai and the Bronx Veterans Administration Hospital, he found their lymphocytes were significantly less responsive to mitogens than those of healthy individuals from the general population matched for age, sex, and race.

We sometimes think humans are uniquely vulnerable to anxiety, but stress seems to affect the immune defenses of lower animals too. In one experiment, for example, behavioral immunologist Mark Laudenslager and colleagues at the University of Denver gave mild electric shocks to 24 rats. Half the animals could switch off the current by turning a wheel in their enclosure, while the other half could not. The rats in the two groups were paired so that each time one rat turned the wheel it protected both itself and its helpless partner from the shock. Laudenslager found that the immune response was depressed below normal in the helpless rats but not in those that could turn off the electricity. What he has demonstrated, he believes, is that lack of control over an event, not the experience itself, is what weakens the immune system.

Other researchers agree. Jay Weiss, a psychologist at Duke University School of Medicine, has shown that animals who are allowed to control unpleasant stimuli don't develop sleep disturbances, ulcers, or changes in brain chemistry typical of stressed rats. But if the animals are confronted with situations they have no control over, they later behave passively when faced with experiences they can control. Such findings reinforce psychiatrists' suspicions that the experience or perception of helplessness is one of the most harmful factors in depression.

One of the most startling examples of how the mind can alter the immune response was discovered by chance. In 1975 psychologist Robert Ader at the University of Rochester School of Medicine and Dentistry conditioned mice to avoid saccharin by simultaneously feeding them the sweetener and injecting them with a drug that while suppressing their immune systems caused stomach upsets. Associating the saccharin with the stomach pains, the mice quickly learned to avoid the sweetener. In order to extinguish the taste aversion, Ader reexposed the animals to saccharin, this time without the drug, and was astonished to find that those rodents that had received the highest amounts of sweetener during their earlier conditioning died. He could only speculate that he had so successfully conditioned the rats that saccharin alone now served to weaken their immune systems enough to kill them.

If you can depress the immune system by conditioning, it stands to reason you can boost it in the same way. Novera Herbert Spector at the National Institute of Neurological and Communicative Disorders and Stroke in Bethesda, Maryland, recently directed a team at the University of Alabama, Birmingham, which confirmed that hypothesis. The researchers injected mice with a chemical that en-

hances natural killer cell activity while simultaneously exposing the rodents to the odor of camphor, which has no detectable effect on the immune system. After nine sessions, mice exposed to the camphor alone showed a large increase in natural killer cell activity.

What mechanism could account for these connections between the psyche and the immune system? One well-known link is the adrenal glands, which the brain alerts to produce adrenaline and other hormones that prepare the body to cope with danger or stress. But adrenal hormones cannot be the only link between mind and body. Research by a group under Neal Miller, professor emeritus of psychology at the Rockefeller University in New York City, has shown that even rats whose adrenal glands have been removed suffer depressed immunity after being exposed to electric shocks.

Anxiety, it seems, can trigger the release of many other hormones, including testosterone, insulin, and possibly even growth hormone. In addition, stress stimulates secretion of chemicals called neuropeptides, which influence mood and emotions. One class of neuropeptides known as endorphins kills pain and causes euphoria. Endorphins have another interesting characteristic: they fit snugly into receptors on lymphocytes, suggesting a direct route through which the mind could influence immunity.

This idea is borne out in the lab, where one of the natural pain-killers, beta-endorphin, can impair the response of lymphocytes in test tubes. Evidence from cancer studies shows that chemicals blocking the normal functions of endorphins can slow the growth of tumors. And other work suggests that tumor cells may be attracted to certain neuropeptides, providing a route for cancer to spread all over the body.

Neuropeptides are turning out to be extraordinarily versatile in their interaction with the immune system. At the National Institutes of Health in Bethesda, Maryland, Michael Ruff has found neuropeptides that attract scavenging white cells called macrophages to the site of injured or damaged tissue. There the macrophages regulate and activate other immune cells as well as gobble up bacteria and debris. What is even more surprising, however, is that the macrophages themselves actually release neuropeptides. This has led Ruff to speculate that these scavenging white cells may also serve as free-floating nerve cells able to communicate with the brain.

But why should that two-way communication sometimes have the effect of allowing stress to upset the body's defenses? One answer may lie in evolution. When early man was attacked by a saber-toothed tiger, for example, it may have been more important from a survival standpoint for his immune system to turn off briefly. In its zeal to get rid of foreign matter and damaged tissue, a revved-up immune system can also attack healthy tissue. Shutting down the immune system for a short time would avert any damage to the body's healthy tissues and would cause no harm, since it takes a while for infection to set in. As soon as the danger had passed, the immune system was able to rebound— perhaps stronger than before—and go about its main business of fighting invading organisms. But the kind of stress we modern humans suffer is of a different kind: it is rarely life threatening and often lasts a long time, weakening our immune defenses for long periods and making us vulnerable to infections and cancer.

The immune system is extraordinarily complex, and the mind is even more so. As Nicholas Hall of George Washington University School of Medicine says, "We're putting together two kinds of black boxes and trying to make sense of what happens."

In the process, researchers are wrestling with three issues of scientific and social import. First, what can be done to protect people at vulnerable times in their lives from a potentially catastrophic failure of their immune defenses? Second, should counseling and psychological support become as important as traditional therapeutic measures in the treatment of disease? And finally, what are the corresponding benefits to health of the positive emotions of hope, affection, love, mirth, and joy?

# NO

Marcia Angell

## DISEASE AS A REFLECTION
## OF THE PSYCHE

Is cancer more likely in unhappy people? Can people who have cancer improve their chances of survival by learning to enjoy life and to think optimistically? What about heart attacks, peptic ulcers, asthma, rheumatoid arthritis, and inflammatory bowel disease? Are they caused by stress in certain personality types, and will changing the personality change the course of the disease? A stranger in this country would not have to be here very long to guess that most Americans think the answer to these questions is yes.

The popular media, stirred by occasional reports in the medical literature, remind us incessantly of the hazards of certain personality types. We are told that Type A people are vulnerable to heart attacks, repressed people (especially those who have suffered losses) are at risk of cancer, worry causes peptic ulcers, and so on. The connection between mental state and disease would seem to be direct and overriding. The hard-driving executive has a heart attack *because* he is pushing for promotion; the middle-aged housewife gets breast cancer *because* she is brooding about her empty nest.

Furthermore, we are told that just as mental state causes disease, so can changes in our outlook and approach to life restore health. Books, magazines, and talk shows abound in highly specific advice about achieving the necessary changes, as well as in explanations about how they work. Norman Cousins, for example, tells us how he managed to achieve a remission of his ankylosing spondylitis by means of laughter and vitamin C—the former, he assumes, operating through reversal of "adrenal exhaustion."[1] Carl and Stephanie Simonton prescribe certain techniques of relaxation and imagery as an adjunct to the conventional treatment of cancer.[2] The imagery includes picturing white cells (strong and purposeful) destroying cancer cells (weak and confused).

Clearly, this sort of postulated connection between mental state and disease is not limited to the effect of mood on our sense of physical well-being. Nor are

From Marcia Angell, "Disease as a Reflection of the Psyche," *The New England Journal of Medicine*, vol. 312, no. 24 (June 13, 1985), pp. 1570–1572. Copyright © 1985 by The Massachusetts Medical Society. Reprinted by permission.

we talking about relaxation as a worthy goal in itself. Cousins, the Simontons, and others of their persuasion advocate a way of thinking not as an end, but rather as a means for defeating disease. The assumption is that mental state is a major factor in causing and curing specific diseases. Is it, and what is the effect of believing that it is?

The notion that certain mental states bring on certain diseases is not new. In her book, *Illness as Metaphor*, Susan Sontag describes the myths surrounding two mysterious and terrifying diseases—tuberculosis in the 19th century and cancer in the 20th.[3] Tuberculosis was thought to be a disease of excessive feeling. Overly passionate artists "consumed" themselves, both emotionally and through the disease. In contrast, cancer is seen today as a disease of depletion. Emotionally spent people no longer have the energy to battle renegade cells. As Sontag points out, myths like these arise when a disease of unknown cause is particularly dreaded. The myth serves as a form of mastery—we can predict where the disease will strike and we can perhaps ward it off by modifying our inner life. Interestingly, when the cause of such a disease is discovered, it is usually relatively simple and does not involve psychological factors. For example, the elaborate construct of a tuberculosis-prone personality evaporated when tuberculosis was found to be caused by the tubercle bacillus.

The evidence for mental state as a cause and cure of today's scourges is not much better than it was for the afflictions of earlier centuries. Most reports of such a connection are anecdotal. They usually deal with patients whose disease remitted after some form of positive thinking, and there is no attempt to determine the frequency of this occurrence and compare it with the frequency of remission without positive thinking. Other, more ambitious studies suffer from such serious flaws in design or analysis that bias is nearly inevitable.[4] In some instances, the bias lies in the interpretation. One frequently cited study, for example, reports that the death rate among people who have recently lost their spouses is higher than that among married people.[5] Although the authors were cautious in their interpretation, others have been quick to ascribe the finding to grief rather than to, say, a change in diet or other habits. Similarly, the known physiologic effects of stress on the adrenal glands are often overinterpreted so that it is a short leap to a view of stress as a cause of one disease or another. In short, the literature contains very few scientifically sound studies of the relation, if there is one, between mental state and disease.

In this issue of the *Journal*, Cassileth et al. report the results of a careful prospective study of 359 cancer patients, showing no correlation between a number of psychosocial factors and progression of the disease.[6] In an earlier prospective study of another disease, Case et al. found no correlation between Type A personality and recurrence of acute myocardial infarction.[7] The fact that these well-designed studies were negative raises the possibility that we have been too ready to accept the venerable belief that mental state is an important factor in the cause and cure of disease.

Is there any harm in this belief, apart from its lack of scientific substantiation? It might be argued that it is not only harmless but beneficial, in that it allows patients some sense of control over their disease. If, for example, patients believe that imagery can help arrest cancer, then they feel less helpless; there is something they can do.

On the other hand, if cancer spreads, despite every attempt to think positively, is the patient at fault? It might seem so. According to Robert Mack, a surgeon who has cancer and is an adherent of the methods of the Simontons, "The patients who survive with cancer or with another catastrophic illness, perhaps even in the face of almost insurmountable odds, seem to be those who have developed a very strong will to live and who value each day, one at a time."[8] What about the patients who *don't* survive? Are they lacking the will to live, or perhaps self-discipline or some other personal attribute necessary to hold cancer at bay? After all, a view that attaches credit to patients for controlling their disease also implies blame for the progression of the disease. Katherine Mansfield described the resulting sense of personal inadequacy in an entry in her journal a year before her death from tuberculosis: "A bad day... horrible pains and so on, and weakness. I could do nothing. The weakness was not only physical. I must *heal my Self* before I will be well.... This must be done alone and at once. It is at the root of my not getting better. My mind is not *controlled*."[3] In addition to the anguish of personal failure, a further harm to such patients is that they may come to see medical care as largely irrelevant, as Cassileth et al. point out, and give themselves over completely to some method of thought control.

The medical profession also participates in the tendency to hold the patient responsible for his progress. In our desire to pay tribute to gallantry and grace in the face of hardship, we sometimes credit these qualities with cures, not realizing that we may also be implying blame when there are reverses. William Schroeder, celebrated by the media and his doctors as though he were responsible for his own renascence after implantation of an artificial heart, was later gently scolded for slackening. Dr. Allan Lansing of Humana Heart Institute worried aloud about Schroeder's "ostrich-like" behavior after a stroke and emphasized the importance of "inner strength and determination."[9]

I do not wish to argue that people have no responsibility for their health. On the contrary, there is overwhelming evidence that certain personal habits, such as smoking cigarettes, drinking alcohol, and eating a diet rich in cholesterol and saturated fats, can have great impact on health, and changing our thinking affects these habits. However, it is time to acknowledge that our belief in disease as a direct reflection of mental state is largely folklore. Furthermore, the corollary view of sickness and death as a personal failure is a particularly unfortunate form of blaming the victim. At a time when patients are already burdened by disease, they should not be further burdened by having to accept responsibility for the outcome.

## REFERENCES

1. Cousins N. Anatomy of an illness as perceived by the patient. New York: WW Norton, 1979.
2. Simonton OC, Matthews-Simonton S, Creighton J. Getting well again: a step-by-step, self-help guide to overcoming cancer for patients and their families. Los Angeles: JP Tarcher, 1978.
3. Sontag S. Illness as metaphor. New York: Farrar, Straus and Giroux, 1977.
4. Fox BH. Premorbid psychological factors as related to cancer incidence. J Behav Med 1978; 1:45–133.
5. Kraus AS, Lilienfeld AM. Some epidemiologic aspects of the high mortality rate in the young widowed group. J Chronic Dis 1959; 10:207–17.

6. Cassileth BR, Lusk EJ, Miller DS, Brown LL, Miller C. Psychosocial correlates of survival in advanced malignant disease. N Engl J Med 1985; 312:1551–5.
7. Case RB, Heller SS, Case NB, et al. Type A behavior and survival after acute myocardial infarction. N Engl J Med 1985; 312:737–41.
8. Mack RM. Lessons from living with cancer. N Engl J Med 1985; 311:1640–4.
9. McLaughlin L. Schroeder kin, doctors try to lift his spirits. Boston Globe. December 17, 1984:1.

# CHALLENGE QUESTIONS
## Can Mental Attitude Affect Biological Disease?

1. When you are ill, what is your typical course of action? What assumptions is this action based on?

2. Under what circumstances, if any, do you feel that people's state of mind affects their physical health?

3. If you were diagnosed with a serious illness, would improving your mental attitude be part of your treatment regimen? Why, or why not?

4. How do stress and anxiety affect a person's quality of life and vice versa?

# PART 2

# Cognitive Processes

*The nature and limitations of our mental (or cognitive) processes pose fundamental questions for psychologists. Are mental capacities, such as intelligence, determined at birth, or can they be increased with the proper form of education? Also, how reliable is memory? For example, are memories of early sexual abuse always reliable? Can they be trusted enough to bring alleged abusers to trial? Some argue, on the other hand, that we can remember more than we know and that this is the underlying process of subliminal advertising. Can an advertiser manipulate our mental processes so that we buy something without full awareness?*

- Are Memories of Sexual Abuse Always Real?

- Is Subliminal Advertising Effective?

- Can Intelligence Be Increased?

# ISSUE 4

# Are Memories of Sexual Abuse Always Real?

**YES: Ellen Bass and Laura Davis,** from *The Courage to Heal: A Guide for Women Survivors of Child Sexual Abuse* (Harper & Row, 1988)

**NO: Lee Coleman,** from "Creating 'Memories' of Sexual Abuse," *Issues in Child Abuse Accusations* (vol. 4, no. 4, 1992)

**ISSUE SUMMARY**

**YES:** Ellen Bass and Laura Davis, both counselors of victims of child sexual abuse, assert that even a faint or vague memory of sexual abuse is prime evidence that sexual abuse has occurred.

**NO:** Psychiatrist Lee Coleman argues that individual memories of sexual abuse are susceptible to manipulation by laypersons and mental health professionals and that "memories" of sexual abuse that never occurred can be created in therapy.

It is hard to imagine a more heinous crime than sexual abuse. Yet, perhaps surprisingly, it is a crime that often goes unpunished. Frequently, sexual abusers are family members and their victims are children who are too young to protest or to know that they are being violated. This is part of the reason why memories have become so significant to the sexual abuse issue. Often, it is not until the victims become adults that they realize they were abused.

The problem is that the reliability of memory itself has come into question. Some cognitive psychologists have expressed doubt about the accuracy of memories when people are formally questioned (such as on the witness stand). Another issue is whether or not memory is subject to manipulation. People under hypnosis, for example, tend to be susceptible to the hypnotist's suggestions as to what they "should" remember. Do therapists of alleged victims of sexual abuse make similar suggestions? Could these therapists be unconsciously or consciously "shaping" through therapeutic suggestion the memories of the people they treat?

In the following selections, Ellen Bass and Laura Davis hold that memories of and what they identify as symptoms of sexual abuse are sufficient evidence that a person was abused. They provide a list of experiences that, if remembered, indicate that a person was probably abused. They also describe a number of the symptoms that they contend are commonly experienced by those who have been abused. Bass and Davis emphasize that a lack of explicit memories about sexual abuse does not mean that abuse did not occur.

Lee Coleman refutes the claims of those who place faith in all memories of sexual abuse. He argues that people can be led to believe that they were sexually abused when, in fact, they were not. Coleman presents a case to show that so-called recovered memories of sexual abuse can be created in therapy with the encouragement of mental health professionals. He holds that professionals who consider themselves specialists in sexual abuse recovery tend to accept without question that sexual abuse has occurred if a client says it has, to encourage as many memories as possible, and to accept all allegations of sexual abuse as real. Coleman views these professionals as manipulative and often without awareness.

| POINT | COUNTERPOINT |
|---|---|
| • If someone says that they believe they were sexually abused, they probably were. | • People can be made to believe that they have been sexually abused when, in fact, they have not. |
| • Memories for traumatic events are likely to be repressed, so they must be "helped" to be recovered. | • "Helping" memories to be recovered can unintentionally create them. |
| • Mental health professionals do not create people's memories for them. | • Mental health professionals sometimes create false memories for their patients. |
| • Memory is like a videotape that records things exactly as they occur. | • Evidence shows that memory is not infallible and can be distorted and inaccurate. |

# YES

Ellen Bass and
Laura Davis

# THE COURAGE TO HEAL

If you have been sexually abused, you are not alone. One out of three girls, and one out of seven boys, are sexually abused by the time they reach the age of eighteen. Sexual abuse happens to children of every class, culture, race, religion, and gender. Children are abused by fathers, stepfathers, uncles, brothers, grandparents, neighbors, family friends, baby-sitters, teachers, strangers, and sometimes by aunts and mothers.[1] Although women do abuse, the vast majority of abusers are heterosexual men.

All sexual abuse is damaging, and the trauma does not end when the abuse stops. If you were abused as a child, you are probably experiencing long-term effects that interfere with your day-to-day functioning.

However, it is possible to heal. It is even possible to thrive. Thriving means more than just an alleviation of symptoms, more than band-aids, more than functioning adequately. Thriving means enjoying a feeling of wholeness, satisfaction in your life and work, genuine love and trust in your relationships, pleasure in your body.

Until now, much of the literature on child sexual abuse has documented the ravages of abuse, talking extensively about "the tragedy of ruined lives," but little about recovery. This [reading] is about recovery—what it takes, what it feels like, how it can transform your life.

People say "time heals all wounds," and it's true to a certain extent. Time will dull some of the pain, but deep healing doesn't happen unless you consciously choose it. Healing from child sexual abuse takes years of commitment and dedication. But if you are willing to work hard, if you are determined to make lasting changes in your life, if you are able to find good resources and skilled support, you can not only heal but thrive. We believe in miracles and hard work.

## HOW CAN I KNOW IF I WAS A VICTIM OF CHILD SEXUAL ABUSE?

When you were a young child or teenager, were you:

- Touched in sexual areas?

Excerpted from Ellen Bass and Laura Davis, *The Courage to Heal: A Guide for Women Survivors of Child Sexual Abuse* (Harper & Row, 1988), pp. 20–22, 70–83. Copyright © 1988 by Ellen Bass and Laura Davis. Reprinted by permission of HarperCollins Publishers, Inc.

- Shown sexual movies or forced to listen to sexual talk?
- Made to pose for seductive or sexual photographs?
- Subjected to unnecessary medical treatments?
- Forced to perform oral sex on an adult or sibling?
- Raped or otherwise penetrated?
- Fondled, kissed, or held in a way that made you uncomfortable?
- Forced to take part in ritualized abuse in which you were physically or sexually tortured?
- Made to watch sexual acts or look at sexual parts?
- Bathed in a way that felt intrusive to you?
- Objectified and ridiculed about your body?
- Encouraged or goaded into sex you didn't really want?
- Told all you were good for was sex?
- Involved in child prostitution or pornography?[2]

If you are unable to remember any specific instances like the ones mentioned above but still have a feeling that something abusive happened to you, it probably did....

Children often cope with abuse by forgetting it ever happened. As a result, you may have no conscious memory of being abused. You may have forgotten large chunks of your childhood. Yet there are things you do remember. When you are touched in a certain way, you feel nauseated. Certain words or facial expressions scare you. You know you never liked your mother to touch you. You slept with your clothes on in junior high school. You were taken to the doctor repeatedly for vaginal infections.

You may think you don't have memories, but often as you begin to talk about what you do remember, there emerges a constellation of feelings, reactions, and recollections that add up to substantial information. To say "I was abused," you don't need the kind of recall that would stand up in a court of law.

Often the knowledge that you were abused starts with a tiny feeling, an intuition. It's important to trust that inner voice and work from there. Assume your feelings are valid. So far, no one we've talked to thought she might have been abused, and then later discovered that she hadn't been. The progression always goes the other way, from suspicion to confirmation. If you think you were abused and your life shows the symptoms, then you were....

\* \* \*

I've looked the memories in the face and smelled their breath. They can't hurt me anymore.

For many survivors, remembering is the first step in healing. To begin with, you may have to remember that you *were* abused at all. Second come specific memories.... The third kind of remembering is the recovery of the feelings you had at the time the abuse took place. Many women have always remembered the physical details of what happened but have forgotten the emotions that went with it. One survivor explained, "I could rattle off the facts of my abuse like a grocery list, but remembering the fear and terror and pain was another matter entirely."

Remembering is different for every survivor. If, as a young woman, you turned your abuser in to the police and testified against him in court, there's not much chance you forgot. Likewise, if you had to raise your abuser's child, or abort it, you've probably always remembered. Or the abuse may have been so present in the daily texture of your life that there was no way to forget.

One woman who'd kept a vivid image of what had happened to her said she sometimes wished she *had* forgotten: "I wish I could have gotten shock treatments like my mother. She had forgotten huge segments of her life, and I used to envy her." On the other hand, this woman said she was glad she'd always known just how bad things were: "At least I knew why I was weird! Knowing what had happened allowed me to work on the damn problem."

You may not have forgotten entirely, but coped by having selective memories.

I always knew that we had an incestuous relationship. I remember the first time I heard the word "incest," when I was seventeen. I hadn't known there was a word for it. I always remembered my father grabbing my breasts and kissing me.

I told my therapist, "I remember every miserable thing that happened to me." It seemed like I remembered so much, how could there be more? I didn't remember anything *but* abuse. But I didn't remember being raped, even though I knew I had been. I categorically told my therapist, "I don't want to remember being raped." We talked about the fact that I didn't want to remember that for months. Yet I knew my father had been my first lover.

There is no right or wrong when it comes to remembering. You may have multiple memories. Or you may just have one. Years of abuse are sometimes telescoped into a single recollection. When you begin to remember, you might have new images every day for weeks on end. Or you may experience your memories in clumps, three or four of them coming

in a matter of days, then not again for months. Sometimes survivors remember one abuser, or a specific kind of abuse, only to remember, years later, a second abuser or a different form of abuse.

There are many women who show signs of having been abused without having any memories. You may have only a vague feeling that something happened but be unable to remember what it was. There are reasons for this, and to understand them, we have to first look at the way early memories are stored.

## ABOUT MEMORIES

The process of storing memories is complex. We store different experiences in the right and left halves of our brain. The left brain stores sequential, logical, language-oriented experience; the right stores perceptual, spatial experiences. When we try to retrieve right-brain information through left-brain techniques, such as logic and language, we sometimes hit a blank. There are some experiences that we are simply not going to remember in an orderly, precise way.

If you were abused when you were pre-verbal, or just as you were learning to talk, you had no way of making sense of what was happening to you. Babies don't know the difference between touching someone's penis and touching someone's leg. If a penis is put in their mouth, they will suck it, much as they would a breast or a bottle. Young children are aware of sensations but cannot come up with a name or a concept—like "sexual abuse"—for what is being done to them.

Another thing that makes remembering difficult is the simple fact that you are trying to remember details of something that happened a long time ago. If you ask friends who weren't abused, you will find that most of them also don't remember a great number of details from their childhood. It is even more difficult to remember the times when we were hurt, humiliated, or otherwise violated.

If the abuse happened only once, or if it was an abuse that is hard to name (inappropriate boundaries, lewd looks, subtler forms of abuse), it can be even harder to remember. For others, the constancy of the abuse prevents detailed naming. As one survivor put it, "Do you remember every time you sat down to eat? What you had for dinner the Tuesday you turned six? I remember the flavor. It was a constant, like eating. It was always there."

## WHAT REMEMBERING IS LIKE

Recovering occluded memories (those blocked from the surface) is not like remembering with the conscious mind. Often the memories are vague and dreamlike, as if they're being seen from far away.

> The actual rape memories for me are like from the end of a tunnel. That's because I literally left my body at the scene. So I remember it from that perspective—there's some physical distance between me and what's going on. Those memories aren't as sharp in focus. It's like they happened in another dimension.

Other times, memories come in bits and pieces.

> I'd be driving home from my therapist's office, and I'd start having flashes of things—just segments, like bloody sheets, or taking a bath, or throwing away my nightgown. For a long time, I remembered all the things around being raped, but not the rape itself.

If memories come to you in fragments, you may find it hard to place them in any kind of chronological order. You may not know exactly when the abuse began, how old you were, or when and why it stopped. The process of understanding the fragments is a lot like putting together a jigsaw puzzle or being a detective.

> Part of me felt like I was on the trail of a murder mystery, and I was going to solve it. I really enjoyed following all the clues. "Okay, I was looking at the clock. It was mid-afternoon. Why was it mid-afternoon? Where could my mother have been? Oh, I bet she was at..." Tracing down the clues to find out exactly what had happened was actually fun.

Ella is a survivor who remembered in snatches. To make sense of her memories, she began to examine some of her own strange ways of coping. She started to analyze certain compulsive behaviors, like staring at the light fixture whenever she was making love:

> I'd be making love and would think, "Why would somebody lay here, when they're supposed to be having a pleasurable experience, and concentrate on a light fixture?" I remember every single lighting fixture in every single house we ever lived in! Why have I always been so obsessed with light under doors, and the interruption of light? That's a crazy thing for an adult woman to be obsessive about—that someone walks past and cracks the light. What's that about?

What it was about was watching to see if her father's footsteps stopped outside her door at night. If they stopped, that meant he'd come in and molest her. Once Ella started to pay attention to these kinds of details, the memories started to fit in place.

## Flashbacks

In a flashback, you reexperience the original abuse. Flashbacks may be accompanied by the feelings you felt at the time, or they may be stark and detached, like watching a movie about somebody else's life.

Frequently flashbacks are visual: "I saw this penis coming toward me," or "I couldn't see his face, just the big black belt he always wore." First-time visual memories can be very dramatic:

My husband was beginning to initiate some lovemaking. I had a flash in my mind. The closest way I can describe it is that it was much like viewing slides in a slide show, when the slide goes by too fast, but slow enough to give you some part of the image. It was someone jamming their fingers up my vagina. It was very vivid, and enough of the feelings came sneaking in that I knew it wasn't a fantasy. There was an element of it that made me stop and take notice. I lay there and let it replay a couple of times.

I felt confused. I was aware that it was something that happened to me. I even had a recollection of the pain. I scrambled around in my mind for an explanation. "Was that a rough lover I had?" Immediately I knew that wasn't the case. So I went back into the flash again. Each time I went back, I tried to open it up to see a little more. I didn't see his face, but I could sense an essence of my father.

Sometimes visual memories are more complete. A survivor who's had them both ways explained the difference:

A flashback is like a slide compared to a film. It's the difference between getting one shot or one look into a room and getting the expanded version. A full memory is more like panning over the whole scene, with all the details, sound, feeling, and visuals rolled into one.

But not everyone is visual. One woman was upset that she couldn't get any pictures. Her father had held her at knifepoint in the car, face down in the dark, and raped her. She had never seen anything. But she had heard him. And when she began to write the scene in Spanish, her native language, it all came back to her—his threats, his brutality, his violation.

## Regression

Another way to regain memory is through regression. Under the guidance of a trustworthy therapist, it is possible to go back to earlier times. Or you may find yourself going back on such a journey on your own, with only the prompting of your own unconscious.

Most of the regressions I experienced felt almost like going on a ride. They'd last maybe three or four hours at a time. One of the most vivid physical regressions I went through was late one evening, when Barbara and I were talking about her going to visit a friend. All of a sudden, I felt like I was being sucked down a drain. And then I felt like a real baby. I started crying and clinging and saying, "You can't go! You have to stay with me!" And I began to talk in a five-year-old's voice, using words and concepts that a five-year-old might use.

All of a sudden I thought I was just going to throw up. I ran to the bathroom, and then I really started to sob. I saw lots of scenes from my childhood. Times I felt rejected flashed by me, almost in slides.

Barb held me, and kind of coached me through it. "It's okay. You can get through this." Having her just sit there and listen really helped me. I just kept crying, and described to Barbara all these slides that were going by. After about twenty minutes, I fell into the deepest sleep I'd had for months. The next morning when I woke up, I felt a million pounds lighter.

## Sense Memory

Often it is a particular touch, smell, or sound that triggers a memory. You might remember when you return to the town, to the house, to the room, where the abuse took place. Or when you smell a certain aftershave the abuser wore.

Thirty-five-year-old Ella says, "It's all real tactile, sensory things that have brought memories back. Textures. Sounds. The smell of my father's house. The smell of vodka on somebody."

Ella had a magic purple quilt when she was a little girl. Her grandmother made it for her. It was supposed to keep her safe—nothing bad could happen to her as long as she was under it. The quilt had been lost for many years, but when Ella finally got it back at twenty-one, it triggered a whole series of memories.

Touch can also reopen memories. Women have had images come up while they were being massaged. You may freeze up and see pictures when you're making love. Your lover breathes in your ear just as your abuser once did, and it all comes spilling back:

Sometimes when we're making love, I feel like my head just starts to float away somewhere. I feel like I literally split off at my shoulders, and I get very lightheaded and dizzy. It's as if someone was blowing a fan down on top of my head. There's a lot of movement down past my hair. It's like rising up out of my head. I get really disoriented.

The other thing I experience is a lot of splitting right at the hips. My legs get very heavy and really solid. They just feel like dead weight, like logs. No energy is passing through them. Then I get real sick to my stomach, just violently ill. I find the minute I get nauseous, whatever it is is very close to me. And if I pay attention to it, I can see it, and move on.

## The Body Remembers What the Mind Chooses to Forget

It is also possible to remember only feelings. Memories are stored in our bodies, and it is possible to physically reexperience the terror of the abuse. Your body may clutch tight, or you may feel the screams you could not scream as a child. Or you may feel that you are suffocating and cannot breathe.

I would get body memories that would have no pictures to them at all. I would just start screaming and feel that something was coming out of my body that I had no control over. And I would usually get them right after making love or in the middle of making love, or right in the middle of a fight. When my passion was aroused in some way, I would remember in my body, although I wouldn't have a conscious picture, just this screaming coming out of me.

## WAYS TO REMEMBER

Memories come up under many different circumstances. You might remember because you're finally in a relationship that feels safe. Or because you've just been through a divorce and everything in your life is unraveling. Women often remember childhood abuse when they are raped or attacked in adult life.

Memories don't always surface in such dramatic ways. While talking with her friend, one woman suddenly heard herself saying something she didn't realize she knew. "It's as though I always knew it," she explained. "It's just that I hadn't thought about it in twenty or thirty years. Up until that moment, I'd forgotten."

You may remember seemingly out of the blue. Or because you're having persistent nightmares that reach up through sleep to tell you:

I'd always had a dream about my brother assaulting me. It was a foggy dream, and I had it over and over again. I'd wake up thinking it was really disgusting because I was enjoying it in the dream. I'd think, "You're sick. Why are you having this dream? Is that what you want?" I'd give myself all those kinds of guilt messages, 'cause it was still a dream. It wasn't history yet.

Then, six months ago, I was sitting in a training meeting for working with sexual assault prevention. I don't even remember what the trainer said, but all of a sudden, I realized that it wasn't a dream, and that it had really happened. I can't tell you anything about the rest of the meeting. I was just in shock.

The fact that this woman remembered in the middle of a training session for sexual assault is significant. As the media focus on sexual abuse has increased, more and more women have had their memories triggered.

## Media Coverage of Sexual Abuse
Jennierose, who remembered in her mid-forties, was sitting with her lover one night, watching a TV program about sexual offenders in prison. The therapist running the group encouraged the offenders to get very emotional, at which time they'd remember the traumatic events in their own childhoods.

In the middle of the program, Jennierose turned to her lover and said, "I wish there was a therapist like that I could go to, because I know there's something I'm not remembering." As soon as she said that, Jennierose had a vision of the first time her father sodom-ized her, when she was four and a half and her mother had gone to the hospital to have another baby. "It was a totally detailed vision, to the point of seeing the rose-colored curtains blowing in the window."

Sobbing, Jennierose said to her lover, "I think I'm making something up." Her lover simply said, "Look at yourself! Look at yourself! Tell me you're making it up." And Jennierose couldn't. She knew she was telling the truth.

This kind of memory is common. Often women become very uncomfortable (nauseated, dizzy, unable to concentrate, emotional) when they hear another survivor's story and realize that what's being described happened to them too.

## When You Break an Addiction
Many survivors remember their abuse once they get sober, quit drugs, or stop eating compulsively. These and other addictions can effectively block any recollection of the abuse, but once you stop, the memories often surface. Anna Stevens explains:

At the point I decided to put down drinking, I had to start feeling. The connection to the abuse was almost immediate. And I've watched other people come to AA and do the same thing. They have just enough time to get through the initial shakes, and you watch them start to go through the memories. And you know what's coming, but they don't....

## When You Become a Mother
Mothers often remember their own abuse when they see their children's vulnerability, or when their children reach the age they were when their own abuse began. Sometimes they remember because their child is being abused. Dana was court-ordered to go for therapy when her three-

year-old daughter, Christy, was molested. Dana first remembered when she unconsciously substituted her own name for her daughter's:

I was in therapy talking about Christy, and instead of saying "Christy," I said "I." And I didn't even catch it. My therapist did. She had always suspected that I was abused too, but she hadn't said anything to me.

She told me what I had said, and I said, "I did? I said 'I?' I hadn't even heard myself. It was really eerie.

What came out was that I was really dealing with Christy's molestation on a level of my own. The things that I was outraged at and that hurt me the most were things that had happened to me, not things that had happened to Christy. Part of the reason I fell apart and so much came back to me when I found out about Christy was because my husband was doing the same things to her that my father had done with me.

### After a Significant Death

Many women are too scared to remember while their abusers are still alive. One woman said, "I couldn't afford to remember until both my parents were dead, until there was nobody left to hurt me." A forty-seven-year-old woman first remembered a year and a half after her mother died: "Then I could no longer hurt my mother by telling her."

### FEELING THE FEELINGS

Although some remembering is emotionally detached, when you remember with feeling, the helplessness, terror, and physical pain can be as real as any actual experience. You may feel as if you are being crushed, ripped open, or suffocated. Sexual arousal may also accompany your memories, and this may horrify you, but arousal is a natural response to sexual stimulation. There is no reason to be ashamed.

You might remember feeling close and happy, wrapped in a special kind of love. Disgust and horror are not the only way to feel when you have memories. There is no *right* way to feel, but you must feel, even if it sends you reeling:

When I first remembered, I shut down emotionally right away. I climbed all the way up into my mind and forgot about the gut level. That's how I protected myself. For a long time it was just an intellectual exercise. "Oh, that's why I have trouble with men and authority. That's why I might not have remembered much about growing up." It took nine months after I first remembered for the feelings to start bubbling up.

I found myself slipping into the feelings I'd had during the abuse, that hadn't been safe to feel at the time. The first was this tremendous isolation. From there, I moved into absolute terror. I got in touch with how frightening the world is. It was the worst of the fear finally coming up. I felt like it was right at the top of my neck all the time, just ready to come out in a scream.

I was right on the edge. I had an encounter with my boss, who said that my performance had been poor. I finally told him what had happened, which was really heavy—telling some male authority figure that you remembered incest in your family. He is a kind and caring person. The best he could do was back off and leave me alone.

I was then carrying around all this external pressure—my job was in jeopardy, my life was falling apart, and I was having all these feelings I didn't know what to do with. In order to keep myself in control, I started compulsively eating. Finally I decided I didn't want to go through this stuff by myself anymore." I got myself into therapy.

Having to experience the feelings is one of the roughest parts of remembering. "It pisses me off that I have to survive it twice, only this time with feelings," one woman said. "This time it's worse. I'm not so effective at dissociating anymore."

Another woman said, "I started off very butch [tough] about remembering. I kicked into my overachiever thing. I was going to lick this thing. I believed getting the pictures was what was important. I got a ton of memories, all on the intellectual level. It was kind of like I was going to 'do' incest, just like I might take up typing."

It was only after a year of therapy that this woman began to realize that *she* was the one who'd been abused. "I finally realized, I finally *felt*, that this was something that had happened to me, and that it had been damaging. I had to realize that just getting the memories was not going to make it go away. *This was about me!*"

## LETTING MEMORIES IN

Few survivors feel they have control over their memories. Most feel the memories have control of them, that they do not choose the time and place a new memory will emerge. You may be able to fight them off for a time, but the price— headaches, nightmares, exhaustion—is not worth staving off what is inevitable.

Not everyone will know a memory is coming, but many survivors do get warnings, a certain feeling or series of feelings, that clue them in. Your stomach may get tight. You may sleep poorly, have frightening dreams. Or you may be warned in other ways:

I always know when they're coming. I get very tense. I get very scared. I get snappy at things that ordinarily wouldn't make me angry. I get sad. Usually it's anger and anxiety and fear that come first. And I have a choice. It's a real conscious choice. It's either I want it or I don't want it. And I said "I don't want it" a lot. And when I did that, I would just get sicker and sicker. I'd get more depressed. I'd get angry irrationally.

Now I don't say I don't want it. It's not worth it. My body seems to need to release it. The more I heal, the more I see these memories are literally stored in my body, and they've got to get out. Otherwise I'm going to carry them forever.

## REMEMBERING OVER TIME

Often when you've resolved one group of memories, another will make its way to the surface.

The more I worked on the abuse, the more I remembered. First I remembered my brother, and then my grandfather. About six months after that I remembered my father. And then about a year later, I remembered my mother. I remembered the "easiest" first and the "hardest" last. Even though it was traumatic for me to realize that everyone in my family abused me, there was something reassuring about it. For a long time I'd felt worse than the initial memories should have made me feel, so remembering the rest of the abuse was actually one of the most grounding things to happen. My life suddenly made sense.

The impact new memories have will shift over time. One woman who has been getting new memories for the past ten years says remembering has become harder over time:

My first flood of memories came when I was twenty-five. The memories I get now are like fine-tuning—more details, more textures. Even though there was more of a feeling of shock and catharsis at first, remembering is harder now. I believe them now. It hurts more. I have the emotions to feel the impact. I can see how it's affected my life.

Laura also says new memories are harder:

Just when I felt that my life was getting back to normal and I could put the incest aside, I had another flashback that was much more violent than the earlier pictures I'd seen. I was furious. I wanted to be finished. I didn't want to be starting in with incest again! And my resistance made the remembering a lot more difficult.

Other survivors say memories have gotten easier to handle:

As I've come to terms with the fact that I was abused, new pictures, new incidents, don't have the same impact. The battle of believing it happened is not one I have to fight each time another piece falls into place. Once I had a framework to fit new memories into, my recovery time got much faster. While my first memories overwhelmed me for weeks, now I might only cry for ten minutes or feel depressed for an hour. It's not that I don't have new memories. It's just that they don't devastate me.

And new memories don't take anything away from the healing you've already done. Paradoxically, *you are already healing from the effects of the things you have yet to remember.*

## "BUT I DON'T HAVE ANY MEMORIES"

If you don't remember your abuse, you are not alone. Many women don't have memories, and some never get memories. This doesn't mean they weren't abused.

If you don't have any memory of it, it can be hard to believe the abuse really happened. You may feel insecure about trusting your intuition and want "proof" of your abuse. This is a very natural desire, but it is not always one that can be met. The unconscious has its own way of unfolding that does not always meet your demands or your timetable.

One thirty-eight-year-old survivor described her relationship with her father as "emotionally incestuous." She has never had specific memories of any physical contact between them, and for a long time she was haunted by the fact that she couldn't come up with solid data. Over time, though, she's come to terms with her lack of memories. Her story is a good model if you don't have specific pictures to draw from:

Do I want to know if something physical happened between my father and me? Really, I think you have to be strong enough to know. I think that our minds are wonderful in the way they protect us, and I think that when I'm strong enough to know, I'll know.

I obsessed for about a year on trying to remember, and then I got tired of sitting around talking about what I couldn't remember. I thought, "All right, let's act as if." It's like you come home and your home has been robbed, and everything has been thrown in the middle of the room, and the window is open and the curtain is blowing in the wind, and the cat is gone. You know somebody robbed you, but you're never going to know who. So what are you going to do? Sit there and try to figure it out while your stuff lies around? No, you start to clean it up. You put bars on the windows. You assume somebody was there. Somebody could come along and say, "Now how do you know someone was there?" You don't know.

That's how I acted. I had the symptoms. Every incest group I went to I completely empathized. It rang bells all the time. I felt like there was something I just couldn't get to, that I couldn't remember yet. And my healing was blocked there.

Part of my wanting to get specific memories was guilt that I could be accusing this man of something so heinous, and what if he didn't do it? How horrible for me to accuse him! That's why I wanted the memories. I wanted to be sure. Societally, women have always been accused of crying rape.

But I had to ask myself, "Why would I be feeling all of this? Why would I be feeling all this anxiety if something didn't happen?" If the specifics are not available to you, then go with what you've got.

I'm left with the damage. And that's why I relate to that story of the burglar. I'm owning the damage. I want to get better. I've been very ill as a result of the damage, and at some point I realized, "I'm thirty-eight years old. What am I go-ing to do—wait twenty more years for a memory?" I'd rather get better.

And then maybe the stronger I am, the more the memories will come back. Maybe I'm putting the cart before the horse. Maybe I've remembered as much as I'm able to remember without breaking down. I don't want to go insane. I want to be out in the world. Maybe I should go with that sense of protection. There is a survivor in here and she's pretty smart. So I'm going with the circumstantial evidence, and I'm working on healing myself. I go to these incest groups, and I tell people, "I don't have any pictures," and then I go on and talk all about my father, and nobody ever says, "You don't belong here."

## NOTES

1. For sources on the scope of child sexual abuse, see the "About Sexual Abuse" section of the Resource Guide. A number of these books cite recent studies to which you can refer for more complete statistics.

2. Between 500,000 and 1,000,000 children are involved in prostitution and pornography in this country; a high percentage of them are victims of incest. See *Sex Work: Writings by Women in the Industry*, edited by Frédérique Dellacoste and Priscilla Alexander (Pittsburgh: Cleis Press, 1987).

# NO

Lee Coleman

# CREATING "MEMORIES" OF
# SEXUAL ABUSE

*ABSTRACT: An analysis of a case of alleged recovered memories of sexual abuse is presented to illustrate how such mental images can be created in therapy. The memories, although believed by the woman to be of actual events, were the result of suggestions from both lay persons and professionals.*

While, just a few years ago, students of child sexual abuse accusations thought they had seen every imaginable brand of irresponsibility on the part of certain mental health professionals, something new and equally terrible has emerged. To the growing number of children trained to say and believe things which never happened is now added a growing number of adults, usually women, being trained to say and believe that they have suddenly "unblocked" memories of childhood sexual abuse.

Just like allegations coming from children, concern about biased and unprofessional methods of eliciting statements from adults should in no way cast doubt on the reality of sexual abuse. There are countless numbers of adults who were molested as children, who did not speak of it, but who now may reveal their experiences as part of our society's belated recognition of such abuse. But to acknowledge the reality of sexual abuse, and the reality of the silence kept by some of the victims, does nothing to mitigate the harm being done by those therapists who are convincing patients that even if sexual abuse is not remembered, it probably happened anyway.

In this article, I will illustrate the process by which a young woman, moderately depressed and unsure of her life goals, but in no way out of touch with reality (psychotic), came to make allegations which were so bizarre that they might easily be thought to be the product of [a] major mental disorder. In such cases, I have repeatedly seen the falsely accused and their closest family and friends make this assumption. This case will show, as have the others I have studied, that the source is not a disorder in the patient, but a "disorder" in the therapist. The problem is the irresponsible adoption by some therapists of a new fad which will be clarified below.

From Lee Coleman, "Creating 'Memories' of Sexual Abuse," *Issues in Child Abuse Accusations,* vol. 4, no. 4 (1992), pp. 169–176. Copyright © 1992 by The Institute for Psychological Therapies. Reprinted by permission of *Issues in Child Abuse Accusations.*

Here, then, is a report I submitted to the Court hearing the civil lawsuit filed by this woman against her cousin. All names and identifying information have been changed.

\* \* \*

Judge John Q. Smith
Superior Court, All American County
Anywhere, USA

The following report concerns the suit between Susan Q. Smith and John V. Public. The opinions expressed are based on a study of the Amended List of Documents of the Plaintiff, dated April 6, 1992, Additional Documents (such as police records and Children's Services Records), Examination for Discovery transcripts of Mrs. Smith and Mr. Public, and my examination of Mrs. Smith on May 4, 1992, which lasted somewhat over three hours. I have also studied several videotapes pertinent to the case, enumerated below.

Based upon all this information, as well [as] my prior professional experience, it is my opinion that the alleged "memories" of Mrs. Smith, relating a variety of sexual and abusive acts perpetrated upon her by Mr. Public and others, are not memories at all. They are, instead, mental images which, however sincerely felt by her to be memories of past events, are nonetheless the result of a series of suggestions from both lay persons and professionals.

That Mrs. Smith has succumbed to these influences in no way implies that she suffers from any mental disorder. By her own account, she has had problems of low self-esteem, depression, and bulimia in her past. She has, however, never suffered and does not now suffer a mental disorder which would imply a loss of contact with reality. If the reliability of her claims are to be best evaluated by the Court, it should be understood that there is another way that a person may say things that may not be true, yet be entirely sincere.

Suggestibility is something we all share as part of our being human, with some persons obviously being more suggestible than others. In this case, Mrs. Smith has been involved with individuals and groups, over a period of years, the end result of which has been to promote a process of accepting the false idea that whatever mental image is conjured up, especially if part of "therapy," is necessarily a valid retrieval of past experience, i.e. a "memory."

Let me now document the evidence which has led me to the above conclusions.

### 1. Mrs. Smith's Suspicions About John Public and His Daughter Alice.

From several sources, such as her deposition, my interview, and investigative interviews, it seems clear that Mrs. Smith suspected for several years that her cousin John Public was engaging in sexual behavior with his daughter Alice. When asked for examples which led to these suspicions, she mentioned alleged comments from him that "a child's hands" felt so good. She also mentioned that no other adults seemed to be concerned about such comments.

Seeing Mr. Public and Alice (approximately eight years old at the time) lying in bed together, in their underwear, reinforced her suspicion, as did the alleged comment from Mr. Public to Mr. Smith (not heard by Mrs. Smith), that his (Smith's) daughter would make him horny. Mrs. Smith also noted that, until age 18 months, her own daughter would cry if Mr. Public attempted to pick her up or get close to her, and Mrs. Smith noted to herself, "She's a smart child." (It should be noted that such behavior in infants of this age is perfectly normal.)

Mrs. Smith told me that she had informed family members on several occasions of her suspicions, but no one else apparently shared her opinions, or felt anything needed to be reported.

The 1986 video of a family Halloween party was the event that convinced Mrs. Smith she should report her suspicions. It is quite important that the Court view this video, in order to judge for itself whether the material could reasonably lead a person to believe something untoward was taking place. My own opinion is there was nothing happening that was unusual or abnormal. It was Alice who first struck a somewhat playful and seductive pose, and such displays are hardly abnormal for a teenage girl. Police investigators likewise saw nothing untoward on this tape.

The question raised, then, is whether Mrs. Smith had for her own personal reasons, upon which I will not attempt to speculate, developed an obsession about Mr. Public and his daughter, one which was leading her (Smith) to overinterpret ordinary behaviors.

It is not surprising, then, that when the report was investigated by Children's Services, no evidence of abuse was uncovered. Mrs. Smith tells me, however, that she was not reassured, and only felt that she had fulfilled an obligation to report something.

## 2. Early Influences Promoting in Mrs. Smith a Belief That Prior Sexual Abuse Might Have Occurred but Not Be Remembered.

From numerous sources (deposition, my interview, journals, therapy records), it is clear that Mrs. Smith was strongly influenced by a statement she says Dr. Gwen Olson made to her regarding bulimia, a problem Mrs. Smith had suffered from to one degree or another since early adolescence.

Mrs. Smith states that Dr. Olson told her, sometime in early 1987 (the records indicate this was in December 1986), that "one hundred percent of my patients with bulimia have later found out that they were sexual abuse victims." Whether these words were actually spoken by Dr. Olson, or instead interpreted this way by Mrs. Smith, I of course do not know. But in either case, the words Mrs. Smith took away with her are extremely important, because the words "found out" would imply that a person could have been sexually abused, not be aware of it, and later recover such an awareness. I will later on be discussing the lack of evidence for, and major evidence against, any such phenomenon being genuine.

Mrs. Smith told me she was seriously affected by this, experiencing crying and feelings of fear. She began to wonder if she might have been sexually abused. When I asked her if she had ever before that time had such a question, she said that she "had no memories" of any such abuse. She had, in fact, told Children's Services shortly before, during the investigation of Alice, that John Public had "never before abused me ... I was relying on my memory."

At this time, Mrs. Smith was being seen in psychotherapy, first by Edna Johnson, and then by Dr. Abraham, for what seems to have been feelings of anxiety and depression. Sexual abuse was apparently not an issue in this therapy. Instead, Mrs. Smith states that her self-esteem was low, and that she was "not functioning" well as a housewife, even though she felt good about her marriage. Both she and Dr. Abraham apparently felt she was "a bored housewife." She decided to start her own business, but this never happened because events leading to the current accusations against John Public interceded.

Mrs. Smith explains that she went to an Entrepreneurs Training Camp in the Fall of 1987, was doing extremely well, but then "sabotaged myself" by performing poorly despite knowing correct answers on an examination. She felt, after the camp, that she needed to work on herself.

In addition, she saw an Oprah Winfrey program on the subject of child abuse. Mrs. Smith told me that she cried as she watched this program, "for me and not for them… I wondered at my feelings and where they were coming from."

Mrs. Smith confirms that it was shortly after seeing this program, with all of the above background in place, that she called the Women's Sexual Assault Center (WSAC) on September 3, 1987.

After a telephone intake, she had a face-to-face contact with Joan Oliver, and told her that "I had concerns, feelings, but no memory of being sexually assaulted…. I thought it would be better to wait (for therapy) until I had a memory. They said OK, and put me on a waiting list."

The records of WSAC generally confirm this account which I received from Mrs. Smith on May 4, 1992. During the first telephone contact, Mrs. Smith related

… strong feelings of abuse as a child came up… She can't remember specific things… her GP told her most bulimics have been sexually abused as children…

A second telephone contact, September 16, include[d]

… occluded memories. Sister was abused by neighborhood man as a child. Susan gets very retriggered by this and by shows about child abuse. Her doctor told her that close to 100% of bulimics have been sexually abused. This really brought up a lot of feelings and some images but not really a memory.

Yet another important event happened around Christmas 1987, before Mrs. Smith had entered the treatments (with Mary Brown and Veronica Erickson) where the mental images alleged to be "memories" started. This was something I had not discovered from any written materials, and learned about for the first time from Mrs. Smith on May 4, 1992.

Mrs. Smith had a friend, Valerie White, who told her about her treatments for back problems. Biofeedback was used at the pain and stress clinic she attended, and Ms. White told Mrs. Smith that she had started to remember being abused. When I asked Mrs. Smith how she reacted to this, she said, "I felt… that if she was in therapy, remembering, maybe I should start as well. I had no memory, but if she was in therapy…"

To summarize, then, the suggestive influences to this point: Mrs. Smith is still not reassured that Alice is not being abused by John Public; Dr. Olson either says or Mrs. Smith believes she says that in her experience all bulimics are sexual abuse victims; finally, after she decides she shouldn't go into therapy "until she has a memory" of sexual abuse, a friend tells her "the remembering" can wait, and Mrs. Smith concludes she should give it a try.

It is my opinion, based on the above material, that Mrs. Smith was at this point being victimized by lay persons and professionals who were representing to her that sexual abuse might not be remembered, when in truth there is no evidence to support such a claim. While

Mrs. Smith may have had her own personal problems and/or motivations for claiming abuse at the hands of Mr. Public (something I will not speculate upon) she was being profoundly influenced by unsound information. It is my opinion that this has persisted to this day.

### 3. Suggestive and Unprofessional Therapy Creates the "Memories."

In March 1988, Mrs. Smith started seeing Mary Brown for individual psychotherapy, and also had interviews with Veronica Erickson, a student who was writing a thesis on "Recovering Memories of Childhood Sexual Abuse." On March 9, 1988, Ms. Erickson commented that Mrs. Smith had done

> ... a lot of great body work. Worked on her anger, hurt about being sexually abused. Has a few memories about it and wants more.

On March 28, the WSAC records show that the

> "memory recovery process" was getting into high gear:... had lots of memories come to her which she feels good about; 2 "rapes," 9 sodomies, and 2 oral sex (she has remembered both rapes and 1 sodomy and oral sex), 8 sodomies and 1 oral sex to go. Can't wait.

Further WSAC records of Ms. Erickson show just as clearly that she has lost all professional objectivity.... The June 14, 1988 note gives an insight as to the position Ms. Erickson was taking with regard to whether Mrs. Smith's increasingly severe claims should be automatically assumed to be accurate:

> ... trying to remember a memory that was just beginning to flash... really scared that this memory is made up... I told her I believed her.

If there is any doubt about the stance being adopted by Ms. Erickson, i.e. that whatever Mrs. Smith "recovers" from week to week is a reliable statement about past events, a reading of her Ph.D. thesis makes it abundantly clear that it was simply a given for her and the selected sources she relies on, that the patient's claims must be taken at face value. She writes, for example:

> Validation, feeling believed, was seen as essential for incest survivors struggling to reconcile their memories.

Nowhere in the thesis is mention made of any concern that false claims may arise in therapy specifically aimed at such "uncovering." Next, she speaks of

> ... the ability of counselor... to facilitate the survivor's recall of the abuse... which of course assumes that abuse has taken place.

Just how broadly based is the source of these allegedly reliable "memories," is indicated by her quoting the book, *The Courage to Heal*, which has been influential in promoting the very ideas at the center of this case:

> "Occluded" memories are vague flashbacks, triggered by touches, smells, sounds, body memories, bodily sensations as "warning signs." Some women just intuitively knew that they had been sexually abused and were struggling to trust their intuition.

It is also clear that the proper role for the therapist, according to Ms. Erickson, is not only to accept all images as "memories," but to actively encourage this process. She writes of her method which

> ... serves to continually promote an atmosphere in which the researcher is spontaneously both receptive and actively stimulating the recollection of

the participant.... The participants and researcher... create the world within which this study is revealed.

Ms. Erickson says of "Victoria" (pseudonym for Mrs. Smith),

> She thought about who might have abused her and when she said his name, she knew who the offender was but she still had no memories as proof (p. 56 of Erickson thesis).

Let me now turn to her other therapist, Mary Brown. Ms. Brown in her intake notes of March 1, 1988 refers to Mrs. Smith having

> ... flashbacks of childhood sexual abuse experiences, she believes by this same cousin.

Ms. Brown's treatment plan was to "assist Susan express and release the emotions associated with the sexual abuse experience." This is important, because it shows that Ms. Brown, from the beginning, assumed the truth of the allegations.

It wasn't too long after this, the night of March 12/13, that Mrs. Smith's calendar indicates she had a "nightmare," and her "first memories." When I asked Mrs. Smith about this, she said it was

> ... the nightmare which triggered the memory.... In the nightmare, the neighbor had shot her husband in the chest. Her cleaning up his blood, I recalled John blotting up my blood after raping me.

There are, of course, no reputable data which would indicate that a patient or therapist can use dream material to reliably "recover memories" of real events. Ms. Brown, however, seems to have utter confidence in the process, for she wrote to the police on August 3, 1988:

> The treatment methods I use enable clients to express and release the very

deepest feelings that may have been stifled.... It is precisely because the emotional intensity of sexual abuse in childhood is greater than what most children can integrate that these experiences are quickly lost to memory. The ensuing, forgetting and denial are the mind's way of protecting the individual from total disruption of their cognitive functioning. This was particularly true of survivors of sexual abuse whose experiences occurred more than ten years ago. The reason for this is that there was not the social awareness nor the professional expertise for dealing with these problems at that time. Children instinctively know when the adults around them are going to be able to help them. When they find themselves in situations where they may either be disbelieved... this forgetting and denial comes into play even more strongly....

> Memories tend to return in fragments and to be unclear or non-specific in the beginning... the blocks in the way of memory are gradually removed.... This is precisely what occurred... with Susan Smith. It is my clinical judgment that Susan had reached a point in her healing process when the memories that were returning were completely reliable.... She was unprepared to report until she herself was certain and until she received validation from me that I was in agreement that the memories could be trusted...

That Ms. Brown was not only accepting all statements as real events, but actively encouraging them, is seen by the following passage from the same letter:

> Susan herself questioned any inconsistency.... It took some education on my part for her to... understand the whole process of how it is that the recall process works...

Ms. Brown was even willing to assure the police that the other persons that Mrs. Smith was gradually naming as victims during that Spring and Summer of 1988 would also need "help" in remembering.

> ... It is highly likely that most or all of the children that Susan remembers... will be unable to remember these experiences. This does not mean they did not occur any more than Susan's former amnesia means that these events had not happened to her. One of these (youngsters) may be precipitated to remember and recapture the experiences through a process similar to what occurred for Susan.

There is, of course, absolutely no evidence that this whole process has anything to do with memory, or a recall of past events. The only professionals who advocate these ideas are those making up a small, fringe group who hold themselves out as "specialists in treating sexual abuse," but who (as this case shows) seem to assume that it is permissible to pass off wild theories, like the ones above, to both patients, families, and investigative agencies.

Most important, however, is that outsiders evaluate the possible impact of such ideas on persons like Mrs. Smith. The evidence is clear that she has raised doubts from time to time, but each time, these "specialists" have told her that her mental images must represent real events. In this sense, I believe the professionals (Brown, Erickson, and others to be mentioned) are most responsible for creating the unreliable information in this case.

Not only do the ideas promoted by Brown and Erickson hold great potential to contaminate information coming from such counseling, but the techniques used with Mrs. Smith would likely heighten this possibility. Mrs. Smith described pounding pillows and being encouraged to express her anger in sessions with Ms. Erickson, and in individual and group sessions with Ms. Brown, she described exercises in which she was using hyperventilation or bending from the waist. The many group sessions she has attended, focusing on "recovery from sexual abuse," have a potentially profound influence on the participants.

In addition, Ms. Brown had a technique, which she called the "denial game," that was used when Mrs. Smith expressed caution about whether her mental images were reliable. This process had the intended effect of causing Mrs. Smith to once more *assume that whatever she could think of had actually happened.*

The police investigation was dropped for lack of evidence, for lack of corroboration from any of the many alleged victims named by Mrs. Smith, and because an outside consultant told the police that the impact of the therapy might be contaminating the information....

Mrs. Smith's statements to police include "trying to see" alleged events, having

> a flash... (a) visual memory of a spirit part of me coming out of me via my mouth and sitting on a head board. I now understand this to be dissociation....

The police, quite understandably, wondered whether this might be a sign of major mental disorder, like a psychosis. Instead, such statements reflect not that Mrs. Smith was suffering a major mental disorder, but simply that she was absorbing unsupported ideas from her therapists. I have studied the process by which some mental health professionals are passing these ideas to patients, via articles, speeches, and in therapy sessions. Many, if not most, patients, will accept these ideas as accepted scientific information, coming as they do from a professional therapist.

Just how much Mrs. Smith had come to believe in this process, already by April, 1988, is seen by her telling the police on April 20, 1988 that

> These are not complete memories at this point but there are bits and pieces of which I would like to tell you now and when I have the complete memory back I will talk to you again.... I would like to add that I expect to have further recall of incidents as I have just begun to have recall in the last five weeks or so....

### 4. The Growth of the Allegations.

The process described above will often lead to a virtual flood of allegations which grow and grow. Particularly if there are emotional rewards for producing more claims, the sky is the limit. In this case, it ultimately led to claims of ritual abuse, animal killings, gang rape, multiple personalities, etc. which Mrs. Smith now seems to disavow but which she at the time was claiming as legitimate memory. A brief review of these developments offers important perspective on the unreliable nature of this entire process.

Dr. Wagner saw Mrs. Smith from May 20, 1988 to January 27, 1989. He used a method Mrs. Smith describes as "regression," and which she now does not trust. She feels that some of the things she said as a result of these methods may not have happened.

For example, Dr. Wagner's notes of November 24, 1988 speak of " ... memory of John and 'Joe.' Tying her up—raping her. Two others came in, Evan and [un-

readable]." Mrs. Smith says she doesn't recall saying this to Dr. Wagner, doesn't believe she said it to him, believes his records are incorrect, and believes she talked about "Sam."

Dr. Wagner, while nowhere in his records expressing any doubt about the reality of these statements, did mention at the outset (June 3, 1988) that he thought Mrs. Smith was: "I suspect getting a lot of mileage out of sexual abuse. Attention and support from home she never got from mom and dad?"

When I questioned Mrs. Smith about other examples of statements drawn from the notes of the many therapists she saw in the coming months, I noted an interesting pattern. Whenever a statement in therapy records referred to events which she now says may not have happened, like seeing a boy with slits for eyes and no face, she says that she cannot recall saying any of this. She repeatedly said it was only her study of the therapy records which allows her to remember what she might have said in therapy.

However, when I asked her about a note from Morton Hunt's evaluation of January 15, 1991, she was quite clear that she did not say the following " ... Then had nightmare. Chose John. Just knew it was him (reviewed possible men)."

Such selective "memory" merely reinforces my opinion that these multiple therapy contacts, of the nature described, make a mockery of the idea that claims growing out of the sessions, or growing out of the mental images of a patient between such sessions, are reliable.

The fact that Mrs. Smith was in much more therapy than I have yet summarized, only deepens the dilemmas. She was in group therapy with Ms. Summers, for 32 sessions, from March 21, 1989 to December 1, 1989, and Ms. Summers, who is another of those who specialize in "working mainly with women recovering from childhood sexual abuse," wrote in her records that "Susan's abuse was the most cruel and degrading I have encountered."

Once again, unquestioning acceptance seems to be the *sine qua non* of many of the therapists in this case. Sadly, such an attitude may be quite destructive to patients. A review of her journals, which I will highlight, shows that (as Dr. Wagner had indicated) Mrs. Smith was getting a lot of positive feedback from more and more "memories." A patient might feel good at the time of such feedback, but the encouragement of this process does not bode well for the long-term welfare of such patients.

May 24, 1988—"Another memory came back—arms tied,... I know there are things I can't even imagine yet that they did to me. I know I still have a lot of memories to go... I know I'll have the strength to handle them... I'm on my way to a happy successful life... I love my strength.

May 26, 1988—This morning at the Mom's Group... another memory came back.... I called WSAC. The more I discover about what I've been through the more I wonder how I ever survived.... You're so strong Susan, so wonderful. You're capable of whatever you believe in. You're OK, Susan Smith. You're strong, you're a survivor, and a winner, you're going straight to the top, head of the class. You're OK, you're a winner. I'm really truly beginning to like myself and I really like that—all these years I hated myself.

May 27—I begin my workshop with my therapist. (Mary Brown)

May 28—... we did rapid breathing... I went to my sexual abuse... my body was twitching and squirming just as if

it were tied up by the hands... I started getting these vague recollections of this blond male being Warren and some occurrence happening.... I wasn't ready to look at it until I could intellectually figure out how this could be...

May 31—Describes Dave* meeting with Smith—He explained to him that these memories had been undisturbed for twenty years and had not been distorted... and that I was not making it up... I knew Dave was not ready to look at his abuse...at WSAC I went into denial mode... Veronica played the denial game with me just to show me that I was crazy to believe I was making this up.

June 14, 1988—Saw Veronica, talked about Yellowstone incident with Gretchen involved, how I was blocking everything because I had no proof John was in Yellowstone and the fact that Gretchen must have repressed and that she would probably deny remembering such an incident... so she had me "hang" and it took a much longer time for the feelings to come, but they did, I cried, pound pillows, yelled, and got back more memories... so much doesn't make sense. Where is everyone else?

Nov. 9, 1988—What I learned in therapy today: When I was abused it happened to my body. It happened to a part of me that I dissociated from. I have separated from and disowned the part of me that it happened to.... I am ashamed of my body... so I abuse it.

April 18, 1989—I love myself and that's something I couldn't have said a year ago. I've come a long way.... Signed Terrific Susan.

May ?, 1989—... I let my little girls talk... etc.

June 8, 1989—attended Conference on Child Sexual Abuse... I learned a lot...

---

* A cousin of Mrs. Smith, and one of the other alleged victims, none of whom had any memories of abuse

talked to Gretchen two weeks ago. More about her "other personalities".... Memories, memories. Where are they. I want to remember all the mean sadistic things John did to me.

July 5, 1989—I know I am going to go on and achieve great things in my life... speak out against abuse of children, especially sexual abuse. l know I'm strong, a survivor, and a successeder. (sic)

Oct. 16, 1989—I got back memories of what happened after John gave my body to the two "tough men" in exchange for drugs.

October 29, 1989—I don't think this can happily, successfully end for me unless I have power over him.

Nov. 29, 1989—Cousin Joe called and told me Warren had memories of being sexually assaulted by John. The memories are just beginning... I told Warren... I was really proud of him.

Nov. 27, 1990—... I don't want any more memories!!! ... I called WSAC this afternoon and bits of memories came up. One was John beside me, and about 5 men, in black robes, or gowns—full length with hoods on their heads.... These men had swordlike daggers in their hands .. a memory of John slitting the throat of a cat with a knife... telling us that this is what would happen to us if we ever told about him.

Dec. 16, 1990—I think I might have multiple personalities. It is something I've wondered about before, but believed you only developed multiples if you were severely abused before age 8.... My first day with Veronica there was this other part of me talking. She named herself Julie... it was really weird cause I knew what was happening... I'm going to get to the other side of this—new and improved. But in the mean time, I'm a nuttsy basketcase.

Dec. 25, 1990—I started back in therapy mid-December, I could no longer contain the memories within me.... I want to write about and keep track of my memo-

ries. I've had a feeling for several months now that there might have been ritual abuse. When I started having flashes of white candles, lots of them, burning, I thought well, this is probably just an image I've seen on TV.... My 2nd day in therapy (3rd time I'd seen June) I had this memory—a faceless boy,... he had no nose and only slits for eyes.... They told us if we didn't behave, or if we ever told they would burn our faces with an iron.... They told the girls they use their genitals as eyes, then when they grow older they'd have furry, hairy eyes and everyone would laugh.

Toward the end of our meeting, I asked Mrs. Smith how she distinguished between the many allegations which she insists took place, and the many allegations which she made but now says she cannot remember saying and isn't sure they are real. The gist of her answer (the tape is of course available) was that "memories" which were like a "videotape," where a picture is complete, from start to finish, and which occurred to her sometimes in therapy but often by herself, are reliable. Brief images, or "flashes," which are incomplete, and which were often in response to therapeutic techniques she now is critical of, like those of June Schreiber and others, she distrusts.

I find this distinction, which I must assume to be sincere on Mrs. Smith's part, to be utterly unreliable. First, the therapy from the beginning has been manipulative, even though I have no doubt that all the therapists were sincere in wanting to help. They all, nonetheless, adopted the position that "the more memory the better."

While this might be interpreted to mean that this is standard practice in the therapeutic community, since so many therapists in this case acted in this manner, it is instead an artifact which resulted when Mrs. Smith sought out or was referred to a selected group of therapists who "specialize in recovery from sexual abuse." Amongst this group, whose work and education I have studied intensively, it is common practice to assume abuse occurs if anyone claims it has, common practice to encourage as many "memories" as possible, common practice to encourage anger and "empowerment," and common practice to accept all allegations, however unlikely, as being real.

All this is terribly unscientific, without general agreement from the mental health community, and in my view highly destructive to many patients. Perhaps most important here, in the context of litigation, is the fact that these techniques absolutely fly in the face of reliable fact-finding.

I cannot emphasize strongly enough how important it is for the Court, in studying this case and deciding what is reliable and what is not, to understand that if commonsense leads to one conclusion about where the truth lies, the use of psychiatric labels and esoteric explanations should not cause the Court to abandon what the facts otherwise seem to show.

\* \* \*

As of this writing, the Court has yet to render a verdict. But whatever is decided in this case, it should be clear that our society is about to experience yet another wave of unreliable sexual abuse allegations. Once again, it is the promulgation of faulty ideas by a small segment of the mental health community (see for example Bass & Davis, 1988; Blume, 1990; Briere & Conte, in press; Cozolino, 1989; Maltz, 1990; Herman & Schatzow, 1987;

Summit, 1987; Young, Sachs, Braun, & Watkins, 1991), coupled with the apathy of the bulk of the mental health community, which promises to create a new form of abuse of patients, families, and the falsely accused. The moral and economic costs are incalculable, and the promotion of pseudoscientific ideas which confuse memory with mental imagery is already confusing the scientific literature.

Fortunately, clearer heads are also in evidence (see Ganaway, 1991; Lanning, 1989 and 1992; Mulhern, 1991a, 1991b, 1991c; Nathan, 1989, 1990, 1991; Passantino, Passantino, & Trott, 1989; Price, 1992; Putnam, 1991; Wakefield & Underwager, 1992 and undated). Given our society's tendency to become infatuated with all manner of fads, it should be obvious that this latest development in the child sexual abuse circus is not going to go away quickly or easily. It will take insight and perseverance to counteract the tendency of the media and most lay persons to uncritically accept the "blocked memory" claims now emerging with increasing regularity. If our society is serious about responding to the reality of childhood sexual abuse, a critical ingredient is the avoidance of irresponsible empire-building by some mental health professionals who have abandoned both science and reason.

## REFERENCES

Bass, E., & Davis, L. (1988). *The courage to heal.* New York, Harper & Row.

Blume, E. (1990). *Secret survivors: Uncovering incest and its aftereffects in women.* New York: J. Wiley & Sons.

Briere, J., & Conte, J. (in press). Self reported amnesia for abuse in adults molested as children. *Journal of Traumatic Stress*

Cozolino, L. (1989). The ritual abuse of children: Implications for clinical practice and research, *The Journal of Sex Research, 26(1),* 131–138.

Ganaway, G. K. (1991, August 19). *Alternate hypotheses regarding satanic ritual abuse memories*. Presented at the 99th Annual Convention of the American Psychological Association, San Francisco.

Herman, J. L., & Schatzow, E. (1987). Recovery and verification of memories of childhood sexual trauma. *Psychoanalytic Psychology, 4(1)*, 1–14.

Lanning, K. V. (1989, October). *Satanic, occult, ritualistic crime: A law enforcement perspective*. National Center for the Analysis of Violent Crime, FBI Academy, Quantico, VA.

Lanning, K. V. (1992). *Investigator's guide to allegations of "ritual" child abuse*. National Center for the Analysis of Violent Crime: Quantico, VA.

Maltz, W. (1990, December). Adult survivors of incest: How to help them overcome the trauma. *Medical Aspects of Human Sexuality, 42–47*.

Mulhern, S. (1991a). *Ritual abuse: Defining a syndrome v. defending a belief*. Unpublished manuscript.

Mulhern, S. (1991b). [Letter to the Editor]. *Child Abuse & Neglect, 15*, 609–610.

Mulhern, S. (1991c). Satanism and psychotherapy: A rumor in search of an inquisition. In J. T. Richardson, J. Best, & D. G. Bromley (Eds.), *The Satanism scare* (pp. 145–172). New York: Aldine de Gruyter.

Nathan, D. (1989, June 21). The Devil and Mr. Mattox, *Texas Observer*, pp. 10–13.

Nathan, D. (1991). Satanism and child molestation: Constructing the ritual abuse scare. In J. T.

Richardson, J. Best, & D. G. Bromley (Eds.), *The Satanism scare* (pp. 75–94). New York: Aldine de Gruyter.

Nathan, D. (1990, June 20). The ritual sex abuse hoax, *Village Voice*, pp. 36–44.

Passantino, G., Passantino, B., & Trott, J. (1989). Satan's sideshow. *Cornerstone, 18(90)*, 23–28.

Price, L. (1992, April 20). Presentation at the Midwest Regional False Memory Syndrome Foundation Meeting. Benton Harbor, Michigan.

Putnam, F. (1991). The satanic ritual abuse controversy. *Child Abuse & Neglect, 15*, 175–179.

Summit, R. (1987, July). Declaration of Roland Summit, MD, Regarding *People v. Dill*.

Wakefield, H., & Underwager, R. (1992, June 20). *Recovered memories of alleged sexual abuse: Lawsuits against parents*. Presentation at 4th Annual Convention of the American Psychological Society, San Diego, CA. (Also, *Behavioral Sciences and the Law*, in press.)

Wakefield, H., & Underwager, R. (undated). Magic, mischief, and memories: Remembering repressed abuse. Unpublished manuscript. (Also see *Issues in Child Abuse Accusations*, 1991, Vol. 3, No. 3.)

Young, W. C., Sachs, R. G., Braun, B. G., & Watkins, R. (1991). Patients reporting ritual abuse in childhood: A clinical syndrome of 37 cases. *Child Abuse & Neglect, 15*, 181–189.

# CHALLENGE QUESTIONS

## Are Memories of Sexual Abuse Always Real?

1. Can a psychologist or other mental health professional lead a patient to believe something that is not true? If so, how can this happen?

2. Can you think of any explanations for the "instances" described by Bass and Davis other than prior sexual abuse?

3. How would you go about "proving" that someone had been sexually abused? What evidence would you need?

4. What are your beliefs about how memories are stored and retrieved?

# ISSUE 5

## Is Subliminal Advertising Effective?

**YES: Roger Crisp,** from "Persuasive Advertising, Autonomy, and the Creation of Desire," *Journal of Business Ethics* (vol. 6, 1987)

**NO: Anthony R. Pratkanis and Elliot Aronson,** from "Subliminal Sorcery: Who Is Seducing Whom?" *USA Today Magazine,* a publication of the Society for the Advancement of Education (September 1991)

### ISSUE SUMMARY

**YES:** Philosopher Roger Crisp argues that persuasive advertising, including subliminal advertising, can influence people's desires and take away their autonomy.

**NO:** Social psychologists Anthony R. Pratkanis and Elliot Aronson argue that there is no clear evidence that subliminal messages in advertisements ever influence people's behavior.

A major record company was taken to court recently for marketing an album that allegedly contained "hidden messages." Lawyers claimed that these hidden messages led two teenage boys to commit suicide. Could hidden messages have caused this extreme behavior? What about other types of hidden messages? Some have accused advertisers of planting subliminal messages (messages that occur below the level of our awareness) encouraging people to buy their products in television commercials and magazine advertisements. There is also a proliferation of subliminal self-help audiotapes on the market that purport to control weight and improve memory *unconsciously.* Do they work?

Such questions are the domain of cognitive psychology. Cognitive psychologists study memory, learning, and other related topics and are thus interested in whether or not we can learn things when we are unaware of them: subliminally. Others in the field of psychology, particularly clinical psychologists, are also interested in subliminal learning and its potential value. For example, if self-help tapes are effective, would they be a useful adjunct to the more traditional forms of psychotherapy? Should they be recommended to patients suffering from depression and other illnesses?

In the selections that follow, Roger Crisp contends that subliminal messages can control our desires. He focuses primarily on one type of subliminal suggestion, which he refers to as "persuasive advertising." Crisp argues that persuasive advertising allows for free action—that is, it does not block a person from carrying through a decision to act—but it strips consumers of free will, or the ability to decide what to do. He criticizes claims that persuasive advertising does not override consumer autonomy, and he argues that because subliminal advertising can sell anything, it is ultimately immoral.

In contrast, Anthony R. Pratkanis and Elliot Aronson argue that there is no clear evidence to support the notion that subliminal messages influence behavior. They reach this conclusion after reviewing and critiquing the available research on subliminal processes. Pratkanis and Aronson also address the current boom in the popularity of subliminal audiotapes, contending that positive effects from the use of these tapes is really a result of the expectations of the user, not subliminal messages.

| POINT | COUNTERPOINT |
|---|---|
| • Subliminal messages ultimately cause behavior. | • No research indicates a causal relationship between subliminal messages and behavior. |
| • Subliminal messages override the autonomy of the consumer. | • Effects attributed to subliminal messages are the result of expectation. |
| • Subliminal messages can sell any product, no matter the quality or price. | • Exaggerated claims of effectiveness ignore the powers of the individual. |

# YES

Roger Crisp

## PERSUASIVE ADVERTISING, AUTONOMY, AND THE CREATION OF DESIRE

In this paper, I shall argue that all forms of a certain common type of advertising are morally wrong, on the ground that they override the autonomy of consumers.

One effect of an advertisement might be the creation of a desire for the advertised product. How such desires are caused is highly relevant as to whether we would describe the case as one in which the autonomy of the subject has been overridden. If I read an advertisement for a sale of clothes, I may rush down to my local clothes store and purchase a jacket I like. Here, my desire for the jacket has arisen partly out of my reading the advertisement. Yet, in an ordinary sense, it is based on or answers to certain properties of the jacket—its colour, style, material. Although I could not explain to you why my tastes are as they are, we still describe such cases as examples of autonomous action, in that all the decisions are being made by me: What kind of jacket do I like? Can I afford one? And so on. In certain other cases, however, the causal history of a desire may be different. Desires can be caused, for instance, by subliminal suggestion. In New Jersey, a cinema flashed sub-threshold advertisements for ice cream onto the screen during movies, and reported a dramatic increase in sales during intermissions. In such cases, choice is being deliberately ruled out by the method of advertising in question. These customers for ice cream were acting 'automatonously', rather than autonomously. They did not buy the ice cream because they happened to like it and decided they would buy some, but rather because they had been subjected to subliminal suggestion. Subliminal suggestion is the most extreme form of what I shall call, adhering to a popular dichotomy, persuasive, as opposed to informative, advertising. Other techniques include puffery, which involves the linking of the product, through suggestive language and images, with the unconscious desires of consumers for power, wealth, status, sex, and so on; and repetition, which is self-explanatory, the name of the product being 'drummed into' the mind of the consumer.

The obvious objection to persuasive advertising is that it somehow violates the autonomy of consumers. I believe that this objection is correct, and that, if one adopts certain common-sensical standards for autonomy, non-persuasive forms of advertising are not open to such an objection. Very high standards for autonomy are set by Kant, who requires that an agent be entirely external to the causal nexus found in the ordinary empirical world, if his or her actions are to be autonomous. These standards are too high, in that it is doubtful whether they allow *any* autonomous action. Standards for autonomy more congenial to common sense will allow that my buying the jacket is autonomous, although continuing to deny that the people in New Jersey were acting autonomously. In the former case, we have what has come to be known in recent discussions of freedom of the will as *both* free will *and* free action. I both decide what to do, and am not obstructed in carrying through my decision into action. In the latter case, there is free action, but not free will. No one prevents the customers buying their ice cream, but they have not themselves made any genuine decision whether or not to do so. In a very real sense, decisions are made for consumers by persuasive advertisers, who occupy the motivational territory properly belonging to the agent. If what we mean by autonomy, in the ordinary sense, is to be present, the possibility of decision must exist alongside.

Arrington (1981) discusses, in a challenging paper, the techniques of persuasive advertising I have mentioned, and argues that such advertising does not override the autonomy of consumers. He examines four notions central to autonomous action, and claims that, on each count, persuasive advertising is exonerated on the charge we have made against it. I shall now follow in the footsteps of Arrington, but argue that he sets the standards for autonomy too low for them to be acceptable to common sense, and that the charge therefore still sticks.

(a) *Autonomous desire:* Arrington argues that an autonomous desire is a first-order desire (a desire for some object, say, Pongo Peach cosmetics) accepted by the agent because it fulfils a second-order desire (a desire about a desire, say, a desire that my first-order desire for Pongo Peach be fulfilled), and that most of the first-order desires engendered in us by advertising are desires that we do accept. His example is an advertisement for Grecian Formula 16, which engenders in him a desire to be younger. He desires that both his desire to be younger and his desire for Grecian Formula 16 be fulfilled.

Unfortunately, this example is not obviously one of persuasive advertising. It may be the case that he just has this desire to look young again rather as I had certain sartorial tastes before I saw the ad about the clothes sale, and then decides to buy Grecian Formula 16 on the basis of these tastes. Imagine this form of advertisement: a person is depicted using Grecian Formula 16, and is then shown in a position of authority, surrounded by admiring members of the opposite sex. This would be a case of puffery. The advertisement implies that having hair coloured by the product will lead to positions of power, and to one's becoming more attractive to the opposite sex. It links, by suggestion, the product with my unconscious desires for power and sex. I may still claim that I am buying the product because I want to look young again. But the real reasons for my purchase are my unconscious desires for power and sex, and the link made between the product and the fulfillment of those desires by the advertisement. These reasons are not reasons I could avow to myself as good reasons for buying the product, and, again, the possibility of decision is absent.

Arrington's claim is that an autonomous desire is a first-order desire which we accept. Even if we allow that it is possible for the agent to consider whether to accept or to repudiate first-order desires induced by persuasive advertising, it seems that all first-order desires induced purely by persuasive advertising will be non-autonomous in Arrington's sense. Many of us have a strong second-order desire not to be manipulated by others without our knowledge, and for no good reason. Often, we are manipulated by others without our knowledge, but for a good reason, and one that we can accept. Take an accomplished actor: much of the skill of an actor is to be found in unconscious body-language. This manipulation we see as essential to our being entertained, and thus acquiesce in it. What is important about this case is that there seems to be no diminution of autonomy. We can still judge the quality of the acting, in that the manipulation is part of its quality. In other cases, however, manipulation ought not to be present, and these are cases where the ability to decide is importantly diminished by the manipulation. Decision is central to the theory of the market-process: I should be able to decide whether to buy product *A* or product *B*, by judging them on their merits. Any manipulation here I shall repudiate as being for no good reason. This is not to say, incidentally, that once the fact that my desires are being manipulated by others has been made transparent to me, my desire will lapse. The people in New Jersey would have been unlikely to cease their craving for ice cream, if we had told them that their desire had been subliminally induced. But they would no longer have voiced acceptance of this desire, and, one assumes, would have resented the manipulation of their desires by the management of the cinema.

*Pace* Arrington, it is no evidence for the claim that most of our desires are autonomous in this sense that we often return to purchase the same product over and over again. For this might well show that persuasive advertising has been supremely efficient in inducing non-autonomous desires in us, which we are unable even to attempt not to act on, being unaware of their origin. Nor is it an argument in Arrington's favour that certain members of our society will claim not to have the second-order desire we have postulated. For it may be that this is a desire which we can see is one that human beings *ought* to have, a desire which it would be in their interests to have, and the lack of which is itself evidence of profound manipulation.

(b) *Rational desire and choice:* One might argue that the desires induced by advertising are often irrational, in the sense that they are not present in an agent in full possession of the facts about the product. This argument fails, says Arrington, because if we require *all* the facts about a thing before we can desire that thing, then all our desires will be irrational; and if we require only the *relevant* information, then prior desires determine the relevance of information. Advertising may be said to enable us to fulfil these prior desires, through the transfer of information, and the supplying of means to ends is surely a paradigm example of rationality.

But, what about persuasive, as opposed to informative, advertising? Take puffery. Is it not true that a person may buy Pongo Peach cosmetics, hoping for an adventure in paradise, and that the product will not fulfil these hopes? Are they really in possession of even the relevant facts? Yes, says Arrington. We wish to purchase *subjective* effects, and these are genuine enough. When I use Pongo Peach, I will experience a genuine feeling of adventure.

Once again, however, our analysis can help us to see the strength of the objection. For a desire to be rational, in any plausible sense, that desire must at least not be induced by the interference of other persons with my system of tastes, against my will and without my knowledge. Can we imagine a person, asked for a reason justifying their purchase of Pongo Peach, replying: 'I have an unconscious desire to experience adventure, and the product has been linked with this desire through advertising'? If a desire is to be rational, it is not necessary that all the facts about the object be known to the agent, but one of the facts about that desire must be that it has not been induced in the agent through techniques which the agent cannot accept. Thus, applying the schema of Arrington's earlier argument, such a desire will be repudiated by the agent as non-autonomous and irrational.

Arrington's claim concerning the subjective effects of the products we purchase fails to deflect the charge of overriding autonomy we have made against persuasive advertising. Of course, very often the subjective effects will be lacking. If I use Grecian Formula 16, I am unlikely to find myself being promoted at work, or surrounded by admiring members of the opposite sex. This is just straight deception. But even when the effects do manifest themselves, such advertisements have still overridden my autonomy. They have activated desires which lie beyond my awareness, and over behaviour flowing from which I therefore have no control. If these claims appear doubtful, consider whether this advertisement is likely to be successful: 'Do you have a feeling of adventure? Then use this brand of cosmetics'. Such an advertisement will fail, in that it appeals to a *conscious* desire, either which we do not have, or which we realise will not be fulfilled by purchasing a certain brand of cosmetics. If the advertisement were for a course in mountain-climbing, it might meet with more success. Our conscious self is not so easily duped by advertising, and this is why advertisers make such frequent use of the techniques of persuasive advertising.

(c) *Free choice:* One might object to persuasive advertising that it creates desires so covert that an agent cannot resist them, and that acting on them is therefore neither free nor voluntary. Arrington claims that a person acts or chooses *freely* if they can adduce considerations which justify their act in their mind; and *voluntarily* if, had they been aware of a reason for acting otherwise, they could have done so. Only occasionally, he says, does advertising prevent us making free and voluntary choices.

Regarding free action, it is sufficient to note that, according to Arrington, if I were to be converted into a human robot, activated by an Evil Genius who has implanted electrodes in my brain, my actions would be free as long as I could cook up some justification for my behaviour. I want to dance this jig because I enjoy dancing. (Compare: I want to buy this ice cream because I like ice cream.) If my argument is right, we are placed in an analogous position by persuasive advertising. If we no longer mean by freedom of action the mere non-obstruction of behaviour, are we still ready to accept that we are engaged in free action? As for whether the actions of consumers subjected to persuasive advertising are voluntary in Arrington's sense, I am less optimistic than he is. It is likely, as we have suggested, that the purchasers of ice cream or Pongo Peach would have gone ahead with their purchase even if they had been made aware that their desires had been induced in them by persuasive advertising. But they would now claim that they themselves had not made the decision, that they were acting on a desire engendered in them which they did not accept, and that there was, therefore, a good reason for them not to make the purchase. The unconscious is not obedient to the commands of the conscious, although it may be forced to listen.

In fact, it is odd to suggest that persuasive advertising does give consumers a choice. A choice is usually taken to require the weighing-up of reasons. What persuasive advertising does is to remove the very conditions of choice.

(d) *Control or manipulation:* Arrington offers the following criteria for control:

A person C controls the behaviour of another person P if (1) C intends P to act in a certain way A, (2) C's intention is causally effective in bringing about A, and (3) C intends to ensure that all of the necessary conditions of A are satisfied. He argues that advertisements tend to induce a desire for X, given a more basic desire for Y. Given my desire for adventure, I desire Pongo Peach cosmetics. Thus, advertisers do not control consumers, since they do not intend to produce all of the necessary conditions for our purchases.

Arrington's analysis appears to lead to some highly counter-intuitive consequences. Consider, again, my position as human robot. Imagine that the Evil Genius relies on the fact that I have certain basic unconscious desires in order to effect his plan. Thus, when he wants me to dance a jig, it is necessary that I have a more basic desire, say, ironically, for power. What the electrodes do is to jumble up my practical reasoning processes, so that I believe that I am dancing the jig because I like dancing, while, in reality, the desire to dance stems from a link between the dance and the fulfilment of my desire for power, forged by the electrodes. Are we still happy to say that I am not controlled? And does not persuasive advertising bring about a similar jumbling-up of the practical reasoning processes of consumers? When I buy Pongo Peach, I may be unable to offer a reason for my purchase, or I may claim that I want to look good. In reality, I buy it owing to the link made by persuasive advertising between my unconscious desire for adventure and the cosmetic in question.

A more convincing account of behaviour control would be to claim that it occurs when a person causes another person to act for reasons which the other person could not accept as good or justifiable reasons for the action. This is how brainwashing is to be distinguished from liberal education, rather than on Arrington's ground that the brainwasher arranges all the necessary conditions for belief. The student can both accept that she has the beliefs she has because of her education and continue to hold those beliefs as true, whereas the victim of brainwashing could not accept the explanation of the origin of her beliefs, while continuing to hold those beliefs. It is worth recalling the two cases we mentioned at the beginning of this paper. I can accept my tastes in dress, and do not think that the fact that their origin is unknown to me detracts from my autonomy, when I choose to buy the jacket. The desire for ice cream, however, will be repudiated, in that it is the result of manipulation by others, without good reason.

It seems, then, that persuasive advertising does override the autonomy of consumers, and that, if the overriding of autonomy, other things being equal, is immoral, then persuasive advertising is immoral.

An argument has recently surfaced which suggests that, in fact, other things are not equal, and that persuasive advertising, although it overrides autonomy, is morally acceptable. This argument was first developed by Nelson (1978), and claims that persuasive advertising is a form of informative advertising, albeit an indirect form. The argument runs at two levels: first, the consumer can judge from the mere fact that a product is heavily advertised, regardless of the form or content of the advertisements, that that product is likely to be a market-winner. The reason for this is that it would not pay to advertise market-losers. Second, even if the consumer is taken in by the content of the advertisement, and buys the product for that reason, he is not being irrational. For he would have bought the product *anyway*, since the very fact that it is advertised means that it is a good product. As Nelson says:

It does not pay consumers to make very thoughtful decisions about advertising. They can respond to advertising for the most ridiculous, explicit reasons and still do what they would have done if they had made the most careful judgements about their behaviour. 'Irrationality' is rational if it is cost-free.

Our conclusions concerning the mode of operation of persuasive advertising, however, suggest that Nelson's argument cannot succeed. For the first level to work, it would have to be true that a purchaser of a product can evaluate that product on its own merits, and then decide whether to purchase it again. But, as we have seen, consumers induced to purchase products by persuasive advertising are not buying those products on the basis of a decision founded upon any merit the products happen to have. Thus, if the product turns out to be less good than less heavily advertised alternatives, they will not be disappointed, and will continue to purchase, if subjected to the heavy advertising which induced them to buy in the first place. For this reason, heavy persuasive advertising is not a sign of quality, and the fact that a product is advertised does not suggest that it is good. In fact, if the advertising has little or no informative content, it might suggest just the opposite. If the product has genuine merits, it should be possible to mention them. Persuasive advertising, as the executives on Madison Avenue know, can be used to sell anything, regardless of its nature or quality.

For the second level of Nelson's argument to succeed, and for it to be in the consumer's interest to react even unthinkingly to persuasive advertising, it must be true that the first level is valid. As the first level fails, there is not even a *prima facie* reason for the belief that it is in the interest of the consumer to be subjected to persuasive advertising. In fact, there are two weighty reasons for doubting this belief. The first has already been hinted at: products promoted through persuasive advertising may well not be being sold on their merits, and may, therefore, be bad products, or products that the consumer would not desire on being confronted with unembellished facts about the product. The second is that this form of 'rational irrationality' is anything but cost-free. We consider it a great cost to lose our autonomy. If I were to demonstrate to you conclusively that if I were to take over your life, and make your decisions for you, you would have a life containing far more of whatever you think makes life worth living, apart from autonomy, than if you were to retain control, you would not surrender your autonomy to me even for these great gains in other values. As we mentioned above in our discussion of autonomous desire, we have a strong second-order desire not to act on first-order desires induced in us unawares by others, for no good reason, and now we can see that that desire applies even to cases in which we would *appear* to be better off in acting on such first-order desires.

Thus, we may conclude that Nelson's argument in favour of persuasive advertising is not convincing. I should note, perhaps, that my conclusion concerning persuasive advertising echoes that of Santilli (1983). My argument differs from his, however, in centering upon the notions of autonomy and causes of desires acceptable to the agent, rather than upon the distinction between needs and desires. Santilli claims that the arousal of a desire is not a rational process, unless it is preceded by a knowledge of actual needs. This, I believe, is too strong. I may well have no need of a new tennis-racket, but my desire for one, aroused by informative advertisements in the newspaper, seems rational enough. I would prefer to claim that a desire is autonomous and at least *prima facie* rational if it is not induced in the agent without his knowledge and

for no good reason, and allows ordinary processes of decision-making to occur.

Finally, I should point out that, in arguing against all persuasive advertising, unlike Santilli, I am not to be interpreted as bestowing moral respectability upon all informative advertising. Advertisers of any variety ought to consider whether the ideological objections often made to their conduct have any weight. Are they, for instance, imposing a distorted system of values upon consumers, in which the goal of our lives is to consume, and in which success is measured by one's level of consumption? Or are they entrenching attitudes which prolong the position of certain groups subject to discrimination, such as women or homosexuals? Advertisers should also carefully consider whether their product will be of genuine value to any consumers, and, if so, attempt to restrict their campaigns to the groups in society which will benefit (see Durham, 1984). I would claim, for instance, that all advertising of tobacco-based products, even of the informative variety, is wrong, and that some advertisements for alcohol are wrong, in that they are directed at the wrong audience. Imagine, for instance, a liquor-store manager erecting an informative bill-board opposite an alcoholics' rehabilitation centre. But these are secondary questions for prospective advertisers. The primary questions must be whether they are intending to employ the techniques of persuasive advertising, and, if so, how those techniques can be avoided.

## ACKNOWLEDGEMENT

I should like to thank Dr. James Griffin for helpful discussion of an earlier draft of this paper.

## REFERENCES

Arrington, R.: 1982, 'Advertising and Behaviour Control,' *Journal of Business Ethics* **I**, 1

Durham, T.: 1984, 'Information, Persuasion, and Control in Moral Appraisal of Advertising Strategy,' *Journal of Business Ethics* **III**, 3

Nelson, P.: 1978, 'Advertising and Ethics,' in *Ethics, Free Enterprise, and Public Policy,* (eds.) R. De George and J. Pichler, New York: Oxford University Press

Santilli, P.: 1983, 'The Informative and Persuasive Functions of Advertising: A Moral Appraisal,' *Journal of Business Ethics* **II**, 1.

# NO

### Anthony R. Pratkanis
### and Elliot Aronson

## SUBLIMINAL SORCERY:
## WHO IS SEDUCING WHOM?

Imagine that it is the 1950s and you are off to see "Picnic," one of the more popular films of the day. However, the movie theater, located somewhere in New Jersey, is unlike any you have been in before. Unbeknownst to you, the projectors have been equipped with a special device capable of flashing short phrases onto the movie screen at such a rapid speed that you are unaware any messages have been presented. During the film, you lean over to your companion and whisper, "Gee, I'd love a tub of buttered popcorn and a Coke right now." To which he replies, "You're always hungry and thirsty at movies, shhhhhh." Then, after a few moments, he says, "You know, some Coke and popcorn might not be a bad idea."

A short time later, you find out that you and your friend weren't the only ones desiring popcorn and Coke in the theater that day. Far from it. According to reports in newspapers and magazines, James Vicary, an advertising expert, secretly had flashed at 1/3,000th of a second the words "Eat Popcorn" and "Drink Coke" onto the movie screen. He claimed that this had produced an increase in Coke sales by 18.1% and in popcorn by 57.7%. Upon reading their newspapers, most people were outraged and frightened. It is a scary world indeed if people can use such a devilish technique to bypass our conscious intellect and beam subliminal commands directly to our subconscious. (The *limen* is the threshold of awareness; thus, subliminal means that the message is so faint or so fast that it actually is below the threshold of awareness.)

In a 1957 article for the *Saturday Review*, "Smudging the Subconscious," Norman Cousins pondered the true meaning of such actions. As he put it, "If the device is successful for putting over popcorn, why not politicians or anything else?" He wondered about the character of men who would dream up such a machine to "break into the deepest and most private parts of the human mind and leave all sorts of scratchmarks." Cousins concluded that the best course of action would be "to take this invention and everything connected to it and attach it to the center of the next nuclear explosive scheduled for testing."

From Anthony R. Pratkanis and Elliot Aronson, "Subliminal Sorcery: Who Is Seducing Whom?" *USA Today Magazine* (September 1991). Copyright © 1991 by The Society for the Advancement of Education. Reprinted by permission.

Cousins was not alone in his concern over the use of subliminal techniques. In a series of four best-selling books, Wilson Bryan Key has brought to national attention the possibility of their widespread use. He argues that such tactics are not limited just to television and movies. Cleverly hidden messages aimed at inducing sexual arousal often are embedded in the pictures of print advertisements. His concern is clear: "Every person reading this book has been victimized and manipulated by the use of subliminal stimuli directed into his unconscious mind by the mass merchandisers of media. The techniques are in widespread use by media, advertising and public relations agencies, industrial and commercial corporations and by the Federal government itself."

Governments have responded to the outcries of the critics. Subliminal advertising has been banned in Australia and Britain. In the U.S., the Federal Communications Commission has ruled that the use of such messages is not in keeping with a broadcast license and could result in its loss. The National Association of Broadcasters has prohibited the use of this type of advertising by its members. A Nevada judge ruled that subliminal messages are not covered by the First Amendment protecting freedom of speech.

Nevertheless, widespread media coverage and governmental laws and rulings have not put an end to these practices. Moreover, not all subliminal devices are designed to manipulate behavior—some are aimed at being helpful to the consumer. Today, a visit to the local bookstore will uncover a vast array of subliminal audio and video tapes designed to accomplish such worthwhile goals as increasing self-esteem, improving memory, reducing weight, controlling anger and temper, and enhancing sexual responsiveness. Such tapes have become quite popular. For example, in their search for better self and health, American consumers spent more than $50,000,000 in 1987 on subliminal tapes designed for therapeutic purposes. The tapes work, according to one manufacturer, because "subliminal messages bypass the conscious mind and imprint directly on the subconscious mind, where they create the basis for the kind of life you want."

Accusations concerning the sinister use of subliminal persuasion continue as well. During the summer of 1990, the rock band Judas Priest was placed on trial for allegedly recording, in one of their songs, the subliminal implant "Do it." This message supposedly caused the suicide deaths of Ray Belknap and James Vance. More trials wait in the wings, including one featuring the rock performer Ozzie Osbourne, scheduled to be heard in Georgia.

## DOES IT REALLY WORK?

Given all the media coverage, governmental involvement, and dollars spent, it is surprising that little public attention has been paid to a most basic question: Does subliminal influence really work?

During the last few years, we have been collecting published articles on subliminal processes. We have gathered more than 100 articles from the mass media and over 200 academic papers on the topic. In none is there clear evidence to support the proposition that subliminal messages influence behavior. Many of the studies fail to find an effect, and those that do either are fatally flawed on methodological grounds or can not be reproduced. Other reviewers of this literature have reached the same conclusion. As cognitive psychologist Timothy Moore puts it, "There is no empirical documentation for stronger subliminal effects, such as inducing particular behaviors or changing motivation. Moreover, such a notion is contradicted by a substantial amount of research and is incompatible with experimentally based conceptions of information processing, learning, and motivation."

If subliminal messages don't change behavior, why do people continue to buy self-help tapes? It seems that many individuals *want* to believe they work. For example, in one study conducted by the Canadian Broadcast Corporation in 1958, the command "Phone Now" was flashed subliminally 352 times during a popular Sunday night television program, "Close-up." Telephone usage did not go up during the period. When asked to guess the message, viewers sent in close to 500 letters, but not one contained the correct answer. Yet, almost half the respondents claimed to be hungry or thirsty during the show. Apparently, they guessed (incorrectly) that the message was aimed at getting them to eat or drink. This not only shows that people *want* to believe the phenomenon works, but demonstrates the power of expectations created by Vicary's theater study. (Interestingly, when confronted with this and other negative findings on subliminal persuasion, Vicary reportedly told the trade newspaper *Advertising Age* that his original "Eat Popcorn/Drink Coke" study was a fabrication intended to increase customers for his failing marketing business!)

What of Key's evidence for the effectiveness of subliminal seduction? Most of the studies he reports lack a control or comparison group. Finding that 62% of all subjects feel sexual, romantic, or satisfied when they see a gin ad with the word "sex" embedded in the ice cubes tells us nothing about the effectiveness of the implant. What would happen if the word "sex" was removed from the cubes? Perhaps 62% of the subjects *still* would feel sexy, romantic, or satisfied. It is possible more or less would feel this way. Without such a comparison, we just don't know.

To illustrate the *in*effectiveness of subliminal audiotapes and to demonstrate the power of expectations, one of the authors [Pratkanis] and his colleagues Jay Eskenazi and Anthony Greenwald conducted a study using mass-marketed audiotapes with subliminal messages designed to improve either self-esteem or memory abilities. Both types contained the same supraliminal (audible) content—various pieces of classical music. However, they differed in their content. According to the manufacturer, the self-esteem tapes contained subliminal messages such as "I have high self-worth and high self-esteem." The memory ones contained subliminal reinforcements such as "My ability to remember and recall is increasing daily."

Using public posters and ads placed in local newspapers, we recruited volunteers who were most interested in the value and potential of subliminal self-help therapies (and who probably would be similar to those most likely to buy such tapes). On the first day of the study, we asked the volunteers to complete various self-esteem and memory measures. Next, each received a subliminal tape, but with an interesting twist. Half were mislabeled so that some of the subjects received a memory tape, but thought it was intended to improve self-esteem, whereas others got a self-esteem one that had been mislabeled memory improvement. The other half of the subjects received correctly labeled tapes.

The volunteers took their tapes home and listened to them every day for five weeks (the period suggested by the manufacturer for maximum effectiveness). Then, they returned to the laboratory and again completed self-esteem and memory tests. They also were asked to indicate if they believed the tapes to be effective. The results showed that the subliminal tapes produced *no* effect (improvement or decrement) on either self-esteem or memory. Yet, the volunteers did not believe this to be the case. Subjects who thought they had listened to a self-esteem tape (regardless of whether they actually did or not) were more likely to be convinced that their self-esteem had improved; those who thought they had listened to a memory one similarly were more likely to believe it had improved their memory. In sum, the subliminal tapes did nothing to improve self-esteem or memory abilities, but, to our subjects, appeared to have an effect. As we put it in the title of the article reporting on this study, "What You Expect Is What You Believe, but Not Necessarily What You Get." These results are not a fluke. We have since repeated our original study twice using different tapes and have yet to find an effect of subliminal messages upon behavior as claimed by the manufacturer.

The history of this controversy teaches us much about persuasion—but not of the subliminal kind. Despite the claims in books and newspapers and on the backs of subliminal self-help tapes, subliminal influence tactics have not been demonstrated to be effective. Of course, it may be that someday, somehow, someone will develop a subliminal technique that may work, just as some day a chemist may find a way to transmute lead to gold. In the meantime, there are many other types of effective persuasion tactics that warrant more attention and scrutiny.

## WIDESPREAD BELIEF

If subliminal devices are so ineffective, why is the belief in their power so widespread? One poll taken around 1970 found that almost 81% of the respondents who had heard of subliminal advertising thought it was a current practice, and more than 68% believed it to be successful in selling products. Most strikingly, surveys also reveal that many people learn about this subject through the mass media and/or courses in high school and college—a further indication of the need for science education in American schools.

A partial answer lies in the coverage that the mass media have given subliminal persuasion. Many of the news stories about it fail to mention negative evidence. When disconfirming proof is presented, it usually is near the end of the article, giving the reader the impression that, at worst, the claims for subliminal effectiveness are somewhat controversial.

A second explanation can be found in our expectations, hopes, and fears. The issue of subliminal influence first emerged as a national concern soon after the Korean War—a time when phenomena like brainwashing and hypnotic suggestion captured the nation's imagination in films such as "The Manchurian Candidate." It is very easy to grasp subliminal seduction as still one more example of brainwashing.

During the post-Watergate years, many Americans felt that their leaders were involved in devious conspiracies and massive cover-ups of the type dramatized in the movie "Network." Key rejuvenated the issue of subliminal influence by portraying it as yet another example that big business and big government were conspiring to get us. Today, there appears to be a growing tendency to turn to quick-fix, "Rambo"-like solutions to complex problems, whether trillion-dollar defense systems in the sky or a $14.95 subliminal cassette tape to improve our self-esteem. Perhaps our theories of what should be have caused us to be a little more accepting and a little less critical of the claims for the power of subliminal influence.

Belief in this process serves a need for many individuals. We live in an age of propaganda. The average American is likely to see more than 7,000,000 ads over a lifetime. Since we provide little education concerning the nature of persuasion, many may feel confused and bewildered by basic social processes.

Subliminal persuasion is presented as an irrational force outside the control of the message recipient. As such, it takes on a supernatural "the devil made me do it" quality capable of justifying and explaining why Americans often are influenced and seemingly can engage in irrational behavior. Why, then, did I buy this worthless product at such a high price?—subliminal sorcery.

However, belief in subliminal persuasion is not without its cost. Perhaps the saddest aspect is that it distracts our attention from more substantive issues.

By looking for subliminal influences, we may ignore more powerful, blatant influence tactics employed by advertisers and sales agents. Consider the suicides of Belknap and Vance brought to light in the trial of Judas Priest. They lived troubled lives, full of drug and alcohol abuse, run-ins with the law, learning disabilities, family violence, and chronic unemployment. What issues did the trial and the subsequent mass media coverage emphasize? There was no discussion of the need for drug treatment centers, evaluation of the pros and cons of America's juvenile justice system, investigation of the schools, inquiry into how to prevent family violence, or examination of the effects of unemployment on a family. Instead, we were mesmerized by an attempt to count the number of subliminal demons that can dance on the end of a record needle.

In this trial, Judge Jerry Carr Whitehead ruled in favor of Judas Priest and CBS Records, stating, "The scientific research presented does not establish that subliminal stimuli, even if perceived, may precipitate conduct of this magnitude. There exist other factors which explain the conduct of the deceased independent of the subliminal stimuli." Perhaps now is the time to lay the myth of subliminal sorcery to rest and direct our attention to other, more scientifically documented, causes of human behavior.

# CHALLENGE QUESTIONS

## Is Subliminal Advertising Effective?

1. Do you believe subliminal messages have any power? How would you feel if you learned you had watched a movie containing subliminal messages?

2. What do you think "causes" people to purchase certain items? In your experiences, what has "caused" you to make certain purchases?

3. Do human beings have free will? Do you feel you are able to make free choices, totally unaffected by "persuasive" techniques?

4. How would our society be different if there were no advertising? Would it be better or worse in your mind?

# ISSUE 6

# Can Intelligence Be Increased?

**YES: Robert J. Sternberg,** from "How Can We Teach Intelligence?" *Educational Leadership* (September 1984)

**NO: Arthur R. Jensen,** from "Compensatory Education and the Theory of Intelligence," *Phi Delta Kappan* (April 1985)

### ISSUE SUMMARY

**YES:** Psychologist Robert J. Sternberg presents his view that intelligence is a changeable and multifaceted characteristic, and he suggests that intelligence can be taught through training programs, three of which he summarizes.

**NO:** Psychologist Arthur R. Jensen contends that efforts to increase intelligence have not resulted in any appreciable gains and that programs designed for this purpose have a faulty understanding of the nature of intelligence.

Are we born with all the intelligence we will ever have? To what extent can we ensure that all healthy people will be able to cope with the increasing complexities of our society? As we become increasingly dependent upon our educational systems, these questions assume special importance.

If intelligence is a capacity fixed by the time of birth, then an efficient educational system should not waste the time, space, money, and resources that teach beyond each student's capacity. It might be appropriate for each individual's educational track to be determined in advance through extensive intelligence testing.

The 1960s in America can be characterized in part by the conviction that the educational disadvantages of poverty could be overcome by special "head start" programs early in a child's life. Early outcomes provided some evidence that intelligence could be increased. However, the long-term results were less encouraging. The question of an unchangeable intelligence is still open.

Robert J. Sternberg complains that psychologists' traditional preoccupation with the measurement of intelligence has prevented them from understanding the nature of intelligence. The most serious error, he says, has been the assumption "that intelligence is, for the most part, a fixed and immutable characteristic of the individual." Sternberg alleges that a vested interest in intelligence tests with stable scores has interfered with the view that intelligence is changeable.

Sternberg asserts that his own research findings suggest that intelligence *can* be trained and focuses on the question of *how* it can be trained. He presents his own theory of what intelligence is, then he reviews three programs that train aspects of intelligence specified by his theory. Finally, he discusses the variables to be considered by educational administrators in the position of choosing programs for their specific school systems.

Arthur R. Jensen claims, "The plain truth is that compensatory programs have not resulted in any appreciable, durable gains in IQ or scholastic achievement for those youngsters who have taken part in them." He points out that these programs have produced positive gains in care, involvement, and attitudes but not in intelligence or academic achievement.

Jensen says the specialists responsible for these compensatory programs were wrong in their understanding of what intelligence is and what IQ tests measure. He says their error was in their view of intelligence as "consisting of a general learning ability of almost unlimited plasticity plus the 'knowledge contents' of memory."

| POINT | COUNTERPOINT |
|---|---|
| • Existing intelligence tests are inadequate. | • Existing intelligence tests have high validity. |
| • Intelligence is plastic. | • Intelligence is fixed. |
| • Intelligence can be trained. | • Intelligence is not subject to manipulation. |

# YES

Robert J. Sternberg

# HOW CAN WE TEACH INTELLIGENCE?

For most of the century, psychologists studying intelligence have been pre-occupied with a single question, "How can we measure intelligence?" In retrospect, this preoccupation has turned out to be a grave mistake for sev-eral reasons. First, it has led to neglect of the more important question, "What is intelligence?" If intelligence tests have not improved much over the years— and the evidence suggests that they haven't (Sternberg, 1979, 1980)—one can scarcely be surprised. Better tests of intelligence could arise only from bet-ter ideas of what intelligence is; curiously enough, few psychologists have sought better tests through better understanding. Rather, they have sought better tests through small refinements of existing technology, which is limited by the inadequacies of the meager theory underlying it (Sternberg, 1977).

Second, the preoccupation with testing has been based on certain assump-tions, at least one of which is seriously in error. This assumption is that intelligence is, for the most part, a fixed and immutable characteristic of the individual. After all, if intelligence is constantly changing, or even potentially changeable, what good could tests be? With scores constantly changing, the usefulness of the tests as measures to rank individuals in a stable way over time would be seriously challenged.

Third, and most important for concerned educators, both the preoccupation with testing and the assumption that intelligence is a fixed entity have led to neglect of an even more productive question, "Can intelligence be trained, and if so, how?" My research findings suggest that intelligence *can* be trained. Thus, the focus of this article is the question of "How?"

Because there is no unanimous agreement among psychologists as to the exact nature of intelligence, my own views are necessarily somewhat id-iosyncratic. Nevertheless, they are accepted in large part by many specialists in the field, and especially those who have set their goal to train intelligence rather than merely to measure it (Brown, 1983; de Bono, 1983; Resnick, 1976; Detterman and Sternberg, 1982).

My "componential" theory of intelligence seeks to understand intelligence in terms of the component processes that make up intelligence performance

From Robert J. Sternberg, "How Can We Teach Intelligence?" *Educational Leadership* (September 1984). Copyright © 1984 by The Association for Supervision and Curriculum Development and funded by The National Institute of Education. Reprinted by permission.

(Sternberg, 1979). I will briefly describe the theory, then review three programs that train aspects of intelligence as specified by the theory. Then I will conclude with general remarks and suggestions on the adoption of an intellectual or thinking skills training program.

## COMPONENTS OF INTELLIGENCE

The view of intelligence as comprising, in part, a set of processes differs in a fundamental way from the view that led to IQ tests. At the turn of the century, the traditional or psychometric view was (and for some continues to be) that intelligence comprises one or more stable, fixed entities (Cattell, 1971; Guilford, 1967; Vernon, 1971). These entities, called *factors*, were alleged to give rise to the individual differences we observe both in IQ test performance and in students' performances at school. The problem with this view is that it does little to suggest how intelligence can be modified. But if intelligence can be broken down into a set of underlying processes, then it is clear what we can do to improve it: we can intervene at the level of the mental process and teach individuals what processes to use when, how to use them, and how to combine them into workable strategies for task solution.

What exactly are these processes? My research suggests they can be divided into three types (Sternberg, 1984). The first type, *metacomponents*, are the higher order or executive processes that we use to plan what we are going to do, monitor what we are doing, and evaluate what we have done. Deciding on a strategy for solving an arithmetic problem or organizing a term paper are examples of metacomponents at work. The second type of processes are *performance compo-*

*nents.* Whereas metacomponents decide what to do, performance components actually do it. So the actual steps we use in, say, solving an analogy or an arithmetic problem, whether on an IQ test or in everyday life, would be examples of sets of performance components in action. The third type of processes are *knowledge-acquisition components*. Processes of this kind are used in learning new material; for example, in first learning how to solve an analogy or a given type of arithmetic problem.

This may seem very abstract, so let's take a concrete example: an analogy. An analogy provides a particularly apt example because virtually everyone who has ever studied intelligence has found the ability to see and solve analogies to be fundamental to intelligent performance. According to the traditional psychometric view, the ability to solve an analogy would be attributed to a static underlying factor of intelligence. Charles Spearman, a famous psychometrician around the turn of the century, called this factor "g," or general intelligence. Some years later, Louis Thurstone, another psychometrician, called the factor "reasoning." The problem with such labels is that they tell us little either about how analogies are solved, or about how the ability to solve analogous problems can be taught.

In contrast, a process-based approach seeks to identify the mental processes used to solve the analogy or other problem. Consider the processes one might use in solving an analogy such as, "*Washington* is to *one* as *Lincoln* is to (a) five, (b) 15, (c) 20, (d) 50." First, we must decide what processes to use, a decision that is metacomponential in nature. Next we must decide how to sequence these processes so as to form a workable strategy for analogy solution, another metacomponential decision. Then we must use the performance components and strategy we have selected to actually solve the problem. It appears, through experimental data we have collected, that what people do is to *encode*, as they need them, relevant attributes of the terms of the analogy: that Washington was the first President of the United States, that he was a Revolutionary War general, and that his is the portrait that appears on a one-dollar bill. Next they *infer* the relation between the first two terms of the analogy, perhaps in this case recognizing that the basis of the analogy might be either Washington as first president or Washington as the portrait on the one-dollar bill. Then they *map* the relation they have inferred in the first part of the analogy to the second part of the analogy (that is, from the Washington part to the Lincoln part), perhaps recognizing that the topic of the analogy is some property of U.S. presidents. Next people *apply* the relation they inferred in the first part of the analogy, as mapped to the second part of the analogy, to the third term so as to select the best alternative. In this case, "five" is the preferred alternative, because it enables one to carry through the relation of portraits on currency (that is, Lincoln's portrait is on the five-dollar bill just as Washington's is on the one-dollar bill). Although this account is a simplification of my model of reasoning by analogy (Sternberg, 1977), it represents the kind of theorizing that goes into a process-based account of intelligent performance.

Now, how can the metacomponents and performance components of intelligence be taught? How can we make students better at structuring and then solving problems than they would be on their own? I recommend three widely disseminated programs, each of which has a unique set of strengths and weaknesses.

## INSTRUMENTAL ENRICHMENT

The first training program, Reuven Feuerstein's (1980) *Instrumental Enrichment (IE)* program, was originally proposed for use with children showing retarded performance; it has since been recognized by Feuerstein and others to be valuable for children at all levels of the intellectual spectrum. It is based on Feuerstein's theory of intelligence, which emphasizes what I refer to as metacomponential and performance-componential functioning.

*Instrumental Enrichment* is intended to improve cognitive functioning related to the input, elaboration, and output of information. Feuerstein has compiled a long list of cognitive deficits his program is intended to correct. This list includes:

• Unplanned, impulsive, and unsystematic exploratory behavior. When presented with a number of cues to problem solving that must be scanned, the individual's approach is disorganized, leaving the individual unable to select those cues whose specific attributes make them relevant for a proper solution to the problem at hand.

• Lack of or impaired capacity for considering two sources of information at once, reflected in dealing with data in a piecemeal fashion rather than as a unit of organized facts.

• Inadequacy in experiencing the existence of an actual problem and subsequently in defining it.

• Lack of spontaneous comparative behavior or limitation of its appearance to a restricted field of needs.

- Lack of or impaired strategies for hypothesis testing.
- Lack of orientation toward the need for logical evidence.
- Lack of or impaired planning behavior.
- Episodic grasp of reality. The individual is unable to relate different aspects of his or her experience to one another. Feuerstein seeks to correct these deficits and, at the same time, to increase the student's intrinsic motivation and feeling of personal competence and self-worth.

What are some of the main characteristics of the Feuerstein program? The materials themselves are structured as a series of units, or instruments, each of which emphasizes a particular cognitive function and its relationship to various cognitive deficiencies. Feuerstein defines an instrument as something by means of which something else is effected; hence, performance on the materials is seen as a means to an end, rather than as an end in itself. Emphasis in analyzing *IE* performance is on processes rather than products. A student's errors are viewed as a source of insights into how the student solves problems. *Instrumental Enrichment* does *not* attempt to teach either specific items of information or formal, operational, abstract thinking by means of a well-defined, structured knowlege base. To the contrary, it is as content-free as possible....

What are the strengths and weaknesses of the *IE* program? On the positive side, it (a) can be used for children in a wide age range (from the upper grades of elementary school to early high school) and for children of a wide range of ability levels (from the retarded to the above average) and socioeconomic groups; (b) is well liked by children and appears to be effective in raising their intrinsic motivation and self-esteem; (c) is well packaged and readily obtainable; and (d) appears effective in raising children's scores on ability tests. Indeed, most of the training exercises contain items similar or identical to those found on intelligence and multiple aptitude tests, so that it should not be totally surprising that intensive practice and training on such items should raise these test scores.

On the more negative side: (a) the program requires extensive teacher training, which must be administered by a designated training authority for the duration of the program; (b) the isolation of the problems from any working knowledge or discipline base (such as social studies or reading, for example) raises questions regarding the transferability of the skills to academic and real-world intellectual tasks, especially over the long term; and (c) despite Feuerstein's aversion to IQ tests, the program trains primarily those abilities that IQ tests tap rather than a broader spectrum of abilities that go beyond intelligence as the tests test it.

To sum up, then, Feuerstein's *Instrumental Enrichment* program is an attractive package in many respects, although with limitations in regard to breadth of skills taught and potential power for generalization. Nevertheless, it is among the best of the available programs that emphasize thinking skill training. Probably it has been the most widely used and field-tested program, both in this country and abroad. As a result, it can be recommended both for members of the majority culture and for members of other cultures and subcultures as well.

## PHILOSOPHY FOR CHILDREN

Matthew Lipman's *Philosophy for Children* program is about as different from *Instru-*

*mental Enrichment* as it could be (Lipman, Sharp, and Oscayan, 1980). Yet it seeks to foster many of the same intellectual skills, albeit in a very different manner.

*Philosophy for Children* consists of a series of texts in which fictional children spend a considerable portion of their time thinking about thinking and about ways in which better thinking can be distinguished from poorer thinking. The keys to learning presented in the program are identification and simulation: through reading the texts and engaging in classroom discussions and exercises that follow the reading, the author's objective is for students to identify with the characters and to join in the kinds of thinking depicted in the program.

Lipman has listed 30 thinking skills that *Philosophy for Children* has intended to foster in children of the upper elementary school, generally grades 5–8. A representative sampling of these skills includes the following:

• *Concept development.* Students clarify their understanding of concepts by applying them to specific cases, learning to identify those cases that are within the boundaries and those that are outside. For example, when considering the concept of friendship, children are asked whether people have to be the same age to be friends, whether two people can be friends and not like each other very much, and whether it is possible for friends ever to lie to one another.

• *Generalizations.* Given a set of facts, students are to note uniformities or regularities and to generalize these regularities from given instances to similar ones. For example, children might be asked to consider generalizations that can be drawn from a set of given facts such as, "I get sick when I eat raspberries; I get sick when I eat strawberries; I get sick when I eat blackberries."

• *Formulating cause-effect relationships.* Students should discern and construct formulations indicating relationships between causes and effects. For example, students might be given a statement such as "He threw the stone and broke the window," and then be asked whether the statement necessarily implies a cause-effect relationship.

• *Drawing syllogistic inferences.* Students should draw correct conclusions from valid syllogisms and recognize invalid syllogisms when they are presented. For example, they might be given the premises, "All dogs are animals; all collies are dogs," and be asked what valid inference they can draw from these premises.

• *Consistency and contradictions.* Students should recognize internal consistencies and inconsistencies within a given set of statements or other data. For example, they might be asked to ponder whether it is possible to eat animals if one genuinely cares about them.

• *Identifying underlying assumptions.* Students should recognize the often hidden assumptions that underlie statements. For example, they might be given the following sentences: "I love your hair that way, Peg. What beauty parlor did you go to?" and be asked to identify the hidden assumption underlying the question.

• *Grasping part-whole and whole-part connections.* Students should recognize relations between parts and wholes and avoid mistakes in reasoning based on identification of the part with the whole, or vice versa. For example, students might be asked to identify the part-whole fallacy underlying the statement,

"If Mike's face has handsome features, Mike must have a handsome face."

• *Working with analogies.* Students should form and identify analogies. For example, they should be able to solve an analogy such as Germ is to Disease as Candle is to (a) Wax, (b) Wick, (c) White, (d) Light.

The skills trained through the *Philosophy for Children* program are conveyed through a series of stories about children. Consider, for example, the first chapter of *Harry Stottlemeier's Discovery*, the first book in the program series. In this chapter about the consequences of Harry's not paying attention in science class, children are introduced to a wealth of thinking skills. For instance:

• *Problem formulation.* Harry says, "All planets revolve about the sun, but not everything that revolves about the sun is a planet." He realizes that he had been assuming that just because all planets revolve about the sun, everything that revolves about the sun must be a planet.

• *Nonreversibility of logical "all" statements.* Harry says that "a sentence can't be reversed. If you put the last part of a sentence first, it'll no longer be true." For example, he cannot convert "all model airplanes are toys" into "all toys are model airplanes."

• *Reversibility of logical "no" statements.* Lisa, a friend of Harry's, realizes that logical "no" statements can be reversed. "No submarines are kangaroos," for example, can be converted to "No kangaroos are submarines."

• *Application of principles to real-life situations.* Harry intervenes in a discussion between two adults, showing how a principle he had deduced earlier can be applied to disprove one of the adult's argument....

The nature of the *Philosophy for Children* program may be further elucidated by comparing it to Feuerstein's program. The notable similarity between the two programs is that both seek to teach thinking skills, especially what was referred to earlier as executive processes (metacomponents) and nonexecutive processes (performance components). But given the basic similarity of goals, the differences between the programs are striking.

First, whereas Feuerstein's program minimizes the role of knowledge base and customary classroom content, Lipman's program maximizes such involvement. Although the introductory volume, *Harry Stottlemeier's Discovery*, is basically philosophical in tone, the subsequent volumes—*Mark, Pixie, Suki,* and *Lisa*—emphasize infusion of thinking skills into different content areas: the arts, social studies, and science.

Second, whereas the material in Feuerstein's program minimizes the use of written language, the material in Lipman's program is conceptually abstract but is presented through wholly verbal text that deals with highly concrete situations.

Third, although both programs involve class discussion, there is much more emphasis on discussion and interchange in Lipman's program than in Feuerstein's. Similarly, the written exercises are less important in Lipman's program.

Fourth, Feuerstein's program was originally designed for retarded learners, although it has since been extended to children at all points along the continuum of intellectual ability. Lipman's program seems oriented toward children of at least average ability on a scale of national norms. Moreover, the reading in *Philosophy for Children* can be a problem for children much below grade level in reading.

What are the strengths and weaknesses of *Philosophy for Children*? The program has outstanding strengths. First, the stories are exciting and highly motivating to upper elementary school children. Second, it is attractively packaged and easily obtainable. Third, tests of the program have shown it to be effective in raising the level of children's thinking skills. Fourth, the infusion of the thinking skills into content areas should help assure durability and at least some transferability of learning attained through the program. Finally, the thinking skills taught are clearly the right ones to teach for both academic and everyday information processing—no one could possibly complain that the skills are only relevant for IQ tests, although, in fact, the skills are also relevant for performance on such tests. . .

In summary, although it is limited somewhat by the range of students for whom it is appropriate, no program I am aware of is more likely to teach durable and transferable thinking skills than *Philosophy for Children*.

## CHICAGO MASTERY LEARNING READING PROGRAM

Whereas *Instrumental Enrichment* and *Philosophy for Children* emphasize thinking skills (metacomponents and performance components), the *Chicago Mastery Learning Reading Program* emphasizes learning strategies and study skills (knowledge-acquisition [Jones, 1982] components)—a fuzzy but nevertheless useful distinction.

The *Chicago* program, developed by Beau Fly Jones in collaboration with others, equips students with the learning strategies and study skills they need to succeed in school and in their everyday lives. Like *Philosophy for Children*, this program is written for children roughly in grades five through eight. There are four books (tan, purple, silver, and gold), each of which teaches somewhat different skills. The emphasis in all four books, however, is on learning to learn. Within each grade (color) level, there are two kinds of units: comprehension and study skills.

Consider, for example, the purple (Grade 7) sequence. The comprehension program contains units on using sentence context, mood in reading and writing, comprehending complex information, comprehending comparisons, analyzing characters, and distinguishing facts from opinions. The study skills program contains units on parts of a book, graphs and charts, preview-question-read, studying textbook chapters, major and minor ideas, and outlining with parallel structure. The silver (Grade 8) sequence for comprehension contains units of figurative language, word meaning from context, reasoning from facts to complex inferences, analyzing stories and plays, completing a story or a play, signs, and symbols. The sequence for study skills contains units on supporting facts, research aids, notetaking in outline form, summaries and generalizations, comprehending road maps, and understanding forms and directions.

The *Chicago* program is based on the belief that almost all students can learn what only the best students currently learn, if only the more typical or less able students are given appropriate learning opportunities. Mastery learning is described as differing from traditional instruction primarily in the systematic and frequent use of formative and diagnostic testing within each of the instructional units. Instruction is done in groups, with individual assistance and remediation as necessary. Because students typically enter the classroom situation with differing skills and levels of proficiency in the exercise of these skills, instructional units begin with simple, concrete, literal, and familiar material and proceed gradually to the more complex, abstract, inexplicit, and unfamiliar material.

Each instructional unit in the *Chicago* program contains several distinct parts: student activities, optional teaching activities, formative tests, additional activities, enrichment activities, retests, and subject-related applications. Students and teachers are thus provided with a wide variety of materials.

The number and variety of exercises is so great as to rule out the possibility of giving a fair sample of materials in the program. Thus, I can make no claim that the following few examples are representative of the program as a whole:

- *Using sentence context.* In one type of exercise, students read a sentence containing a new word for them to learn. They are assisted in using cues in the sentence to help them determine the word's meaning.
- *Mood in reading and writing.* Students are given a sentence from either expository or fictional text. They are asked to choose which of three words or phrases best describes the mood conveyed by the sentence.
- *Comprehending comparisons.* Students are taught about different kinds of comparisons. They are then given some sample comparisons and asked to elaborate on the meanings, some of which are metaphorical.
- *Facts and opinions.* Students are taught how to distinguish facts from opinions. They are given a passage to read, along with some statements following the passage. Their task is to indicate which statements represent facts and which opinions.

The *Chicago* program is similar to the *Instrumental Enrichment* and *Philosophy for Children* programs in its direct teaching of cognitive skills. The program differs in several key respects, however. First, it resembles typical classroom curriculum more than either of the other two programs. Whereas implementation of either of the others would almost certainly have to follow an explicit policy decision to teach thinking skills as an additional part of the curriculum, the *Chicago* program could very well be implemented as part of an established program, such as the reading curriculum. Second, the program does fit into a specific curriculum area that is common in schools, namely, reading. The Lipman program would fit into a philosophy curriculum, if any school offered such instruction. The Feuerstein program would be unlikely to fit into any existing curricular program, except those explicitly devoted to teaching thinking skills. Third, the *Chicago* program emphasizes learning strategies, whereas the emphasis of the other two programs tends to be on thinking skills. Finally, the *Chicago* program seems most broadly applicable to a wide range of students, including those who are above and below grade level.

Like all programs, the *Chicago* program has both strengths and weaknesses. Its most notable strengths are (1) the wide range of students to whom it can be administered, both in terms of intellectual levels and socio-economic backgrounds; (2) the relatively lesser amount of teacher training required for its implementation; (3) the ease with which the program can be incorporated into existing curricula;

and (4) the immediate applicability of the skills to school and other life situations. Students in the program have shown significant pretest to pretest gains in achievement from the program (Jones, 1982).

As for weaknesses, or at least limitations, compared to the *IE* and Lipman's programs, (1) the materials applied are less likely to be intrinsically motivating to students; (2) the skills trained by the *Chicago* program are within a non-limited domain (reading and performing verbal comprehension) than in some other programs; and (3) the program is less clearly based on a psychological theory of cognition.

In conclusion, the *Chicago Mastery Learning Program* offers an attractive means for teaching learning skills, in the context of a reading program. The materials are carefully prepared to be wide ranging and should meet the needs of a wide variety of schools.

## CHOOSING THE RIGHT PROGRAM

Do we really need intervention programs for teaching students intellectual skills? The answer is clearly "yes." During the last decade or so we have witnessed an unprecedented decline in the intellectual skills of our school children (Wigdor and Garner, 1982). This is evident, of course, from the decline in scores on tests such as the Scholastic Aptitude Test (SAT); but college professors don't need SAT scores to be apprised of the decline: they can see it in poorer class performance and particularly in the poorer reading and writing of their students. Moreover, thinking skills are needed by more than the college-bound population. Perhaps intellectual skills could be better trained through existing curricula than they are

now. But something in the system is not working, and I view programs such as those described here as exciting new developments for reversing the declines in intellectual performance we have witnessed in recent years.

How does one go about choosing the right program for one's particular school and student needs? I believe that wide-ranging research is needed before selecting any one of several programs for school or districtwide implementation. Which program to select will depend on the grade level, socioeconomic level, and intellectual level of the students; the particular kinds of skills one wishes to teach; the amount of time one can devote to training students; one's philosophy of intellectual skills training (that is, whether training should be infused into or separated from regular curricula); and one's financial resources, among other things. Clearly, the decision of which program to use should be made only after extensive deliberation and outside consultation, preferably with people who have expertise, but not a vested interest, in the implementation of one particular program or another.

The following general guidelines can be applied in selecting a program (see also Sternberg, 1983):

• The program should be based on a psychological theory of the intellectual processes it seeks to train and on an educational theory of the way in which the processes will be taught. A good pair of theories should state what processes are to be trained, how the processes work together in problem solving, and how the processes can be taught so as to achieve durability and transfer of training. Innumerable programs seek to train intelligence, but most of them are worth little or nothing. One can immediately rule out large numbers of the low-value programs by investigating whether they have any theoretical basis. The three programs described here are both strong psychological and educational foundations.

• The program should be sociocul-turally appropriate. It should be clear from the examples described here that programs differ widely in terms of the student populations to whom they are targeted. The best intentions in such a program may be thwarted if the students cannot relate the program both to their cognitive structures and to the world in which they live.

• The program should provide explicit training both in the mental processes used in task performance (performance components and knowledge-acquisition components) and in self-management strategies for using these components (metacomponents). Many early attempts at process training did not work because investigators assumed that just teaching the processes necessary for task performance would result in improved performance on intellectual tasks. The problem was that students often did not learn when to use the processes or how to implement them in tasks differing even slightly from the ones on which they had been trained. In order to achieve durable and transferable learning, it is essential that students be taught not only how to perform tasks but also when to use the strategies they are taught and how to implement them in new situations.

• The program should be responsive to the motivational as well as the intel-lectual needs of the students. A program that does not adequately motivate students is bound not to succeed, no matter how excellent the cognitive component may be.

• The program should be sensitive to individual differences. Individuals differ greatly in the knowledge and skills they bring to any educational program. A program that does not take these individual differences into account will almost inevitably fail to engage large numbers of students.

• The program should provide explicit links between the training it provides and functioning in the real world. Psychologists have found that transfer of training does not come easily. One cannot expect to gain transfer unless explicit provisions are made in the program so as to increase its likelihood of occurrence.

• Adoption of the program should take into account demonstrated empirical success in implementations similar to one's own planned implementation. Surprisingly, many programs have no solid data behind them. Others may have data that are relevant only to school or student situations quite different from one's own. A key to success is choosing a program with a demonstrated track record in similar situations.

• The program should have associated with it a well-tested curriculum for teacher training as well as for student training. The best program can fail to realize its potential if teachers are insufficiently or improperly trained.

• Expectations should be appropriate for what the program can accomplish. Teachers and administrators often set themselves up for failure by setting expectations that are inappropriate or too high.

Programs are now available that do an excellent, if incomplete, job of improving children's intellectual skills. The time has come for supplementing the standard curriculum with such programs. We can continue to use intelligence tests, but we will provide more service to children by developing their intelligence than by testing it.

## REFERENCES

Brown, A. L. "Knowing When, Where, and How to Remember: A Problem of Metacognition." In *Advances in Instructional Psychology, Vol 1*. Edited by R. Glaser. Hillsdale, N.J.: Erlbaum, 1978.

Brown, J. L. "On Teaching Thinking Skills in the Elementary and Middle Schools." *Phi Delta Kappan* 64 (1983): 709–714.

Cattell, R. B. *Abilities: Their Structure, Growth, and Action.* Boston: Houghton-Mifflin, 1971.

de Bono, E. "The Direct Teaching of Thinking as a Skill." *Phi Delta Kappan* 64 (1983): 703–08.

Detterman, D. K., and Sternberg, R. J., eds. *How and How Much Can Intelligence Be Increased?* Norwood, N.J.: Ablex, 1982.

Feuerstein, R. *Instrumental Enrichment: An Intervention Program for Cognitive Modifiability.* Baltimore: University Park Press, 1980.

Guilford, J. P. *The Nature of Intelligence.* New York: McGraw-Hill, 1967.

Jones, B. F. *Chicago Mastery Learning: Reading.* 2nd ed. Watertown, Mass.: Mastery Education Corporation, 1982.

Lipman, M.; Sharp, A. M.; and Oscanyan, F. S. *Philosophy in the Classroom.* 2nd ed. Philadelphia: Temple University Press, 1980.

Resnick, L. B. *The Nature of Intelligence.* Hillsdale, N.J.: Erlbaum, 1976.

Sternberg, R. J. *Intelligence, Information Processing, and Analogical Reasoning: The Componential Analysis of Human Abilities.* Hillsdale, N.J.: Erlbaum, 1977.

Sternberg, R. J. "The Nature of Mental Abilities." *American Psychologist* 34 (1979): 214–230.

Sternberg, R. J. "The Construct Validity of Aptitude Tests: An Information-Processing Assessment." In *Construct Validity in Psychological Measurement.* Princeton, N.J.: Educational Testing Service, 1980.

Sternberg, R. J. "Criteria for Intellectual Skills Training." *Educational Researcher* 12 (1983): 6–12, 26.

Sternberg, R. J. *Beyond IQ: A Triarchic Theory of Human Intelligence.* New York: Cambridge University Press, 1984.

Vernon, P. E. *The Structure of Human Abilities.* London: Methuen, 1971.

Wigdor, A. K., and Garner, W. R., eds. *Ability Testing: Uses, Consequences, and Controversies* (2 volumes). Washington, D.C.: National Academy Press, 1982.

# NO

### Arthur R. Jensen

# COMPENSATORY EDUCATION AND THE THEORY OF INTELLIGENCE

The past 20 years have been a period of unparalleled affluence for public education and educational research in the U.S. When the history of this era is written, two features will stand out prominently: racial desegregation of the schools and large-scale experimentation with compensatory education.

The nation focused its educational resources during this period primarily on extending the benefits of education to every segment of the population—especially to those groups that historically have derived the least benefit from the traditional system of schooling. During the past 20 years more young people have gone to school for more years and have obtained more diplomas, per capita, in the U.S. than in any other nation. Fifty percent of U.S. high school graduates in the 1970s went on to college.

These proud facts are one side of the picture. The other side is much less complimentary and should shake any complacency we Americans might feel. The past 20 years, which have brought the most energetic large-scale innovations in the history of U.S. education, have also brought an accelerating decline in Scholastic Aptitude Test scores. And there are other signs of malaise as well. On objective measures of the average level of educational achievement, the U.S. falls below all other industrialized nations, according to the International Association for the Evaluation of Educational Achievement.[1] In fact, average levels of educational achievement lower than that of the U.S. are found only in the industrially under-developed nations of the Third World.

Illiteracy in the U.S. has been grossly underestimated. Until recently, the U.S. Census Bureau routinely estimated the rate of illiteracy as the percentage of Americans with fewer than six years of schooling. The 1980 Census found that only two-tenths of 1% (0.2%) of the U.S. population between the ages of 14 and 24 met this definition of illiteracy—a rate that was the same for both black and white Americans.

Simple tests of actual reading ability reveal a much less rosy picture, however. According to lawyer and psychologist Barbara Lerner, evidence collected by the National Assessment of Educational Progress shows that "the overall rate of illiteracy for cohorts reaching their 18th birthday in the 1970s

From Arthur R. Jensen, "Compensatory Education and the Theory of Intelligence," *Phi Delta Kappan* (April 1985). Copyright © 1985 by Arthur R. Jensen. Reprinted by permission.

can safely be estimated to have been at least 20%.... [Moreover, the] black-white gap was still dramatic: 41.6% of all black 17-year-olds still enrolled in school in 1975 were functionally illiterate."[2] Lerner goes on to emphasize the broad implications of this finding:

> On this basis, it would have seemed reasonable to predict serious shortages of literate workers throughout the 1980s and perhaps beyond, along with high levels of structural unemployment, particularly among younger black workers, and increasing difficulty in meeting economic competition from foreign countries with more literate work forces.[3]

Clearly, those conditions that originally gave rise to the aims and aspirations of compensatory education are as relevant today as they were 20 years ago. Of the many lessons that can be learned from assessments and meta-analyses of the results of 20 years of compensatory education, I intend to dwell in this article on what seems to me to be one of the most important. Because the lesson on which I will dwell is one of the clearest and seemingly least-debatable findings of studies of compensatory education programs of all kinds and because this lesson has important implications for both theory and practice, it is peculiar that this lesson has been soft-pedaled in most published summaries of compensatory education outcomes.

The lesson to which I refer is this: compensatory education has made its least impressive impact on just those variables that it was originally intended (and expected) to improve the most: namely, I.Q. and scholastic achievement. The plain truth is that compensatory programs have not resulted in any appreciable, durable gains in I.Q. or scholastic achievement for those youngsters who have taken part in them. This is an important discovery, and the fact that we do not like this outcome or that it is not what we expected neither diminishes its importance nor justifies downplaying it. Rather, we are challenged to try to understand its theoretical implications for the study of intelligence and its practical implications for the practice of education.

Let us not be distracted from trying to understand the discrepancy between the expected and the actual outcomes of compensatory education programs by the too-easy response of retroactively revising our original expectations. We should gain more from our 20 years of experience than just a list of excuses for the disappointing discrepancy between our expectations and the actual results.

To be sure, Head Start and other compensatory education programs have produced some positive gains. The fact that the bona fide benefits of compensatory education have not been primarily cognitive in nature and not strongly reflected in academic achievement per se should not detract from the social importance of these gains. The positive outcomes of Head Start and similar programs include such things as the improvement of participants' nutrition and of their medical and dental care. The list of positive outcomes also includes greater involvement of parents in their children's schooling, noticeable improvement in the children's attitude toward school and in their self-esteem, fewer behavioral problems among participants, fewer retentions in grade, and a smaller percentage of special education placements.[4]

These socially desirable outcomes have not been accompanied by marked or lasting improvement in either I.Q. or academic performance, however. Even the smaller percentage of special education placements may be attributable to teachers' and administrators' knowledge that certain children have taken part in Head Start or other compensatory education programs, because such children are less apt than nonparticipating peers to be labeled as candidates for special education. Gene Glass and Mary Ellwein offer an insightful observation on this point in their review of *As the Twig Is Bent*, a book on 11 compensatory education programs and their outcomes, as assessed by the Consortium for Longitudinal Studies. According to Glass and Ellwein:

> [T]hose whose ideas are represented in *As the Twig Is Bent* see themselves as developmental psychologists molding the inner, lasting core of the individual—one can almost visualize the cortical wiring they imagine being rearranged by ever-earlier intervention. And yet the true lasting effects of a child's preschool experiences may be etched only in the attitudes of the professionals and in the records of the institutions that will husband his or her life after preschool.[5]

Even studies of those compensatory programs that involve the most intensive and prolonged educational experience show the effects of such programs on I.Q. to be relatively modest and subject to "fadeout" within one to three years. The highly publicized "Miracle in Milwaukee" Study by Rick Heber and Howard Garbert appears to be a case in point. In that study, the researchers gave intensive training designed to enhance cognitive development to children who were deemed at risk for mental retardation because of their family backgrounds. The training lasted from birth until the participants entered school. Unfortunately,

no detailed account of the conduct of the Milwaukee Study or of its long-term outcomes has yet appeared in any refereed scientific journal. Because the data are not available for full and proper critical review, I cannot legitimately cite this study with regard to the effects of early intervention on subsequent intelligence and scholastic achievement.

Fortunately, a similar study—the Abecedarian Project,[6] currently under way in North Carolina—is being properly reported in the appropriate journals, and the researchers conducting this study promise the kind of evaluation that Heber and Garber have failed to deliver. From infancy to school age, children in the Abecedarian Project spend six or more hours daily, five days a week, 50 weeks a year, in a cognitive training program. Their I.Q. gains, measured against a matched control group at age 3, look encouraging. However, the possibility exists that the program has merely increased participants' I.Q. scores and not the underlying factor of intelligence that the I.Q. test is intended to measure and upon which its predictive and construct validity depend.[7]

Probably the most scholarly, thorough, and up-to-date examination of the variety of experimental attempts to improve intelligence and other human abilities is *How and How Much Can Intelligence Be Increased?* edited by Douglas Detterman and Robert Sternberg.[8] In a review of this book, I said:

> What this book may bring as something of a surprise to many psychologists who received their education in the 1950s and '60s, in the heyday of what has been termed "naive environmentalism" in American educational psychology, is the evident great difficulty in effecting practically substantial and durable gains

in individuals' intelligence. In terms of some conceptions of human intelligence as predominantly a product of cultural learning, this fact should seem surprising.... The sum total of the wide-ranging information provided in this book would scarcely contradict the conclusion that, as yet, investigators have not come up with dependable and replicable evidence that they have discovered a psychological method by which they can increase "intelligence" in the sense of Spearman's $g$.[9]

Thus current claims regarding the plasticity of human intelligence are notably more subdued than were the promises of only 20 years ago. Edward Zigler, one of the founders of and leaders in compensatory education, and his colleague, Winnie Berman, have recently warned that workers in the field "must be on guard never again to make the errors of overpromising and overselling the positive effects of early childhood intervention."[10]

Despite their personal enthusiasm for compensatory education, Zigler and Berman have surveyed the history and developments of this field with critical objectivity. Of the beginning of preschool intervention in the 1960s, they say:

It was widely believed that a program of early environmental enrichment would give lower SES [socioeconomic status] children the boost they needed to perform on a par with their middle SES peers. Intervention was supposed to impart immediate benefits so that class differences would be eliminated by the time of school entry. Furthermore, many expected that the brief preschool experience would be so potent a counteraction to the deficits in poor children's lives that it could prevent further attenuation in age-appropriate performance and a recurrence of the gap between social classes in later grades.... What we witnessed in

the 1960s was the belief that intelligence quotients can be dramatically increased with minimal effort.... Unfortunately, "knowing more" was easily translated into "becoming smarter."[11]

Elsewhere, Zigler describes the thinking in the early days of Head Start, a program that he helped to initiate:

... J. McV. Hunt, Benjamin Bloom, and others constructed for us a theoretical view that conceptualized the young child as possessing an almost unlimited degree of plasticity. Joe Hunt continued to assert that the norm of reaction for intelligence was 70 I.Q. points ... and that relatively short-term intervention efforts could result in I.Q. gains of 49 or 63 points. With such environmental sugarplums dancing in our heads, we actually thought we could compensate for the effects of several years of impoverishment as well as inoculate the child against the future ravages of such impoverishment, all by providing a six- or eight-week summer Head Start experience.[12]

This theoretical view of human intelligence—a view that governed the design and expectations of compensatory education programs in the 1960s—has been put to the test during the past 20 years. And the outcome seems remarkably clear. It turns out that the prevailing views of most psychologists and educators in the 1960s were largely wrong with regard to such questions as, What is the nature of intelligence? What is it that our I.Q. tests measure primarily? Why is the I.Q. so highly predictive of scholastic performance?

The error lay in believing that the disadvantage with which many poor or culturally different children entered school—and the disadvantage that compensatory education was intended to remedy—was mainly a deficiency in *knowledge*. Implicit in this belief was a view of intelligence as consisting of a general learning ability of almost unlimited plasticity plus the "knowledge contents" of memory, particularly those kinds of knowledge that serve to improve scholastic performance. Holders of this view saw the information content of I.Q. tests as an arbitrary sample of the specific items of knowledge and skill normally acquired by members of the white middle and upper classes.

In this highly behavioristic conception of intelligence, which I have elsewhere termed the *specificity doctrine*,[13] intelligence is erroneously identified with the content of the test items that psychologists have devised for assessing intelligence. These test items cover such things as general information, vocabulary, arithmetic, and the ability to copy certain geometric figures, to make block designs, and to work puzzles. To acquire the knowledge and skills to do these things—or to learn other, similar things that would have positive transfer to performance on I.Q. tests or in coursework—is to become more intelligent, according to this deceptive view of intelligence. As Zigler and Berman have put it, "knowing more" is erroneously translated into "becoming smarter."

Striking findings from two recent lines of research—that on test bias and that on mental chronometry—clearly contradict the view of individual and group differences in intelligence as differences primarily in knowledge.

The research on test bias has shown that the level of difficulty of I.Q. and achievement test items is consistent across all American-born, English-speaking ethnic and social-class groups. Moreover, I.Q. and achievement tests do not differ in their predictive validity for these groups. These findings are highly inconsistent with the hypothesis that cultural differences exist in the knowledge base that these tests sample. Available evidence from studies of test bias makes it extremely implausible that racial and social-class differences can be explained by cultural differences in the knowledge base or by differential opportunity for acquiring the knowledge that existing tests sample.[14] For every American-born social class and racial group, highly diverse test items maintain the same relative standing on indices of item difficulty, regardless of the culture loadings of the items. This phenomenon requires that we find some explanation for group differences on I.Q. and achievement tests other than cultural differences in exposure to the various kind of knowledge sampled by the tests.

We must seek the explanation, I believe, at the most basic level of information processing. In recent years, both the theory and the technology of research on cognitive processes have afforded powerful means for analyzing individual and group differences in abilities. Within the framework of cognitive processes research, the kinds of questions that we can investigate are quite different and more basic than those we can study through traditional psychometric tests and factor analysis. Mental chronometry, or measurement of the time required for various mental events in the course of information processing, permits us to investigate individual differences at the level of elementary cognitive processes—those processes through which individuals attain the complex learning, knowledge, and problem-solving skills that I.Q. tests sample.

Researchers devise the tasks used to measure individual differences in various elementary cognitive processes in such a way as to rule out or greatly minimize individual differences in knowledge. These tasks are so simple, and the error rates on them are so close to zero, that individual differences can be studied only by chronometric techniques. For example, the cognitive tasks that we use in our laboratory are so easy that they typically require less than one second to perform.[15] Yet these very brief response latencies, derived from a number of elementary processing tasks, together can account for some 70% of the variance in scores on untimed standard psychometric tests of intelligence. Very little of the true score variance on such tests can be attributed to the knowledge covered by the tests' content per se.

It is important to understand that the items of standardized psychometric tests are mainly vehicles for reflecting the past and present efficiency of mental processes. That these items usually include some knowledge content is only an incidental and nonessential feature. The fact is that individual differences on these content-laden tests correlate with response latencies on elementary cognitive-processing tasks that have minimal intellectual content. This means that our standard I.Q. tests—and the scholastic achievement tests with which these I.Q. tests are highly correlated—reflect individual differences in the speed and efficiency of basic cognitive processes more than they reflect differences in the information content to which test-takers have been exposed. In fact, we can account for a substantial portion of the variance in I.Q. scores by measuring the evoked electrical potentials of the brain, using an electrode attached to the scalp—a measure that is not only free of any knowledge content but that is not even dependent on any voluntary or overt behavior by the subject.[16]

Thus I suggest that the design of compensatory education and the assessment of its effects should be informed by the recent studies on information processing. The variables that have been measured by researchers in this field to date have correlated not only with I.Q., but with scholastic achievement as well.[17] An important question for future research is, What proportions of the variance in I.Q. and in scholastic achievement are associated with elementary cognitive processes and with meta-processes respectively? A second but equally important question is, What possible effects can various types of compensatory training have on these two levels of cognitive processes?

*Elementary cognitive processes* include such variables as perceptual speed, stimulus scanning, stimulus encoding, mental rotation or transformation of visual stimuli, short-term memory capacity, efficiency of information retrieval from long-term memory, generalization, discrimination, comparison, transfer, and response execution. *Meta-processes* include those planning and executive functions that select and coordinate the deployment of the elementary cognitive processes to handle specific situations, e.g., strategies for problem recognition, for selecting and combining lower-order cognitive processes, for organizing information, for allocating time and resources, for monitoring one's own performance, and the like.

Meta-processes are thought to be more amenable than elementary processes to improvement through training, but no solid evidence currently exists on this question. And, though much is already known about social-class and racial-group differences in I.Q. and scholastic achievement, psychologists have scarcely begun to try to understand the nature and locus of these differences in terms of the cognitive processes and meta-processes involved.[18] As yet, virtually nothing is known about the effects of compensatory education on the various levels of cognitive processing or about the extent to which the levels of cognitive processing can be influenced by training especially designed for that purpose.

I suspect that a substantial part of the individual variance in I.Q. and scholastic achievement—probably somewhere between 50% and 70%, according to the best evidence on the heritability of I.Q.—is not subject to manipulation by any strictly psychological or educational treatment. The reason for this, I assume, is that the main locus of control of that unyielding source of variance is more biological than psychological or behavioral.

At an even more fundamental level, we might ask why variance in intelligence should be so surprisingly resistant to experimental manipulation. As I have suggested elsewhere,[19] this apparent resistance to manipulation seems less surprising if we view human intelligence as an outcome of biological evolution. Genetic variation is the one absolutely essential ingredient to enable evolution to occur. If intelligence has evolved as a fitness characteristic in the Darwinian sense—that is, as an instrumentality for the survival of humankind—it is conceivable that the biological basis of intelligence has a built-in stabilizing mechanism, rather like a gyroscope, that safeguards the individual's behavioral capacity for coping with the exigencies of survival. If that were the case, mental development would not be wholly at the mercy of often erratic environmental happenstance. A too-malleable fitness trait would afford an organism too little protection against the vagaries of its environment. Thus, as humanity evolved, processes may also have evolved to buffer intelligence from being pushed too far in one direction or another, whether by adventitiously harmful or by intentionally benevolent environmental forces.

## NOTES

1. Barbara Lerner, "Test Scores as Measures of Human Capital," in Raymond B. Cattell, ed., *Intelligence and National Achievement* (Washington, D.C.: Cliveden Press, 1983).

2. Ibid., p. 73.

3. Ibid., p. 74.

4. Consortium for Longitudinal Studies, *As the Twig Is Bent... Lasting Effects of Preschool Programs* (Hillsdale, N.J.: Erlbaum, 1983); and Edward Zigler and Jeanette Valentine, *Project Head Start* (New York: Free Press, 1979).

5. Gene V. Glass and Mary C. Ellwein, review of *As the Twig Is Bent..., by the Consortium for Longitudinal Studies*, in *Science*, 20 January 1984, p. 274.

6. Craig T. Ramey et al., "The Carolina Abecedarian Project: A Longitudinal and Multidisciplinary Approach to the Prevention of Developmental Retardation," in Theodore D. Tjossem, ed., *Intervention Strategies for High Risk Infants and Young Children* (Baltimore: University Park Press, 1976).

7. Craig T. Ramey and Ron Haskins, "The Modification of Intelligence Through Early Experience," *Intelligence*, January/March 1981, pp. 5–19; and Arthur R. Jensen, "Raising the I.Q.: The Ramey and Haskins Study," *Intelligence*, January/March 1981, pp. 29–40.

8. Douglas K. Detterman and Robert J. Sternberg, eds., *How and How Much Can Intelligence Be Increased?* (Norwood, N.J.: Ablex, 1982).

9. Arthur R. Jensen, "Again, How Much Can We Boost I.Q.?" review of *How and How Much Can Intellignce Be Increased?* edited by Douglas K. Detterman and Robert J. Sternberg, in *Contemporary Psychology*, October 1983, p. 757.

10. Edward Zigler and Winnie Berman, "Discerning the Future of Early Childhood Intervention," *American Psychologist*, August 1983, p. 897.

11. Ibid., pp. 895–96.

12. Quoted in Peter Skerry, "The Charmed Life of Head Start," *Public Interest*, Fall 1983, pp. 18–39.

13. Arthur R. Jensen, "Test Validity: *g* Versus the Specificity Doctrine," *Journal of Biological Structures*, vol. 7, 1984, pp. 93–118.

14. Arthur R. Jensen, *Bias in Mental Testing* (New York: Free Press, 1980); and Cecil R. Reynolds and Robert T. Brown, *Perspectives on Bias in Mental Testing* (New York: Plenum, 1984).

15. Arthur R. Jensen, "Chronometric Analysis of Intelligence," *Journal of Social and Biological Structures*, April 1980, pp. 103–22; idem, "The Chronometry of Intelligence," in Robert J. Sternberg, ed., *Advances in the Psychology of Human Intelligence* (Hillsdale, N.J.: Erlbaum, 1982); and idem, "Reaction Time and Psychometric *g*," in Hans J. Eysenck, ed., *A Model for Intelligence* (Heidelberg: Springer-Verlag, 1982).

16. Donna E. Hendrickson and Alan E. Hendrickson, "The Biological Basis of Individual Differences in Intelligence," *Personality and Individual Differences*, January 1980, pp. 3–34.

17. Jerry S. Carlson and C. Mark Jensen, "Reaction Time, Movement Time, and Intelligence: A Replication and Extension," *Intelligence*, July/September 1982, pp. 265–74.

18. John G. Borkowski and Audrey Krause, "Racial Differences in Intelligence: The Importance of the Executive System," *Intelligence*, October/December 1983, pp. 379–95; Arthur R. Jensen, "Race Differences and Type II Errors: A Comment on Borkowski and Krause," *Intelligence*, in press; and Philip A. Vernon and Arthur R. Jensen, "Individual and Group Differences in Intelligence and Speed of Information Processing," *Personality and Individual Differences*, in press.

19. Jensen, "Again, How Much Can We Boost I.Q.?" p. 758.

# CHALLENGE QUESTIONS

## Can Intelligence Be Increased?

1. If you had a child about to enter school and you had the choice between one administered by Jensen and one administered by Sternberg, which school would you choose? Why?

2. If you were a school administrator with concern for efficiently using your resources to make the most of each student's potential, would you give each student an intelligence test to determine which classes are most appropriate for him or her?

3. If programs for improving the thinking skills of students are successful, has the intelligence of the students been increased?

4. Should it be taken for granted that college students already have mature thinking skills?

5. Should programs with goals similar to those described in Sternberg's article be a part of a college education? If so, should they be separate courses or part of all courses?

# PART 3

# Human Development

*The goal of developmental psychologists is to document the course of our physical, social, and intellectual changes over a life span. Considerable attention has been paid to the childhood part of that life span because this period of development seems to set the stage for later periods. Three potential influences on childhood are debated here: television, formal schooling, and parental divorce.*

- Is Television Harmful to Children?

- Should Formal Schooling Begin at an Earlier Age?

- Are Children of Divorced Parents at Greater Risk?

# ISSUE 7

# Is Television Harmful to Children?

**YES: Marie Winn,** from *Unplugging the Plug-In Drug* (Viking Penguin, 1987)

**NO: Daniel R. Anderson,** from "How TV Influences Your Kids," *TV Guide* (March 3, 1990)

## ISSUE SUMMARY

**YES:** Marie Winn, author and children's advocate, asserts that television negatively influences children because it robs them of opportunities for family activities and for the development of intellectual and social skills.

**NO:** Professor of psychology Daniel R. Anderson contends that there is no consistent evidence that television turns children into mindless "vidiots." Instead, he believes that television can be an effective tool for educating children.

Television is considered responsible for much of society's ills, especially the ills of children, by many people. Some researchers and social scientists have hypothesized a variety of negative effects of television: children supposedly suffer shortened attention span, increased aggression, and decreased school performance, all as a result of watching television. Moreover, many parents worry about the poor quality of many current television programs. Does poor-quality television harm children? If so, what are the specific negative effects, and what programs are the most harmful? Does television in general, regardless of the quality, harm children?

Psychologists have been attempting to answer these questions for a long time. Social and developmental psychologists, particularly, have conducted long programs of research on these issues. They have been especially interested in television experiences that may prove harmful to children and their development. However, they have also investigated the potential positive effects of television, particularly the effects of programs considered educational in nature.

In her critique of television, Marie Winn argues that parents commonly use television to make childrearing less burdensome and that television serves a number of purposes for today's families, including that of time filler, tranquilizer, problem solver, escape mechanism, and punishment. Winn describes eight specific ways in which television negatively influences children and their families. Her general concern is that the time spent watching television represents a loss of opportunities for more meaningful family interaction and for the development of important social skills.

Daniel R. Anderson, on the other hand, argues that there is no consistent evidence that television makes children mentally passive or shortens their attention span. Instead, he claims that television is useful in educating children, and he points to such programs as *Sesame Street* and *Mr. Rogers' Neighborhood* as evidence of this. Anderson also reviews the many studies on television violence and finds that children are not equally susceptible to the effects of television violence. He concludes that negative effects attributed to television are actually the result of broader societal issues.

| POINT | COUNTERPOINT |
|---|---|
| • Television prevents children from engaging in other activities. | • Television does not turn children into mindless robots. |
| • Television has a negative effect on children's academic performance. | • There is no consistent evidence that television impairs children's interest in education or their ability to think. |
| • Television allows kids to grow up less civilized and less resourceful. | • Television can be an effective tool for education. |
| • Because television socializes children, its violence can have a powerful effect on their behavior. | • Children are not equally susceptible to television violence. |

# YES

Marie Winn

## THE TROUBLE WITH TELEVISION

Of all the wonders of modern technology that have transformed family life during the last century, television stands alone as a universal source of parental anxiety. Few parents worry about how the electric light or the automobile or the telephone might alter their children's development. But most parents do worry about TV.

Parents worry most of all about the programs their children watch. If only these weren't so violent, so sexually explicit, so cynical, so *unsuitable*, if only they were more innocent, more educational, more *worthwhile*.

Imagine what would happen if suddenly, by some miracle, the only programs available on all channels at all hours of day and night were delightful, worthwhile shows that children love and parents wholeheartedly approve. Would this eliminate the nagging anxiety about television that troubles so many parents today?

For most families, the answer is no. After all, if programs were the only problem, there would be an obvious solution: turn the set off. The fact that parents leave the sets on even when they are distressed about programs reveals that television serves a number of purposes that have nothing to do with the programs on the screen.

Great numbers of parents today see television as a way to make child-rearing less burdensome. In the absence of Mother's Helper (a widely used nineteenth-century patent medicine that contained a hefty dose of the narcotic laudanum), there is nothing that keeps children out of trouble as reliably as "plugging them in."

Television serves families in other ways: as a time-filler ("You have nothing to do? Go watch TV"), a tranquilizer ("When the kids come home from school they're so keyed up that they need to watch for a while to simmer down"), a problem solver ("Kids, stop fighting. It's time for your program"), a procrastination device ("I'll just watch one more program before I do my homework"), a punishment ("If you don't stop teasing your little sister, no TV for a week"), and a reward ("If you get an A on your composition you can watch an extra hour of TV"). For parents and children alike it serves as an avoidance mechanism ("I can't discuss that now—I'm watching my

From Marie Winn, *Unplugging the Plug-In Drug* (Viking Penguin, 1987). Copyright © 1987 by Marie Winn. Reprinted by permission of Viking Penguin, a division of Penguin Books USA, Inc. Some notes omitted.

program"), a substitute friend ("I need the TV on for company"), and an escape mechanism ("I'll turn on the TV and try to forget my worries").

Most families recognize the wonderful services that television has to offer. Few, however, are aware that there is a heavy price to pay. Here are eight significant ways television wields a negative influence on children and family life:

### 1. TV Keeps Families from Doing Other Things

The primary danger of the television screen lies not so much in the behavior it produces—although there is danger there—as in the behavior it prevents: the talks, the games, the family festivities and arguments through which much of the child's learning takes place and through which his character is formed. Turning on the television set can turn off the process that transforms children into people.[1]

Urie Bronfenbrenner's words to a conference of educators almost two decades ago focus on what sociologists call the "reduction effects" of television—its power to preempt and often eliminate a whole range of other activities and experiences. While it is easy to see that for a child who watches 32 hours of television each week, the reduction effects are significant—obviously that child would be spending 32 hours doing *something* else if there were no television available—Bronfenbrenner's view remains an uncommon and even an eccentric one.

Today the prevailing focus remains on improving programs rather than on reducing the amount of time children view. Perhaps parents have come to depend so deeply on television that they are afraid even to contemplate the idea that something might be wrong with their use of television, not merely with the programs on the air.

### 2. TV Is a Hidden Competitor for All Other Activities

...Almost everybody knows that there are better, more fulfilling things for a family to do than watch television. And yet, if viewing statistics are to be believed, most families spend most of their family time together in front of the flickering screen.

Some social critics believe that television has come to dominate family life because today's parents are too selfish and narcissistic to put in the effort that reading aloud or playing games or even just talking to each other would require. But this harsh judgment doesn't take into consideration the extraordinary power of television. In reality, many parents crave a richer family life and are eager to work at achieving this goal. The trouble is that their children seem to reject all those fine family alternatives in favor of television.

To be sure, the fact that children are likely to choose watching television over having a story read aloud to them, or playing with the stamp collection, or going out for a walk in the park does not mean that watching television is actually more entertaining or gratifying than any of these activities. It does mean, however, that watching television is easier.

In most families, television is always there as an easy and safe competitor. When another activity is proposed, it had better be *really special;* otherwise it is in danger of being rejected. The parents who have unsuccessfully proposed a game or a story end up feeling rejected as well. They are unaware that television is still affecting their children's enjoyment of other activities, even when the set is off.

Reading aloud is a good example of how this competition factor works. Virtually every child expert hails reading aloud as a delightful family pastime. Educators encourage it as an important way for parents to help their children develop a love for reading and improve their reading skills. Too often, however, the fantasy of the happy family gathered around to listen to a story is replaced by a different reality: "Hey kids, I've got a great book to read aloud. How about it?" says the parent. "Not now, Dad, we want to watch 'The Cosby Show,'" say the kids.

It is for this reason that one of the most important *Don'ts* suggested by Jim Trelease in his valuable guide *The Read-Aloud Handbook* is the following:

> Don't try to compete with television. If you say, "Which do you want, a story or TV?" they will usually choose the latter. That is like saying to a 9-year-old, "Which do you want, vegetables or a donut?" Since *you* are the adult, *you* choose. "The television goes off at eight-thirty in this house. If you want a story before bed, that's fine. If not, that's fine too. But no television after eight-thirty." But don't let books appear to be responsible for depriving children of viewing time.[2]

### 3. TV Allows Kids to Grow Up Less Civilized

...It would be a mistake to assume that the basic child-rearing philosophy of parents of the past was stricter than that of parents today. American parents, in fact, have always had a tendency to be more egalitarian in their family life than, say, European parents. For confirmation, one has only to read the accounts of eighteenth- or nineteenth-century European travelers who comment on the freedom and audacity of American children as compared to their European counterparts. Why then do parents today seem far less in control of their children than parents not only of the distant past but even of a mere generation ago? Television has surely played a part in this change.

Today's parents universally use television to keep their children occupied when they have work to do or when they need a break from child care. They can hardly imagine how parents survived before television. Yet parents *did* survive in the years before TV. Without television, they simply had to use different survival strategies to be able to cook dinner, talk on the telephone, clean house, or do whatever work needed to be done in peace.

Most of these strategies fell into the category social scientists refer to as "socialization"—the civilizing process that transforms small creatures intent upon the speedy gratification of their own instinctive needs and desires into successful members of a society in which those individual needs and desires must often be left ungratified, at least temporarily, for the good of the group.

What were these "socialization" strategies parents used to use? Generally, they went something like this: "Mommy's got to cook dinner now (make a phone call, talk to Mrs. Jones, etc.). Here are some blocks (some clay, a pair of blunt scissors and a magazine, etc.). Now you have to be a good girl and play by yourself for a while and not interrupt Mommy." Nothing very complicated.

But in order to succeed, a certain firmness was absolutely necessary, and parents knew it, even if asserting authority was not their preferred way of dealing with children. They knew they had to work steadily at "training" their child to behave in ways that allowed them to do those normal things that needed to be done. Actually, achieving this goal was not terribly difficult. It took a little effort to set up certain patterns—perhaps a few days or a week of patient but firm insistence that the child behave in certain ways at certain times. But parents of the past didn't agonize about whether this was going to be psychologically damaging. They simply had no choice. Certain things simply *had to be done*, and so parents stood their ground against children's natural struggle to gain attention and have their own way.

Obviously it is easier to get a break from child care by setting the child in front of the television set than to teach the child to play alone for certain periods of time. In the first case, the child is immediately amused (or hypnotized) by the program, and the parent has time to pursue other activities. Accustoming children to play alone, on the other hand, requires day-after-day perseverance, and neither parent nor child enjoys the process very much.

But there is an inevitable price to pay when a parent never has to be firm and authoritative, never has to use that "I mean business" tone of voice: socialization, that crucial process so necessary for the child's future as a successful member of a family, a school, a community, and a nation is accomplished less completely. A very different kind of relationship between parent and child is established, one in which the parent has little control over the child's behavior.

The consequences of a large-scale reduction in child socialization are not hard to see in contemporary society: an increased number of parents who feel helpless and out of control of their children's lives and behavior, who haven't established the parental authority that might protect their children from involvement in such dangerous activities as drug experimentation, or from the physical and emotional consequences of precocious sexual relationships.

## 4. Television Takes the Place of Play

...Once small children become able to concentrate on television and make some sense of it—usually around the end of their second year of life—it's not hard to understand why parents eagerly set their children before the flickering screen: taking care of toddlers is hard! The desperate and tired parent can't imagine *not* taking advantage of this marvelous new way to get a break. In consequence, before they are three years old, the opportunities of active play and exploration are hugely diminished for a great number of children—to be replaced by the hypnotic gratification of television viewing.

Yet many parents overlook an important fact: children who are suddenly able to sustain attention for more than a few minutes on the TV screen have clearly moved into a new stage of cognitive development—their ability to concentrate on TV is a sign of it. There are therefore many other new activities, far more developmentally valuable, that the child is now ready for. These are the simple forms of play that most small children enjoyed in the pre-television era: cutting and pasting, coloring and drawing, building with blocks, playing games of make-believe with toy soldiers or animals or dolls. But the parent who begins to fill in the child's time with television at this point is unlikely to discover these other potential capabilities.

It requires a bit of effort to establish new play routines—more effort, certainly, than plunking a child in front of a television screen, but not really a great deal. It requires a bit of patience to get the child accustomed to a new kind of play—play on his own—but again, not a very great deal. It also demands some firmness and perseverance. And a small amount of equipment (art materials, blocks, etc.), most of it cheap, if not free, and easily available.

But the benefits for both parent and child of *not* taking the easiest way out at this point by using television to ease the inevitable child-care burdens will vastly outweigh the temporary difficulties parents face in filling children's time with less passive activities. For the parent, the need for a bit more firmness leads to an easier, more controlled parent-child relationship. For the child, those play routines established in early childhood will develop into lifelong interests and hobbies, while the skills acquired in the course of play lead to a sense of accomplishment that could never have been achieved if the child had spent those hours "watching" instead of "doing."

## 5. TV Makes Children Less Resourceful

...Many parents who welcome the idea of turning off the TV and spending more time with the family are still worried that without TV they would constantly be on call as entertainers for their children. Though they *want* to play games and read aloud to their children, the idea of having to replace television minute-for-minute with worthwhile family activities is daunting. They remember thinking up all sorts of things to do when they were kids. But their own kids seem different, less resourceful, somehow. When there's nothing to do, these parents observe regretfully, their kids seem unable to come up with anything to do besides turning on the TV.

One father, for example, says, "When I was a kid, we were always thinking up things to do, projects and games. We certainly never whined to our parents, 'I have nothing to do!'" He compares this with his own children today: "They're simply lazy. If someone doesn't entertain them, they'll happily sit there watching TV all day."

There is one word for this father's disappointment: unfair. It is as if he were disappointed in them for not reading Greek though they have never studied the language. He deplores his children's lack of inventiveness, as if the ability to play were something innate that his children are missing. In fact, while the *tendency* to play is built into the human species, the actual *ability* to play—to imagine, to invent, to elaborate on reality in a playful way—and the ability to gain fulfillment from it, these are skills that have to be learned and developed.

Such disappointment, however, is not only unjust, it is also destructive. Sensing their parents' disappointment, children come to believe that they are, indeed, lacking something, and that this makes them less worthy of admiration and respect. Giving children the opportunity to develop new resources, to enlarge their horizons and discover the pleasures of doing things on their own is, on the other hand, a way to help children develop a confident feeling about themselves as capable and interesting people.

It is, of course, ironic that many parents avoid a TV Turn-Off out of fear that their children won't know what to do with themselves in the absence of television. It is television watching itself that has allowed them to grow up without learning how to be resourceful and television watching that keeps them from developing those skills that would enable them to fill in their empty time enjoyably.

## 6. TV Has a Negative Effect on Children's Physical Fitness

...Not long ago a study that attracted wide notice in the popular press found a direct relationship between the incidence of obesity in children and time spent viewing television. For the 6–11 age group, "children who watched more television experienced a greater prevalence of obesity, or superobesity, than children watching less television. No significant differences existed between obese, superobese, and nonobese children with respect to the number of friends, their ability to get along with friends, or time spent with friends, alone, listening to the radio, reading, or in leisure time activities," wrote the researchers. As for teenagers, only 10 percent of those teenagers who watched TV an hour or less a day were obese as compared to 20 percent of those who watched more than five hours daily. With most other variables eliminated, why should this be? The researchers provided a commonsense explanation: Dedicated TV watchers are fatter because they eat more and exercise less while glued to the tube.[3]

## 7. TV Has a Negative Effect on Children's School Achievement

...It is difficult if not impossible to prove that excessive television viewing has a direct negative effect on young children's cognitive development, though by using cautionary phrases such as "TV will turn your brain to mush" parents often express an instinctive belief that this is true.

Nevertheless an impressive number of research studies demonstrate beyond any reasonable doubt that excessive television viewing has an adverse effect on children's achievement in school. One study, for instance, shows that younger children who watch more TV have lower scores in reading and overall achievement tests than those who watch less TV.[4]

Another large-scale study, conducted when television was first introduced as a mass medium in Japan, found that as families acquired television sets children showed a decline in both reading skills and homework time.

But it does not require costly research projects to demonstrate that television viewing affects children's school work adversely. Interviews with teachers who have participated in TV Turn-Offs provide confirmation as well.

Almost without exception, these teachers testify that the quality of homework brought into class during the No-TV period was substantially better. As a fifth grade teacher noted: "There was a real difference in the homework I was getting during No-TV Week. Kids who usually do a good job on homework did a terrific job. Some kids who rarely hand in assignments on time now brought in surprisingly good and thorough work. When I brought this to the class's attention during discussion time they said, 'Well, there was nothing else to do!'"

## 8. Television Watching May Be a Serious Addiction

...A lot of people who have nothing but bad things to say about TV, calling it the "idiot box" and the "boob tube," nevertheless spend quite a lot of their free time watching television. People are often apologetic, even shamefaced about their television viewing, saying things like, "I only watch the news," or "I only turn the set on for company," or "I only watch when I'm too tired to do anything else" to explain the sizable number of hours they devote to TV.

In addition to anxiety about their own viewing patterns, many parents recognize that their children watch too much television and that it is having an adverse effect on their development and yet they don't take any effective action to change the situation.

Why is there so much confusion, ambivalence, and self-deception connected with television viewing? One explanation is that great numbers of television viewers are to some degree addicted to the *experience* of watching television. The confusion and ambivalence they reveal about television may then be recognized as typical reactions of an addict unwilling to face an addiction or unable to get rid of it.

Most people find it hard to consider television viewing a serious addiction. Addictions to tobacco or alcohol, after all, are known to cause life-threatening diseases—lung cancer or cirrhosis of the liver. Drug addiction leads to dangerous behavioral aberrations—violence and crime. Meanwhile, the worst physiological consequences of television addiction seem to be a possible decline in overall physical fitness, and an increased incidence of obesity.

It is in its psychosocial consequences, especially its effects on relationships and family life, that television watching may be as damaging as chemical addiction. We all know the terrible toll alcoholism or drug addiction takes on the families of addicts. Is it possible that television watching has a similarly destructive potential for family life?

Most of us are at least dimly aware of the addictive power of television through our own experiences with the medium: our compulsive involvement with the tube too often keeps us from talking to each other, from doing things together, from working and learning and getting involved in community affairs. The hours we spend viewing prove to be curiously unfulfilling. We end up feeling depressed, though the program we've been watching was a comedy. And yet we cannot seem to turn the set off, or even *not* turn it on in the first place. Doesn't this sound like an addiction?

## NOTES

1. Urie Bronfenbrenner, "Who Cares for America's Children?" Address presented at the Conference of the National Association for the Education of Young Children, 1970.

2. Jim Trelease, *The Read-Aloud Handbook.* Penguin, 1985.

3. W. H. Dietz and S. L. Gortmaker, "Do We Fatten Our Children at the Television Set? Obesity and Television Viewing in Children and Adolescents." *Pediatrics* 75 (1985).

4. S. G. Burton, J. M. Calonico, and D. R. McSeveney, "Effects of Preschool Watching on First-Grade Children." *Journal of Communications* 29:3 (1979).

# NO
Daniel R. Anderson

## HOW TV INFLUENCES YOUR KIDS

A few months ago, when she was 23 months old, Sarah started to watch TV. "She *cries* when *Mister Rogers' Neighborhood* goes off the air," her mother wrote me. "The first time she saw it, she sat quietly with me and watched the whole show. She talked about it for the rest of the day."

Children typically begin paying consistent attention to a few television programs at about age 2. If Sarah continues to be a typical American child, she will spend about 30 percent of her waking hours in front of a TV, watching a wider range of programs as she matures. In terms of sheer exposure, television has the potential to be a major influence on Sarah's, and most children's, development. In recent years, researchers have begun to clarify the nature of that influence. The news is both good and bad.

The good news is that, contrary to a widespread theory, TV doesn't transform children into mindless "vidiots." The theory first gained popularity in the 1970s when social critics began to write that television mesmerizes young children by its rapid scene changes. A consequence, so these critics believe, is that children watch TV mindlessly and passively, with little thought and reflection. And they believe the long-term effects are worse: a short attention span and a diminished intellect.

But the theory has a flaw. It's been based mostly on anecdotes, never convincingly proved. And more than 100 studies on TV and children's attention span, comprehension and intellectual development have largely discredited it. In other words, there is no consistent evidence that TV makes children mentally passive, shortens their attention span, reduces their interest in education or otherwise impairs their ability to think. In fact, researchers are finding that young children aren't mesmerized by TV. Children seem to pay the greatest attention when they are most mentally involved with the program. The studies also show that young children tend to ignore or reject programs that they don't understand.

Sarah's TV viewing illustrates this. She now enjoys watching many children's TV shows, her mother reports, but not all. When a science program directed at older kids comes on, Sarah asks her mother, " 'Change? Change TV?' She doesn't just turn away," her mother wrote. "She's insistent we get rid of that program."

The fact that children actively think about television indicates that television can be an effective tool for education, an idea supported by a great deal of research. For 20 years PBS's *Sesame Street* has helped preschoolers learn elementary reading and arithmetic, and *Mister Rogers' Neighborhood,* also on public TV, has helped them deal with emotions and self-control. The potential of television for teaching children is beginning to be demonstrated with such science programs as *3-2-1 Contact* and the math program *Square One TV,* both on PBS.

Despite the lack of evidence that TV impairs intellectual development, many educators blamed TV when national achievement-test scores declined. While it is true that heavy viewers have lower achievement scores, studies suggest that heavy TV viewing is more a symptom of poor achievement than a cause. Poor achievers tend to come from disrupted families or have parents who fail to provide intellectually stimulating activities. Such families tend to be heavy TV viewers.

Unfortunately, much of what kids watch is intended for adults and may not be limited or interpreted by their parents. When it comes to adult-oriented TV, young children take in the information but jumble up the meaning. Consider my conversation with 6-year-old Sebastian. He had just seen a commercial in which a young couple sitting on the grass share a sumptuous lunch in front of their new Mercedes. When asked what the ad meant, Sebastian answered unhesitatingly, "They want you to buy picnics!"

Sebastian's misunderstanding was benign and amusing. Less amusing is the realization that uncontrolled TV viewing can expose a child to large doses of violence, antisocial values and sexual imagery. To the adult, this fare may have entertainment value. A given violent program may even deliver the implicit message that criminals get punished, so crime doesn't pay. The problem is that the child may see the violence of the crime and the criminal's glamorous lifestyle but not make the connection between those things and the criminal's subsequent downfall.

We know a lot about the effects of television violence. Studies suggest that TV has a role in producing aggressive play and real-life violence. Children who watch a lot of TV violence are described by other children as more aggressive. And some long-term studies find that viewing violent programming contributes to later aggressive behavior. Some of the most disturbing incidents occurred in 1973 after the movie "Fuzz" was aired. Apparently reenacting scenes in which youths set homeless people on fire, teenagers in Boston and Miami fatally burned two people.

Most researchers who study the effects of TV violence suggest that children are not equally susceptible to its influence. If parents are loving and discourage aggressive behavior, their children are unlikely to be influenced. But if parents are unavailable or permissive of violence, children are more likely to be influenced.

For many children from broken homes and poor neighborhoods, television may be the only window to the world outside. At its worst, television provides these children images of violence and crime associated with wealth and glamour. At its best, television provides these children with knowledge of positive alternatives in life and gives them hope.

Sarah, who just began watching TV, has loving parents who will monitor and limit her viewing. They will discuss programs with her and instill social values that will enable her to evaluate the things she experiences from TV. TV won't be her only entertainment and learning resource. For Sarah, TV will provide positive education and wholesome entertainment.

# CHALLENGE QUESTIONS

## Is Television Harmful to Children?

1. Have you ever watched a television program that you felt could have had negative effects? If so, what made you feel that way?

2. Does viewing television violence necessarily lead children to become violent? What evidence supports your conclusion?

3. Winn argues that there are negative effects of watching television; Anderson refutes these claims. Can you add any arguments supporting Winn's position? Anderson's position?

4. Should parents be concerned about the television shows their children watch? Why, or why not?

5. Why is television so often blamed for societal problems? Are there any alternative explanations for societal problems?

# ISSUE 8

## Should Formal Schooling Begin at an Earlier Age?

**YES: Albert Shanker,** from "The Case for Public School Sponsorship of Early Childhood Education Revisited," in Sharon L. Kagan and Edward F. Zigler, eds., *Early Schooling: The National Debate* (Yale University Press, 1987)

**NO: Edward F. Zigler,** from "Formal Schooling for Four-Year-Olds? No," *American Psychologist* (March 1987)

### ISSUE SUMMARY

**YES:** Albert Shanker, president of the American Federation of Teachers, argues that early childhood education is a necessity and that public education is its best sponsor.

**NO:** Edward F. Zigler, a professor of psychology and one of the planners of Project Head Start, contends that schooling for 4-year-olds is a bad idea that could prove harmful to children.

There is perhaps no greater influence on a child's development than schooling. Formal schooling occurs during the crucial formative years of a child's life, usually from the ages of 5 to 18 years. At school we learn vital information about our culture (as well as academic information), how to get along with our peers, and how to interact with authority figures.

Child development researchers have become particularly interested in the effects of formal schooling. Some researchers have been struck by the benefits of formal schooling for young children, especially in comparison to day care, which is often the only alternative for working parents to provide daytime care for their very young children. These researchers advocate an earlier entrance into formal schooling, such as at age 4, but others reject this idea as harmful to the child. What are the advantages of early childhood schooling? What are the disadvantages? The answers to these questions are relevant not only to the child development literature but also to the parents and teachers of young children.

In the following selections, Albert Shanker focuses on the benefits of early childhood education. In his view, the chief argument for making such schooling available concerns the high percentage of mothers with preschool-aged children who have entered the work force in the past two decades. Unfortunately, he contends, the supply of quality day care for these children is inadequate. Shanker also points to evidence that early childhood education can increase IQ scores and improve academic performance in later years. Although delivering this type of childhood education may be a problem, Shanker argues that the setup of the public education system would support early schooling programs well.

In contrast, Edward F. Zigler argues that the issue of universal schooling for all preschool-aged children requires more careful consideration than it has been given. He presents evidence suggesting that such schooling has little if any advantage for certain children. He feels that early schooling denies children the freedom to develop at their own pace and ultimately harms their development. He also feels that many of the supposed benefits of early education programs are the result of other programs that have little to do with formal education.

| POINT | COUNTERPOINT |
|---|---|
| • There are good reasons for establishing early childhood education programs, such as the inadequacies of day care. | • The issue of universal early schooling has not been sufficiently investigated. |
| • There are many benefits of early childhood education programs. | • Such benefits result from other services provided with these programs. |
| • Evidence shows that good pre-schools can raise IQ scores and improve later academic performance. | • There is little conclusive evidence that early schooling affects intellectual functioning. |
| • The solution lies in making a variety of early childhood programs available to anyone who wants them. | • Only the populations who need the programs should be targeted. |

# YES
### Albert Shanker

## THE CASE FOR PUBLIC SCHOOL SPONSORSHIP OF EARLY CHILDHOOD EDUCATION REVISITED

Early childhood education has had a long and bumpy history in the United States, much of it spent debating whether it would undermine the "natural" order of mothers' staying at home to care for their young children. The idea that early childhood education is unnatural or un-American has not entirely died, but reality has overtaken ideology. Now that the majority of American mothers of preschool children work outside the home, it has become harder for policymakers to be indifferent to the lack of affordable, quality child care available to families. It is therefore not surprising that early childhood education is making a comeback as a national issue.

Early childhood education is also enjoying a new respectability. The idea that the early childhood years have a profound impact on human development is an ancient one, but modern social science findings have confirmed that young children who are deliberately exposed to stimulating experiences fare better than children who are not. Although many still would prefer that these experiences take place at home under the loving tutelage of a mother, the accumulating research findings about the positive effects of educationally sound preschool programs have dissipated much of the fear of institutional child care. The latest and most dramatic evidence of the benefits of such programs, particularly for disadvantaged youngsters, comes from the Perry Preschool Project. Not only has this news heartened child advocates, it also has broadened the potential constituency for early childhood education. Usually identified only with the needs of working mothers and the interests of educators, early childhood education now also engages policymakers and citizens concerned about the costs and consequences of the large numbers of disadvantaged children who grow up to become liabilities to themselves and to society.

Early childhood education ought therefore to be a political winner. It bridges the interests of parents from all economic levels, of married and single mothers, of mothers who work and those who need or want to work. It has implications for non-parents and for the elderly who also bear the costs

From Albert Shanker, "The Case for Public School Sponsorship of Early Childhood Education Revisited," in Sharon L. Kagan and Edward F. Zigler, eds., *Early Schooling: The National Debate* (Yale University Press, 1987). Copyright © 1987 by Yale University Press. Reprinted by permission.

if other people's children grow up to become dependent or deviant adults. It obviously touches education, welfare, health, and other social service professionals. Slowly but steadily, and with a recent push from the National Governors' Association, the political community is indeed rousing itself to the issue of early childhood education. Not since the 1960s has the potential for developing a coherent and caring policy toward preschoolers seemed so bright.

Yet despite the signs of popular and political support for early childhood education, it is not at all clear that a consensus surrounds the issue. What exactly do we mean by early childhood education? The dominant image now comes from the Perry Preschool Project, a high-quality, high-cost educational program for disadvantaged youngsters in a public school setting. But the more usual model of early childhood education is a low-quality, low-cost proprietary program. Similarly, the rhetoric of some policymakers focuses on the custodial needs of working parents—which implies full-day, year-round child-care programs. Yet the rhetoric of others concerns the developmental needs of youngsters, which denotes preschool programs of half a school day or less. Some conceptualize early childhood education as an academic readiness program. Others prefer a whole-child approach that involves attending to the social, emotional, cognitive, and health needs of preschoolers and often includes a parent education component. Differences of opinion (and cost) also exist over whether programs should be compulsory, universally available, or targeted only to the poor and disadvantaged.

Less philosophically complex but even more controversial than questions about the nature and purpose of early childhood education is the issue of sponsorship. Historically, the battles over turf have been between the public schools and community-based organizations, between elementary educators and early childhood educators. The transcendent interest in restoring early childhood education to the national agenda has submerged these differences, but the attacks on public schools heard at the 1986 annual meeting of the National Association for the Education of Young Children suggested that a renewal of old antagonisms is not out of the question.

Some of these differences over early childhood education may not be as intractable as they appear or as they once seemed. Ignoring them, however, or acting as if all early childhood education programs or sponsorship arrangements are equal surely will do nothing to reconcile these differences. Indeed, the failure to revisit these issues may mean that in the name of developing a coherent and caring policy toward young children and promoting equity, policymakers will instead be further institutionalizing our present patchwork of policy and exacerbating inequalities. The challenge we now face is to expand both the quantity and the quality of early childhood education. That means insisting on standards while avoiding standardization. It involves promoting flexibility while ending fragmentation. And it means equalizing the opportunity for disadvantaged youngsters to be integrated into the mainstream of American life without further segregating them in poverty programs.

## THE SOURCES OF DEMAND AND THE FAILURE OF SUPPLY

Recent arguments on behalf of expanding early childhood education are fueled by a number of sources, but chief among them is the influx of mothers of preschool-age children into the labor force. In 1975, 38.8 percent of mothers with children under the age of six were employed. Five years later, the proportion had climbed to 46.8 percent. In the early 1980s, the 50 percent mark was reached, and by 1986 it was 54.4 percent. Almost 60 percent of women with children between the ages of three and five are now in the labor force (U.S. Bureau of Labor Statistics, 1986; Grubb, 1986).

The rise in the proportion of working mothers cannot be explained solely by the increase in single mothers. in fact, whether because of women's liberation or, more demonstrably, the need for a second income, the increase in labor force participation of married mothers of preschoolers has been particularly dramatic. In 1948, the proportion of married mothers who worked outside the home was 13 percent. By 1965, the figure had almost doubled to 23 percent, reaching 37 percent a decade later. In 1986, it was 54 percent, with no sign of abating (U.S. Bureau of Labor Statistics, 1986; Grubb, 1986).

Not surprisingly, the proportion of young children enrolled in child-care programs has also increased. Although it is difficult to sort out participation by type of program, we know that between 1970 and 1983, the enrollment rate of three- and four-year-olds in some kind of program increased from 21 to 38 percent. Seven out of ten children of working mothers are cared for in their own homes or in the homes of others. Two out of five children are minded by relatives. Fifteen percent are in day-care centers, and nearly one out of ten accompanies the mother to work (Hechinger, 1986).

Although what falls under the category of preschool education varies from study to study, it is clear that preschool attendance is highly associated with family income. The preschool enrollment rate for families earning below twenty thousand dollars a year is 46 percent and drops to 29 percent for families with annual incomes below ten thousand dollars. In sharp contrast, the preschool enrollment rate for families earning over twenty thousand dollars annually is 64 percent. Viewed from the perspective of parents' educational attainment, the unequal access to preschool is also apparent. Whereas the enrollment rate for three- and four-year-old children of elementary school dropouts was 23 percent, it was 58 percent for children of college graduates (Hechinger, 1986; Schweinhart & Koshel, 1986).

Not only is the supply of child care inadequate and strongly associated with ability to pay, but the quality of many programs fails to live up to the rhetoric about our devotion to children. Many experts have warned about the detrimental effects of substandard child care. Mere custodial care, even in well-maintained facilities, does not provide a child with the experiences necessary for sound cognitive, social, and emotional development. As suggested by a recent headline, "Fatal Fire Renews Debate on Child-care Standards" (*Education Week*, Dec. 3, 1986), when facilities and staffing quality or ratios do not meet even minimal standards, the problem may go beyond the quality of life to life itself. As late as 1986, child advocates were still pressing not only for the enforcement of the Federal

Interagency Day Care Requirements but also for a more adequate set of standards.

The low-quality custodial model of early childhood "education" owes its existence in no small part to the ill-repute with which the very people child care was supposed to help were regarded for much of American history: working mothers. Although women's participation in the labor force has been steadily increasing since the turn of the century, it was not until recently, when the proportion of mothers who worked outside the home approached 50 percent, that this condition was viewed as something other than a symptom of pathology. To be sure, concern for the welfare of poor children of working mothers was certainly evident from the beginning of American history. But compassion could not overcome the prejudices against these children's poverty-stricken families nor the prevailing view that women, no matter how desperate their circumstances, ought not to put paid work over their child-rearing responsibilities. As a result, the few model programs earlier in this century that accounted for both a child's developmental and custodial needs either disappeared or degenerated into solely custodial programs branded by the perceived deficits of working mothers.

While mothers working and therefore institutional child care were viewed as a perversion of a healthy mother-child relationship, the obverse situation also came to be regarded as true. If the mother-child relationship was "abnormal," for reasons either of poverty or of family breakdown, then institutional child care could be an antidote to "bad" mothers; it could even be a means of allowing poor mothers to get out of the house and work. But whether mothers were damned if they worked or damned if they didn't work, the legacy of childcare programs as essentially baby-sitting operations remained the same....

Throughout the 1960s, federal spending for children increased significantly. Yet, with the exception of Head Start, federal policy reinforced a by-then unequal system of services in which the poor received low-cost, low-quality custodial day care, the affluent patronized private nursery schools, and those families who fell in neither category were left to fend for themselves. There is no evidence to suggest that this pattern has changed (Grubb, 1986).

## QUALITY EARLY CHILDHOOD EDUCATION

In contrast to the traditional custodial model of early childhood programs is the educational or developmental model most commonly associated with good preschools but also characteristic of good day care.[1] Indeed, if the major demographic influence on the revival of interest in early childhood education has been the increased labor force participation of mothers of young children, then another significant influence has been the steadily accumulating research findings about the benefits of educationally sound preschool programs.

The notion that the preschool years are crucial to a child's emotional and intellectual development is, of course, not novel. Even before the research confirming this perception was available, and as early as the 1920s, some middle-class and affluent families availed their children of the enriching experiences offered by nursery schools. Initially open only part time, nursery schools steadily increased their hours of operation as even their clientele began to work outside the home. Although they became more similar to custodial child-care programs in hours of operation, however, nursery schools' affluent clientele and quality programs meant that they escaped the stigma attached to day care (Grubb, 1986).

Researchers confirmed what nursery school advocates and wise mothers involved in full-time child rearing already knew. Within the last thirty years, the work of educators like Jean Piaget and Benjamin Bloom supported the idea that young children should have available to them a variety of guided stimulating experiences and that such early learning was implicated in children's subsequent development.

Although this line of thinking did not generally produce a reexamination of the traditional custodial model of child care, it did shape Head Start, one of the major programs of the War on Poverty in the 1960s. The inauguration of Head Start with the passage of the Economic Opportunity Act of 1964 marked the beginning of a federal recognition that child-care services for poor children, like those for the more affluent, should have educational content.

Over the past two decades, the primary source of governmental support of early childhood programs has been federal, with Head Start the flagship of this effort. Much research has been devoted to Head Start, and most of it has confirmed the expectations of the program's supporters. Yet despite the largely positive research findings about the effects of Head Start, the political shifts and budgetary vicissitudes afflicting identifiable poverty programs have meant that Head Start now serves a mere 24 percent (and probably less) of the three- and four-year-olds living in poverty (Schweinhart & Koshel, 1986).

The success of Head Start spurred a number of other experiments offering disadvantaged youngsters educationally sound preschool programs. The results thus far have been encouraging, some of them even electrifying. For example, a 1985 study of 175 disadvantaged children conducted by the University of North Carolina concluded that good preschools can raise IQs by as much as 15 points and significantly improve school achievement in later grades. Other studies also confirm that the educational model of preschool programs can help boost children's intellectual and social development (for reviews, see Berrueta-Clement, Schweinhart, Barnett, Epstein, & Weikart, 1986, pp. 30–36; Schweinhart & Koshel, 1986, pp. 6–7).

Many of the preschool programs represented by these studies have had their day in the sun. None, however, has captured as much political attention as the High/Scope Educational Research Foundation's Perry Preschool Program study (Berrueta-Clement et al., 1986). Although a few studies have analyzed the long-term results of early childhood education programs, the Perry Preschool study is the first longitudinal cost-benefit analysis of such a program. It is in no small part due to the stunningly positive outcomes of the Perry Preschool Program that there has been a growing receptivity to expanding early childhood education.

Initiated in 1962, the study examined the long-term effects of participation and nonparticipation in a developmentally based preschool program on 123 disadvantaged black youths who were at risk of school failure. Researchers collected in-depth information about the children starting at age three up to age nineteen.

Of prime concern were the children's attitudes and academic and vocational accomplishments.

According to the researchers, preschool attendance altered performance by nearly a factor of two on four major variables at age nineteen. The preschoolers' subsequent rates of employment and participation in college or vocational training were nearly double those of the group without preschool. Moreover, for those who attended preschool, the rate of teenage pregnancy (including live births) and the percentage of years spent in special education classes were about half of what they were for those who did not attend preschool. Preschool attendance was associated with a reduction of twenty percentage points in the detention and arrest rate and nearly that much in the high school drop-out rate. Scores on a test of functional competence were also superior for those who attended preschool (Berrueta-Clement et al., 1986).

Considered in terms of their economic value, these benefits make the preschool program a worthwhile investment for society. Indeed, over the lifetimes of the participants, preschool is estimated to yield economic benefits with a percentage value that is over seven times the cost of one year of the program (Berrueta-Clement et al., 1986).

The key to the extraordinary individual and social benefits of the Perry Preschool Program—in fact, of all the preschool programs that have received similar evaluations—is quality. The Perry program was based on solid principles about the cognitive and social development of young children. Teachers were intensively trained, and child-staff ratios were no more than 6:1. Weekly home visits also were a part of the program. On the one hand, the program was expensive:

$4,818 per child a year in 1981 dollars. On the other hand, the lifetime benefit was about $29,000 per participant. Extraordinarily, just the savings realized from the program participants' reduced need for special education placements in school were sufficient to reimburse taxpayers for the cost of running the program for one year.

Still, the short-term costs of the Perry Preschool Program have had an astringent effect on some of the enthusiasm initially expressed about its results. This is not entirely surprising. Americans are becoming habituated to looking to the immediate bottom line and ignoring the future. The question is, in being pennywise are we becoming pound-foolish? Do we prefer to be niggardly when it comes to expenditures on young children and instead incur the high economic, social, and, potentially, political costs associated with our high rates of school failure and dropouts, teenage pregnancy, youth unemployment or underemployment, delinquency and criminal behavior, and welfare dependency?

Society's answer thus far is that we do. High-quality preschool programs are not the magic bullets that will wipe out poverty. But the evidence is powerful indeed that they can significantly and even permanently revise the grim life sentence stamped on so many children of poverty....

## PUBLIC SCHOOL SPONSORSHIP OF EARLY CHILDHOOD EDUCATION

The first advantage of this proposal is that the public education system already has in place organizations experienced in administering large and complex programs. Many state and local education agencies have child development experts on staff. Those that do not would have to hire such people to ensure that programs are age- and need-appropriate or utilize the expertise of such staff in other agencies through interagency agreements. The experience of states such as California and Connecticut suggests that education departments that use an advisory group composed of educators, child development experts, representatives from welfare departments, and other groups whose activities touch the lives of young children are particularly successful at mounting appropriate and flexible programs.

Under the sponsorship of public education and with the formal cooperation of other relevant agencies and groups, order can be brought out of the chaos and fragmentation now characterizing early childhood policies, and the divorce between day-care programs and developmental programs can be reconciled. For example, a public school can run both a preschool program, with its approximately three hours of a deliberately developmental "curriculum," and a quality day-care program whose hours account for the remainder of the working day. Parents would be free to choose whether their child attended only the preschool portion or remained throughout the working day....

A second advantage of this proposal is that public schools are universally available. They exist in urban, suburban, small-town, and rural areas. This means that early childhood education could be universally available, although it should not be compulsory. Ideally, of course, programs would be free of cost to all who desired to attend. Short of this ideal, it may be necessary to design a plan that is based on the ability to pay.... Since a number

of school districts currently charge some sliding-scale fees for child-care services, thoughtful models already exist.

Third, the public education system is best equipped to offer or coordinate the variety of services, such as health and nutrition, that support a child's development. The safety and health record of public schools is also superlative, especially in light of the millions of children they serve every day. Moreover, public schools are more ready (and willing) than other providers to respond to the special needs of handicapped and non-English-speaking children, both in the mainstream and through special services.

The public education system is also in a better position to address the problems of staffing that have characterized many programs and undercut confidence in early childhood education. For one, the licensing or credential-checking systems in place in state and local departments of education could help ensure that quality standards for early childhood education staff are both promulgated and monitored.... Similarly, although public education is hardly saintly in adhering to agreements about appropriate child-adult ratios, its performance is better than most child-care operations and, again, has the capacity to be rigorously monitored and called to account. And no other existing arrangement can surpass the public schools' ability to deliver in-service training, which could keep the staff abreast of current child development theory and practices.

\* \* \*

There are those who will argue that it is tantamount to madness to call for public school sponsorship of early childhood education during a time of intense criticism of public education. The education reform movement of the 1980s has produced a stack of reports documenting the shortcomings of the public schools. My own voice as president of the AFT [American Federation of Teachers] has been loud and clear about the necessity of fundamental reform. But, as in the past, the response to the criticisms of the last few years, although not always adequate or thoughtful, illustrates that public education is a strikingly accountable institution. We do not hear much about what goes on in other institutions of government. We know even less about the private and other organizations sponsoring early childhood education that are subject only to loose controls or no democratic controls at all. Yet we always know the condition of public education, and we have an array of democratic policy mechanisms to improve its condition.

Still, the fears about the structural and educational rigidities that would beset early childhood programs under public school sponsorship are worth exhuming. According to the charges leveled during the 1970s, particularly around the time the federally proposed Child and Family Services Act of 1975 was being considered, public schools were bureaucratic, authoritarian institutions that revolved more around the interests of educators than the needs of children and their parents. Elementary education, critics contended, was narrowly conceived in terms of basic cognitive skills imparted through fixed lessons by teachers who essentially lectured to orderly rows and columns of too numerous children in self-contained classrooms. The schedule and time clock ruled expectations about the progress of children, as well as the day. Children who did not keep pace uniformly, usually according to the criteria of standardized tests, were labeled failures.

The ideals of individualized instruction were espoused, but the legacy of the factory model of schooling prevailed.

Of course, this stereotypical image of the public schools ignored some important realities. For one, only the worst schools fit the stereotype. Second, many public schools were already running exemplary preschool programs, none of which was "contaminated" by the rigidities of the upper elementary grades. And third, there were many factorylike preschool programs outside the public schools and others of such poor quality that introducing some of the worst features ascribed to the public schools would have represented an improvement. More than a decade later and with many more successful experiences with public schools sponsoring preschools, those realities are still with us.

Yet some of the groups that raised these criticisms about the rigidities of the public schools had a point. If the factory model of schooling is not pervasive, it nonetheless represents the dominant organizing principle of public education. It should under no circumstances be extended downward to the preschool level, and it should by all means be repudiated in the entire system. Given the recent report and efforts of the Carnegie Task Force on the Teaching Profession (1986) and considering the new tenor of the second stage of education reform in the 1980s, there is reason to believe that the structural and educational rigidities of the public school system will be addressed. Indeed, new models of school organization and learning are already being tried, and some of them owe much to the lessons learned from the flexible, developmental, child-centered approach that the best of the early childhood education community pioneered.

The renewed interest in early childhood education brings us another chance to reconcile the conflicts over early childhood. Our failure to do so will not stop mothers from working and needing quality child care. It will not materially harm the parties to the conflict. It will, however, hurt young children and perpetuate the problems of meeting their economic, developmental, and custodial needs. There is no reason for the lack of coordination between day care and preschool education, save a set of policies that have irrationally fragmented the planning and administration of such programs and maintained the historic and unequally applied distinctions between a child's custodial and educational needs. There is every reason to expect more incidences of fatality, abuse, and just plain neglect if we continue to be indifferent to standards and implicitly delegate our responsibility for the welfare of the nation's children to organizations concerned only for their own welfare.

It is possible to have standards without standardization and flexibility without fragmentation in early childhood education policy. The solution lies in making a variety of quality early childhood education programs universally available to all parents who want these services. A large part of the means to that end involves the early childhood education community recognizing that the public education system is the best prime sponsor. Another part involves the continuing willingness of the public school system to recognize child development–based approaches to learning and to make the structural and educational changes indicated by the best of these approaches. By drawing on their strengths rather than hurling charges about their weaknesses,

child advocates might this time actually cooperate on behalf of effective, caring policies toward children.

## REFERENCES

Berrueta-Clement, J. R., Schweinhart, L. J., Barnett, W. S., Epstein, A. S., and Weikart, D. P. (1986). Changed lives: The effects of the Perry Preschool Program on youths through age 19. In F. M. Hechinger (Ed.). *A better start: New choices for early learning* (pp. 11–40). New York: Walker.

Carnegie Task Force on the Teaching Profession. (1986). *Teachers for the 21st century* (A Report of the Carnegie Forum on Education and the Economy). New York: Carnegie Corporation of New York.

Grubb, W. N. (1986, August). *Young children face the states: Issues and options for early childhood programs.* Draft paper for Rutgers University, The Center for Policy Research in Education.

Hechinger, F. M. (Ed.). (1986). *A better start: New choices for early learning.* New York: Walker.

National Governors' Association. (1986). *Time for results: The governors' 1991 report on education.* Washington, DC: Author.

Schweinhart, L. J., & Koshel, J. J. (1986). *Policy options for preschool programs.* Ypsilanti, MI: High/Scope Early Childhood Policy Papers No. 5.

U.S. Bureau of Labor Statistics. (1986, August 20). *Half of mothers of children under three now in labor force.* Washington, DC: U.S. Department of Labor 86–345.

U.S. Department of Labor. *Labor force statistics derived from the current population survey: A databook* (Vol. 1, Table C-11). Washington, DC: U.S. Government Printing Office.

## NOTE

1. Although my characterization of the custodial model of early childhood education is clearly pejorative, it should in no way he construed to denigrate either the function of custodianship or day-care programs in a generic sense. Clearly, meeting a child's custodial needs is very important. Equally clearly, many day-care programs offer developmentally sound activities, while many preschools do not. But although the difference between day-care and preschool programs is frequently only nominal, the distinction between the custodial and developmental models is historical and real. By custodial model, then, I mean low-quality programs that are no more and sometimes less than mere baby-sitting operations, indifferent to or ignorant of the unique developmental needs of preschoolers.

# NO

Edward F. Zigler

## FORMAL SCHOOLING FOR FOUR-YEAR-OLDS? NO

A developing momentum is moving our nation toward universal preschool education (Zimiles, 1985). Many decision makers are advocating the downward extension of public schooling to four-year-olds. New York's Mayor Koch not only made all-day kindergarten mandatory but also appointed a commission charged with reorganizing and broadening access to all early intervention and preschool programs in New York City. A *New York Times* editorial entitled "School at 4: A Model for the Nation" hailed Koch's initiative as the most sensible way to "save the next generation" (1985, p. 22). American Federation of Teachers president Albert Shanker also endorsed preschool education. So many positive voices have been heard that it is easy to assume that schooling for four-year-olds is an uncomplicated issue that has met only with popular support and enthusiasm. Indeed, the commissioner for education in New York State, Gordon Ambach (1985), stated that it was impossible to find anyone to uphold the negative side of the issue.

There are some negative voices, however, and they are beginning to be heard. Herbert Zimiles (1985), a leading thinker in the field of early childhood education, has argued that the movement toward universal preschool education is characterized more by enthusiasm than thought. The commissioner of education for the state of Connecticut, Gerald Tirozzi, another champion of public education for four-year-olds, established a committee to study the issue within the general context of children's services. In their recommendations, this committee concluded that "under no circumstances do we believe it appropriate for all four-year-olds to be involved in a 'kindergarten-type' program within the public schools" (Kagan, 1985, p. 3).... I will add my voice to those who have argued that the issue of universal schooling for four-year-olds requires more thought than it has been accorded.

The current impetus for earlier schooling has two sources. The first is the concern generated by the increasing criticism of our public secondary schools. The National Commission on Excellence in Education report, *A Nation at Risk* (1983), detailed the failures of secondary schooling in America. Similar studies (for example, Boyer, 1983; Sizer, 1984) soon followed. These reports emphasized the need for higher academic standards, more attention

Adapted from Edward F. Zigler, "Formal Schooling for Four-Year-Olds? No," *American Psychologist* (March 1987). Copyright © 1987 by The American Psychological Association, Inc. Reprinted by permission. References omitted.

to basics, more rigor in teaching, and longer school days and years. Few of them proposed earlier schooling as a solution to our educational problems.

An ostensible exception, Mortimer Adler's thoughtful *Paideia Proposal* (1983), did link school reform and early childhood education. Adler stated: "preschool deprivation is the cause of backwardness or failure in school.... Hence at least one year—or better, two or three years of preschool tutelage must be provided for those who do not get such preparation from favorable environments" (pp. 37–38). Too often, however, Adler's caveat with regard to the purely remedial nature of preschool for the disadvantaged is ignored. It is not Adler's opinion, nor is it mine, that the more advantaged children in our society require a year of preschool education at the state's expense.

A second source of the momentum toward universal preschool education is the inappropriate generalization of the effects of some excellent remedial programs for the economically disadvantaged. Several preschool intervention programs—such as Head Start (Lazar & Darlington, 1982), the New York University Institute for Developmental Studies (Deutsch, Deutsch, Jordan, & Grallo, 1983), the Ypsilanti-based Perry Preschool Program (Berrueta-Clement, Schweinhart, Barnett, Epstein & Weikart, 1984), the New York State prekindergarten program (Ambach, 1985), and the Brookline Early Education Program (Pierson, Tivnan, & Walker, 1984)—have succeeded in spurring the developmental and cognitive growth of economically disadvantaged three- and four-year-old children. But extrapolation to all children from these programs is inappropriate for two reasons. First, benefits were obtained only for economically disadvantaged

children. Second, these intervention programs differ from standard school fare in a number of important ways, since they provide primary health and social services. In addition, unlike conventional schooling, this assistance is provided to the family as a whole, not simply to a target child. These are vital differences, as many theorists believe that preschool programs are most successful when parents participate and that the basic needs of children and their families must be met before schooling can have any effect (Bronfenbrenner, 1974; Deutsch, Deutsch, Jordan, & Grallo, 1983; Radin, 1969; Slater, 1971; Sparrow, Blachman, & Chauncey, 1983; Valentine & Stark, 1979; Waksman, 1980).

Public preschool education shares few of these services and concerns, nor can they become the primary focus of the educational establishment. It is an open question whether early school-based programs will result in the same increases in social competence found by the Cornell Consortium (Royce, Darlington, & Murray, 1983) following early intervention programs for the economically disadvantaged, increases which may well be a consequence of services having very little to do with formal education. It was precisely those differences between Head Start and formal schooling that I have outlined here that led many of us to oppose President Carter's proposal to move Head Start into the new Department of Education, and that in the end prevented its inclusion.

## THE PERRY PRESCHOOL PROGRAM

Other differences, too, must be considered when interpreting the benefits of the Perry Preschool Program in Ypsilanti, Michigan, an intervention program involving either one or two years of half-day preschool for seven months each year and periodic home visits for high-risk four- and five-year-olds. This well-known exemplary intervention effort achieved remarkable success, and it deserves the praise it has received from many quarters. It is one of the few intervention efforts that attempted to assign participants randomly to experimental and control groups. Further, it is one of the few intervention efforts that have met my dictum that the assessment of early intervention efforts should include a cost-benefit analysis (Zigler & Berman, 1983). But generalizing from the results of this unique effort to typical public programs is highly problematic for three reasons.

First, it is very unlikely that a preschool program mounted in the typical public school will be of the quality represented by the Perry Preschool Project. The program's experimental character ensured that it would be exceptionally well planned, monitored, and managed. Further, the very fact that staff members are participating in an experiment can stimulate and motivate them. For example, researchers worked extensively with the direct child care givers in analyzing and constructing the program (Barnett, personal communication, 1985), and visiting experts held weekly seminars for the entire preschool staff (Weikart, 1967). Although the consequences of these aspects of the program were not analyzed, their potential effect on program outcome may well have been substantial.

Second, there are questions concerning the Perry sample. It was not only nonrepresentative of children in general; there is some doubt that it was representative of even the bulk of economically disadvan-

taged children. The sample was limited to black youngsters, when in fact the majority of low-income children are white (U.S. Bureau of the Census, 1984); it is even problematic as to whether the sample was representative of low-income black children. The Perry Project was limited to children with IQs between 61 and 88. Yet the median IQ of black children in the United States was 80–85 in the early 1960s (Kennedy, Van de Riet, & White, 1963). A further argument against generalization from the Perry Preschool Project lies in the fact that participation was fully voluntary, which introduced a self-selection phenomenon (how families that did not choose to volunteer differed from the final project sample is an open question).

Finally, the Perry Project poses a number of methodological difficulties. First, to be assigned to the intervention group, children had to have a parent at home during the day, resulting in a significant difference between control and intervention groups on the variable of maternal employment. Second, as noted by Haskins and Gallagher (1984) assignment to experimental and control groups was not wholly random. Although this departure from random assignment is probably of minor consequence, it does render interpretation of program effects problematic. Finally, criticisms have been advanced that the Perry program's cost-benefit analyses overestimated the benefits attributed to the intervention (Hanke & Anwyll, 1980).

I concur with the Gottfrieds (1984) and Larsen (1985) that caution should be exercised in generalizing from one group to another. (I would like to see the outcome of the High/Scope model when mounted by people with less expertise than those employed in the Perry project.) Furthermore, evaluations of any intervention should be conducted by researchers not involved in the development of the model being evaluated (Zigler & Berman, 1983). Given the pervasiveness of self-fulfilling prophecies (Rosenthal & Jacobson, 1968; Merton, 1948), this is merely a commonsense concern. I should note, however, that Campbell (in press) has recently argued that it is appropriate for those who mount programs to do their own evaluations in order to retain their qualitative subjective insights in their analyses.

## APPROPRIATE CANDIDATES FOR INTERVENTION

The High/Scope data generate the intriguing hypothesis that preschool intervention is particularly effective for the most economically disadvantaged children, a view supported by the New York State evaluation of its experimental preschool program (Irvine, Flint, Hick, Horan, & Kikuk, 1982). The New York study indicated that the only cognitive gains that lasted beyond the preschool period were among children whose mothers scored extremely low on measures of education.

This view has apparently not escaped the attention of educational decision makers. Almost all the states that now provide school-sponsored programs for four-year-olds limit enrollment to low-income, handicapped, and, in some cases, non-English-speaking youngsters (Kagan, 1985). Even the Ypsilanti group recognized that these are the children who can most profit from intervention (Berrueta-Clement et al., 1984, p. 7). Although Pierson et al. (1984) have made some claims for the effectiveness of preschool programs for middle-class children, their criterion for this status

is questionable. In any case, the gains made by children of educated parents in their study were far less than those made by the children of less educated parents. What is more, such differences as were found may turn out to be short-lived, as no long-term assessment of the intervention and control groups has been carried out.

In contrast, there is a large body of evidence indicating that there is little if anything to be gained by exposing middle-class children to early education (see Adler, 1982; Caruso & Detterman, 1981; Clarke, 1984; Darlington, Royce, Snipper, Murray, & Lazar, 1980; Swift, 1964). For example, the only advantage Swift (1964) could find as a result of preschool education was a small degree of enhanced social development when the children entered school; those not involved in preschool reached the same level of social adjustment in less than two years. Similarly, Abelson, Zigler, and DeBlasi (1974) found that while an extensive four-year intervention program benefited low-income children, it had no effect on middle-class youngsters. In his review of research on preschool intervention, English specialist on child development and education Martin Woodhead (1985) states:

> Three main considerations affect the validity of drawing general conclusions for early education policy. First, the populations served by these projects were severely disadvantaged, mainly black children, and the evidence for wider replicability is inconclusive. Secondly, the projects all featured a carefully designed, well-supported programme with low ratios of children to teachers. Finally the effectiveness of pre-school may also be conditional on features of

the educational and family context in which intervention took place. (p. 133)

American schools are already under great financial pressure and must make the most efficient use possible of limited economic resources. I have long been an advocate of cost-benefit analyses for all types of social programs (Zigler & Berman, 1983). As previously stated, our best thinking suggests we can make the most effective use of limited funds by investing them in intervention programs that target three overlapping groups: (1) the economically disadvantaged child, (2) the handicapped child, and (3) the bilingual child (Casto & Mastropieri, 1984; Kagan, 1985; White & Casto, 1984). Spreading education budgets to include all four-year-olds would spread them too thin. Such an extension would not only have little effect on the more advantaged mainstream, but would diminish our capacity to intervene with those who could benefit the most.

There is, however, one potential advantage to universal preschool education. A weakness of Head Start and Head Start-like programs is their built-in economic segregation of children. Poor children go to Head Start, while more affluent children go elsewhere. Universal preschools would better integrate children across socioeconomic lines and, as Zimiles (1985) has noted, would introduce equity into early childhood programs. Although this would waste funding on children who have little to gain from early education, it would also guarantee its availability to those who could not otherwise afford it. Furthermore, Abelson et al. (1974) and Coleman et al. (1966) suggest there are educational advantages to mixed socioeconomic and racial groupings. Nevertheless, although we would be well-advised to promote the integration of children from diverse social and ethnic backgrounds, the cost of doing so through universal preschool education outweighs its potential benefits.

## THE REAL NEED: HIGH QUALITY CHILD CARE

Educators in several states point to parental pressure for all-day kindergarten as evidence of the value parents place on early education, but I believe that they have misread this demand. What many parents are expressing is less a burning desire for preschool education than their desperate need for quality day care. Fifty-nine percent of the mothers of three- and four-year-olds are now employed outside their homes, and many of these mothers have enrolled their children in child-care programs that provide organized educational activities (Chorvinsky, 1982). Yet, ironically, not even all-day kindergarten programs are able to fill the day-care needs of families with both parents working outside the home. Schools tend to adjourn around 3:00, two hours before most working days end. Thus, the day-care problem has only been partly solved, and this token improvement may actually lead parents to take fewer precautions, given the relatively short period of time children are alone.

Day care can be prohibitively expensive for many families, and it is not surprising that many would prefer to shift the cost to the public school system. The Perry Preschool Project was estimated by its originators to cost approximately fifteen hundred dollars per year per child in 1963. Given the number of three- and four-year-olds in the nation today, and adjusting the figures for inflation, the total cost of a universal child development program would be many billions of dollars per year. Unfortunately, advocates of universal preschool education continue to behave as though these vast sums will magically appear. Fiscal reality demands we target populations who can most benefit from care and provide them with the more general programs best suited to their particular needs.

We must also listen to those families who neither need nor want their young children placed in preschool. The compulsory aspect of many of the proposed early education plans has angered many parents and set them in opposition to school officials—a poor beginning to the positive home-school relation that is vital to the educational process (Bronfenbrenner, 1974; Lazar & Darlington, 1982). Decision makers must be sensitive to the individual needs of children and parents and recognize that, whenever the family situation permits it, the best place for a preschool child is often at home.

We must strive also to be sensitive to the individual differences among young children. Some four-year-olds can handle a five- or six-hour school day. Many others cannot. Whenever it is best for the children to be at home with their parents, we should not needlessly deprive families of valuable time they could spend together. This is not to ignore the fact that home may be a place of abuse or neglect, a welfare hotel, or a confusing and insecure environment without what we have come to accept as adequate resources. For these children, day care may be the best available alternative. Yet many competent, caring parents who are at home resent school administrators' proposals to keep their preschool children in a full-day early education program. In fact,

recent work by Tizard and her colleagues has demonstrated that the conversations children carry on at home may be the richest source of linguistic and cognitive enrichment for children from all but the most deprived backgrounds (Hughes, Carmichael, Pinkerton, & Tizard, 1979; Tizard, Carmichael, Hughes, & Pinkerton, 1980; Tizard & Hughes, 1984; Tizard, Mortimore, & Burchell, 1981; Tizard, Hughes, Carmichael, & Pinkerton, 1982, 1983). This body of work highlights the vast scope of information and ideas that are transmitted at home, as opposed to the circumscribed agenda of the school. The fact that parent and child share a common life and frame of reference allows them to explore events and ideas in intimate, individualistic conversations with great personal meaning. At a time when universal early education, the earlier the better, is being advocated, the Tizard work reminds us of other, equally important roots of cognitive development.

## A TIME FOR CHILDHOOD

I concur with Elkind (1981) and Winn (1983) that we are driving our young children too hard and thereby depriving them of their most precious commodity—their childhood. The image of the four-year-old in designer jeans and miniature executive briefcase in hand may seem cute, but rushing children from cradle to school denies them the freedom to develop at their own pace. Children are growing up too fast today, and prematurely placing four- and five-year-olds into full-day preschool education programs will only compound this problem.

Those who argue in favor of universal preschool education ignore evidence that indicates early schooling is inappropriate for many four-year-olds and that it may even be harmful to their development (Ames, 1980; Collins, 1984; Elkind, 1981; Gesell, 1928; Yarrow, 1964; Zimiles, 1985). Marie Winn (1983) notes in *Children without Childhood* that premature schooling can replace valuable playtime, potentially slowing or reducing the child's overall development. This is an especial danger given the present cognitive thrust in education, increasing the possibility of an overemphasis on formal and highly structured academics (Ames, 1980; Zimiles, 1985). The supervision of very young children must be a distinctive form of care suited to the rapid developmental changes and high dependency of these children, not a scaled-down version of a grade-school curriculum.

At the same time we must remember that although early childhood is an important and sensitive time, it is not uniquely so. In the 1960s we believed early childhood was a magic period during which minimal intervention efforts would have maximal indelible effects on the child. In the current push toward early formal education we can see the unfortunate recurrence of this idea.

Every age in a child's life is a magic age. We must be just as concerned for the six-year-old, the ten-year-old, and the sixteen-year-old as we are for the four-year-old (Clarke & Clarke, 1976). In fact, the proposed New York plan is especially troubling in that it includes a suggestion to add a year of education at the beginning of formal schooling and to drop a year at the end of high school. The work of Feuerstein (1970; Feuerstein, Rand, Hoffman, & Miller, 1980) and Hobbs and Robinson (1982), to name but a few scholars in this area, has demonstrated that adolescence is itself a sensitive and fluid period in the life of the child. We must guard against short-changing one age group in our efforts to help another.

## THE EASY WAY OUT

This is not the first time universal preschool education has been proposed. Wilson Riles, then California state superintendent of schools, advocated early childhood education ten years ago, as school superintendents in New York and Connecticut are doing today. Then, as now, the arguments in favor of preschool education were that it would reduce school failure, lower drop-out rates, increase test scores, and produce a generation of more competent high school graduates. I have reached the same conclusion in interpreting the evidence as did the state of California finally: preschool education will achieve none of these results. I am not simply saying that universal preschool education will be a waste of time and money. Rather there is a positive danger in asserting that the solution to the poor school and later life performance of the disadvantaged will be solved by a year of preschool education. The nation is on the verge of falling into the over-optimistic trap that ensnared us in the mid-sixties, when expectations were raised that an eight-week summer program could solve all the problems of the poor. If we wish to improve the lives of the economically disadvantaged, we must abandon the short-term "solutions" of the sixties and work for much deeper social reforms (Zigler & Berman, 1983). The purely symbolic function served by relying on educational innovations alone to solve the problems of poor children has been noted by historian Marvin Lazerson:

Too often discussions of educational reform appear to be a means of avoiding more complex and politically dangerous issues.... Education is... cheaper than new housing and new jobs. We are left with greater school responsibility while the social problems which have the greatest effect on schooling are largely ignored. The schools—in this case, preschool—are asked to do too much, and given too little support to accomplish what they are asked. A variety of interest groups, however, are satisfied: educators, because they get status and funds, social reformers, because they believe in education, and government officials because they pass positive legislation without upsetting traditional social patterns. (1970, p. 84)

We simply cannot inoculate children in one year against the ravages of a life of deprivation. Even champions of early childhood education have made sobering statements warning us not to expect too much while doing too little. Fred Hechinger wrote, "Part of the problem is to overpromise and underfinance. The hard fact is that there are no educational miracles for the effects of poverty" (1985, p. C10). In an incisive analysis, Sen. Daniel Patrick Moynihan agreed, warning that exaggerated reports of success in the field of early childhood education lead inevitably to near nihilism when these extravagant hopes are unfulfilled: "From finding out that not everything works, we rush to the judgment that nothing works or can be made to work" (1984, p. 8). Moynihan noted that the Ypsilanti researchers were restrained in their claims of the benefits of early childhood education, stating that such programs are "part of the solution, not the whole solution" (quoted in Moynihan, 1984, p. 13). In editorializing these results, however, Moynihan unabashedly stated, "Yes, after all the years of experiment and disappointment, American society does know one sure way to lead poor children out of a life of poverty" (p. 13). Moynihan's point that research is threatened when results are exaggerated in this fashion is well taken. Just as the credibility of researchers can be damaged, so too can the credibility of educators if they insist on promising more than they can possibly deliver. Barbara Tizard states:

Insofar, then, as the expansion of early schooling is seen as a way of avoiding later school failure or of closing the social class gap in achievement, we already know it to be doomed to failure. It would perhaps be sensible for research workers to point this out very clearly to public authorities at an early stage. This is not, of course, to say that such an expansion has no value—no one would agree that a young child should not be fed well, because his present diet may not affect his adult weight and height. Nursery schooling, or particular forms of it, may help to develop the child's social and cognitive skills as well as add to the happiness of both child and mother. What seems certain, however, is that without continuous reinforcement in the primary school or home, pre-school education has no longterm effect on later school achievement. (Tizard, 1974, p. 4)

## A REALISTIC SOLUTION

Educators must realize they cannot reform the world or change the basic nature of children. The real question is how to provide the best experience during the day for a four-year-old—specifically for those who cannot remain at home with a consistent, competent care giver. Parents do not need children who read at age four, but they do need affordable, good-quality child care. The most cost-effective way to provide universally available—again, not compulsory—care would be to work through the school. I am advocating a return to the concept of the community school as a local center for all the social services required by the surrounding neighborhood. These full-service schools would, in addition to supplying other programs, provide full-day, high-quality child care for four- and even three-year-old children in their facilities, since they are already present in the community. Although such preschool programs would include a developmentally appropriate educational component, they would be places primarily for recreation and socialization—the real business of preschoolers. In-school day care could also easily accommodate older children after school is dismissed. Another investigator summarizes the need in this way: "We must... align the goals of programs for infants, preschoolers, and early elementary school-aged pupils so that such programs become components of an integrated, consistent plan for educating young children" (Weinberg, 1979, p. 915).

Such a program, although operating on school grounds, should not be staffed solely by teachers. Instead I propose that we staff school-based day-care programs with teachers in a supervisory capacity and with Child Development Associates (CDAs), the certified care givers currently employed in our nation's Head Start program. The National Day Care Study (Ruopp, Travers, Glantz, & Coelen, 1979) found that the one background characteristic of teachers that related to program quality was their training for early childhood programs. Certification of CDAs is based on both educational attainment and proven competence in meeting all the needs of children.

Finally, in thinking of three- and four-year-olds, let us not neglect the needs of five-year-olds. I believe that a full day of formal schooling is too much even for these children. Instead, I would propose a half-day kindergarten program to be followed by a half day in school day care for those who need it. The extra cost could be borne by parents on a sliding-fee basis, with financial assistance available to needy families. Licensed qualified teachers would teach a half day in the morning and certified CDAS would care for the children in the afternoon. A half day of education is plenty for a five-year-old. Again, let me emphasize that the day-care element should be strictly voluntary; no parent who wants his or her child at home after school ends at noon should be denied this. Furthermore, such a program would do well to adopt a whole-child approach, recognizing the child's socio-emotional needs in the course of development, as exemplified by Biber (1984) in her Bank Street model, rather than treating kindergarten like a miniature elementary school with a heavy cognitive-academic orientation. New York University's Institute for Developmental Studies educational enrichment program is another excellent example of a program using a sound whole-child approach.

On a larger scale, many aspects of the funding issue will have to be addressed, such as the tax base and licensing procedures. Federal support might be expected to subsidize costs for economically disadvantaged children. Cost containment would also be enhanced by making use of existing school facilities.

In short, we must ask ourselves— what would we be buying for our children in universal preschool education programs, and at what cost? The family-oriented, multiservice community school could meet the many different needs of preschoolers and their families with a variety of programs from which parents could select to suit their needs and desires. Such services could include comprehensive intervention programs, health and nutrition components, and high-quality, affordable day care, to name only a few possibilities. Our four-year-olds do have a place in school, but it is not at a school desk.

# CHALLENGE QUESTIONS

## Should Formal Schooling Begin at an Earlier Age?

1. If you were the parent of a 4-year-old child, would you want your child to participate in formal schooling of some kind? Why, or why not? If you would, what characteristics would you look for in such schooling?

2. What should our government do regarding early childhood education?

3. What, if anything, do you see as potential harms of early childhood education? Can potential problems be minimized? If so, how?

4. What does the push for early childhood education by some people reveal about our society? Does it say anything about today's parents?

5. Shanker believes there are benefits of early childhood education. Do you agree? Can you think of any potential benefits not discussed by Shanker?

# ISSUE 9

## Are Children of Divorced Parents at Greater Risk?

**YES: Judith S. Wallerstein,** from "Children of Divorce: The Dilemma of a Decade," in Elam W. Nunnally, Catherine S. Chilman, and Fred M. Cox, eds., *Troubled Relationships* (Sage Publications, 1988)

**NO: David H. Demo and Alan C. Acock,** from "The Impact of Divorce on Children," *Journal of Marriage and the Family* (August 1988)

### ISSUE SUMMARY

**YES:** Judith S. Wallerstein, a clinician, researcher, and the senior consultant to the Marin County Community Mental Health Center, contends that children of divorced parents are at greater risk of developing mental and physical problems than are children of intact families.

**NO:** Sociologists David H. Demo and Alan C. Acock question the idea that intact, two-parent families are always best for children, and they argue that any negative effects of divorce are short-lived and that divorce often produces many positive changes.

Over half of all marriages now end in divorce. What effect do these divorces have upon the young children involved? Many people assume that the changes involved in divorce would naturally lead to some emotional problems, with potentially permanent ramifications. Hidden in this view, however, is the assumption that the traditional, two-parent family is the most appropriate environment in which to raise children. Indeed, most research on children of divorce has been based on this assumption.

Several developmental psychologists have begun to question this assumption. They suggest that nontraditional families—single-parent families, for example—can also produce happy, emotionally stable children. This could mean that divorce is not always negative. In fact, the effects of living in a highly conflictual environment—such as the environment of a couple contemplating divorce—could be more damaging than the actual act of divorce itself. In this sense, the level of family conflict would have more to do with a child's adjustment than would the number of parents he or she has.

Judith S. Wallerstein, while acknowledging certain limitations on the relevant research, contends that children of divorce are at great risk of developing problems. She argues that increased attention to education, treatment, and prevention programs is needed for this special population of children. She identifies three broad stages in the divorcing process along with the effects each stage has on the children. Wallerstein also chronicles changes in the parent-child relationship that occur during the divorce process. These include a diminished capacity of adults to parent their children, a decline in emotional sensitivity and support for the children, decreased pleasure in the parent-child relationship, and less interaction with the children. All of these changes, she concludes, have a negative impact on the development of the children. She asserts that for most children, divorce is "the most stressful period of their lives."

David H. Demo and Alan C. Acock, on the other hand, argue that "it is simplistic and inaccurate to think of divorce as having uniform consequences for children." They contend that most current research is based upon Freudian or social learning concepts that emphasize that both parents are necessary for a child to develop normally. Demo and Acock, however, question the necessity of the traditional, two-parent family. They cite evidence showing that parental separation is actually beneficial for children when the alternative is continued familial conflict. Other studies reveal that factors such as maternal employment and social support are more important than the actual divorce in determining how successfully a child develops following a family breakup. Unfortunately, most studies do not distinguish between the effects of family structure (one- versus two-parent families, for example) and the effects of divorce. Demo and Acock maintain that studies that make this distinction are required before any final conclusions can be drawn about the effects of divorce on children.

| POINT | COUNTERPOINT |
|---|---|
| • Children of divorce are at greater risk of developing problems than are children in traditional, two-parent families. | • Nontraditional families can also produce healthy, emotionally stable children. |
| • Children experience parental separation and its aftermath as the most stressful period of their lives. | • Children who experience divorce indicate that it is preferable to living in conflict. |
| • There are significant, negative changes in the parent-child relationship during the divorce process. | • There are positive outcomes of divorce, such as greater assumption of responsibility and internal locus of control. |
| • A child's age and developmental stage appear to be the most important factors affecting his or her response to divorce. | • These factors are not as important as family characteristics in understanding the effects of divorce. |

# YES
## Judith S. Wallerstein

# CHILDREN OF DIVORCE:
# THE DILEMMA OF A DECADE

It is now estimated that 45% of all children born in 1983 will experience their parents' divorce, 35% will experience a remarriage, and 20% will experience a second divorce (A. J. Norton, Assistant Chief, Population Bureau, United States Bureau of the Census, personal communication, 1983)....

Although the incidence of divorce has increased across all age groups, the most dramatic rise has occurred among young adults (Norton, 1980). As a result, children in divorcing families are younger than in previous years and include more preschool children....

Although many children weather the stress of marital discord and family breakup without psychopathological sequelae, a significant number falter along the way. Children of divorce are significantly overrepresented in outpatient psychiatric, family agency, and private practice populations compared with children in the general population (Gardner, 1976; Kalter, 1977; Tessman, 1977; Tooley, 1976). The best predictors of mental health referrals for school-aged children are parental divorce or parental loss as a result of death (Felner, Stolberg, & Cowen, 1975). A national survey of adolescents whose parents had separated and divorced by the time the children were seven years old found that 30% of these children had received psychiatric or psychological therapy by the time they reached adolescence compared with 10% of adolescents in intact families (Zill, 1983).

A longitudinal study in northern California followed 131 children who were age 3 to 18 at the decisive separation. At the 5-year mark, the investigators found that more than one-third were suffering with moderate to severe depression (Wallerstein & Kelly, 1980a). These findings are especially striking because the children were drawn from a nonclinical population and were accepted into the study only if they had never been identified before the divorce as needing psychological treatment and only if they were performing at age-appropriate levels in school. Therefore, the deterioration observed in these children's adjustment occurred largely following the family breakup....

Divorce is a long, drawn-out process of radically changing family relationships that has several stages, beginning with the marital rupture and its immediate aftermath, continuing over several years of disequilibrium, and finally coming to rest with the stabilization of a new postdivorce or remarried family unit. A complex chain of changes, many of them unanticipated and unforeseeable, are set into motion by the marital rupture and are likely to occupy a significant portion of the child or adolescent's growing years. As the author and her colleague have reported elsewhere, women in the California Children of Divorce study required three to three-and-one-half years following the decisive separation before they achieved a sense of order and predictability in their lives (Wallerstein & Kelly, 1980a). This figure probably underestimates the actual time trajectory of the child's experience of divorce. A prospective study reported that parent–child relationships began to deteriorate many years prior to the divorce decision and that the adjustment of many children in these families began to fail long before the decisive separation (Morrison, 1982). This view of the divorcing process as long lasting accords with the perspective of a group of young people who reported at a 10-year follow-up that their entire childhood or adolescence had been dominated by the family crisis and its extended aftermath (Wallerstein, 1978).

**Stages in the Process**
The three broad, successive stages in the divorcing process, while they overlap, are nevertheless clinically distinguishable. *The acute phase* is precipitated by the decisive separation and the decision to divorce. This stage is often marked by steeply escalating conflict between the adults, physical violence, severe distress, depression accompanied by suicidal ideation, and a range of behaviors reflecting a spilling of aggressive and sexual impulses. The adults frequently react with severe ego regression and not unusually behave at odds with their more customary demeanor. Sharp disagreement in the wish to end the marriage is very common, and the narcissistic injury to the person who feels rejected sets the stage for rage, sexual jealousy, and depression. Children are generally not shielded from this parental conflict or distress. Confronted by a marked discrepancy in images of their parents, children do not have the assurance that the bizarre or depressed behaviors and moods will subside. As a result, they are likely to be terrified by the very figures they usually rely on for nurturance and protection.

As the acute phase comes to a close, usually within the first 2 years of the divorce decision, the marital partners gradually disengage from each other and pick up the new tasks of reestablishing their separate lives. *The transitional phase* is characterized by ventures into new, more committed relationships; new work, school, and friendship groups; and sometimes new settings, new lifestyles, and new geographical locations. This phase is marked by alternating success and failure, encouragement and discouragement, and it may also last for several years. Children observe and participate in the many changes of this period. They share the trials and errors and the fluctuations in mood. For several years life may be unstable, and home may be unsettled.

Finally, *the postdivorce phase* ensues with the establishment of a fairly stable single-parent or remarried household. Eventually three out of four divorced women and four out of five divorced men reenter wedlock (Cherlin, 1981). Unfortunately, though, remarriage does not bring immediate tranquility into the lives of the family members. The early years of the remarriage are often encumbered by ghostly presences from the earlier failed marriages and by the actual presences of children and visiting parents from the prior marriage or marriages. Several studies suggest widespread upset among children and adolescents following remarriage (Crohn, Brown, Walker, & Beir, 1981; Goldstein, 1974; Kalter, 1977). A large-scale investigation that is still in process reports long-lasting friction around visitation (Jacobson, 1983).

## Changes in Parent–Child Relationships

Parents experience a diminished capacity to parent their children during the acute phase of the divorcing process and often during the transitional phase as well (Wallerstein & Kelly, 1980a). This phenomenon is widespread and can be considered an expectable, divorce-specific change in parent–child relationships. At its simplest level this diminished parenting capacity appears in the household disorder that prevails in the aftermath of divorce, in the rising tempers of custodial parent and child, in reduced competence and a greater sense of helplessness in the custodial parent, and in lower expectations of the child for appropriate social behavior (Hetherington, Cox, & Cox, 1978; 1982). Diminished parenting also entails a sharp decline in emotional sensitivity and support for the child; decreased pleasure in the parent–child relationship; decreased attentiveness to the child's needs and wishes; less talk, play, and interaction with the child; and a steep escalation in inappropriate expression of anger. One not uncommon component of the parent–child relationship coincident with the marital breakup is the adult's conscious or unconscious

wish to abandon the child and thus to erase the unhappy marriage in its entirety. Child neglect can be a serious hazard.

In counterpoint to the temporary emotional withdrawal from the child, the parent may develop a dependent, sometimes passionate, attachment to the child or adolescent, beginning with the breakup and lasting throughout the lonely postseparation years (Wallerstein, 1985). Parents are likely to lean on the child and turn to the child for help, placing the child in a wide range of roles such as confidante, advisor, mentor, sibling, parent, caretaker, lover, concubine, extended conscience or ego control, ally within the marital conflict, or pivotal supportive presence in staving off depression or even suicide. This expectation that children should not only take much greater responsibility for themselves but also should provide psychological and social support for the distressed parent is sufficiently widespread to be considered a divorce-specific response along with that of diminished parenting. Such relationships frequently develop with an only child or with a very young, even a preschool, child. Not accidentally, issues of custody and visitation often arise with regard to the younger children. While such disputes, of course, reflect the generally unresolved anger of the marriage and the divorce, they may also reflect the intense emotional need of one or both parents for the young child's constant presence (Wallerstein, 1985).

Parents may also lean more appropriately on the older child or adolescent. Many youngsters become proud helpers, confidantes, and allies in facing the difficult postdivorce period (Weiss, 1979b). Other youngsters draw away from close involvement out of their fears of engulfment, and they move precipitously out of the family orbit, sometimes before they are developmentally ready....

## CHILDREN'S REACTIONS TO DIVORCE

### Initial Responses
Children and adolescents experience separation and its aftermath as the most stressful period of their lives. The family rupture evokes an acute sense of shock, intense anxiety, and profound sorrow. Many children are relatively content and even well-parented in families where one or both parents are unhappy. Few youngsters experience any relief with the divorce decision, and those who do are usually older and have witnessed physical violence or open conflict between their parents. The child's early responses are governed neither by an understanding of issues leading to the divorce nor by the fact that divorce has a high incidence in the community. To the child, divorce signifies the collapse of the structure that provides support and protection. The child reacts as to the cutting of his or her lifeline.

The initial suffering of children and adolescents in response to a marital separation is compounded by realistic fears and fantasies about catastrophes that the divorce will bring in its wake. Children suffer with a pervasive sense of vulnerability because they feel that the protective and nurturant function of the family has given way. They grieve over the loss of the noncustodial parent, over the loss of the intact family, and often over the multiple losses of neighborhood, friends, and school. Children also worry about their distressed parents. They are concerned about who will take care of the parent who has left and whether the custodial parent will be able to manage alone. They experience intense anger toward one or both parents whom they hold responsible for disrupting the family. Some of their anger is reactive and defends them against their own feelings of powerlessness, their concern about being lost in the shuffle, and their fear that their needs will be disregarded as the parents give priority to their own wishes and needs. Some children, especially young children, suffer with guilt over fantasied misdeeds that they feel may have contributed to the family quarrels and led to the divorce. Others feel that it is their responsibility to mend the broken marriage (Wallerstein & Kelly, 1980a).

The responses of the child also must be considered within the social context of the divorce and in particular within the loneliness and social isolation that so many children experience. Children face the tensions and sorrows of divorce with little help from anybody else. Fewer than 10% of the children in the California Children of Divorce study had any help at the time of the crisis from adults outside the family although many people, including neighbors, pediatricians, ministers, rabbis, and family friends, knew the family and the children (Wallerstein & Kelly, 1980a). Thus, another striking feature of divorce as a childhood stress is that it occurs in the absence of or falling away of customary support.

Developmental factors are critical to the responses of children and adolescents at the time of the marital rupture. Despite significant individual differences in the child, in the family, and in parent–child relations, the child's age and developmental stage appear to be the most important factors governing the initial response. The child's dominant needs, his or her capacity to perceive and understand family events, the central psychological preoccupation and conflict, the available repertoire of defense and coping strategies, and the dominant patterning of relationships and expectations all reflect the child's age and developmental stage.

A major finding in divorce research has been the common patterns of response within different age groups (Wallerstein & Kelly, 1980a). The age groups that share significant commonalities in perceptions, responses, underlying fantasies, and behaviors are the preschool ages 3 to 5, early school age or early latency ages 5 1/2 to 8, later school age or latency ages 8 to 11, and, finally, adolescent ages 12 to 18 (Kelly & Wallerstein, 1976; Wallerstein, 1977; Wallerstein & Kelly, 1974; 1975; 1980a). These responses, falling as they do into age-related groupings, may reflect children's responses to acute stress generally, not only their responses to marital rupture.

Observations about preschool children derived from longitudinal studies in two widely different regions, namely, Virginia and northern California, are remarkably similar in their findings (Hetherington, 1979; Hetherington et al., 1978; 1982; Wallerstein & Kelly, 1975, 1980a). Preschool children are likely to show regression following one parent's departure from the household, and the regression usually occurs in the most recent developmental achievement of the child. Intensified fears are frequent and are evoked by routine separations from the custodial parent during the day and at bedtime. Sleep disturbances are also frequent, with preoccupying fantasies of many of the little children being fear of abandonment by both parents. Yearning for the departed parent is intense. Young children are likely to become irritable and demanding and to behave aggressively with parents, with younger siblings, and with peers.

Children in the 5- to 8-year-old group are likely to show open grieving and are preoccupied with feelings of concern and longing for the departed parent. Many share the terrifying fantasy of replacement. "Will my daddy get a new dog, a new mommy, a new little boy?" were the comments of several boys in this age group. Little girls wove elaborate Madame Butterfly fantasies, asserting that the departed father would some day return to them, that he loved them "the best." Many of the children in this age group could not believe that the divorce would endure. About half suffered a precipitous decline in their school work (Kelly & Wallerstein, 1979).

In the 9- to 12-year-old group the central response often seems to be intense anger at one or both parents for causing the divorce. In addition, these children suffer with grief over the loss of the intact family and with anxiety, loneliness, and the humiliating sense of their own powerlessness. Youngsters in this age group often see one parent as the "good" parent and the other as "bad," and they appear especially vulnerable to the blandishments of one or the other parent to engage in marital battles. Children in later latency also have a high potential for assuming a helpful and empathic role in the care of a needy parent. School performances and peer relationships suffered a decline in approximately one-half of these children (Wallerstein & Kelly, 1974).

Adolescents are very vulnerable to their parents' divorce. The precipitation of acute depression, accompanied by suicidal preoccupation and acting out, is frequent enough to be alarming. Anger can be intense. Several instances have been reported of direct violent attacks on custodial parents by young adolescents who had not previously shown such behavior (Springer & Wallerstein, 1983). Preoccupied with issues of morality, adolescents may judge the parents' conduct during the marriage and the divorce, and they may identify with one parent and do battle against the other. Many become anxious about their own future entry into adulthood, concerned that they may experience marital failure like their parents (Wallerstein & Kelly, 1974). By way of contrast, however, researchers have also called attention to the adolescent's impressive capacity to grow in maturity and independence as they respond to the family crisis and the parents' need for help (Weiss, 1979a)....

## Long-Range Outcomes

The child's initial response to divorce should be distinguished from his or her long-range development and psychological adjustment. No single theme appears among all of those children who enhance, consolidate, or continue their good development after the divorce crisis has finally ended. Nor is there a single theme that appears among all of those who deteriorate either moderately or markedly. Instead, the author and her colleague (Wallerstein & Kelly, 1980a) have found a set of complex configurations in which the relevant components appear to include (a) the extent to which the parent has been able to resolve and put aside conflict and anger and to make use of the relief from conflict provided by the divorce (Emery, 1982; Jacobson, 1978 a, b, c); (b) the course of the custodial parent's handling of the child and the resumption or improvement of parenting within the home (Hess & Camara, 1979); (c) the extent to which the child does not feel rejected by the noncustodial or visiting parent and the extent to which this relationship has continued regularly and kept pace with the child's growth; (d) the extent to which the divorce has helped to attenuate or dilute a psychopathological parent–child relationship; (e) the range of personality assets and deficits that the child brought to the divorce, including both the child's history in the predivorce family and his or her capacities in the present, particularly intelligence, the capacity for fantasy, social maturity, and the ability to turn to peers and adults; (f) the availability to the child of a supportive human network (Tessman, 1977); (g) the absence in the child of continued anger and depression; and (h) the sex and age of the child....

## FUTURE DIRECTIONS

Despite the accumulating reports of the difficulties that many children in divorced families experience, society has on the whole been reluctant to regard children of divorce as a special group at risk. Notwithstanding the magnitude of the population affected and the widespread implications for public policy and law, community attention has been very limited; research has been poorly supported; and appropriate social, psychological, economic, or preventive measures have hardly begun to develop. Recently the alarm has been sounded in the national press about the tragically unprotected and foreshortened childhoods of children of divorce and their subsequent difficulties in reaching maturity (Winn, 1983). Perhaps this reflects a long-overdue awakening of community concern.

The agenda for research on marital breakdown, separation, divorce, and remarriage and the roads that families travel between each of these way stations [are] long and [have] been cited repeatedly in this [article]. The knowledge that we have acquired is considerable but the knowledge that we still lack is critical. More knowledge is essential in order to provide responsible advice to parents; to consult effectively with the wide range of other professionals whose daily work brings them in contact with these families; to design and mount education, treatment, or prevention programs; and to provide guidelines for informed social policy.

**AUTHOR'S NOTE:** The Center for the Family in Transition, of which the author is the Executive Director, is supported by a grant from the San Francisco Foundation. The Zellerback Family Fund supported the author's research in the California Children of Divorce Project, one of the sources for this [article]. A slightly different version of this paper has been published in *Psychiatry Update: The American Psychiatric Association Annual Review, Vol. III.* L. Grinspoon (Ed.), pp. 144–158, 1984.

## REFERENCES

Cherlin, A. J. (1981). *Marriage, divorce, remarriage.* Cambridge, MA: Harvard University Press.

Crohn, H., Brown, H., Walker, L., & Beir, J. (1981). Understanding and treating the child in the remarried family. In I. R. Stuart & L. E. Abt (Eds.), *Children of separation and divorce: Management and treatment.* New York: Van Nostrand Reinhold.

Emery, R. E. (1982). Interparental conflict and children of discord and divorce. *Psychological Bulletin, 92,* 310–330.

Felner, R. D., Stolberg, A. L., & Cowen, E. L. (1975). Crisis events and school mental health referral

patterns of young children. *Journal of Consulting and Clinical Psychology, 43,* 303–310.

Gardner, R. A. (1976). *Psychotherapy and children of divorce.* New York: Jason Aronson.

Goldstein, H. S. (1974). Reconstructed families: The second marriage and its children. *Psychiatric Quarterly, 48,* 433–440.

Hess, R. D., & Camara, K. A. (1979). Post-divorce relationships as mediating factors in the consequences of divorce for children. *Journal of Social Issues, 35,* 79–96.

Hetherington, E. (1979). Divorce: A child's perspective. *American Psychology, 34,* 79–96.

Hetherington, E., Cox, M., & Cox, R. (1978). The aftermath of divorce. In H. Stevens & M. Mathews (Eds.), *Mother–child relations.* Washington, DC: National Association for the Education of Young Children.

Hetherington, E. M., Cox, M., & Cox, R. (1982). Effects of divorce on parents and children. In M. E. Lamb (Ed.), *Nontraditional families: Parenting and child development.* Hillsdale, NJ: Lawrence Erlbaum Associates.

Jacobson, D. (1978a). The impact of marital separation/divorce on children: I. Parent–child separation and child adjustment. *Journal of Divorce, 1,* 341–360.

Jacobson, D. (1978b). The impact of marital separation/divorce on children: II. Interparent hostility and child adjustment. *Journal of Divorce, 2,* 3–20.

Jacobson, D. (1978c). The impact of marital separation/divorce on children: III. Parent–child communication and child adjustment, and regression analysis of findings from overall study. *Journal of Divorce, 2,* 175–194.

Jacobson, D. S. (1983). *Conflict, visiting and child adjustment in the stepfamily: A linked family system.* Paper presented at annual meeting of the American Orthopsychiatric Association, Boston.

Kalter, N. (1977). Children of divorce in an outpatient psychiatric population. *American Journal of Orthopsychiatry, 47,* 40–51.

Kelly, J. B., & Wallerstein, J. S. (1976). The effects of parental divorce: Experiences of the child in early latency. *American Journal of Orthopsychiatry, 46,* 20–32.

Kelly, J. B., & Wallerstein, J. S. (1979). The divorced child in the school. *National Principal, 59,* 51–58.

Morrison, A. L. (1982). *A prospective study of divorce: Its relation to children's development and parental functioning.* Unpublished dissertation, University of California at Berkeley.

Norton, A. J. (1980). The influence of divorce on traditional life cycle measures. *Journal of Marriage and the Family, 42,* 63–69.

Springer, C., & Wallerstein, J. S. (1983). Young adolescents' responses to their parents' divorces. In L. A. Kurdek (Ed.), *Children and divorce.* San Francisco: Jossey-Bass.

Tessman, L. H. (1977). *Children of parting parents.* New York: Jason Aronson.

Tooley, K. (1976). Antisocial behavior and social alienation post divorce: The "man of the house" and his mother. *American Journal of Orthopsychiatry, 46,* 33–42.

Wallerstein, J. S. (1977). Responses of the pre-school child to divorce: Those who cope. In M. F. McMillan & S. Henao (Eds.), *Child psychiatry: Treatment and research.* New York: Brunner/Mazel.

Wallerstein, J. S. (1978). Children of divorce: Preliminary report of a ten-year follow-up. In J. Anthony & C. Chilland (Eds.), *The child in his family* (Vol. 5). New York: Wiley.

Wallerstein, J. S. (1985). Parent–child relationships following divorce. In E. J. Anthony & G. Pollock (Eds.), *Parental influences in health and disease* (pp. 317–348). Boston: Little, Brown.

Wallerstein, J. S., & Kelly, J. B. (1974). The effects of parental divorce: The adolescent experience. In J. Anthony & C. Koupernik (Eds.), *The child in his family: Children at psychiatric risk* (Vol. 3). New York: Wiley.

Wallerstein, J. S., & Kelly, J. B. (1975). The effects of parental divorce: The experiences of the preschool child. *American Journal of Orthopsychiatry, 46,* 256–269.

Wallerstein, J. S., & Kelly, J. B. (1980a). *Surviving the breakup: How children and parents cope with divorce.* New York: Basic Books.

Weiss, R. S. (1979a). *Going it alone: The family life and social situation of the single parent.* New York: Basic Books.

Weiss, R. S. (1979b). Growing up a little faster. *Journal of Social Issues, 35,* 97–111.

Winn, M. (8 May 1983). The loss of childhood. *The New York Times Magazine.*

Zill, N. (22 March 1983). *Divorce, marital conflict, and children's mental health: Research findings and policy recommendations.* Testimony before Subcommittee on Family and Human Services, United States Senate Subcommittee on Labor and Human Resources.

# NO

David H. Demo and
Alan C. Acock

# THE IMPACT OF DIVORCE
# ON CHILDREN

*With the acceleration of the divorce rate from the mid-1960s to the early 1980s, the number of nontraditional families (such as single-parent families and reconstituted families) have increased relative to intact, first-time nuclear families. This article reviews empirical evidence addressing the relationship between divorce, family composition, and children's well-being. Although not entirely consistent, the pattern of empirical findings suggests that children's emotional adjustment, gender-role orientation, and antisocial behavior are affected by family structure, whereas other dimensions of well-being are unaffected. But the review indicates that these findings should be interpreted with caution because of the methodological deficiencies of many of the studies on which these findings are based. Several variables, including the level of family conflict, may be central variables mediating the effect of family structure on children.*

The purpose of this article is to review and assess recent empirical evidence on the impact of divorce on children, concentrating on studies of nonclinical populations published in the last decade. We also direct attention to a number of important theoretical and methodological considerations in the study of family structure and youthful well-being. We begin by briefly describing some of the theoretical propositions and assumptions that guide research in this area.

## THEORETICAL UNDERPINNINGS

Consistent with the Freudian assumption that a two-parent group constitutes the minimal unit for appropriate sex-typed identification, anthropologists, sociologists, and social psychologists have long maintained the necessity of such a group for normal child development. Representative of structural-functional theorizing, Parsons and Bales argued that one of the basic functions of the family is to serve as a stable, organically integrated "factory" in which human personalities are formed.

From David H. Demo and Alan C. Acock, "The Impact of Divorce on Children," *Journal of Marriage and the Family,* vol. 50, no. 3 (August 1988). Copyright © 1988 by The National Council on Family Relations, 3989 Central Avenue, NE, Suite #550, Minneapolis, MN 55421. Reprinted by permission. Notes and references omitted.

Similarly, social learning theory emphasizes the importance of role models, focusing on parents as the initial and primary reinforcers of child behavior (Bandura and Walters, 1963). Much of the research adopting this perspective centers on parent-child similarities, analyzing the transmission of response patterns and the inhibitory or disinhibitory effect of parental models. The presence of the same-sex parent is assumed to be crucial in order for the child to learn appropriate sex-typed behavior. This assumption is shared by developmental and symbolic interactionist theories, various cognitive approaches to socialization, and confluence theory, as well as anthropological theories.

It logically follows that departures from the nuclear family norm are problematic for the child's development, especially for adolescents, inasmuch as this represents a crucial stage in the developmental process. Accordingly, a large body of research literature deals with father absence, the effects of institutionalization, and a host of "deficiencies" in maturation, such as those having to do with cognitive development, achievement, moral learning, and conformity. This focus has pointed to the crucial importance of both parents' presence but also has suggested that certain causes for parental absence may accentuate any negative effects...

**Divorce and Family Structure**

In examining [the] research,... it is important to distinguish between studies investigating the effects of family structure and those investigating the effects of divorce. Most studies compare intact units and single-parent families, guided by the assumption that the latter family structure is precipitated by divorce. Of course, this is not always the case. Single-parent families consist of those with parents who have never married, those formed by the permanent separation of parents, and those precipitated by the death of a parent. Simple comparisons between one- and two-parent families are also suspect in that *two*-parent families are not monolithic. First-time or nondivorced units differ from divorced, remarried units in which stepparents are involved. In addition, little recognition has been given to the fact that families of different types may exhibit varying levels of instability or conflict, a potentially confounding variable in establishing the effects of family structure. In short, most investigations of the linkage between family structure and youthful well-being have failed to recognize the complexity of present-day families....

Bearing in mind these conceptual distinctions, we now move to a systematic review of recent evidence on the impact of divorce on children and adolescents.

## EXISTING RESEARCH

A substantial amount of research has examined the effects of family structure on children's social and psychological well-being. Many studies document negative consequences for children whose parents divorce and for those living in single-parent families. But most studies have been concerned with limited dimensions of a quite complex problem. Specifically, the research to date has typically (a) examined the effects of divorce or father absence on children, ignoring the effects on adolescents; (b) examined only selected dimensions of children's well-being; (c) compared intact units and single-parent families but not recognized important variations (e.g., levels of marital instability and conflict) within these structures; and (d) relied on cross-sectional designs to assess developmental processes.

Social and psychological well-being includes aspects of personal adjustment, self-concept, interpersonal relationships, antisocial behavior, and cognitive functioning....

### Personal Adjustment

Personal adjustment is operationalized in various ways by different investigators but includes such variables as self-control, leadership, responsibility, independence, achievement orientation, aggressiveness, and gender-role orientation....

On the basis of her review of research conducted between 1970 and 1980, Cashion (1984: 483) concludes: "The evidence is overwhelming that after the initial trauma of divorce, the children are as emotionally well-adjusted in these [female-headed] families as in two-parent families." Investigations of long-term effects (Acock and Kiecolt, 1988; Kulka and Weingarten, 1979) suggest that, when socioeconomic status is controlled, adolescents who have experienced a parental divorce or separation have only slightly lower levels of adult adjustment....

While their findings are not definitive, Kinard and Reinherz speculate that either "the effects of parental divorce on children diminish over time; or that the impact of marital disruption is less severe for preschool-age children than for school-age children" (1986: 291). Children's age at the time of disruption may also mediate the impact of these events on other dimensions of their well-being (e.g., self-esteem or gender-role orientation) and thus will be discussed in greater detail below.... But two variables that critically affect children's adjustment to divorce are marital discord and children's gender.

*Marital discord.*... [E]xtensive data on children who had experienced their parents' divorce indicated that, although learning of the divorce and adjusting to the loss of the noncustodial parent were painful, children indicated that these adjustments were preferable to living in conflict. Many studies report that children's adjustment to divorce is facilitated under conditions of low parental conflict—both prior to *and* subsequent to the divorce (Guidubaldi, Cleminshaw, Perry, Nastasi, and Lightel, 1986; Jacobson, 1978; Lowenstein and Koopman, 1978; Porter and O'Leary, 1980; Raschke and Raschke, 1979; Rosen, 1979).

*Children's gender.* Children's gender may be especially important in mediating the effects of family disruption, as most of the evidence suggests that adjustment problems are more severe and last for longer periods of time among boys (Hess and Camara, 1979; Hetherington, 1979; Hetherington, Cox, and Cox, 1978, 1979, 1982; Wallerstein, 1984; Wallerstein and Kelly, 1980b). Guidubaldi and Perry (1985) found, controlling for social class, that boys in divorced families manifested significantly more maladaptive symptoms and behavior problems than boys in intact families. Girls differed only on the dimension of locus of control; girls in divorced households scored significantly higher than their counterparts in intact households....

While custodial mothers provide girls with same-sex role models, most boys have to adjust to living without same-sex parents. In examining boys and girls living in intact families and in different custodial arrangements, Santrock and

Warshak (1979) found that few effects could be attributed to family structure per se, but that children living with opposite-sex parents (mother-custody boys and father-custody girls) were not as well adjusted on measures of competent social behavior....

Along related lines, a number of researchers have examined gender-role orientation and, specifically, the relation of father absence to boys' personality development. Most of the evidence indicates that boys without adult male role models demonstrate more feminine behavior (Biller, 1976; Herzog and Sudia, 1973; Lamb, 1977a), except in lower-class families (Biller, 1981b). A variety of studies have shown that fathers influence children's gender role development to be more traditional because, compared to mothers, they more routinely differentiate between masculine and feminine behaviors and encourage greater conformity to conventional gender roles (Biller, 1981a; Biller and Davids, 1973; Bronfenbrenner, 1961; Heilbrun, 1965; Lamb, 1977b; Noller, 1978).... But it should be reiterated that these effects have been attributed to father absence and thus would be expected to occur among boys in all female-headed families, not simply those that have experienced divorce....

[M]ost of the research on boys' adjustment fails to consider the quality or quantity of father-child contact or the availability of alternative male role models (e.g., foster father, grandfather, big brother, other male relatives, coach, friend, etc.), which makes it difficult to assess the impact of changing family structure on boys' behavior. There are also limitations imposed by conceptualizing and measuring masculinity-femininity as a bipolar construct (Bem, 1974; Constantinople, 1973; Worell,

1978), and there is evidence that boys and girls in father-absent families are better described as androgynous (Kurdek and Siesky, 1980a).

*Positive outcomes of divorce....* [T]he tendency of children in single-parent families to display more androgynous behavior may be interpreted as a beneficial effect. Because of father absence, children in female-headed families are not pressured as strongly as their counterparts in two-parent families to conform to traditional gender roles. These children frequently assume a variety of domestic responsibilities to compensate for the absent parent (Weiss, 1979), thereby broadening their skills and competencies and their definitions of gender-appropriate behavior. Divorced parents also must broaden their behavioral patterns to meet increased parenting responsibilities, thereby providing more androgynous role models. Kurdek and Siesky (1980a: 250) give the illustration that custodial mothers often "find themselves needing to acquire and demonstrate a greater degree of dominance, assertiveness, and independence while custodial fathers may find themselves in situations eliciting high degrees of warmth, nurturance, and tenderness."

Aside from becoming more androgynous, adolescents living in single-parent families are characterized by greater maturity, feelings of efficacy, and an internal locus of control (Guidubaldi and Perry, 1985; Kalter, Alpern, Spence, and Plunkett, 1984; Wallerstein and Kelly, 1974; Weiss, 1979). For adolescent girls this maturity stems partly from the status and responsibilities they acquire in peer and confidant relationships with custodial mothers....

There is evidence (Kurdek et al., 1981) that children and adolescents with an internal locus of control and a high level of interpersonal reasoning adjust more easily to their parents' divorce and that children's divorce adjustment is related to their more global personal adjustment.

## Self-Concept...

*Marital discord....* [F]amily structure is unrelated to children's self-esteem (Feldman and Feldman, 1975; Kinard and Reinherz, 1984; Parish, 1981; Parish, Dostal, and Parish, 1981), but parental discord is negatively related (Amato, 1986; Berg and Kelly, 1979; Cooper, Holman, and Braithwaite, 1983; Long, 1986; Raschke and Raschke, 1979; Slater and Haber, 1984). Because this conclusion is based on diverse samples of boys and girls of different ages in different living arrangements, the failure to obtain effects of family structure suggests either that family composition really does not matter for children's self-concept or that family structure alone is an insufficient index of familial relations. Further, these studies suggest that divorce per se does not adversely affect children's self-concept. Cashion's (1984) review of the literature indicates that children living in single-parent families suffer no losses to self-esteem, except in situations where the child's family situation is stigmatized (Rosenberg, 1979)....

## Cognitive Functioning

... Many... studies find that family conflict and disruption are associated with inhibited cognitive functioning (Blanchard and Biller, 1971; Feldman and Feldman, 1975; Hess and Camara, 1979; Kinard and Reinherz, 1986; Kurdek, 1981; Radin, 1981).... In this section we summarize the differential effects of family disruption on academic performance by gender and social class and offer some insights as to the mechanisms by which these effects occur.

*Children's gender.* Some studies suggest that negative effects of family disruption on academic performance are stronger for boys than for girls (Chapman, 1977; Werner and Smith, 1982), but most of the evidence suggests similar effects by gender (Hess and Camara, 1979; Kinard and Reinherz, 1986; Shinn, 1978). While females traditionally outscore males on standardized tests of verbal skills and males outperform females on mathematical skills, males who have experienced family disruption generally score higher on verbal aptitude (Radin, 1981). Thus, the absence of a father may result in a "feminine" orientation toward education (Fowler and Richards, 1978; Herzog and Sudia, 1973). But an important and unresolved question is whether this pattern results from boys acquiring greater verbal skills in mother-headed families or from deficiencies in mathematical skills attributable to father absence. The latter explanation is supported by evidence showing that father-absent girls are disadvantaged in mathematics (Radin, 1981).

*Children's race....* [M]ost studies show academic achievement among black children to be unaffected by family structure (Hunt and Hunt, 1975, 1977; Shinn, 1978; Solomon, Hirsch, Scheinfeld, and Jackson, 1972). Svanum, Bringle, and McLaughlin (1982) found, controlling for social class, that there are no significant effects of father absence on cognitive performance for white or black children. Again, these investigations focus on family composition and demonstrate that the effects of family structure on academic performance do not vary as much by race as by social class, but race differences in the impact of divorce remain largely unexplored....

*Family socioeconomic status....* When social class is controlled, children in female-headed families fare no worse than children from two-parent families on measures of intelligence (Bachman, 1970; Kopf, 1970), academic achievement (Shinn, 1978; Svanum et al., 1982), and educational attainment (Bachman, O'Malley, and Johnston, 1978).... In order to disentangle the intricate effects of family structure and SES [socioeconomic status] on children's cognitive performance, family researchers need to examine the socioeconomic history of intact families and those in which disruption occurs, to examine the economic resources available to children at various stages of cognitive development, and to assess changes in economic resources and family relationships that accompany marital disruption.

*Family processes....* First, family disruption alters daily routines and work schedules and imposes additional demands on adults and children living in single-parent families (Amato, 1987; Furstenberg and Nord, 1985; Hetherington et al., 1983; Weiss, 1979) Most adolescents must assume extra domestic and child care responsibilities, and financial conditions require some to work part-time. These burdens result in greater absenteeism, tardiness, and truancy among children in single-parent households (Hetherington et al., 1983). Second, children in recently disrupted families are prone to experience emotional and behavioral problems such as aggression, distractibility, dependency, anxiety, and withdrawal (Hess and Camara, 1979; Kinard and Reinherz, 1984), factors that may help to explain problems in school conduct and the propensity of teachers to label and stereotype children from broken families (Hess and Camara, 1979; Hetherington et al., 1979, 1983). Third, emotional problems may interfere with study patterns, while demanding schedules reduce the time available for single parents to help with homework....

## Interpersonal Relationships...

*Peer relations.* Studies of preschool children (Hetherington et al., 1979) and preadolescents (Santrock, 1975; Wyman, Cowen, Hightower, and Pedro-Carroll, 1985) suggest that children in disrupted families are less sociable: they have fewer close friends, spend less time with friends, and participate in fewer shared activities. Stolberg and Anker (1983) observe that children in families disrupted by divorce exhibit psychopathology in interpersonal relations, often behaving in unusual and inappropriate ways. Other studies suggest that the effects are temporary. Kinard and Reinherz (1984) found no differences in peer relations among children in intact and disrupted families, but those in recently disrupted families displayed greater hostility. Kurdek et al. (1981) conducted a two-year follow-up of children whose parents had divorced and showed that relationships with peers improved after the divorce and that personal adjustment was facilitated by opportunities to discuss experiences with peers, some of whom had similar experiences....

*Dating patterns.* Hetherington (1972) reported that adolescent girls whose fathers were absent prior to age 5 had difficulties in heterosexual relations, but Hainline and Feig's (1978) analyses of female college students indicated that early and later father-absent women could not be distinguished on measures of romanticism and heterosexual attitudes.

An examination of dating and sexual behavior among female college students found that women with divorced parents began dating slightly later than those in intact families, but women in both groups were socially active (Kalter, Riemer, Brickman, and Chen, 1985). Booth, Brinkerhoff, and White (1984) reported that, compared to college students with intact families, those whose parents were divorced or permanently separated exhibited higher levels of dating activity, and this activity increased further if parental or parent-child conflict persisted during and after the divorce.... Regarding adolescent sexual behavior, the findings consistently demonstrate that males and females not living with both biological parents initiate coitus earlier than their counterparts in intact families (Hogan and Kitagawa, 1985; Newcomer and Udry, 1987). But Newcomer and Udry propose that, because parental marital status is also associated with a broad range of deviant behaviors, these effects may stem from general loss of parental control rather than simply loss of control over sexual behavior. Studies of antisocial behavior support this interpretation.

## Antisocial Behavior

Many studies over the years have linked juvenile delinquency, deviancy, and antisocial behavior to children living in broken homes (Bandura and Walters, 1959; Glueck and Glueck, 1962; Hoffman, 1971; McCord, McCord, and Thurber, 1962; Santrock, 1975; Stolberg and Anker, 1983; Tooley, 1976; Tuckman and Regan, 1966). Unfortunately, these studies either relied on clinical samples or failed to control for social class and other factors related to delinquency. However,... a number of studies involving large representative samples and controlling for social class provide similar findings (Dornbusch, Carlsmith, Bushwall, Ritter, Leiderman, Hastorf, and Gross, 1985; Kalter et al., 1985; Peterson and Zill, 1986; Rickel and Langner, 1985). Kalter et al. (1985) studied 522 teenage girls and found that girls in divorced families committed more delinquent acts (e.g., drug use, larceny, skipping school) than their counterparts in intact families. Dornbusch et al. (1985) examined a representative national sample of male and female youth aged 12–17 and found that adolescents in mother-only households were more likely than their counterparts in intact families to engage in deviant acts, partly because of their tendency to make decisions independent of parental input. The presence of an additional adult (a grandparent, an uncle, a lover, a friend) in mother-only households increased control over adolescent behavior and lowered rates of deviant behavior, which suggests that "there are functional equivalents of two-parent families—nontraditional groupings that can do the job of parenting" (1985: 340)....

A tentative conclusion based on the evidence reviewed here is that antisocial behavior is less likely to occur in families where two adults are present, whether as biological parents, stepparents, or some combination of biological parents and other adults. Short-term increases in antisocial behavior may occur during periods of disruption, however, as children adjust to restructured relationships and parents struggle to maintain consistency in disciplining (Rickel and Langner, 1985).... Peterson and Zill (1986) demonstrated that, when social class was controlled, behavior problems were as likely to occur among adolescents living in intact families characterized by persistent conflict as among those living in disrupted families.... Peterson and Zill found that "poor parent-child relationships lead to more negative child behavior, yet maintaining good relationships with parents can go some way in reducing the effects of conflict and disruption" (1986: 306). Hess and Camara's (1979) analyses of a much smaller sample yielded a similar conclusion: aggressive behavior in children was unrelated to family type but was more common in situations characterized by infrequent or low-quality parent-child interaction and parental discord....

## CONCLUSIONS

There is reason to question the validity of the family composition hypothesis. Theoretically, it has been assumed that the nuclear family is the norm and, by implication, that any departure from it is deviant and therefore deleterious to those involved. Even if this were the case, no theoretical perspective recognizes that these effects may be short-lived or otherwise mitigated by compensatory mechanisms and alternative role models. In the absence of a parent, it is possible that developmental needs are met by other actors.

It is simplistic and inaccurate to think of divorce as having uniform consequences for children. The consequences of divorce vary along different dimensions of well-being, characteristics of children (e.g., predivorce adjustment, age at the time of disruption) and characteristics of families (e.g., socioeconomic history, pre- and postdivorce level of conflict, parent-child relationships, and maternal employment). Most of the evidence reviewed here suggests that some sociodemographic characteristics of chil-

dren, such as race and gender, are not as important as characteristics of families in mediating the effects of divorce. Many studies report boys to be at a greater disadvantage, but these differences usually disappear when other relevant variables are controlled. At present, there are too few methodologically adequate studies comparing white and black children to conclude that one group is more damaged by family disruption than the other.

Characteristics of families, on the other hand, are critical to youthful well-being. Family conflict contributes to many problems in social development, emotional stability, and cognitive skills (Edwards, 1987; Kurdek, 1981), and these effects continue long after the divorce is finalized. Slater and Haber (1984) report that ongoing high levels of conflict, whether in intact or divorced homes, produce lower self-esteem, increased anxiety, and a loss of self-control. Conflict also reduces the child's attraction to the parents (White, Brinkerhoff, and Booth, 1985). Rosen (1979) concludes that parental separation is more beneficial for children than continued conflict.... Such conflict and hostility may account for adolescent adjustment problems whether the family in question goes through divorce or remains intact (Hoffman, 1971). The level of conflict is thus an important dimension of family interaction that can precipitate changes in family structure and affect children's well-being.

Maternal employment is another variable mediating the consequences of divorce for children. Divorced women often find the dual responsibilities of provider and parent to be stressful (Bronfenbrenner, 1976). But studies indicate that women who work prior to the divorce do not find continued employment problematic (Kinard and Reinherz, 1984); the problem occurs for women who enter the labor force after the divorce and who view the loss of time with their children as another detriment to the children that is caused by the divorce (Kinard and Reinherz, 1984). As a practical matter, the alternative to employment for single-parent mothers is likely to be poverty or, at best, economic dependency. The effects of maternal employment on children's well-being need to be compared to the effects of nonemployment and consequent poverty.

Other bases of social support for single-parent mothers and their children must also be examined. The presence of strong social networks may ease the parents' and, presumably, the child's adjustment after a divorce (Milardo, 1987; Savage et al., 1978). However, women who are poor, have many children, and must work long hours are likely to have limited social networks and few friends. Typically, the single mother and her children are also isolated from her ex-husband's family (Anspach, 1976). By reuniting with her family of origin, the mother may be isolated from her community and new social experiences for herself and her children (McLanahan, Wedemeyer, and Adelberg, 1981). Kinship ties are usually strained, as both biological parents and parents-in-law are more critical of the divorce than friends are (Spanier and Thompson, 1984). Little has been done to relate these considerations about kinship relations and social networks of divorced women to the well-being of children and adolescents. We believe that these social relations are important, but empirical verification is needed.

# CHALLENGE QUESTIONS

## Are Children of Divorced Parents at Greater Risk?

1. How should parents help their children adjust to divorce? What types of educational and treatment programs should be established to support children of divorce?

2. Which do you feel is more damaging to children, divorce or continuing to live in a conflictual environment? Give reasons (and possibly research) to support your stance.

3. What do you feel is the most significant factor affecting children's adjustment following divorce? Why? How would this affect treatment strategies for children?

4. Demo and Acock list several positive outcomes of divorce. Why do you think these occur, and can you think of other possible positive outcomes?

# PART 4

# Mental Health

*A mental disorder is often defined as a pattern of thinking or behaving that is either disruptive to others or uncomfortable for the person with the disorder. This definition seems straightforward; however, is it universally applicable? Certain patterns of sexuality and drinking behavior fit this definition, but does this make them "diseases" in the medical sense? Some researchers have recently argued that stress related to abortion is often severe enough to be labeled a disorder—specifically, "postabortion syndrome." Is this a legitimate disease requiring treatment?*

- Can Sex Be an Addiction?

- Is Alcoholism a Disease?

- Does Abortion Have Severe Psychological Effects?

# ISSUE 10

## Can Sex Be an Addiction?

**YES: Patrick Carnes,** from "Progress in Sex Addiction: An Addiction Perspective," *SIECUS Report* (June/July 1986)

**NO: Marty Klein,** from "Why There's No Such Thing as Sexual Addiction—And Why It Really Matters," *Annual Meeting of the Society for the Scientific Study of Sex* (November 1989)

### ISSUE SUMMARY

**YES:** Patrick Carnes, a therapist who has established an inpatient program for sexual dependency, argues that sexual addictions do exist and that their treatment should be handled in a way similar to other addictions.

**NO:** Marty Klein, a nationally certified sex educator, claims that promoting the concept of sexual addictions has negative consequences, such as relieving people of the responsibility for controlling their sexual impulses and trivializing sexuality.

Sex and sexual behavior have always been hot topics. Sex in advertising, sex on television and in the movies, and sex education are but a few of the specific areas of controversy. In recent years, controversies have been brewing around whether or not sex can be addictive. Some therapists argue that alcoholism and problems like overeating have been viewed as addictions, so why couldn't certain sexual behaviors sharing the same characteristics also be seen as addictions? Why couldn't a person's excessive masturbation or constant sexual activity be an indication that he or she is "addicted" to sex?

This way of understanding people with sexual problems has many significant implications. For clinical psychologists, viewing patients as sexual addicts would indicate the type of treatment they should use. Group-oriented, "12-step" treatment programs—such as that used by Alcoholics Anonymous—would probably be the treatment of choice. An addiction approach would also make some sexual behaviors pathologies; that is, the "disease" that causes the addiction would also be viewed as causing the sexual behaviors. Therefore, the person exhibiting the behaviors would not be held responsible for them, and no moral judgments about the behaviors could be rendered.

In the selections that follow, Patrick Carnes affirms the addiction view of problematic sexual behavior. He argues that "a significant number of people have identified themselves as sexual addicts: people whose sexual behavior has become 'unstoppable' despite serious consequences." He explores progress in the field of sexual addiction from what he calls an "addiction-ologist" point of view. Carnes proposes that sexual addictions gain their momentum from certain personal belief systems, where shame about sex and sex-negative messages are prevalent. Because of this, he suggests that treatment of sexual addiction should include the addict's family and significant others. He also sees 12-step approaches and inpatient rehabilitation as viable treatment options.

In opposition, Marty Klein denies that sexual addictions even exist. He maintains that the very concept of sexual addiction has serious flaws. According to Klein, the sexual addiction model is "moralistic, arbitrary, misinformed, and narrow." Not only does this addiction concept have negative effects and implications for the mental health community, he argues, but it also has many unwanted political ramifications. Foremost, perhaps, is the notion that sex is dangerous. Klein explains why this and other implications are false.

| POINT | COUNTERPOINT |
|---|---|
| • Sexual addiction is a valid concept referring to a specific set of symptoms exhibited by a number of people. | • The concept of sexual addiction is arbitrary and misinformed. |
| • Sexual addicts are persons for whom sexual behavior has become "unstoppable." | • Virtually everyone has the ability to control and express her or his sexual impulses. |
| • Sexual addiction as a diagnostic category is valid and useful for treatment. | • The diagnosis of sexual addiction leads people to deny responsibility for their sexuality. |
| • Sexual addiction can be viewed as a disease. | • Sexual addiction makes a disease out of what often falls into a normal range of behavior. |

# YES

Patrick Carnes

## PROGRESS IN SEX ADDICTION: AN ADDICTION PERSPECTIVE

Over the last fifteen years the new professional discipline of addictionology has emerged from the extensive foundations laid in both research and treatment of alcohol and drug addictions. Led by organizations like the American Academy of Addictionology and scholarly publications like the *Journal of Addictive Behaviors*, researchers have found that different addictive behaviors (e.g. compulsive eating, alcoholism, compulsive gambling, smoking) have much in common. It is not surprising that sex has only recently been added to the list, given the guilt and shame still attached to the subject. Nor should it surprise us that the professional controversy far exceeds that of other forms of addiction.

### DEFINING SEXUAL ADDICTION

The fact remains that a significant number of people have identified themselves as sexual addicts: people whose sexual behavior has become "unstoppable" despite serious consequences. These consequences include the physical (self-mutilation, sexual violence, disease, unwanted pregnancy), occupational (large financial losses, job losses, sexual abuse and harassment, withdrawal of professional licenses), and familial (loss of relationships, impaired family functioning, sexual abuse, sexual dysfunction). In addition to those problems, one of the most frequent mental health complaints of sexual addicts is suicidal ideation.

Another frequent complaint of "recovering" sex addicts is that the mental health community does not acknowledge their problem. They become enraged when sexologists dismiss sexual addiction as a problem of sexual misinformation, or excessive guilt due to a cultural dissonance, or not a serious or widespread problem. I recently spoke at a Sexaholics Anonymous convention in which participants were rageful and moved to tears over statements made by professionals in a *New York Times* article. Stepping back from the intensity of their feelings, I had to reflect that compared to the amount of time taken to gain acceptance for the concept of alcoholism, the progress made in sexual addiction is remarkable.

From Patrick Carnes, "Progress in Sex Addiction: An Addiction Perspective," *SIECUS Report*, vol. 14, no. 6 (June/July 1986). Copyright © 1986 by Sex Information and Education Council of the U.S., Inc., 130 West 42nd Street, New York, NY 10036. 212/819-9770. Reprinted by permission.

My purpose here is to summarize this progress from an addictionologist's point of view and to specify further challenges which will require the close cooperation of specialists in addiction and professionals in human sexuality.

## CASE STUDY

Consider the case of Larry, a 45-year-old manager of a computer programming department. Larry was arrested for exhibitionism and sent to a court-mandated group for eight sessions. The group focused on the exposing behavior, but from Larry's point of view it was merely the tip of the iceberg. He had a 15-year collection of pornography, carefully cataloged and indexed. He saw prostitutes three to four times a month and masturbated daily—sometimes five times in one day. His sexual relationship with his wife, Joan, had diminished largely due to her rage at his increasing sexual demands and his sexual affairs with other women. Part of her response was to overeat so much that she gained over 125 pounds.

Larry also used marijuana and cocaine, ironic considering his intense hatred of his dad's drinking problem, another form of substance abuse. A further irony was that his wife bought the drugs for Larry because, as she later reported, it was better to have him stoned at home than out cruising around.

Larry lived in constant fear of discovery that his children, wife, or church community would find out about the range of his activities. He hated his life and was constantly trying to cope financially to support his sexual activities and drug use.

Venereal disease created a crisis in the marriage, and with the help of their physician, Larry and Joan entered a hospital outpatient program for sexual addiction. Larry found that he was not alone in his problems. Many of the patients had the same or similar issues. In an interview with Larry two-and-a-half years later, upon completion of his treatment, he recounted that there were three main changes in his life since he began treatment. First, his sexuality had shifted dramatically. No longer was he pursuing a desire that he never seemed able to satisfy. Now he and Joan were learning and enjoying sex in different ways than they had believed possible. Second, he had time for work and play. And third, he was no longer living in constant jeopardy of being discovered or running out of money.

In *Out of the Shadows: Understanding Sexual Addiction*, I describe a model (see Figure 1) in which the principle momentum for the addiction in addicts like Larry comes from a personal belief system. This belief system captures all the cultural and familial messages about sex and relationships. When these messages are very sex negative and are coupled with low self esteem, core beliefs about one's own innate shamefulness emerge. Shame is basically a problem of mastery (why is it other kids can do this and I can't?). When the shame is sexual (why is it other people seem to be in control of their sexual feelings and I am not?), the environment for obsessive behavior is at its optimum.

## IMPAIRED THINKING

Through these lenses the addict's thinking becomes impaired, literally, to the point of loss of contact with reality. Addicts talk of entering an altered state parallel to the Jekyll-Hyde shift where even common sense considerations disappear. Denial and delusion govern their

*Figure 1*

**The Addictive System**

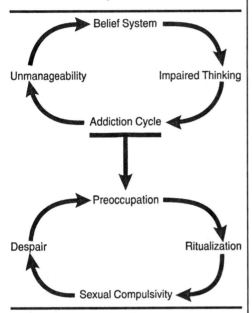

From Patrick Carnes, *Out of the Shadows: Understanding Sexual Addiction* (MInneapolis, MN: CompCare Publishers, 1983). Copyright © 1983 by Patrick Carnes, Ph.D. Reprinted by permission of CompCare Publishers.

lives. One addict, for example, told of following a woman into what he thought was a restaurant only to discover himself standing in the lobby of a police station to which the woman had fled.

Because of the impaired thinking, an addiction cycle perpetuates itself through four phases:

• preoccupation in which the addict enters a trance-like obsession

• ritualization that enhances the trance

• sexual behavior that is often not rewarding

• despair that, once again, the behavior has been repeated.

One way to stave off the despair is to start the preoccupation over again. And the cycle becomes the recursive series of events which dominates the addict's life. With this process underway, the addict's life becomes more and more unmanageable, thus confirming the basic feelings of unworthiness that are the core of the addict's belief system.

Larry's secretive life was embedded in this process of shame, powerlessness, and despair. He wanted very much to stop the pain, but the only things that seemed to help were his rituals of indexing his pornography, finding a prostitute, or, when unable to pay for sex, exposing himself. Larry's addictive process presents a very common model familiar to addiction professionals. Shame is a key factor in all addictions. Sexual shame, especially in a sex-negative culture, is particularly virulent.

## MULTIPLE ADDICTIONS

Other familiar factors in Larry's case are multiple addictions, both in the addict and his immediate family members. Golden Valley Health Center, a suburban Minneapolis hospital, has a twenty bed in-patient treatment program for sexual addiction called the Sexual Dependency Unit. I serve as a program consultant to that facility. Seventy-one percent of the patient population reports multiple addiction or compulsive behaviors. In fact, thirty-eight percent of the program's patients are chemically dependent; another thirty-eight percent have eating disorders. Compulsive gambling, spending, caffeine use, and smoking are also frequent complaints.

The Golden Valley Program represents, in a concrete manner, the emerging recognition among addictionologists that not only do addictions occur concurrently, but in mutually reinforcing ways. Clinicians often observe that the treatment of one addiction will result in the flourishing of another. Patients, for example, who have both alcoholism and sexual addiction often observe that their alcohol use was a way to anesthetize their pain around their out-of-control sexual behavior. They further comment that their alcoholism was relatively easy to deal with compared to their sexual acting out.

Such observations are at odds significantly with the traditional "disease" model of chemical dependency in which alcoholism and drug addiction are perceived as the primary "illness" and the sexual behavior as resulting from it. Unfortunately, there are still alcoholism treatment centers where patients are told that their sexual behavior will straighten out once they get sober.

Major progress is being made, however, in terms of understanding the relationships among the various addictions. One exciting example is the research of Milkman and his colleagues (*Advances in Alcohol and Substance Abuse*, 1983) on the psychobiological impact of hormone interactions on addiction pathology. For their research purposes, they use a matrix developed around three categories of addictions: the arousal addictions (e.g., gambling, sex, stimulant drugs, and high risk behaviors), the satiation addictions (e.g., overeating, depressant drugs, and alcohol), and the fantasy addictions (e.g., psychedelic drugs, marijuana, and mystical/artistic preoccupations). Beyond their research method of categorization, the conceptualization of models of poly-addiction will go far in broadening traditional models of addiction. They will also as-sist in answering the questions many practitioners have about cross-tolerance effects.

## FAMILY SYSTEM THEORY

Many addiction professionals are using systems theory as a conceptual foundation for their work not only because it is an integrative paradigm but also because it is a *growth* versus *illness* model. One of the systems identified, for example, by most addiction specialists as key to the self-defeating patterns of the addiction is the family system. Note in Larry's story how other family members had their own addiction patterns (father's drinking and wife's overeating). Observe also Joan's co-participation in the illness through the purchasing of Larry's drugs. Even her weight gain was a statement about their sexuality.

As part of the etiology of the addictive system, extreme family behavior such as extreme rigidity or chaos are common to people who have dependency problems. Further, I describe in a new book now in press a survey of 300 sexual addicts and the incidence of childhood sexual abuse. Sixty-five percent of the women and forty-five percent of the men report having been sexually abused. For a number of reasons I specify in the book, I believe that this is, in fact, underreported.

As part of treatment, the family or significant others are vital to the recovery process. When Golden Valley Health Center staff conducted six-month post-treatment evaluations, they discovered only one common denominator to all the patients who suffered relapse: no family members, partners, or significant others had participated in the family week of treatment.

Systems theory also allows a more organic approach to treatment. For example, comparisons between alcoholism and sexual addiction treatment can create misperceptions about the course of treatment. A better comparison can be made by looking at eating disorders. There are 34 million obese and 14 million morbidly obese persons in the United States. Yet, like sexual addiction, we have been very slow to address this problem. In compulsive overeating, patients are not asked to give up eating, but rather to learn how to eat differently. Eating patterns, environments, foods, and rituals shift so that they enhance rather than destroy the patient's life.

Similarly, sexual addiction treatment helps patients reclaim their sexuality by a primary refocusing of their sexual behavior. Some have assumed that the abstinence focus of alcohol programs has been directly translated to sex addiction programs, and they feared that treatment in these programs would be a sex-negative experience. Of the four hospital based programs I know, treatment staff work very hard to help their patients achieve the goal of sexual enhancement. Part of review criteria for all such programs should include treatment goals that encourage healthy and varied forms of sexual expression.

## TREATMENT OUTCOME

In terms of treatment outcomes, the early six-month evaluation of Golden Valley Health Center patients is encouraging. This internal study of 30 patients has all the obvious limitations of a preliminary study done on the first patient cohort to reach six months. It is also not a large sample, nor is it conducted over a long period of time. Nor were the forms con-

sistently completed. But the information obtained from this preliminary study is positive. For quality of life indicators, patients reported significant improvement in the following areas:

- Family Life 76%
- Job Performance 81%
- General Physical Health 80%
- Self-Image 71%

For program outcomes, patients reported:

- Having no or minimal problems maintaining recovery 86%
- Recommending program to others 100%
- Attending regular or frequent 12-step meetings 76%

The last program outcome requires some explanation. Addiction programs often rely on community support groups based on the 12 steps of Alcoholics Anonymous or as they are translated (e.g., Overeaters Anonymous, Gamblers Anonymous). In the case of sexual addiction, there are a number of groups, such as Sex Addicts Anonymous or Sexaholics Anonymous. The fact that 76 percent of Golden Valley's patients could find local groups is remarkable, given that the majority of them came from all over the United States and Canada. It is a testimony to the rapid expansion of resources for this problem.

## CONCLUSION

Some professionals are mistrustful of self-help groups, especially when they have had no experience with them. The fact is they are of uneven quality. However, a good group is hard to beat in terms of helping addicts cope with their shame. The 12 steps are particularly effective with shame-based addictive disorders. Perhaps the best brief explanation of the process is Ernst Kurtz's class article "Why AA Works" (*Journal of Studies on Alcohol*, 43:38-80) for those readers with no 12-step group experience.

Definitional problems abound in sexual addiction. Eli Coleman elaborates upon them in his companion article to this piece. Questions of normalcy, cross-cultural comparisons, special populations are all familiar terrain to the addiction specialist. In fact, Jim Orford, one of the very first to articulate a theory on sexual dependency, comments in his recent book *Excessive Appetites* (1985):

> Debate over definitions in this area is intriguingly reminiscent of debates on the same subject when drugtaking, drinking, or gambling are under discussion. In none of these areas is there agreement about the precise points on the continuum at which normal behaviour, heavy use, problem behaviour, excessive behaviour, "mania" or "ism" are to be distinguished one from another. When reading of the supposed characteristics of the "real nymphomaniac," one is haunted by memories of attempts to define the "real alcoholic" or the "real compulsive gambler."

Current research trends are abandoning the traditional disease oriented typologies in favor of recognizing that natural systems are varied even in pathologies. To find the model "sex addict" that everyone can agree on will take us down a trail the professional addictionologist has been on before. There is not one kind of alcoholic but actually a variety of types who have excessive use of alcohol in common. So I believe that we will find similar patterns in sexual addiction.

The risk is that addiction specialists look skeptically at sex therapists and their lack of training in addictive delusional thought processes and relapse prevention while sexual scientists criticize addictionologists as having inadequate knowledge of sexuality. Meanwhile, people who are struggling with the issue are asking for help. And no progress will be made.

Therein is the opportunity. Some years ago the Italian psychiatrist Mara Palazolli (1981) appealed for professionals to work for what she termed "transdisciplinary" knowledge as contrasted with interdisciplinary efforts in which different specialists focused on a common problem. From her point of view "transdisciplinary" meant creating a new body of knowledge through the cooperation of different disciplines. Sexual addiction presents us with a great challenge and opportunity for addictionologists and sexual scientists to develop the new body of knowledge that Palazolli envisioned.

# NO
## Marty Klein

# WHY THERE'S NO SUCH THING AS SEXUAL ADDICTION—AND WHY IT REALLY MATTERS

If convicted mass murderer Ted Bundy had said that watching Bill Cosby reruns motivated his awful crimes, he would have been dismissed as a deranged sociopath. Instead, Bundy said his pornography addiction made him do it—which many people treated as the conclusions of a thoughtful social scientist. Why?

There's a phenomenon emerging in America today that affects us and our profession whether we like it or not. Not caring about it, or having no opinion about it, is no longer an option for us.

I am not interested, by the way, in trashing 12-step programs. AA performs a great service every year in helping people handle their addiction to alcohol and other drugs. The two-part question that has been put to us—again, whether we like it or not—is, is the addiction model a good one for diagnosing sexual problems, and is the 12-step model a good one for treating sexual problems?

If it is, is it as appropriate for treating rapists as it is for people who masturbate too much?

## HOW THE SEXUAL ADDICTION MOVEMENT AFFECTS PROFESSIONALS

*People are now self-diagnosing as "sex addicts."

They're also diagnosing their partners. Non-sexologist professionals such as ministers and doctors are diagnosing some of their clientele as sex addicts, too. As a result of these trends, many people who should be seeing therapists or sexologists are not. And many who don't need "treatment" *are* getting it.

*The sexual addiction movement is aggressively training non-sexologists, such as marriage counselors, in the treatment of sexual problems.

Many professionals are now taking these programs instead of those offered by sexologists. Also, some professionals now feel incompetent to treat certain systemic problems without this sexual addiction "training."

From the Annual Meeting of the Society for the Scientific Study of Sex, November 1989. Copyright © 1989 by Marty Klein. Reprinted by permission.

It is important to note that the content of this sexual addiction training is sexologically inadequate: there is little or no discussion of systems, physiology, diagnoses, cultural aspects, etc.

*The concept of sexual addiction affects the sexual climate of the new society in which we work—negatively.

This negativity is reflected in anti-sex education legislation, anti-pornography ordinances, homophobic industry regulations, etc.

*Sex addicts now have cachet as sex experts.

Mass murderer Ted Bundy, widely quoted as an expert on the effects of pornography, is only one example. Right-wing crusaders now routinely quote "sex addicts" to justify repressive beliefs and public policy suggestions.

## DEFINING SEXUAL ADDICTION

In the literature, the sex addict is typically described as:

• Someone who frequently does or fantasizes sexual things s/he doesn't like

• Someone whose sexual behavior has become unstoppable despite serious consequences (including, according to Patrick Carnes, unwanted pregnancy)

• Someone whose sexual behavior and thoughts have become vastly more important than their relationships, family, work, finances, and health

• Someone whose sexual behavior doesn't reflect her/his highest self, the grandest part of her/his humanness

• According to the National Association of Sexual Addiction Problems, "6% or 1 out of 17 Americans are sexual addicts." That's about 14 million people.

From this literature and from meetings of groups like Sexaholics Anonymous (SA), the beliefs of people committed to the sexual addiction model appear to include:

• Sex is most healthy in committed, monogamous, loving, heterosexual relationships;

• The "goal" of sex should always be intimacy and the expression of our highest self;

• There are limits to healthy sexual expression, which are obvious (e.g., masturbation more than once a day);

• Choosing to use sex to feel better about yourself or to escape from problems is unhealthy.

## CLINICAL IMPLICATIONS OF THE CONCEPT

*It sees powerlessness as a virtue.

Step 1 of the traditional "12 steps" of all AA-type groups is "we admitted we were powerless over X (alcohol, our sexual impulses, etc.)..."

Controlling our sexuality can be painful, not because we lack self-control or will power, but because sexual energy is powerful and demands expression. The primitive, infantile forces behind those demands often make sexuality feel like a matter of life and death—which, in the unconscious, it is.

"Sex addicts" say they are "out of control," but this is just a *metaphor*—i.e., they *feel* out of control; controlling their impulses is very painful. We've all had that experience, with sex and with other things. *Virtually everyone* has the ability to choose how to control and express their sexual impulses (we'll discuss the small group who can't later).

The concept of sexual addiction colludes with peoples' desire to shirk responsibility for their sexuality. But powerlessness is far too high a price to pay.

*It prevents helpful analysis by patients and therapists.

The concept of sexual addiction prevents any examination of the personality dynamics underlying sexual behavior. It prevents the assessment and treatment of sexual or personality problems, because identifying and dealing with the "addiction" is the goal.

By encouraging people to "admit" that they *are* powerless, the concept of sexual addiction prevents people from examining how they come to *feel* powerless—and what they can do about that feeling. This careful examination, ultimately, is the source of personality growth and behavior change.

The expression "That's my addiction talking" is creeping into the popular vocabulary. This translates into "don't confront or puncture my defenses."

*It trivializes sexuality.

The concept of sexual addiction ignores the childhood passions at the source of sexual guilt. Aggression, lust for power, and greedy demands to be pleasured are all part of normal sexuality, which every adult needs to broker in some complex fashion.

People learn to feel guilty about their sexual impulses as infants. "Sex addicts" are told they have nothing to feel guilty about, that they can learn to feel better one day at a time But people know all the "good" reasons they have for feeling sexual guilt. By denying the dark side of normal, healthy sexuality that most people know they have, the concept of sexual addiction *increases* guilt.

Self-identified "sex addicts" want us to remove the darkness from their sexuality, leaving only the wholesome, non-threatening part—which would, of course, also leave them as non-adults.

Rather than collude with this understandable desire, competent therapists are willing to confront this darkness. Instead of snatching it away from patients, we can help them approach it, understand it, and ultimately feel less afraid of it.

Another way to describe this is that

*It lets people split—i.e., externalize their "bad" sexuality.

Once a person describes her/himself as a "sex addict," s/he can say "*I* don't want that sexual feeling or behavior over there; *the disease* wants it." Good therapists know how to recognize splitting, how it blocks adult functioning, and how to move patients away from it.

*It makes a disease out of what is often within reasonable limits of sexual behavior.

High levels of masturbating and *any* patronage of prostitutes, for example, are typically condemned as "abnormal" and reflecting a "disease," according to SA-type groups. Which experts get to make judgments about acceptable sexual behavior? Exactly where do their criteria come from?

*It doesn't teach sexual decision-making skills, or how to evaluate sexual situations.

Rather, the concept uses a "just say no" approach. As Planned Parenthood's Faye Wattleton says, "just say no" helps people abstain from self-destructive sex about as well as "have a nice day" helps people deal with depression.

SA-type groups say that ultimately, sexual abstinence is more like abstinence from compulsive eating—that is, moderation—than it is like abstinence from compulsive drinking—that is, zero participation. On what theoretical basis has this critical judgment been made? Simple expediency.

*Where is the healthy model of sexuality?

The sexual addiction model of human sexuality is moralistic, arbitrary, misinformed, and narrow. *Excluded* from this model are using sex to feel good; having "bad" fantasies; and enjoying sex without being in love. Where is the theoretical justification for this moralistic position?

We've seen this before: the concept of sin as sickness. It has led to sincere attempts to "cure" homosexuality, nymphomania, and masturbation—by the world's leading social scientists, within our own lifetime.

It is outrageous to treat sexual problems without a healthy model of sexuality that relates to most people's experience. The sexual addiction concept shows a dramatic ignorance of the range of typical human sexuality.

At the end of competent sex therapy or psychotherapy treatment, the patient is a grown-up, able to make conscious sexual choices. Sex addiction treatment offers a patient the chance to be a recovering sex addict. Which would you rather be?

## PROFESSIONAL IMPLICATIONS OF THE CONCEPT

*It reduces the credibility of sexologists.

Prospective patients are now asking therapists a new kind of question: "Are you in recovery yourself?" "Have you treated sex addicts before?" What if a therapist is emotionally/sexually healthy and therefore *not* "in recovery"? Is s/he then disqualified as a professional?

The public, I'm afraid, is also getting a picture of us as being ivory tower types out of touch with the real—i.e., *destructive*—sexuality out on the street.

They're feeling "You want to waste time discussing systems, regression, defenses, and meanwhile there are kids buying *Playboy* out there!"

*It replaces professional sexologists as relevant sex experts.

There are two groups of people behind this:

a) Addictionologists, often in recovery themselves (i.e., they have unresolved sexual and impulse control issues). They typically have little or no training in sexuality (e.g., I am told that Patrick Carnes' Ph.D. is in Counselor Education and Staff Development); and

b) 12-steppers themselves, lay people who love being in recovery. Their missionary zeal has nothing to do with science or clinical expertise. They freely generalize their own experience with sexual problems and "recovery" to all people and to human sexuality.

Both groups of people are now being quoted—and are actively portraying themselves—as sex experts.

By offering training from people with little or no sexological background, the concept suggests that all we offer is just another "theory" about sexual functioning. Just as creationists now want (and frequently get) "equal time" when scientists teach or discuss evolution, addictionologists now want—and are beginning to get—"equal time" regarding sexual functioning.

Graduates of such training programs believe that they have learned something about sexuality, when they haven't. They have learned something about *addiction*. And they are taught that they are competent to treat addiction in any form, whether its vehicle alcohol, food, gambling, love, or sex.

Addictionologists admit they lack skills in differential diagnosis. They and their 12-step programs let anyone define him/herself as a "sex addict." How many personality disorders, how much depression, how many adjustment reactions are being treated as "sex addiction"?

## POLITICAL IMPLICATIONS OF THE CONCEPT

*It strengthens society's anti-sex forces.

"Sexual addiction" is the Right's newest justification for eliminating sex education, adult bookstores, and birth control clinics. They are using the same arguments to eliminate books like *The Color Purple* from school libraries. Businessman Richard Enrico, whose group Citizens Against Pornography eliminated the sale of *Playboy* magazine from all 1800 7–11 stores, did so, he says, "because smut causes sex addiction." And he was able to convince one of America's largest corporations of this complete fiction.

We should not be colluding with this destructive force.

*It emphasizes negative aspects of sex.

Sex addiction treatment is essentially creating a special interest group of people who feel victimized by their own sexuality. Not *others'* sexuality, like rape victims—their *own* sexuality. This lobby/interest group is growing as increasing numbers of people are recruited into identifying themselves as sex addicts. With the agenda of protecting people from their *own* sexuality, they are a dangerous group, easily exploited by the Right and other sex-negative points of view.

*It frightens people about the role of sexuality in social problems.

Increasingly, "sex addicts" and trainers are talking in public about how sexual impulses took over their lives and made them do things like steal money, take drugs, and see prostitutes.

This also frightens people about their ability to control their own sexuality—as if they're vulnerable to being taken over.

*It supports public ignorance about sexuality.

"Sex addicts" and trainers spread stories about how childhood masturbating to *Playboy* leads to porn addiction, and about how prostitutes become so alluring that people destroy their marriages. The public, of course, takes the additional step that this could happen to anyone—even though there is no data to support this idea.

The movement continues to spread dangerous lies about sex, even though the ultra-conservative Meese Commission was unable to find any evidence that pornography leads to child molestation, and even though no medical society in the world has ever proven that masturbation of any kind is harmful.

*It focuses on the "dignified" "purpose" of sex.

These words always seem to mean a rigid sex role system, with sex needing love to give it meaning. Sweating and moaning never seem dignified to people concerned with the dignity of sex. Ultimately, the "purpose" of sex can only be a political, rather than scientific, concept.

*It obscures the role of society in distorting our sexuality.

Sexologists understand that our moralistic American society constricts healthy sexual expression. We all know the sexual and intimacy problems this creates; in fact, we are now beginning to understand how such distortion even helps create sex offenders.

But the sexual addiction movement only sees society as encouraging promiscuity, instead of discouraging pleasure and healthy sexuality. This simplistic analysis cannot see how the media and other institutions make guilt-free sex almost impossible.

The sexual addiction concept attempts to heal society's sexual pain while keeping its economic, political, and social foundations intact. This is not only naive and ineffective, but dangerous.

## WHY IS THE SEXUAL ADDICTION CONCEPT SO POPULAR?

*It distances personal responsibility for sexual choices.

As Dr. Domeena Renshaw says, "my illness makes me have affairs" is a very popular concept.

The concept seems to allow sexual expression without the punishment our infantile side fears. This is a great childhood fantasy. But the price is too high.

*It provides fellowship.

SA-type meetings provide structure and relaxed human contact for people who have trouble finding these in other ways.

The program also allows alcoholics in AA to work the steps again. This is one of the single biggest sources of self-described "sex addicts." In fact, Patrick Carnes claims that 83% of all sex addicts have some other kind of addiction.

*It provides pseudo-"scientific" support for the intuitive belief that sex is dangerous.

In doing so it legitimizes sex-negative attitudes, and supports sexual guilt.

*It lets people self-diagnose.

This is very American, very democratic. People like to feel they are taking charge of their lives, and self-diagnosing gives them the illusion that they are.

*It encourages people to split.

When people are troubled by their sexuality, it is comforting to imagine the problem "out there" rather than "in here." A striking example is Jimmy Swaggart, who railed against immorality out in the world, while behaving in the very ways he was condemning.

It also encourages a kind of splitting among *non*-"sex addicts." In answering the defensive question "how can people be sexual like *that*?," it makes people who behave in certain ways essentially *different* (they're "addicted") from us "normal" folk. Basically, people use the concept of sexual addiction as a projection of their fear about their own sexuality. Its very existence is sort of an exorcism of sexuality on a societal level.

*It helps people get distance from their sexual shame.

Most of us have deep shame about our sexuality—either our overt behavior, or the more primitive urges and images left over from childhood that we've never accepted. This profound sense of shame is what people would really like to get rid of; the behavioral symptoms they're supposedly addicted to are just a symbol of that shame.

SA-type groups reframe this shame into a positive thing. It becomes a badge for membership; it lets "addicts" know they're heading toward a solution; it affirms that a sex-crazed society is victimizing them; and it suggests they're being too hard on themselves.

Good therapy does the opposite. It helps people feel their shame, relate it to an even deeper pain, and temporarily feel worse—before helping them resolve it.

## WHY DO SO MANY PEOPLE CLAIM TO GET RELIEF FROM SEXUAL ADDICTION PROGRAMS?

First, we should keep in mind that simply because people claim that something gives them emotional relief doesn't mean it works in the way they claim. Astrology apparently helped reduce Nancy Reagan's anxiety about Ron's career; but that doesn't mean it actually helped him make better decisions.

*The recovery process can be emotionally reassuring for many people.

It offers structure, goals, fellowship, and an accepting social environment. In fact, since most of the talk at SA-type groups is about sex and relationships, it's a relatively easy place to meet people for dating. And that *does* go on.

Conversation at SA-type meetings is exclusively about material that each individual is already focusing on. Thus, *all* conversation feels like it's about the individual "addict," and so participants can feel connected with others without having to abandon their own narcissistic focus. This feels intimate, and gives the illusion that an individual is making progress.

And, of course, virtually everyone gets to hear stories of people who are worse off than they are, and so they feel better.

*People enjoy feeling like they're heading somewhere.

While "addicts" learn to enjoy the *process* of recovery, they also learn they're never going to fully *get* there. So they set their sights lower—and *do* accomplish never being cured.

Because the sexual addiction movement is not interested in personality change, it can offer symptom relief without any ethical conflicts. In many cases people do get that relief—although it's at the expense of the rest of their character structure.

Finally, as "addicts" continue learning how to distance themselves from their "bad" sexuality, they feel an increasing sense of direction and relief.

*Addicts transfer some of their compulsivity to the SA-type group meeting itself.

For many "sex addicts," meetings (sometimes many times per week) are the most important part of the week. In a predictable setting and way, with comforting regularity, they get to listen to and talk about sexual feelings and behavior they dislike.

This feeling is perfectly conveyed by a "sex addict" quoted in *Contemporary Sexuality*. He notes that "Every Thursday night for the past year and a half I have repeated that statement [about his so-called "addiction"] to my 12-step support group." By itself this is a trivial point; in the context of a program supposed to heal compulsive behavior, it is troubling.

## WHAT ABOUT SEXUAL COMPULSIVITY?

Most self-described sex addicts aren't out of control; they are relatively "normal" neurotics for whom being in control is *painful*. In fact, as the National Association of Sexual Addiction Problems says, "most addicts do not break the law, nor do they satisfy their need by forcing themselves upon others."

Those who are *really* sexually compulsive are typically psychotic, sociopathic, character-disordered, etc. Some of these people have impaired reality testing. Others have absolutely no concern about the consequences of their behavior. Dr. Renshaw states that "undifferentiated sexual urgency is a symptom of manic-depression."

These people don't need help laying off one day at a time. They need deep therapy, medication, structured behavioral interventions, or other intensive modalities. Dr. Eli Coleman, for example, reports treatment success with lithium, comparable to the clinical results lithium produces with other compulsives.

It is absolutely indefensible to suggest that the same mechanism is operating in the rapist and the guy who masturbates "too often." The concept of sexual addiction does nothing to diagnose serious problems, assess danger, discuss beliefs about sex, take a history, or change personality. There are no treatment statistics on *true* obsessive-compulsives via the sexual addiction model.

We must also, and this is much harder, continue to resist and interpret society's demand for simple answers and easy solutions about sex offenders.

Sexual energy scares people; distorted expressions of that energy terrify people. We need to continually educate policymakers and the public as to why the treatment of sex offenders is so complex and difficult, and why quick-fix solutions are worse than partial solutions. We must find a way to say "I don't know" or "We're still working on it" without apologizing. Cancer researchers, for example, have done a good job of making partial answers—like early detection and quitting smoking—acceptable.

## SUMMARY

The concept of "sex addiction" really rests on the assumption that sex is dangerous. There's the sense that we frail humans are vulnerable to the Devil's temptations of pornography, masturbation, and extramarital affairs, and that if we yield, we become "addicted."

Without question, being a sexual person is complex, and we *are* vulnerable—to our sex-negative heritage, shame about our bodies, and conflict about the exciting sexual feelings we can't express without risking rejection. Sexuality per se, however, is not dangerous—no matter how angry or frightened people are.

Professional sexologists should reject any model suggesting that people must spend their lives 1) in fear of sexuality's destructive power; 2) being powerless about sexuality; 3) lacking the tools to relax and let sex take over when it's appropriate.

Addictionologists have cynically misled the public into thinking that "sexual addiction" is a concept respected and used by professional therapists and educators. Even a brief look at our literature, conferences, and popular writing shows how rarely this is true. But addictionologists don't care about sexual truth or expertise—only about addiction.

The sexual addiction movement is not harmless. These people are missionaries who want to put everyone in the missionary position.

In these terrible anti-sex times, one of our most important jobs is to reaffirm that sexuality—though complicated—is precious, not dangerous. Now more than ever, our job is to help people just say yes.

# CHALLENGE QUESTIONS

## Can Sex Be an Addiction?

1. What types of sexual behaviors, if any, do you feel are problematic? Why? What should be done about such behaviors?

2. If you were diagnosed as a sex addict, how would you react? What would you do?

3. According to Klein, why is the concept of sexual addiction so popular? Do you agree?

4. Does our society seem to promote or disregard the idea of sexual addiction? What is the basis for your answer?

# ISSUE 11

## Is Alcoholism a Disease?

**YES: George E. Vaillant,** from "We Should Retain the Disease Concept of Alcoholism," *Harvard Medical School Mental Health Letter* (August 1990)

**NO: Herbert Fingarette,** from "We Should Reject the Disease Concept of Alcoholism," *Harvard Medical School Mental Health Letter* (September 1990)

### ISSUE SUMMARY

**YES:** Physician George E. Vaillant argues that viewing alcoholism as a disease is appropriate and consistent with available research on the genetic transmission of alcoholism.

**NO:** Professor emeritus of philosophy Herbert Fingarette maintains that alcoholism is not a disease and that such a view is neither scientifically valid nor useful.

Understanding alcoholism is a priority for psychologists because the consequences of alcoholism have been catastrophic for society. Some experts estimate that alcohol is involved in more than 50 percent of the fatal car accidents that occur in the United States every year. Additionally, alcohol is involved in a substantial number of murders, assaults, rapes, suicides, and child abuse cases. Obviously, effective treatment is vital, but treatment cannot proceed until the causes of alcoholism are known.

Currently, there is a heated debate surrounding the causes of alcoholism. The most prevalent view is that alcoholism is a biologically determined disease. This is the basis on which most physicians, psychologists, and self-help groups like Alcoholics Anonymous (AA) treat alcoholism. Unfortunately, this view seems to imply that alcoholics have no control over or responsibility for their disease or related behaviors. This implication tends to relieve the alcoholic of guilt, but it also relieves the alcoholic of any responsibility. Is this the best way to understand alcoholism? Is there any evidence supporting this model? What does biological and genetic research indicate? These questions have great importance for the tragic individual and societal problem of alcoholism.

In the following selections, George E. Vaillant argues that viewing alcoholism as a disease is useful for persuading problem drinkers to acknowledge their problem. If alcoholism were not a disease, he says, then alcoholics would have difficulty gaining entry into the health care system for treatment. Vaillant claims that a medical diagnosis leads to hope and improved morale.

Indeed, alcoholics who understand their disease, according to Vaillant, are more willing to take responsibility for their own care.

On the other hand, Herbert Fingarette views the disease position as scientifically invalid. He feels strongly that it promotes false beliefs about and inappropriate attitudes toward alcoholism. He discusses research that he feels disproves biological causes of alcoholism. When behavior is labeled a disease, cautions Fingarette, "it becomes excusable because it is regarded as involuntary." He maintains that alcoholism is not involuntary and that alcoholics have as much control over their drinking behavior as nonalcoholics. Fingarette concludes that the disease position promotes harmful, wasteful, and ineffective social policies.

| POINT | COUNTERPOINT |
|---|---|
| • Alcoholism is a disease like any other physical disease. | • The disease position is an attempt to make a medical problem out of a social problem. |
| • Considering alcoholism a disease encourages those with drinking problems to get help. | • Considering alcoholism a disease discourages alcoholics from taking responsibility for their behavior. |
| • Alcoholism is a disease because alcoholics do not have the capacity to control how much they drink. | • Alcoholic behavior is always voluntary and can be controlled. |
| • The disease model of alcoholism reflects the fact that genetic factors are the source of problem drinking. | • Although a link exists between alcoholism and genetic factors, this link is less significant than other factors. |

# YES

George E. Vaillant

# WE SHOULD RETAIN THE DISEASE CONCEPT OF ALCOHOLISM

When I read expert discussions of why alcoholism is not a disease, I am reminded of the equally learned discussions by "the best and the brightest" of why the Viet Nam War was a good idea. These discussants had intelligence, advanced degrees, scholarship, prestige, literacy—every qualification but one. They lacked experience. None had spent much time in Viet Nam. Just so, the philosopher Herbert Fingarette, the psychoanalyst Thomas Szasz, the sociologist and theoretician Robin Room, and provocative, thoughtful psychologists like Stanton Peele and Nicholas Heather have every qualification but one for explaining why alcoholism is not a disease—they have never worked in an alcohol clinic. Why, I wonder, do experienced alcohol workers and recovering alcoholics, the thousands of competent common folk in the trenches, accept the view that alcoholism is a disease? Why is it mainly less competent people, the active alcoholics, who agree with Professor Fingarette that they are just "heavy drinkers"?

Let me summarize the evidence provided by the learned academics who have pointed out the folly of the medical model of alcoholism. First, alcohol abuse—unlike coughing from pneumonia, for example—is a habit under considerable volitional control. Second, there is compelling evidence that variations in alcohol consumption are distributed along a smooth continuum, although a medical model would suggest that in any individual, alcoholism is either present or absent. Third, when alcoholism is treated as a disease it can be used both by individuals and by society to explain away major underlying problems—poverty, mental deficiency, crime, and the like—which require our attention if efforts at prevention, treatment and understanding are to succeed. Fourth, to diagnose people as alcoholic is to label them in a way that can damage both self-esteem and public acceptance. Fifth, alcoholism should not be considered a disease if it is regarded as merely a symptom of underlying personality or depression.

From George E. Vaillant, "We Should Retain the Disease Concept of Alcoholism," *Harvard Medical School Mental Health Letter* (August 1990). Copyright © 1990 by the President and Fellows of Harvard College. Reprinted by permission of the *Harvard Medical School Mental Health Letter*, 164 Longwood Avenue, Boston, MA 02115.

## REFUTATION OF OBJECTIONS

Let me try to refute these objections one by one. First, it may be true that there is no known underlying biological defect in alcoholism. Rather, alcohol abuse is a multidetermined continuum of drinking behaviors whose causes are differently weighted for different people and include culture, habits, and genes. But the same can be said of high blood pressure and coronary heart disease. The incidence of hypertension varies with measurement procedures and psychological circumstances. It lies on a physiological continuum which defies precise definition. It has no known specific cause. It is powerfully affected by social factors; for example, it has become epidemic among young urban black males. The point of using the term 'disease' for alcoholism is simply to underscore that once a person has lost the capacity to control consistently how much and how often he or she drinks, continued use of alcohol can be both a necessary and a sufficient cause of a syndrome that produces millions of invalids and causes millions of deaths.

The second objection to the medical model of alcoholism is that only opinion separates the alcoholic from the heavy drinker. Supposedly one either has a disease or does not have it; diagnosis should depend on signs and symptoms, not value judgments. But consider the example of coronary heart disease. We regard it as a medical illness, although its causes are diverse and often poorly understood and there is no fixed point at which we can decide that coronary arteries become abnormal. So it is with alcoholism. Normal drinking merges imperceptibly with pathological drinking. Culture and idiosyncratic viewpoints will always determine where the line is drawn.

The third objection is that alcoholism is affected by so many situational and psychological factors that the drinking must often be viewed as reactive. Some people drink uncontrollably only after a serious loss or in certain specific situations, and some alcoholics return to normal drinking by an act of will. But these observations are equally true of hypertension, which often has an extremely important psychological component. Nevertheless, prospective studies show that alcohol dependence causes depression, anxiety, and poverty far more often than the other way around. In citing psychological problems as a cause of alcoholism, Fingarette reverses the position of cart and horse.

The fourth objection to calling alcoholism a disease is that it involves both labeling and a disparagement of free will. But in this case both labeling and the denial of free will are therapeutic. Some people believe that the label 'alcoholic' transforms a person into an outcast, akin to a leper. Well, should a doctor who knows that a person has leprosy keep the fact secret lest the patient be labeled a leper? Some people believe that if alcoholics are taught to regard alcoholism as a disease they will use this label as an excuse to drink or a reason why they should not be held responsible for their own recovery. It does not work out that way. Like people with high blood pressure, alcoholics who understand that they have a disease become more rather than less willing to take responsibility for self-care. That is why the self-help group, Alcoholics Anonymous, places such single-minded emphasis on the idea that alcoholism is a disease.

## DIAGNOSIS HELPS

Once patients accept the diagnosis, they can be shown how to assume responsibility for their own care. Physicians stress the value of diagnosing hypertension early because it can provide a rational explanation for headaches and other symptoms that were hitherto regarded as neurotic or irrational. For years alcoholics themselves have labeled themselves 'wicked,' 'weak,' and 'reprehensible.' The offer of a medical explanation does not lead to irresponsibility, only to hope and improved morale.

The fifth argument against calling alcoholism a disease is the most compelling; it is said that uncontrolled maladaptive ingestion of alcohol is not a biological disorder but a disorder of behavior. Like compulsive fingernail biting, gambling, or child molesting, this form of deviant behavior can often be better classified by sociologists than by physiologists, and better treated by psychologists skilled in behavior therapy than by physicians with their medical armamentarium.

But unlike giving up gambling or fingernail biting, giving up alcohol abuse often requires skilled medical attention during acute withdrawal. Unlike gamblers and fingernail biters, most alcoholics develop secondary symptoms that do require medical care. Unlike child molesters, but like people with high blood pressure, alcoholics have a mortality rate two to four times as high as the average. In order to receive the medical treatment they require, alcoholics need a label that will allow them unprejudiced access to emergency rooms, detoxification clinics, and medical insurance.

The final argument for regarding alcoholism as a disease rather than a behavior disorder is that it often causes alcoholics to mistreat persons they love. Very few sustained human experiences involve as much abuse as the average close family member of an alcoholic must tolerate. Fingarette's "heavy drinking" model (which conveys a concept of misbehavior) only generates more denial in the already profoundly guilt-ridden alcoholic. Calling alcoholism a disease rather than a behavior disorder is a useful device both to persuade the alcoholic to acknowledge the problem and to provide a ticket for admission to the health care system. In short, in our attempts to understand and study alcoholism, we should employ the models of the social scientist and the learning theorist. But in order to treat alcoholics effectively we need to invoke the medical model.

Let me close with an anecdote. My research associate, reviewing the lives of 100 patients who had been hospitalized eight years previously for detoxification from alcohol, wrote to me that she mistrusted the diagnosis of alcoholism. To illustrate, she described one man who drank heavily for seven years after his initial detoxification. Although the alcohol clinic's staff agreed that his drinking was alcoholic, neither he nor his wife acknowledged that it was a problem. Finally he required a second detoxification, and the clinic staff claimed that they had been right.

"How can you call such behavior a disease," my associate wrote, "when you cannot decide if it represents a social problem [that is, requires a value judgment] or alcohol-dependent drinking?" Then she shifted her attention to the ninety-nine other tortured lives she had been reviewing. Oblivious of the contradiction, she concluded: "I don't think I ever fully realized before I did this follow-up what an absolutely devastating disease alcoholism is." I respectfully submit that if Professor Fingarette were to work in an alcohol clinic for two years, he would agree with the last half of my research associate's letter rather than the first half.

# NO

Herbert Fingarette

## WE SHOULD REJECT THE DISEASE CONCEPT OF ALCOHOLISM

Why do heavy drinkers persist in their behavior even when prudence, common sense, and moral duty call for restraint? That is the central question in debates about alcohol abuse. In the United States (but not in other countries such as Great Britain) the standard answer is to call the behavior a disease, "alcoholism," whose key symptom is a pattern of uncontrollable drinking. This myth, now widely advertised and widely accepted, is neither helpfully compassionate nor scientifically valid. It promotes false beliefs and inappropriate attitudes, as well as harmful, wasteful, and ineffective social policies.

The myth is embodied in the following four scientifically baseless propositions: 1) Heavy problem drinkers show a single distinctive pattern of ever greater alcohol use leading to ever greater bodily, mental, and social deterioration. 2) The condition, once it appears, persists involuntarily: the craving is irresistible and the drinking is uncontrollable once it has begun. 3) Medical expertise is needed to understand and relieve the condition ("cure the disease") or at least ameliorate its symptoms. 4) Alcoholics are no more responsible legally or morally for their drinking and its consequences than epileptics are responsible for the consequences of their movements during seizures.

The idea that alcoholism is a disease has always been a political and moral notion with no scientific basis. It was first promoted in the United States around 1800 as a speculation based on erroneous physiological theory, and later became a theme of the temperance movement. It was revived in the 1930s by the founders of Alcoholics Anonymous (AA), who derived their views from an amalgam of religious ideas, personal experiences and observations, and the unsubstantiated theories of a contemporary physician.

The AA doctrine won decisive support in the 1940s when a reputable scientist, E. M. Jellinek, published an elaborate statistical study of the "phases of alcoholism." He portrayed an inevitable sequence of ever more uncontrollable drinking that led progressively to such symptoms as black-outs, tolerance, and withdrawal distress, until the drinker "hit bottom" as a derelict, became insane, or died. Jellinek's work seemed to put a scientific seal of confirmation on the AA portrait of the alcoholic. That was hardly surprising, since he had taken his data from questionnaires that were prepared and distributed by

From Herbert Fingarette, "We Should Reject the Disease Concept of Alcoholism," *Harvard Medical School Mental Health Letter* (September 1990). Copyright © 1990 by the President and Fellows of Harvard College. Reprinted by permission of the *Harvard Medical School Mental Health Letter*, 164 Longwood Avenue, Boston, MA 02115.

AA and answered by fewer than 100 self-selected members. Jellinek conscientiously acknowledged the source of his data and his reservations about its scientific adequacy. Nevertheless, his dramatic-tragic portrait of the alcoholic became widely accepted and is now part of American folk beliefs.

## NO CONSISTENT PATTERN

Recent scientific literature shows that in reality the typical pattern of heavy drinking fluctuates. Some drinkers with numerous and severe problems deteriorate; others markedly improve, or develop different problems. Some claim loss of control; others do not. Many heavy drinkers report no serious social problems associated with their drinking and are not recognized as alcoholics by friends, colleagues, or even their families.

The idea that alcoholics are constantly drunk is quite false. One leading researcher points out that "in any given month, one half of alcoholics will be abstinent, with a mean of four months of being dry in any one-year to two-year period." During any ten- to twenty-year period, about a third of alcoholics "mature out" into various forms of moderate drinking or abstinence. The rate of maturing out is even higher among heavy problem drinkers not diagnosed as alcoholics. Undoubtedly there is a small group who follow a pattern resembling Jellinek's four phases; one objection to the disease concept of alcoholism is that it focuses attention mainly on this marginal group.

It is now widely believed that a biological cause of alcoholism has been discovered; some people are said to have a biochemistry or a genetic predisposition that dooms them to be alcoholics if they drink. The truth is less dramatic. There are certain so-called biological markers associated with heavy drinking, but these have not been shown to cause it. One supposed marker is the metabolism of alcohol into acetaldehyde, a brain toxin, in the bodies of people who are independently identifiable as being at higher risk of becoming alcoholics. Another proposed marker is the high level of morphine-like substances supposedly secreted by alcoholics when they metabolize alcohol. But almost all people with serious drinking problems have intermittent periods of sobriety during which all metabolic products of alcohol have been excreted. It is implausible that any residual effects, whether physical or psychological, could be so powerful as to override a sober person's rational, moral, and prudential inclination to abstain.

Recent studies have also been said to imply that alcoholism is a hereditary disease. But that is not what the genetic research shows. In the first place, these studies provide no evidence of a genetic factor in the largest group of heavy drinkers—those who have significant associated problems but are not diagnosable as alcoholics. Even among the minority who can be so diagnosed, the data suggest that only a minority have the pertinent genetic background. And even in this category, a minority of a minority, studies report that the majority do not become alcoholics.

It is not only misleading but dangerous to regard alcoholism as a genetic disorder. Heavy drinkers without alcoholism in their genetic backgrounds are led to feel immune to serious drinking problems, yet they have the greatest total number of problems. On the other hand, people who do have some hereditary disposition to alcoholism could easily become defeatist. Their risk is higher, and they should be aware of that, but their fate is still very much in their own hands.

## NO SINGLE CAUSE

The idea of a single disease obscures the scientific consensus that no single cause has ever been established. Heavy drinking has many causes which vary from drinker to drinker, from one drinking pattern to another. Character, motivation, family environment, personal history, ethnic and cultural values, marital, occupational, and educational status all play a role. As these change, so do patterns of drinking, heavy drinking, and "alcoholism." For example, alcohol is used in many so-called "primitive" societies, but their drinking patterns are not ours, and what we call alcoholism does not exist among them before contact with Europeans. That would not be true if alcoholism were a disease caused by chemical and neurological effects of drinking in conjunction with individual genetic vulnerability. The crucial role of psychology in alcoholics' drinking is demonstrated by experiments in which they are deceived about whether the beverage they are drinking contains alcohol. Their drinking patterns then reflect their beliefs; the actual presence or absence of alcohol is irrelevant.

Alcoholics do not "lack control" in the ordinary sense of those words. Studies show that they can limit their drinking in response to appeals and arguments or rules and regulations. In experiments they will reduce or eliminate drinking in return for such rewards as money, social privileges, or exemption from boring tasks. To object that these experiments are invalid because they occur in protected settings is to miss the point, which is precisely that the drinking patterns of alcoholics can vary dramatically in different settings.

True, alcoholics often resist appeals to cease their alcohol abuse, and they ignore obvious prudential and moral considerations. The simplistic explanation that attributes this to an irresistible craving obscures a more complicated reality: they have developed a way of life in which they use drinking as a major strategy for coping with their problems. They have become accustomed to values, friends, settings, and beliefs that protect and encourage drinking. When they encounter drastically changed circumstances in a hospital, clinic, or communal group, they are capable of following different rules. Even some who "cheat" where abstention is expected nevertheless limit their drinking to avoid being found out. They do not automatically lose control because of a few drinks. Our focus of attention must shift from drinking per se to the meaning of drink for certain persons and the way of life in which its role has become central.

## TERMS REDEFINED

Responsible scientists who are familiar with the research but want to preserve the disease concept of alcoholism have had to redefine their terms. What they now mean by "disease" and "loss of control" no longer coincides either with the customary meaning of those words or with what the public is encouraged to believe. Thus Mark Keller, one of the early leaders of the alcoholism movement, now reinterprets loss of control to mean that alcoholics who have decided to stop "cannot be sure they will stand by their resolution" This is said to be compatible with anything from constant heavy drinking to remission in the form of permanent moderation or total abstention. Although the medical term "remission" is used, this is not a medical or scientific explanation: we all know that someone who resolves to change a long-standing way of life cannot be sure whether the promise will be kept. Similarly, craving, still popularly understood as an overwhelming and irresistible desire, has now been extended by researchers to include mild inclinations, although this makes nonsense of the supposed compulsion to drink.

The disease concept is sometimes justified on the ground that although scientifically invalid, it is a practical way of encouraging alcoholics to enter treatment. This argument is based on false assumptions and has harmful consequences. The many heavy drinkers who see themselves (often correctly) as not fitting the criteria for alcoholism under some current diagnostic formula are likely to conclude that they have no cause for concern. Their inclination to deny their problems is thus encouraged. As for people who are diagnosable as alcoholics, the vast majority never become permanently abstinent, even after treatment or after they join AA. Yet the disease doctrine may cause them to develop a fatalistic conviction that even one slip is a disaster, since they have been led to believe, falsely, that occasional or moderate drinking is never possible for them.

When behavior is labeled a disease, it becomes excusable because it is regarded as involuntary. This is an important result of the disease concept of alcoholism, and indeed an important reason for its promulgation. Thus special benefits are provided to alcoholics in employment, health, and civil rights law, provided they can prove that their drinking is persistent and very heavy. The effect is to reward people who continue to drink heavily. This policy is insidious precisely because it is well intended, and those who criticize it may seem to lack compassion.

## SUPREME COURT VIEW

The United States Supreme Court, after reviewing detailed briefs pro and con, has consistently held in favor of those who say that alcoholics are responsible for their behavior, and has concluded that medical evidence does not demonstrate their drinking to be involuntary. Spokesmen for the National Council on Alcoholism (NCA) state publicly that they too believe alcoholics should be held responsible for their misdeeds, but they are being hypocritical. In the less visible forum of the federal courts, the NCA has repeatedly argued that alcoholics should be protected from criminal and civil liability for their acts and excused from the normal regulatory requirements.

But the greatest scandal of the argument for the disease concept as a useful lie is the claim that it helps alcoholics by inducing them to enter treatment. On the contrary, both independent and government research show expensive disease-oriented treatment programs to be largely a waste of money and human resources. Their apparent success proves illusory when they are compared in statistically rigorous studies with other programs, and with the rate of improvement in untreated alcohol abusers (which is much higher than the disease concept has led the public to believe). Very often, perhaps always, brief outpatient counseling works just as well as a long stay in a hospital or other residential clinic costing thousands of dollars. Some studies conclude that professional intervention is slightly better than no treatment, although the treatment method, duration, setting, or cost makes no difference. Other studies find no significant difference in results whether or not there is treatment.

We must refocus our compassion and redefine our policies on alcohol abuse. While continuing biological research, we should loosen the grip of physicians on the chief government agencies and research funding sources, and we should reject their deep bias in favor of the disease concept. Greater resources must be shifted to psychological and sociocultural research. We should consider promising new approaches to treatment that are being used in other countries. The public should be better informed about the scientific facts and above all about our scientific ignorance. Our policies should reflect the fact that heavy drinking is not primarily a biochemical or medical problem but a human and social one.

# CHALLENGE QUESTIONS

## Is Alcoholism a Disease?

1. What is your definition of an alcoholic? How is this definition affected by whether or not you believe alcoholism is a disease?

2. If a family member or a friend were diagnosed as alcoholic, what type of treatment would you encourage that person to pursue? Why?

3. What do you see as the role of mental health professionals in the treatment of problem drinkers?

4. Who seems to have the stronger argument, Vaillant or Fingarette? Has your personal experience with people who drink alcohol affected your conclusion? If so, how?

# ISSUE 12

## Does Abortion Have Severe Psychological Effects?

**YES: Anne C. Speckhard and Vincent M. Rue,** from "Postabortion Syndrome: An Emerging Public Health Concern," *Journal of Social Issues* (vol. 48, no. 3, 1992)

**NO: Nancy E. Adler, Henry P. David, Brenda N. Major, Susan H. Roth, Nancy F. Russo, and Gail E. Wyatt,** from "Psychological Responses After Abortion," *Science* (April 6, 1990)

### ISSUE SUMMARY

**YES:** Psychotherapists Anne C. Speckhard and Vincent M. Rue argue that abortion has serious psychological consequences for women, including what they term "postabortion syndrome" (PAS).

**NO:** Psychologists Nancy E. Adler et al. contend that severe negative psychological reactions following abortion are infrequent.

Despite the controversy that induced abortion regularly raises, the procedure is still performed frequently. Currently, almost one-quarter of all pregnancies in the United States are terminated by legal, induced abortion, which equals 1.6 million annual abortions. Twenty-four percent of American women who abort are teenagers, 57 percent are younger than 25 years old, and almost 80 percent of these women are unmarried. Most abortions are performed sometime during the first trimester (the first three months), but a small percentage—about 10 percent—are performed later on in the pregnancy, when the fetus is more developed. Regardless of when a woman chooses to terminate a pregnancy, what psychological effects might be attached to abortion?

For many people, the subject of abortion is not just a psychological issue; it is also a moral and political issue. Those who consider themselves pro-life often claim that women who abort suffer many negative effects. They view abortion as a trauma with many permanent consequences. Those who consider themselves pro-choice, on the other hand, usually argue that any negative effects of abortion are minimal. Indeed, from the pro-choice perspective, abortion offers relief from the stress of pregnancy and the burden of caring for an unwanted child.

In the selections that follow, Anne C. Speckhard and Vincent M. Rue describe the sociopolitical context of abortion research. They argue that "there is a reluctance to call attention to the negative effects of abortion for fear of providing support to anti-abortion groups." They criticize recent research showing few negative effects of abortion as methodologically flawed and not representative of most women who undergo abortions. Speckhard and Rue maintain that women suffer negative psychological consequences after undergoing abortion much more often than people believe and that, in fact, many women experience symptoms of postabortion syndrome (PAS), including flashbacks, "anniversary reactions," and guilt.

Nancy E. Adler and her colleagues, basing their conclusions on a review of what they feel are methodologically sound studies, argue that psychological distress for women is usually greatest *before* an abortion and that the actual incidence of severe negative responses to abortion is quite low. Adler et al. claim that "the weight of the evidence... indicates that legal abortion of an unwanted pregnancy in the first trimester does not pose a psychological hazard for most women." The authors also describe some of the risk factors that may contribute to any distress that is experienced following abortion, but they suggest that this distress reflects typical strategies for coping with normal life stress.

| POINT | COUNTERPOINT |
|---|---|
| • Abortion is a stressor that often has severe negative consequences. | • Distress is generally greater before abortion; thus, abortion is a stress reliever. |
| • Some psychological consequences of abortion can be permanent. | • Any negative psychological consequences are infrequent and limited in duration. |
| • The research on the effects of abortion is methodologically flawed. | • Methodologically sound studies do exist. |
| • Certain groups of women are underrepresented in the available research. | • The amount of bias from underrepresentation is minor. |
| • Psychology needs postabortion recovery treatment centers. | • Counseling and support is more useful before abortion, when the stress is greatest. |

# YES

Anne C. Speckhard
and Vincent M. Rue

## POSTABORTION SYNDROME: AN EMERGING PUBLIC HEALTH CONCERN

*Elective abortion, the most common surgical procedure in the United States, continues to generate considerable moral, legal, medical, and psychological controversy. This article reviews the pertinent literature, defines and describes postabortion syndrome (PAS) as a type of Post-Traumatic Stress Disorder....*

In the United States, prior to the liberalization and legalization of abortion, permission for an abortion sometimes required psychiatric determination of individual psychopathology (Stotland, 1989). When abortion became decriminalized and liberalized in the U.S. in 1973, psychiatric indications for abortion were eliminated. Today the abortion decision is private and requires no evidence of psychological impairment. In fact, psychiatric illness may be a contraindication (Moseley, Follingstad, & Harley, 1981; Ney & Wickett, 1989; Zakus & Wilday, 1987). In the current context, it is paradoxical but possible that the decision to elect abortion can generate significant resulting psychosocial distress (Rue, 1986; Speckhard, 1987b).

Clinical reports and recent studies have indicated that men, women, families, and even health care providers can sometimes experience negative psychological responses following abortion that do not appear to be linked back to individual pathology (Michels, 1988; Rue, 1986, 1987; Selby, 1990; Speckhard, 1987a, 1987b; Stanford-Rue, 1986). On the other hand, when psychopathology is present preabortion, increasing evidence suggests that abortion does not ameliorate individual dysfunction, but may worsen it (De-Veber, Ajzenstat, & Chisholm, 1991; Mall & Watts, 1979; Ney & Wickett, 1989).

Other recent studies have reported, however, minimal negative outcomes and even relief following abortion (Adler et al., 1990; David, 1985; Major, Mueller, & Hildebrandt, 1985). Not usually examined however, is the question of whether abortion may function in a dual role—as both coping mechanism *and* stressor. While abortion may indeed function as a stress reliever by eliminating an unwanted pregnancy, other evidence suggests that it may also simultaneously or subsequently be experienced by some individuals as a psychosocial stressor, capable of causing posttraumatic stress disorder

From Anne C. Speckhard and Vincent M. Rue, "Postabortion Syndrome: An Emerging Public Health Concern," *Journal of Social Issues*, vol. 48, no. 3 (1992). Copyright © 1992 by The Society for the Psychological Study of Social Issues. Reprinted by permission of Plenum Press, New York

(PTSD)—(Barnard, 1990; Rue, 1985, 1986, 1987; Selby, 1990; Speckhard, 1987a, 1987b; Vaughan, 1991). We suggest that this constellation of dysfunctional behaviors and emotional reactions should be termed "postabortion syndrome" (PAS).

## SOCIOPOLITICAL CONTEXT OF ABORTION RESEARCH

Like the decision to abort, the scientific study of the stress effects of abortion does not occur in a vacuum. The politicization of abortion has significantly restricted scientific investigation of the effects of abortion, and has produced a profound interpersonal and interprofessional schism in American society, including media reporting biases and public misinformation (Shaw, 1990).

There is a reluctance to call attention to negative consequences of abortion for fear of providing support to anti-abortion groups. Minimizing acknowledgment and discussion of postabortion trauma may result in women feeling abandoned by their counselors and isolated from other women experiencing similar difficulties. This may discourage women from revealing their postabortion feelings and may result in labeling women with emotional difficulties after their abortion as deviant and in need of psychotherapy (Lodl, McGettigan, & Bucy, 1985).

Ironically, the politicization of abortion research may be leading us to stigmatize and label women who experience postabortion stress as pathological. This would indeed be unfortunate given the many years of feminist-oriented research that attempted to remedy the "a priori" definition of women who choose abortion as pathological. Neither should those who experience abortion as trau-

matic now be defined as pathological without first considering the potential of abortion to act as a trauma even for some healthy women. Steinberg (1989) has cautioned, "We must examine the impact on these women because their numbers are so great and because the political and social volatility of this issue locks so many of them into silence" (p. 483).

Additionally, there is a danger of professional denial concerning the negative effects of abortion (Mester, 1978). The prevailing opinion espoused by the American Psychological Association (APA) is characteristic of the position held by most national and international mental health associations—i.e., that abortion, "particularly in the first trimester, does not create psychological hazards for most women undergoing the procedure" (Fox, 1990, p. 843); that "psychological sequelae [complications or conditions resulting from the event] are usually mild and tend to diminish over time without adversely affecting general functioning"; and that "severe emotional responses are rare" (American Psychological Association, 1987, p. 25). In the authors' opinion, the APA's position is an unwarranted overgeneralization that cannot be logically supported because it is based on a body of research that is methodologically flawed. David (1987) acknowledged,

Regardless of personal convictions about abortion, there is general agreement that uncertainty persists about the psychological sequelae of terminating pregnancies. Inconsistencies of interpretation stem from lack of consensus regarding the symptoms, severity, and duration of mental disorder; from opinions based on individual case studies; and from the lack of a national reporting system for adequate follow-up monitoring.... The literature abounds with methodological problems, lack of controls, and sampling inadequacies.... (p. 1)

Similarly, Adler et al. (1990) cautioned consumers of abortion regarding the psychological health risks by noting that "no definitive conclusions can be drawn about longer effects," and that "women who are more likely to find the abortion experience stressful may be underrepresented in volunteer samples" (p. 43).

Having gone "on record" supporting abortion, it may now be difficult for these professional groups to be open to reexamining their position. This has certainly been true of the American Psychological Association in its abortion advocacy positions, clearly stated in its U.S. Supreme Court amicus curiae briefs (i.e., in *Thornburgh v. ACOG*, *Hartigan v. Zbaraz*, and *Hodgson v. Humphrey*). In our opinion, the APA has been correctly criticized for overly extending the weight of scientific authority with respect to its statements and generalizations regarding adolescents and abortion (Gardner, Sherer, & Tester, 1989). On balance, Wilmoth (1988) concluded, "The most scientific conclusion about the psychological sequelae of abortion would be that the research permits no conclusions" (p. 9).

In 1989, U.S. Surgeon General Koop reported on his findings from meetings with scientists and clinicians, and from reviewing over 250 articles pertaining to the health risks of abortion. He concluded, "all these studies were reviewed... the data do not support the premise that abortion does or does not cause or contribute to psychological problems" (Koop, 1989a, p. 2). Later Koop testified in the U.S. House of Rep-

resentatives: "there is no doubt about the fact that there are those people who do have severe psychological problems after abortion" (Koop, 1989b, p. 232), and stated, "if you study abortion the way many people have and see how well women feel about their decision 3 months after the actual procedure, you can be very badly misled" (p. 241).

## RECENT ABORTION RESEARCH

Some recent reviews of the literature corroborate Koop's assessment (APA, 1987; Huckeba & Mueller, 1987), though others do not (Adler et al., 1990). Rue, Speckhard, Rogers, and Franz (1987) made an empirical assessment of the literature presented to Surgeon General Koop, which included (a) clinical evidence describing PAS; (b) a systematic analysis by Rogers that quantified threats to validity in 239 postabortion studies; and (c) a meta-analysis by Rogers of the controlled studies. (Excluding the meta-analysis, these data were later refined and published by Rogers, Stoms, & Phifer, 1989). In the paper by Rue et al. (1987), after excluding anecdotal and review articles, there remained 13 postpartum control-group studies, which were meta-analyzed, and 31 prospective and 32 retrospective uncontrolled studies, which were systematically analyzed.

The incidence of 20 methodological shortcomings in the above-mentioned 76 studies is presented in Table 1. For instance, in 69 of 76 studies insufficient sample size was evident (an $N \leq 385$), and in 33 studies substantial sample attrition was evident. Of the total number of studies, 49% used no baseline measurement and 25% had unclear outcome criteria. The mean number of method-

*Table 1*

**Percentage of Methodological Shortcomings in Comparison, Prospective, and Retrospective Studies of Abortion**

| Limitations in studies | Comparison studies ($N = 13$) | Prospective studies ($N = 31$) | Retrospective studies ($N = 32$) | Total ($N = 76$) |
|---|---|---|---|---|
| Sample size ($N \leq 385$) | 77 | 94 | 94 | 91 |
| Sample attrition | 31 | 45 | 47 | 43 |
| Selection bias | 23 | 35 | 28 | 30 |
| No baseline measurement | 31 | 35 | 69 | 49 |
| No demographics | 8 | 19 | 19 | 17 |
| Abortion granted on psychiatric grounds | 69 | 52 | 47 | 53 |
| History of psychiatric instability | 54 | 65 | 34 | 50 |
| No/low instrument reliability | 8 | 35 | 41 | 33 |
| No/low interrater reliability | 38 | 19 | 6 | 17 |
| Interviewer bias | 23 | 39 | 56 | 43 |
| Recall distortion | 15 | 3 | 59 | 29 |
| Indirect data | 31 | 16 | 13 | 17 |
| Incomplete data | 38 | 52 | 44 | 46 |
| Contradiction | 0 | 29 | 16 | 18 |
| Unclear outcome criteria | 23 | 29 | 22 | 25 |
| Recovery room follow-up | 0 | 16 | 0 | 7 |
| Follow-up varies | 15 | 10 | 38 | 22 |
| Concomitant sterilization | 31 | 32 | 28 | 30 |
| No incidence data | 23 | 26 | 0 | 15 |
| Multiple abortions | 23 | 39 | 38 | 36 |

*Note.* Unpublished table from data set of James Rogers originally used in Rue et al. (1987). Data set later refined and published in Rogers, Stroms, and Phifer (1989).

those uncontrolled studies with the greatest methodological weaknesses were more likely to report higher rates of positive experiences after abortion (Rue et al., 1987)....

After considering (a) prospective and retrospective studies, (b) postpartum control-group studies, and (c) the study that appeared to have used the best methodology of the various investigations reviewed (David, Rasmussen & Holst, 1981), Rue et al. (1987) concluded the following: (1) that the abortion literature is largely flawed as to design and methodology, (2) that all psychological studies of abortion display some negative outcomes for at least a proportion of those women studied, (3) that the clinical literature and experience with postabortion trauma are convergent in suggesting the need for the diagnostic category of PAS, and (4) that the types of errors found in the many studies examined *underestimate* the negative responses to abortion.

After reviewing the conclusions of the authors, Dr. Koop directed that the paper by Rue et al. (1987) be peer reviewed by health scientists within the federal government. Various anonymous criticisms of it were later reluctantly and unofficially provided to us (the identity of these reviewers was subsequently revealed in a congressional hearing and published in the committee report; the published versions are cited here). Some of the reviewers' criticisms displayed considerable bias: "Abortion is a moral issue (although all may not agree on this point either) and it must be removed from academic exercises of proof and disproof" (Dever, 1989, p. 165). Other reviewers concurred with the authors "that the issue could have important implications for public health" (Kleinman, 1989, p. 157). Some reviewers objected to the appropriateness of the meta-analytic technique. Meta-analysis, however, is now widely used and generally accepted as a means to obtain a numerical estimate of the overall effect size of a particular variable on a defined outcome. Indeed, in 1988 the authors conducted a computer search of the psychological, medical, health, biological, sociological, and family relations abstracts from 1980 to 1988, and found 895 citations, including approximately 528 meta-analyses that were reported in article titles. More recently, Posavac and Miller (1990) conducted a meta-analysis of the literature on the psychological effects of abortion and concurred that existing research is flawed methodologically, and that comparison group designs may tend to show more negative outcomes for abortion.

Perhaps the methodologically best-designed study completed to date is the Danish study reported by David et al. (1981), and David (1985). In it, admissions to psychiatric hospitals were tracked for a three-month period after either delivery or abortion for all Danish women under the age of 50, and then compared with the three-month admission rate to psychiatric hospitals for all Danish women of similar age. The authors found, "at all parities, women who obtained abortions are at higher risk for admission to psychiatric hospitals than are women who delivered" (David, 1985, p. 155). For abortion women, the psychiatric admission rate was 18.4 per 10,000 compared to 12.0 for delivering women and 7.5 for all Danish women aged 15–49. Of even more concern were the findings pertaining to women who were divorced, separated, or widowed at the time of abortion or delivery. The corresponding rates of psychiatric admission were 63.8 per 10,000 for these women aborting vs. 16.9 for these women [undergoing] delivery.

Four points require emphasis regarding this study (David et al., 1981): (1) it was relatively short-term and provided no long-term assessment of differences between women who aborted vs. those who delivered; (2) it most likely underreported the incidence and degree of postabortion traumatization because women may often be in denial for a considerable period of time after their abortion...; (3) the outcome measure used was admission to a psychiatric hospital, the worst-case circumstance—one could expect substantial quantitative differences between these two groups if less-severe dependent variables like depressive symptomatology or outpatient treatment in psychotherapy were used; and (4) women who elected abortion at all ages, parities, and relationship strata (except women aged 35–39, those with five pregnancies, and those who were married) had higher rates of admission to psychiatric hospitals than women who delivered.

An example of a methodologically unsound study is one in which 60% of 247 women surveyed failed to complete the study protocol three weeks postabortion (Major et al., 1985). Yet the authors concluded that the majority of women felt relief postprocedure. They did, however, caution:

> Of course, the possibility that women who returned to the clinic for their checkup were coping more successfully three weeks later than women who did not return cannot be ruled out, because we were unable to contact the women who did not return. (p. 594)

This high attrition rate could be attributed to avoidant behavior due to an abortion trauma, and it conforms to the view that women who are more likely to find the abortion experience stressful may be underreported in volunteer samples (Adler et al., 1990).

In 1987, Reardon conducted an exploratory survey of 252 high-stress, postabortion women. Although nonrandomly chosen and self-selected from 42 states, his sample compared favorably to national incidence data on women obtaining abortions by age, family size, race, marital status, and number of previous abortions. He found the majority of respondents experienced some of 28 negative outcomes including the following: flashbacks (61%), anniversary reactions (54%), suicidal ideation (33%), feelings of having less control of their lives (78%), difficulty in maintaining and developing relationships (52%), first use or increased use of drugs (49%), and delayed onset of stress, with most reporting their worst reactions as occurring one year or more postabortion (62%).

Likewise, Speckhard (1987b) found that all of the 30 women in her self-selected descriptive sample had long-term grief reactions, some lasting for over five years. Participants were women who described themselves as experiencing high-stress reactions, recruited through referrals from clinicians and other participants. In structured telephone interviews, the majority reported feelings of depression (100%), anger (92%), guilt (92%), fears that others would learn of the abortion (89%), preoccupation with the aborted child (81%), feelings of low self-worth (81%), discomfort around small children (73%), frequent crying (81%), flashbacks (73%), sexual dysfunction (69%), suicidal thoughts (65%), and increased alcohol usage (61%). The majority of the women studied reported being surprised at such intense reactions to their abortions.

These studies, though done with small, nonrandom groups, show that high-stress postabortive women can be doubly stigmatized by themselves—first by their fear of sharing their abortion experiences with one another and/or being viewed as deviant, and second by feeling that their negative reactions are a sign of maladjustment to what appears a relatively simple, common, and benign procedure (Speckhard, 1987a, 1987b). Koop (1989b) noted that in U.S. government reproductive surveys, the rate at which women reported having had an abortion was only half that expected based on abortion statistics.

Assessing the impact of abortion on the psychological health of women and men may not be as simple as some have suggested. In her book, *Parental Loss of a Child*, Rando included a chapter on the loss from induced abortion. In it, Harris (1986) described three obstacles to the clinical identification of negative responses following abortion: (1) masking of emotional responses may occur both at the time of the abortion and in later contacts with professionals; (2) if grief persists, it may surface in disguised form and be expressed behaviorally or in psychosomatic complaints; and (3) if the caregiver has ambivalent or unresolved feelings about abortion, this may interfere with the accurate assessment of postabortion trauma and the establishment of trust and the ability to be patient and empathic. Because of the self-insulation associated with the abortion experience, it is important that the caregiver be aware of the potential for grief, and take the initiative in exploring the client's perceptions and reactions. Joy (1985) stressed the need to be alert to women who are requesting counseling for depression resulting from unresolved grief over a prior abortion, i.e., a delayed grief reaction.

Vaughan (1991) studied 232 women from 39 states who by self-report suffered stress, guilt, grief, depression, and anger, which were defined as symptoms of PAS. The sample was purposive and was recruited primarily through a national network of crisis pregnancy centers affiliated with the Christian Action Council. The mean length of time since the abortion was 11 years. Vaughan employed the technique of canonical correlation between antecedent variables and postabortion variables. She found the following: (1) two different profiles of anger, guilt, and stress; (2) postabortion, 45% of respondents reported negative feelings toward subsequent pregnancies, difficulty bonding, and obsessive thoughts of having a replacement child; (3) only 5.9% of those not married but in a relationship at the time of the abortion continued their relationship postabortion; (4) 24% of the postabortive women

had medical problems perceived as having been caused by the abortion; (5) 36% were suicidal postabortion; (6) 42% indicated negative interaction with the abortion clinic staff and felt the counseling received there was misleading and deceptive—this dissatisfaction was significantly related to high anger and guilt scores; and (7) the onset of the symptoms suggested as indicative of PAS was often several years postprocedure.

Mattinson (1985) reported on case studies from the Tavistock Institute in London. She found that, for some patients, the existence of postabortion grief placed interpersonal relationships at risk. Delayed grief reactions causing interpersonal stress took many different forms. Some were mild but persistent; others of a more extreme nature were triggered many years later by a loss of a different nature. Sometimes husbands were more affected than wives.

The first study to use standardized outcome measures of PTSD compared to the diagnostic criteria for PAS developed by Rue was conducted by Barnard (1990). She randomly selected 984 women from a Maryland abortion clinic for a follow-up questionnaire. Interestingly, 60% apparently gave the wrong telephone number at the time of their abortion. After administering a 48-item questionnaire designed to measure PAS (the Impact of Event Scale) and the Millon Clinical Multiaxial Inventory, Barnard reported 45% of her sample of 80 women had symptoms of avoidance and intrusion, and 19% met the full diagnostic criteria for PTSD three to five years following an abortion. She also noted that 68% of these women had little or no religious involvement at the time of the abortion.

Even representatives of Planned Parenthood, an organization that has historically denied the legitimacy of postabortion traumatization and the idea that abortion involves a human death experience, has affirmed that

> women can have a variety of emotions following an abortion (grief, depression, anger, guilt, relief, etc.). It is important to give her the opportunity to air these feelings and be reassured that her feelings are normal. The counselor can also help by letting the woman know that a sense of loss or depression following an abortion is common, due to both the end of the pregnancy as well as the physical and hormonal changes that occur after a pregnancy is over. (Saltzman & Policar, 1985, p. 94)

Because there has never been a national epidemiological study of the psychological health risks of abortion in this country, it is impossible to estimate with any accuracy the incidence of negative abortion sequelae. Lodl et al. (1985) estimated a range of 10%–50% experiencing distress following abortion. A recent APA task force on women and depression (McGrath, Keita, Strickland, & Russo, 1990) concluded that "abortion's relative risk of mental disorder compared with other reproductive events has not been fully ascertained" (p. 12).

Symptoms of traumatization have also been documented in populations of women aborting for genetic reasons, suggesting that the wantedness of the pregnancy at the time of the abortion may not be the key issue in whether or not a woman is traumatized by her abortion, as some have suggested. In a study of couples who elected prostaglandin induction abortion for genetic reasons, i.e., fetal anomalies, Magyari, Wedehase, Ifft, and Callanan (1987) reported negative psychological sequelae in their sample. Interestingly, the psychologi-

cal intervention protocol developed by Magyari et al. (1987) for these parents of wanted children identified the following: (1) the need for grief counseling that is anticipatory in nature, individualized, and emphasizes the normalcy of feelings; and (2) facilitation of the mourning process by affirming the pregnancy and providing memories central to the grief process. The latter included the options of seeing or holding the fetus, knowing the sex of the fetus, viewing a photo of the fetus, and naming the fetus. The majority of couples elected to see their aborted offspring.

As is often the case with abortion for nongenetic reasons, common feelings in these couples after abortion for genetic reasons included relief and a sense of conclusion to the crisis. Yet Magyari et al. (1987) cautioned, "We tell them that they face a difficult time and that recovery may not be as smooth as their friends and family may assume it will be" (p. 78). At six to eight weeks postabortion, the intervention team discussed unmet grief reactions thus far and assisted the couple by discussing future events including anniversary reactions. Immediate reproductive replacement was discouraged and the couple was warned "not to pursue a subsequent pregnancy as a replacement for the lost child" (Magyari et al., 1987, p. 80). Even with this intervention protocol in operation, within one year of the abortion, two out of three couples were pregnant again, suggesting the existence of a "replacement child phenomenon." Peppers (1987) has corroborated that grief over a perinatal loss, including abortion can occur irrespective of the wantedness of the pregnancy. In his study, 80 women having abortions at a clinic in Atlanta completed a 13-item grief scale....

## ABORTION EXPERIENCED AS A STRESSOR

"Researchers tend to agree that, at some level, abortion is a stressful experience for all women" (APA, 1987, p. 18). The American Psychiatric Association (1987), in its *Diagnostic and Statistical Manual of Mental Disorders* (3rd ed., rev.; DSM-III-R), listed abortion as an example of a psychosocial stressor, but has not included the category of PAS. As a psychosocial stressor, abortion may lead some women to experience reactions ranging from mild distress to severe trauma, creating a continuum that we conceptualize as progressing in severity from postabortion distress (PAD), to PAS, to postabortion psychosis (PAP).

The concept of PAS is in the formative stages of understanding and operationalization (Wilmoth, 1988). It took the American Psychiatric Association over a decade to officially recognize posttraumatic stress disorder (PTSD). PAD, PAS, and PAP may currently be making a similar transition, though none of them are currently recognized even as subtypes or examples in the DSM-III-R. The following definitions are proposed:

### Postabortion Distress

PAD may be defined as the manifestation of symptoms of discomfort following an abortion, resulting from three aspects: (a) the perceived physical pain and emotional stress of the pregnancy and abortion; (b) the perception of a loss from the abortion (i.e., loss of a role, dream, relationship, parts or perception of self, potential life, etc.); and (c) the conflict in personality, roles, values, and relationships that results from a changed perception of the appropriateness of the abortion decision.

PAD might be categorized as an adjustment disorder when impairment in occupational functioning or in usual social activities occurs. In order for it to be considered an adjustment disorder, the onset of distress must occur within three months of the abortion and persist no longer than six months, and persistent reexperience of the abortion stressor cannot be present (American Psychiatric Association, 1987).

### Postabortion Psychosis

PAP is suggested as a generic designation for major affective or thought disorders not present before an abortion, and directly and clinically attributable to the induced abortion. PAP is characterized by chronic and severe symptoms of disorganization and significant personality and reality impairment, including hallucinations, delusions, and severe depression. Decompensation occurs when the individual becomes aware of, overwhelmed by, and unable to communicate the feelings of guilt, grief, fear, anger, and responsibility for the traumatic death of her/his unborn child. Other manifestations may include intolerable levels of affect, self-condemnation, anxiety, and terror at feeling unable to face the trauma, and also paranoia about being found out. Although PAP is not a commonly encountered reaction to abortion traumatization, clinical evidence of it has been reported (Sim & Neisser, 1979; Spaulding & Cavenar, 1978; Speckhard & Rue, in press).

### Postabortion Syndrome

PAS is proposed as a type of PTSD that is characterized by the chronic or delayed development of symptoms resulting from impacted emotional reactions to the perceived physical and emotional trauma of abortion. We propose four basic components of PAS as a variant of PTSD: (1) exposure to or participation in an abortion experience, i.e., the intentional destruction of one's unborn child,[1] which is perceived as traumatic and beyond the range of usual human experience; (2) uncontrolled negative reexperiencing of the abortion death event, e.g., flashbacks, nightmares, grief, and anniversary reactions; (3) unsuccessful attempts to avoid or deny abortion recollections and emotional pain, which result in reduced responsiveness to others and one's environment; and (4) experiencing associated symptoms not present before the abortion, including guilt about surviving.

The proposed diagnostic criteria for PAS... were developed from the diagnostic assessment of PTSD in the DSM-III-R (American Psychiatric Association, 1987). The course of PAS conforms to the diagnostic criteria for PTSD—i.e., the symptoms of reexperience, avoidance, and associated symptoms must persist more than one month, or the onset may be delayed (i.e., greater than six months after the abortion). Clinical experience suggests that spontaneous recovery from PAS is not characteristic. Although PAS is categorized here as a type of PTSD, additional diagnoses including anxiety, depressive, or organic mental disorder may concurrently be made.

More than an accidental grab bag of isolated symptoms, PAS is conceptualized here as a clustering of related and unsuccessful attempts to assimilate and gain mastery over an abortion trauma. The resulting lifestyle changes involve partial to total cognitive restructuring and behavioral reorganization.

Wilmoth, Bussell, and Wilcox (1991) argue that PAS is not a type of PTSD because abortion is volitional. Peterson, Prout, and Schwarz (1991) have pointed out, however, that there are situations when patients suffering with PTSD in fact have reasons to feel guilty. They identify among many pathological identifications a "killer self" (p. 90). We submit that the volitional nature of the abortion decision is largely responsible for the perceived degree of traumatization. On the other hand, some women with PAS perceive their abortions as less than totally volitional. Some women feel their abortion was coerced, forced, or the only option available to them (Luker, 1975), and others feel their consent was not informed (Reardon, 1987; Speckhard, 1987b). Moreover, the DSM-III-R does not preclude volitional stressors in the criteria for PTSD (e.g., divorce and accidental homicide). In fact, it clearly indicates that PTSD is apparently more severe and longer lasting when the stressor is of human design (American Psychiatric Association, 1987, p. 248). We hold that abortion, intentionally caused and yielding unintended consequences, is one such example.

## CONCLUSION

The psychological impact of abortion trauma on women, men, and children is far more complex than previously realized. Flawed studies and political pressure have produced an informational deficit concerning postabortion trauma. It is essential that the aftereffects of abortion be thoroughly reexamined. Failure to do so may lead women into making decisions about abortion that could be detrimental to them, decisions lacking in informed consent and free choice. Even critics like Wilmoth (1988, p. 12) have conceded that "after further study, PAS may become an accepted diagnostic category."

In addition to the need for improved research on this topic, the authors believe there is a growing need for specialized postabortion recovery treatment models and services—for example, postabortion counseling centers, peer support groups, and educational workshops for both the general public and professionals. A growing need is evident; the resistance to this viewpoint, however, may be formidable.

## NOTE

1. The term fetal or unborn child is used throughout this article to indicate the differing stages of development, embryo to fetus, at which abortion occurs. This term is used in deference to the perceptions of women and men distressed by the loss of their psychological attachment to what they often refer to as "our baby."

## REFERENCES

Adler, E., David, H., Major, B., Roth, S., Russo, N., & Wyatt, G. (1990). Psychological responses after abortion. *Science, 248*, 41–44.

American Psychiatric Association. (1987). *Diagnostic and statistical manual of mental disorders* (3rd ed., rev.). Washington, DC: Author.

American Psychological Association (1987). *Research review: Psychological sequelae of abortion*. Unpublished testimony presented to the Office of the U.S. Surgeon General. Washington, DC: Author.

Barnard, C. A. (1990) *The long-term psychosocial effects of abortion*. Portsmouth, NH: Institute for Pregnancy Loss.

David, H. (1985). Post-abortion and post-partum psychiatric hospitalization. *Ciba Foundation Symposium, 115*, 150–164.

David, H. (1987). Post-abortion syndrome? *Abortion Research Notes, 16*, 1–6.

David, H., Rasmussen, N., & Holst, E. (1981). Post-partum and postabortion psychotic reactions. *Family Planning Perspectives, 13*, 88–91.

DeVeber, L., Ajzenstat, J., & Chisholm, D. (1991). Postabortion grief: Psychological sequelae of induced abortion. *Humane Medicine, 7*, 203–209.

Dever, G. (1989, March 16). A report on *The psychological aftermath of abortion:* An evaluation. Written testimony submitted to the Human Resources and Intergovernmental Relations Subcommittee of the Committee on Government Operations, U.S. House of Representatives. In *Medical and psychological impact of abortion* (pp. 162–173). Washington, DC: U.S. Government Printing Office.

Fox, R. (1990). Proceedings of the American Psychological Association, Incorporated for the year 1989: Minutes of the annual meeting of the Council of Representatives. *American Psychologist, 45*, 817–847.

Gardner, W., Sherer, D., & Tester, M. (1989). Asserting scientific authority. *American Psychologist, 44*, 895–902.

Huckeba, W., & Mueller, C. (1987). *Systematic analysis of research on psycho-social effects of abortion reported in refereed journals 1966–1985*. Unpublished manuscript. Washington, DC: Family Research Council.

Kleinman, J. (1989, March 16). Written testimony submitted to the Human Resources and Intergovernmental Relations Subcommittee of the Committee on Government Operations, U.S. House of Representatives. In *Medical and psychological impact of abortion* (pp. 156–157). Washington, DC: U.S. Government Printing Office.

Koop, C. (1989a, January 9). Letter to President Ronald Reagan concerning the health effects of abortion. In *Medical and psychological impact of abortion* (pp 68–71). Washington, DC: U.S. Government Printing Office.

Koop, C. (1989b, March 16). Testimony before the Human Resources and Intergovernmental Relations Subcommittee of the Committee on Government Operations, U.S. House of Representatives. In *Medical and psychological impact of abortion* (pp. 193–203, 218, 223–250). Washington, DC: U.S. Government Printing Office.

Lodl, K., McGettigan, A., & Bucy, J. (1985). Women's responses to abortion: Implications for postabortion support groups. *Journal of Social Work and Human Sexuality, 3*, 119–132.

Magyari, P., Wedehase, B., Ifft, R., & Callanan, N. (1987). A supportive intervention protocol for couples terminating a pregnancy for genetic reasons. *Birth Defects, 23*, 75–83.

Mall, D., & Watts, W. (Eds.). (1979). *The psychological aspects of abortion*. Washington, DC: University Publications of America.

Major, B., Mueller, P., & Hildebrandt, K. (1985). Attributions, expectations and coping with abortion. *Journal of Personality and Social Psychology, 48*, 585–599.

Mattinson, J. (1985). The effects of abortion on a marriage. *Ciba Foundation Symposium, 115,* 165–177.

McGrath, E., Keita, G., Strickland, B., & Russo, N. (Eds.). (1990). *Women and depression: Risk factors and treatment issues.* Washington, DC: American Psychological Association.

Mester, R. (1978). Induced abortion in psychotherapy. *Psychotherapy and Psychosomatics, 30,* 98–104.

Michels, N. (1988). *Helping women recover from abortion.* Minneapolis: Bethany House.

Moseley, D., Follingstad, D., & Harley, H. (1981). Psychological factors that predict reaction to abortion. *Journal of Clinical Psychology, 37,* 276–279.

Ney, P., & Wickett, A. (1989). Mental health and abortion: Review and analysis. *Psychiatric Journal of the University of Ottawa Press, 14,* 506–516.

Peppers, L. (1987). Grief and elective abortion: Breaking the emotional bond? *Omega, 18,* 1–12.

Peterson, K., Prout, M., & Schwarz, R. (1991). *Posttraumatic stress disorder: A clinician's guide.* New York; Plenum.

Posavac, E., & Miller, T. (1990). Some problems caused by not having a conceptual foundation for health research: An illustration from studies of the psychological effects of abortion. *Psychology and Health, 5,* 13–23.

Rando, T. (Ed.). (1986). *Parental loss of a child.* Champaign, IL: Research Press.

Reardon, D. (1987). *Aborted women: Silent no more.* Chicago: Loyola University Press.

Rogers, J., Stomis, G., & Phifer, J. (1989). Psychological impact of abortion. *Health Care for Women International, 10,* 347–376.

Rue, V. (1985). Abortion in relationship context. *International Journal of Natural Family Planning, 9,* 95–121.

Rue, V. (1986, August). *Post-abortion syndrome.* Paper presented at Conference on Post-Abortion Healing, University of Notre Dame.

Rue, V. (1987, August). *Current trends and status of post-abortion syndrome.* Paper presented at Conference on Post Abortion Healing, University of Notre Dame.

Rue, V., Speckhard, A., Rogers, J., & Franz, W. (1987). *The psychological aftermath of abortion: A white paper.* Testimony presented to the Office of the Surgeon General, U.S. Department of Health and Human Services, Washington, DC.

Saltzman, L., & Policar, M. (Eds.). (1985). *The complete guide to pregnancy testing and counseling.* San Francisco: Planned Parenthood of Alameda/San Francisco.

Selby, T. (1990). *The mourning after: Help for post-abortion syndrome.* Grand Rapids, MI: Baker Book House.

Shaw, D. (1990). Abortion bias seeps into news. Investigative series. *Los Angeles Times.* July 1, pp. 1, A30, A50; July 2, pp. 1, A20; July 3, pp. 1, A22, A23; July 4, pp. 1, A28, A38.

Sim, M., & Neisser, R. (1979). Post-abortive psychoses: A report from two centers. In D. Mall & W. Watts (Eds.), *The psychological aspects of abortion* (pp. 1–14). Washington, DC: University Publications of America.

Spaulding, J., & Cavenar, J. (1978). Psychoses following therapeutic abortion. *American Journal of Psychiatry, 135,* 364–365.

Speckhard, A. C. (1987a). *Post-abortion counseling.* Portsmouth, NH: Institute for Pregnancy Loss.

Speckhard, A. C. (1987b). *Psycho-social stress following abortion.* Kansas City, MO: Speed & Ward.

Speckhard, A., & Rue, V. (in press). Complicated mourning: Dynamics of impacted post-abortion grief. *Pre- & Peri-natal Psychology Journal.*

Stanford-Rue, S. (1986). *Will I cry tomorrow: Healing post-abortion trauma.* Old Tappan, NJ: Fleming Revell.

Steinberg, T. (1989). Abortion counseling: To benefit maternal health. *American Journal of Law and Medicine, 15,* 483–517.

Stotland, N. (1989). Psychiatric issues in abortion, and the implications of recent legal changes for psychiatric practice. In N. Stotland (Ed.), *Psychiatric aspects of abortion* (pp. 1–16). Washington, DC: American Psychiatric Press.

Vaughan, H. (1991). *Canonical variates of post-abortion syndrome.* Portsmouth, NH: Institute for Pregnancy Loss.

Wilmoth, G. (1988). Depression and abortion: A brief review. *Population and Environmental Psychology News, 14,* 9–12.

Wilmoth, G., Bussell, D., & Wilcox, B. (1991). Abortion and family policy: A mental health perspective. E. A. Anderson & R. C. Hula (Eds.), *The reconstruction of family policy* (pp. 111–127). New York: Greenwood

Zakus, G., & Wilday, S. (1987). Adolescent abortion option. *Social Work in Health Care, 12,* 77–91.

# NO

## Nancy E. Adler, Henry P. David, Brenda N. Major, Susan H. Roth, Nancy F. Russo, and Gail E. Wyatt

## PSYCHOLOGICAL RESPONSES AFTER ABORTION

*A review of methodologically sound studies of the psychological responses of U.S. women after they obtained legal, nonrestrictive abortions indicates that distress is generally greatest before the abortion and that the incidence of severe negative responses is low. Factors associated with increased risk of negative response are consistent with those reported in research on other stressful life events.*

Abortion has been a legal medical procedure throughout the United States since the 1973 Supreme Court decision in *Roe v. Wade*, with 1.5 million to 1.6 million procedures performed annually. U.S. abortion patients reflect all segments of the population. In 1987, almost 60% of abortion patients were under 25 years of age. Most (82%) were not married, and half had no prior births. Nearly 69% of women obtaining abortions were white (1). Abortions are most often performed in the first trimester; the median gestational age is 9.2 weeks; 97% of abortions are performed by instrumental evacuation (2).

Although much literature exists on the psychological consequences of abortion, contradictory conclusions have been reached. Disparate interpretations are due in part to limitations of the research methods and in part to political, value, or moral influences. In this review of studies with the most rigorous research designs, we report consistent findings on the psychological status of women who have had legal abortions under nonrestrictive circumstances (3). This article is limited to U.S. studies; however, results from a study in Denmark are also relevant because of the existence of a uniform national population registration system not available in the United States (4).

## RESPONSES AFTER ABORTION

Responses after abortion reflect the entire course of experiencing and resolving an unwanted pregnancy. Although there may be sensations of regret, sadness, or guilt, the weight of the evidence from scientific studies (3) indicates that legal abortion of an unwanted pregnancy in the first trimester does not pose a psychological hazard for most women.

Descriptive studies have shown the incidence of severe negative responses after abortion to be low (5–10). After first-trimester abortion, women most frequently report feeling relief and happiness. In a study by Lazarus (5), 2 weeks after first-trimester abortions, 76% of women reported feeling relief, while the most common negative emotion, guilt, was reported by only 17%. Negative emotions reflecting internal concerns, such as loss, or social concerns, such as social disapproval, typically are not experienced as strongly as positive emotions after abortion (5–8). For example, Adler (6) obtained ratings of feelings over a 2- to 3-month period after abortion on Likert-type scales, with 5 representing strongest intensity. Mean ratings were 3.96 for positive emotions, 2.26 for internally based negative emotions, and 1.89 for socially based negative emotions.

Women show little evidence of psychopathology after abortion. For example, on the short form of the Beck Depression Inventory, scores below 5 are considered nondepressed (11). In a sample of first-trimester patients, Major et al. (9) obtained mean scores of 4.17 (SD* = 3.92) immediately after the abortion and 1.97 (SD = 2.93) 3 weeks later.

---

* [SD = standard deviation.—Ed.]

Measures used in most studies were not designed to assess psychopathology, but, rather, emotional distress within normal populations. These indicators show significant (12) decreases in distress from before abortion to immediately after and from before abortion or immediately after to several weeks later (9, 10). For example, Cohen and Roth (10) found a drop in the depression subscale of the Symptom Checklist 90 (SCL-90) from a mean of 24.1 (SD = 11.8) at the time of arrival at a clinic to a mean of 18.4 (SD = 12.2) in the recovery room. Similar drops were shown on the anxiety scale of the SCL-90 and on the Impact of Events scale, an indicator of distress.

Only two studies compared responses after abortion with those after birth. Athanasiou et al. (13) studied women after early (suction) abortion, late (saline) abortion, and term birth. Starting with 373 women, researchers matched 38 patients in each group for ethnicity, age, parity, and marital and socioeconomic status. Thirteen to sixteen months after abortion or delivery, women completed the Minnesota Multiphasic Personality Inventory (MMPI) and the SCL. None of the groups had a mean score on any subscales of the MMPI above 70, the cutoff indicating psychopathology. Few differences among groups were shown (14), and the authors concluded that the three groups were "startlingly similar."

Zabin et al. (15) interviewed 360 adolescents seeking pregnancy tests and compared those who had negative results, those who were pregnant and carried to term, and those who were pregnant and aborted. All three groups showed higher levels of state (transient) anxiety at base line than they did 1 or 2 years later (for example, for the abortion group $\bar{X}$ = 74.6 at base line versus 45.6

and 43.6 at 1 and 2 years later). Two years after the initial interview, the abortion group showed, if anything, a more positive psychological profile than either of the other two groups. There were no differences on state anxiety, but the abortion group was significantly lower on trait anxiety than either of the other two groups, was higher on self-esteem than the negative pregnancy group, and had a greater sense of internal control than the childbearing group.

## FACTORS RELATING TO PSYCHOLOGICAL RESPONSES

Although most women do not experience negative psychological responses after abortion, case studies document some negative experiences. Various aspects of the abortion experience may contribute to distress. Ambivalence about the wantedness of the pregnancy may engender a sense of loss. Conflict about the meaning of abortion and its relation to deeply held values or beliefs, perceived social stigma, or lack of support may also induce negative reactions.

*The decision process.* The greater the difficulty of deciding to terminate a pregnancy, the more likely there will be negative responses after abortion (6–8, 16). For example, Adler (6) found that the difficulty of deciding to abort, reported several days before abortion, was positively associated with the experience of negative emotions reflecting loss 2 to 3 months after abortion ($r = 0.37$), but was not related to a statistically significant extent to the experience of positive emotions or of negative emotions reflecting social disapproval.

Although most women do not find the decision to abort difficult, some do (16), and it appears to be more difficult

for women seeking termination later in pregnancy. Whereas only 7% of 100 first-trimester patients studied by Osofsky et al. (17) reported initial indecision and 12% reported difficulty in deciding about abortion, corresponding figures among 200 second-trimester patients were 36 and 51%. Women undergoing second-trimester abortions also report more emotional distress after abortion than do those terminating first-trimester pregnancies (17–19).

Women who perceive more support for the decision to abort are more satisfied with their decision (7, 20). Those with fewer conflicts over abortion are also more satisfied; in a sample of adolescents, Eisen and Zellman (21) found that satisfaction with the decision 6 months after an abortion was associated with a favorable opinion of abortion in general as well as for themselves.

The more a pregnancy is wanted and is viewed as personally meaningful by the woman, the more difficult abortion may be. Major et al. (9) found that among 247 first-trimester abortion patients, women who described their pregnancy as being "highly meaningful" compared to those who found their pregnancy to be less personally meaningful reported more physical complaints immediately after the abortion and anticipated more negative consequences. Three weeks after the abortion, women who had indicated having had no intention to become pregnant scored significantly lower on the Beck Depression Inventory ($\bar{X} = 1.68$, SD = 2.33) than did the minority of women who had at least some intention to become pregnant ($\bar{X} = 3.71$, SD = 5.03).

In summary, women who report little difficulty in making their decision, who are more satisfied with their choice, and who are terminating pregnancies that were unintended and hold little personal meaning for them show more positive responses after abortion. Women with negative attitudes toward abortion and who perceive little support for their decision have more difficulty deciding about abortion. These factors may also contribute to delay in obtaining abortions (19), potentially subjecting women to the greater stress of second-trimester procedures (17–19).

*Perceived social support.* Perceived social support can buffer some adverse effects of stressful life events (22). However, social support is complex. Support for having the abortion needs to be differentiated from support in general; the former is associated with more favorable outcomes; the latter may not be.

Women with greater support for their abortion from parents and the male partner generally show more positive responses after abortion (8, 23, 24). Intimacy with and involvement of the male partner was a significant predictor of emotional reaction in two samples (8). Together with satisfaction with the decision and the woman's initial emotional response to becoming pregnant, partner support accounted for almost 40% of the variance in psychological response 2 to 3 weeks after abortion. Moseley et al. (24) found that having negative feelings toward one's partner, making the abortion decision alone, and experiencing opposition from parents were associated with greater emotional distress on the Multiple Affective Adjective Check List both before a first-trimester abortion and immediately after. However, Robbins (25) found that single women who maintained a strong relationship with their partner reported more negative change on the MMPI 6 weeks after abortion and

more regret 1 year later than those whose relationships deteriorated.

In a study of actual social support, Major et al. (9) recorded whether women were accompanied to the clinic by a male partner. Out of 247 women, 83 were accompanied. Compared to unaccompanied women, those with partners were younger and expected to cope less well beforehand; women who were more distressed about the abortion may have expressed a greater need for their partners to accompany them. Accompanied women were significantly more depressed and reported more physical complaints immediately after abortion than unaccompanied women. Differences in depression after abortion remained after controlling for age and coping expectations, but they did not remain in a 3-week follow-up of a subset of women.

*Coping processes and expectancies.* Generalized positive outcome expectancies and situation-specific coping expectancies and processes have been linked to a variety of health-relevant outcomes (26). Major et al. (9) found that among abortion patients, those who expected to cope well scored lower on the Beck Depression Inventory than those with more negative expectations ($\bar{X} = 2.98$, SD = 3.04 versus $\bar{X} = 5.93$, SD = 4.41, respectively). Those expecting to cope well also showed more positive mood, anticipated fewer negative consequences, and had fewer physical complaints both immediately after abortion and 3 weeks later.

Cohen and Roth (10) examined coping styles and levels of anxiety and depression before and immediately after abortion. As noted earlier, anxiety and depression decreased significantly from before the abortion to afterwards for all women, but those who used approach strategies (for example, thinking about the procedure, talking about it) showed a greater decrease in anxiety from before to after abortion than those not using these strategies. Women who used denial scored significantly higher in depression and anxiety than did those who did not deny.

## LIMITATIONS OF RESEARCH AND FUTURE DIRECTIONS

Although each study has methodological shortcomings and limitations, the diversity of methods used provides strength in drawing general conclusions. Despite the diversity, the studies are consistent in their findings of relatively rare instances of negative responses after abortion and of decreases in psychological distress after abortion compared to before abortion. However, weaknesses and gaps found among studies provide challenges for future research.

First, samples of well-defined populations and information on subjects who choose not to participate are needed. Studies have sampled women from specific clinics or hospitals. Both public and private clinics have been used, and samples have varied in their ethnic and socioeconomic character. Women whose abortions are performed by private physicians are not represented; they are estimated to be about 4% of women having abortions (27).

Of more concern is the necessary use of volunteers, which can introduce bias if women who agree to participate in research differ from those who do not on characteristics linked to more positive or negative outcomes. An analysis of studies that provide data on characteristics of research participants versus the population from which the sample was drawn suggests that women who are more likely to find the abortion experience stressful may be underrepresented in volunteer samples. However, the amount of bias introduced by this underrepresentation appears to be minor and unlikely to influence the general conclusions (28).

Second, the timing of measurement has been limited. Many studies lack base-line date from before the abortion. We know of no studies with data collected before the pregnancy, making it impossible to control for variables that may be associated with the initial occurrence of the pregnancy and which could influence responses after abortion. One of the best predictors of a woman's psychological status after abortion is likely to be her functioning before the occurrence of the unwanted pregnancy (29). Former Surgeon General C. Everett Koop has called for a prospective study of a nationally representative sample of women of child-bearing age (30). Such a study would address both issues of representativeness and of base-line measurement.

Timing of assessment after abortion has also been limited. Some studies obtained measures within a few hours after the procedure, while the woman was still in the clinic. Responses at this time may not be indicative of longer term response. A few studies have obtained measures a few weeks or months after abortion; the longest follow-up is 2 years. Therefore, no definitive conclusions can be drawn about longer term effects. Although individual case studies have identified instances in which individuals develop severe problems that they attribute to an earlier abortion experience (31), the number of such cases is comparatively small. Moreover, research on other life stresses suggests that women who do not experience severe negative responses within a few months after the event are unlikely to develop future significant psychological problems related to the event (32). Longer term studies are needed to confirm this observation and to ascertain the influence of other life events attributed retrospectively to the abortion experience.

Finally, in studying psychological responses after abortion, it is important to separate the experience of abortion from the characteristics of women seeking abortion and from the context of resolving an unwanted pregnancy. A useful comparison would be women who carry an unwanted pregnancy to term and surrender the child for adoption; this would control both for the unwantedness of the pregnancy and the experience of loss. The study by Athanasiou et al. (13) matched women who were terminating pregnancies with those carrying to term on key demographic variables, but they were not matched on "wantedness" of the pregnancy. Similarly, the comparison used in the Danish study (4) for women aborting their pregnancies was women carrying to term, most of whom were likely to be delivering wanted pregnancies. One would expect more adverse outcomes for women carrying unwanted pregnancies to term (33).

A number of questions can be addressed without a comparison group. Theoretically grounded studies testing conditional hypotheses about factors that may put women at relatively greater risk for negative responses are particularly important. Such studies can address critical questions about the nature of the abortion experience and its aftermath, and can point the way to interventions if needed.

## CONCLUSION

Scientific studies on psychological responses to legal, nonrestrictive abortion in the United States suggest that severe negative reactions are infrequent in the immediate and short-term aftermath, particularly for first-trimester abortions. Women who are terminating pregnancies that are wanted and personally meaningful, who lack support from their partner or parents for the abortion, or who have more conflicting feelings or are less sure of their decision beforehand may be at relatively higher risk for negative consequences.

Case studies have established that some women experience severe distress or psychopathology after abortion and require sympathetic care. As former Surgeon General C. Everett Koop testified before Congress regarding his review of research on psychological effects of abortion, such responses can be overwhelming to a given individual, but the development of significant psychological problems related to abortion is "minuscule from a public health perspective" (34).

Despite methodological shortcomings of any single study, in the aggregate, research with diverse samples, different measures of response, and different times of assessment have come to similar conclusions. The time of greatest distress is likely to be before the abortion. Severe negative reactions after abortions are rare and can best be understood in the framework of coping with a normal life stress.

## REFERENCES AND NOTES

1. S. K. Henshaw and J. Silverman, *Fam. Plann. Perspect.* **20**, 158 (1988).

2. S. Henshaw, *ibid.* **19**, 5 (1987); C. Tietze and S. K. Henshaw, *Induced Abortion: A World Review* (Alan Guttmacher Institute, New York, 1986); E. Powell-Griner, *Mon. Vital Stat.* **36** (no. 5), 1 (1987).

3. Studies included in this article had to meet the following three criteria: (i) the research was empirical and based on a definable sample; (ii) the sample was drawn from the United States; and (iii) the women studied had undergone abortions under legal and nonrestrictive conditions (for example, women did not have to qualify for the procedure on the basis of threat to physical or mental health). These criteria allow for maximal generalizability to U.S. women under current conditions.

4. Through the use of computer linkages to national abortion and birth registers, the admissions register to psychiatric hospitals was tracked for women 3 months after abortion ($n = 27,234$) or delivery ($n = 71,370$) and for all women 15 to 49 years of age residing in Denmark ($n = 1,169,819$). To determine incidence rates, only first admissions to psychiatric hospitals were recorded, excluding women who had been admitted within the 15 previous months. The key finding was that for both never-married women and currently married women, the psychiatric admission rate after pregnancy was roughly the same for abortions or deliveries—about 12 per 10,000 compared to 7 per 10,000 for all women of reproductive age. Among the much smaller group of separated, divorced, or widowed women, those who had terminated pregnancies (which perhaps were originally intended) experienced a fourfold higher admissions rate (64 per 10,000) than the group of separated, divorced, or widowed women who delivered (17 per 10,000). However, because there may be a bias against hospitalizing a new mother, particularly if she is nursing, the relative psychological risk of delivery may be underestimated [H. P. David, N. Rasmussen, E. Holst, *Fam. Plann. Persect.* **13**, 88 (1981)].

5. A. Lazarus, *J. Psychosom. Obstet. Gynaecol.* **4**, 141 (1985).

6. N. E. Adler, *Am. J. Orthopsychiatry* **45**, 446 (1975).

7. J. D. Osofsky and H. Osofsky, *ibid.* **42**, 48 (1972).

8. L. R. Shusterman, *Soc. Sci. Med.* **13A**, 683 (1979).

9. B. Major, P. Mueller, K. Hildebrandt, *J. Pers. Soc. Psychol.* **48**, 585 (1985). Means for 3-week follow-up interviews reported here do not match means published in the original article. Due to an error in the original publication, standard deviations were reported instead of means, but all tests of significance were accurate. The correct means are reported here.

10. L. Cohen and S. Roth, *J. Hum. Stress.* **10**, 140 (1984).

11. A. T. Beck and R. W. Beck, *Postgrad. Med.* **52**, 81 (1972).

12. In this article, significance is used in terms of statistical significance and may not represent clinically significant changes or associations.

13. R. Athanasiou, W. Oppel, L. Michaelson, T. Unger, M. Yager, *Fam. Plann. Persect.* **5**, 227 (1973).

14. The only statistically significant differences found were as follows: (i) women who had experienced term birth scored higher on the paranoia subscale of the MMPI ($\bar{X} = 61.7$, SD $= 14.6$) than did women in either abortion group ($\bar{X} = 58.9$, SD $= 12.2$ for suction patients and $\bar{X} = 54.6$, SD $= 9.4$ for saline patients) and (ii) suction abortion patients reported fewer somatic complaints on the SCL ($\bar{X} = 10.6$, SD $= 8.0$) than either the saline abortion or delivery patients ($\bar{X} = 14.7$, SD $= 8.1$ and $\bar{X} = 14.8$, SD $= 9.3$, respectively).

15. L. S. Zabin, M. B. Hirsch, M. R. Emerson, *Fam. Plann. Persect.* **21**, 248 (1989).

16. M. B. Bracken, *Soc. Psychiatry* **13**, 135 (1978).

17. J. D. Osofsky, H. J. Osofsky, R. Rajan, D. Spitz, *Mt. Sinai J. Med.* **42**, 456 (1975).

18. J. B. Rooks and W. Cates, Jr., *Fam. Plann. Persect.* **9**, 276 (1977); N. B. Kaltreider, S. Goldsmith, A. Margolis, *Am. J. Obstet. Gynecol.* **135**, 235 (1979).

19. M. Bracken and S. Kasl, *ibid.* **121**, 1008 (1975).

20. M. B. Bracken, L. V. Klerman, M. Bracken, *ibid.* **130**, 251 (1978).

21. M. Eisen and G. L. Zellman, *J. Gen. Psychol.* **145**, 231 (1984).

22. S. Cohen and T. A. Wills, *Psychol. Bull.* **98**, 310 (1985); R. C. Kessler and J. D. McLeod, *Social Support and Health*, S. Cohen and S. L. Syme, Eds. (Academic Press, Orlando, FL, 1985), pp. 219–240.

23. M. B. Bracken, M. Hachamovitch, G. Grossman, *J. Nerv. Ment. Dis.* **158**, 154 (1974).

24. D. T. Moseley *et al.*, *J. Clin. Psychol.* **37**, 276 (1981).

25. J. M. Robbins, *Soc. Probl.* **31**, 334 (1984).

26. M. F. Scheier and C. S. Carver, *J. Pers.* **55**, 169 (1987); A. Bandura, *Psychol. Rev.* **84**, 191 (1977).

27. S. K. Henshaw, J. D. Forrest, J. Van Vort, *Fam. Plann. Persect.* **19**, 63 (1987).

28. N. E. Adler, *J. Appl. Soc. Psychol.* **6**, 240 (1976); E. W. Freeman, *Am. J. Orthopsychiatry* **47**, 503 (1977).

29. E. C. Payne, A. R. Kravitz, M. T. Notman, J. V. Anderson, *Arch. Gen. Psychiatry* **33**, 725 (1976); E. M. Belsey, H. S. Greer, S. Lal, S. C. Lewis, R. W. Beard, *Soc. Sci. Med.* **11**, 71 (1977).

30. C. E. Koop, letter to R. W. Reagan, 9 January 1989.

31. A. C. Speckhard, *The Psycho-Social Aspects of Stress Following Abortion* (Sheed and Ward, Kansas City, MO, 1987).

32. C. B. Wortman and R. C. Silver, *J. Consult. Clin. Psychol.* **57**, 349 (1989).

33. One may also find more adverse consequences for the children born as a result of

unwanted pregnancy [H. P. David. Z. Dytrych, Z. Matejcek, V. Schuller, *Born Unwanted: Developmental Effects of Denied Abortion* (Springer, New York, 1988)].

34. Committee on Government Operations, House of Representatives, *The Federal Role in Determining the Medical and Psychological Impact of Abortions on Women,* 101st Cong., 2d sess., 11 December 1989, House Report 101-392, p. 14.

35. This article is based on a review conducted by a panel convened by the American Psychological Association. The authors were members of the panel. We thank J. Gentry and B. Wilcox for contributions to the manuscript and G. Markman and A. Schlagel for manuscript preparation.

# CHALLENGE QUESTIONS

## Does Abortion Have Severe Psychological Effects?

1. If someone you know were considering terminating a pregnancy, what advice would you offer? Why?

2. What potential problems do you see in research on abortion effects? How would you design an experiment to minimize these problems?

3. Is abortion a moral, psychological, or political issue? What is the basis of your conclusion? How does this answer affect your position regarding whether abortion is harmful or not?

4. What do you see as the strengths and weaknesses of Speckhard and Rue's proposal that postabortion syndrome occurs in some women following abortion?

# PART 5

# Psychological Treatment

*Psychotherapists have always been concerned about the safety and effectiveness of their treatments. But not all therapists are in agreement about which treatments are the safest and most effective. For example, some people have argued that electroconvulsive therapy, which is often used to treat depression, has significant, lasting physical side effects. Other treatments, while not always as physically invasive, can nevertheless be emotionally harmful or simply a waste of time. For example, is it more appropriate to treat drug addicts and alcoholics by modifying their problem behavior or by stopping it altogether? Also, is psychological treatment through self-help groups effective?*

- Are Self-Help Groups Helpful?

- Is Abstinence the Best Treatment for Drug Addiction?

- Is Electroconvulsive Therapy Safe?

# ISSUE 13

## Are Self-Help Groups Helpful?

**YES: Frank Riessman,** from "The New Self-Help Backlash," *Social Policy* (Summer 1990)

**NO: Susan Baxter,** from "The Last Self-Help Article You'll Ever Need," *Psychology Today* (March/April 1993)

### ISSUE SUMMARY

**YES:** Frank Reissman, a professor of education and sociology and the director of the Peer Research Laboratory, maintains that self-help groups have the ability to empower people and the potential to benefit society.

**NO:** Psychotherapist Susan Baxter criticizes self-help groups because they give everyone the status of victim and they have great potential for abuse.

Imagine that you recently lost one of your parents to cancer. The past few weeks have been very difficult, so you talk with a friend about your grief, and she suggests that you go to a local self-help group: the "Loss of a Parent" group. You are understandably a bit skittish about discussing such a personal matter with a group of complete strangers. Yet, you are curious, and you wonder if such a group might help. What would you do? How would you decide whether or not to go?

Many people have experienced this dilemma. Self-help groups are everywhere, for almost every sort of problem—from alcoholism to overeating to single parenting. Sometimes, mental health professionals conduct such groups, but at other times, nonprofessionals who have experienced the problems of the membership lead self-help groups. Supporters generally feel that these groups serve a great number of people who might be unable or unwilling to obtain mental health services. Detractors see the proliferation of these self-help groups as reflective of people's tendency to focus on their own, individual problems.

Frank Reissman clearly disagrees with the latter position. He argues that self-help groups have helped many people overcome problems that were not solvable outside the group, and he describes the benefits of 12-step recovery programs like that of Alcoholics Anonymous (AA). He feels that AA and similar groups empower their members and contribute to positive changes in their lifestyles and feelings of self-worth. Furthermore, he believes that self-help groups have the "potential to be a stepping stone toward political organization." That is, self-help groups may lead to beneficial political changes in society as a whole.

In opposition, Susan Baxter criticizes the self-help group movement. Although she agrees that individuals with life-threatening, chronic illnesses may benefit from such groups, she believes that the effectiveness of the self-help model is greatly diminished when it is applied to all problems. She maintains that the proliferation of self-help groups promotes the idea that we are all victims (of one thing or another). This, Baxter argues, could ultimately prevent us from taking personal responsibility for our behavior. She also feels that because self-help group programs lack adequate controls, there is a potential for abuse of group members. In this light, Baxter criticizes the American Psychological Association (APA) for not establishing standards for such groups.

| POINT | COUNTERPOINT |
|---|---|
| • Self-help groups are potentially beneficial to a great number of people. | • The proliferation of self-help groups has decreased their effectiveness. |
| • Self-help groups empower participants to take responsibility for their own recovery. | • Self-help groups prevent people from taking personal responsibility for their problems. |
| • Self-help groups are relatively harmless and often have many benefits. | • Self-help groups can be counterproductive and even harmful to members. |

# YES

### Frank Riessman

# THE NEW SELF-HELP BACKLASH

Twenty-odd years ago, most professionals rejected the concept of self-help groups by saying the blind could not lead the blind. In the 1980s, as the ranks of self-help groups burgeoned, the most common critique was that self-help was a poor substitute for the greatly-needed professional services cut by the Reagan Administration. But, despite these fears and concerns, the self-help movement has swept forward around the country and around the world. In its February 5, 1990, cover story, *Newsweek* reported over 15 million people in 500,000 self-help groups in the US, and there are currently over 70 self-help clearinghouses. The Alcoholics Anonymous model is being adopted as far away as the Soviet Union; Mothers Against Drunk Driving (MADD) has had a significant impact on drunk-driving legislation; treatment of drug addiction at Lincoln Hospital in New York City combines acupuncture with participation in Narcotics Anonymous; popular self-help books have dominated bestseller lists for weeks on end; and at least one report on self-help has become almost mandatory for every popular magazine and talk show.

These groups have had a significant "empowering" effect on people at the personal level: participants are able to overcome problems (addictions) they have not been able to overcome alone. And note that recovery is a *collective* action; only by banding together and recognizing their common problems are participants able to deal with their problems....

## THE CRITICS TAKE ON SELF-HELP

Self-help groups have benefited an enormous number of people, and have the potential to be a stepping stone toward political organization—though clearly this potential has not been fully realized. Critics have often failed to recognize the optimistic and empowering effect of self-help. The first step in the "12-Step" process (the model AA and many other groups follow)[1]—admitting and accepting powerlessness over your problem—has often convinced outsiders that the approach is disempowering (12-step theory holds that alcoholism and other "addictions" are biologically rooted, and the biological basis cannot be overcome and should not be denied). But admitting their powerlessness over the "disease" can empower 12-steppers to *do something about themselves*. Self-help groups allow participants to say "Responsibility starts now: I am not responsible for being an alcoholic, but I am responsible for my recovery from alcoholism."

A new wave of criticism of self-help has emerged, directed mostly at this 12-step model, and with a particularly strong emphasis on codependency, the latest addiction attacked by self-helpers. Deeply critical articles have appeared in the *New York Times Book Review, The Nation, Seven Days, The American Spectator,* and *Readings* (the review of the American Orthopsychiatric Association).

What are the main features of the present-day backlash?

1. Members of self-help groups are becoming addicted to these groups themselves.

2. Recovery therapists are packaging and selling 12-step principles, building a huge clientele and publication market.

3. By conceptualizing addiction in biomedical terms the problems require a lifetime of continuous intervention—as the AA phrase has it, "always recovering, never recovered." Moreover, the addiction model that originated from alcohol addiction is now (presumably inappropriately) applied to other behaviors ranging from gambling to codependency (the diseasing of America).

4. The number of people supposedly affected by dysfunctional families is being exaggerated out of all proportion, and participation in 12-step groups is advocated by some recovery writers as *the* path to recovery.

5. Contrary to the group model, many people recover on their own, as indicated by 40 million people who quit smoking.

6. The emphasis on powerlessness and the presumed religious aura of 12-step groups is a roadblock for many people in seeking help.

7. It is pointed out—correctly—that Alcoholics Anonymous as a key example has success rates proportionally no higher than those of a variety of other treatments.

8. Self-help is a psychologically-focused diversion from societal criticism and structural change.

## A RESPONSE

Although these points are not always accurate in their understanding of self-help, many of the criticisms should be considered closely by people involved in the self-help movement.

Taking the points up individually:

1. Because self-helpers attend many meetings does not *necessarily* make them self-help junkies, any more than a frequent church-goer is necessarily a "religious junkie" (though, of course, it is *possible* to be addicted to church or self-help). The experience of the vast majority of self-helpers and church-goers is more of benefit than addiction. Involvement, even dependence, on such groups need not be addicting, nor perceived negatively. Rather it may be seen as a way for individuals to become less isolated, to increase their connection to others, and to find a positive source for growth and reinforcement.

2. There is no question that self-help principles are being packaged and sold by recovery therapists. This practice commodifies the processes of recovery, taking away one of the most empowering aspects of self-help: the person seeking help is a (free) participant, not a (paying) patient. The uses of self-help meth-

## THE TWELVE STEPS OF ALCOHOLICS ANONYMOUS

1. We admitted we were powerless over alcohol—that our lives had become unmanageable.

2. Came to believe that a Power greater than ourselves could restore us to sanity.

3. Made a decision to turn our will and our lives over to the care of God as we understood Him.

4. Made a searching and fearless moral inventory of ourselves.

5. Admitted to God, to ourselves, and to another human being the exact nature of our wrongs.

6. Were entirely ready to have God remove all these defects of character.

7. Humbly asked Him to remove our shortcomings.

8. Made a list of all persons we had harmed, and became willing to make amends to them all.

9. Made direct amends to such people wherever possible, except when to do so would injure them or others.

10. Continued to take personal inventory and when we were wrong promptly admitted it.

11. Sought through prayer and meditation to improve our conscious contact with God, as we understood Him, praying only for knowledge of His will for us and the power to carry that out.

12. Having had a spiritual awakening as the result of these steps, we tried to carry this message to alcoholics, and to practice these principles in all our affairs.

tant to remember that recovery therapy arose primarily because other methods were failing to reach large numbers of people. Self-help has influenced recovery therapists to let go of the distance therapists traditionally have maintained from their patients—the attitude that "I'm OK, you're not." As therapists disclose some of their own issues, a more symmetrical relationship results that many people find productive. In addition, recovery therapists frequently urge their clients to join local self-help groups, thus encouraging a source of support from peers.

3. The AA position that alcoholism is a disease an alcoholic is biologically unable to overcome, but which he or she can control, is indeed open to question—all the more so when parallel arguments are made for overeating, gambling, or codependency. But while it is important not to overlook the substantive issues of whether alcoholism (or gambling) can be considered a biological disease in the scientific sense, it is equally important not to overlook AA's action perspective—it is interested primarily in what works. To some extent, the biological position can be seen as a "metaphor" that gives people permission to be powerless. And while powerlessness is a critical first step, it is not a powerlessness that calls for passivity and inaction. Alcoholics are indeed, as critics often complain, seen to be recovering for life. But although this has a clear disadvantage, it also enables the individual to relapse and yet remain within the orbit of treatment. It doesn't stop people from leaving, but it does enable them to return.

4. These estimates may seem far-fetched, but we should look more carefully into whether tens of millions of people grew up in dysfunctional families. The numbers may be exaggerated; on the

ods by therapists should be scrutinized and reported on carefully. But it is impor-

other hand, dysfunctional families may be close to the norm in our society. It may turn out to be useful to conceptualize the issue in these terms. The real question is an empirical one: are people in fact recovering through interventions based on the assumption that their problems arose from dysfunctional family life?

5. Anti-smoking groups such as Smokers Anonymous have not been particularly effective, yet 40 million people have given up smoking in the last 20 years. Why self-help fell short here is a question worth looking into, and perhaps not so easily answered. But it is dangerously misleading to say all these people gave up smoking on their own. An enormous campaign was mounted by the Surgeon General's office, the American Cancer Society, the American Lung Association, the American Heart Association, and many others to create a dramatically different atmosphere for smoking. One legislature after another passed bans on smoking in public spaces and forced the creation of nonsmoking work and travel settings. Bette Davis or Jimmy Stewart could hardly be seen in a film without a cigarette; Geena Davis or Tom Hanks could hardly be seen with one. The cumulative effect of this change in atmosphere is significant; if we want to attack addictive behaviors today we should pay attention to what is surely one of the largest-scale successes we know. And while we should admit that the self-help *group* approach is not the answer for every addiction, neither did 40 million smokers kick the habit "alone."

6. There is much to be said about 12-step groups and religion. Most 12-step supporters vigorously claim the 12 steps are not religious, but rather spiritual. The groups are not involved in promot-ing institutional religions—it should be as easy to accept the orientation of a 12-step group whether one is Buddhist, Muslim, Jewish, Christian, or Native American. However, it is hard to ignore the nonspecific religious underpinnings, for instance, of AA: the ritual format of the meetings ("My name is John and I am an alcoholic..."), the possibility of redemption via acceptance (confession) of one's sin, the 12 crucial steps that mention God six times and a religion-like cast of making amends, and nonsectarian "prayers" like the serenity prayer ("God, grant me the serenity to accept the things I cannot change, courage to change the things I can, and wisdom to know the difference").... Twelve-step groups encourage people to interpret the notion of God and a higher power in whatever way they feel comfortable with. But while the approach is strongly nonsectarian, it is hard to see how these notions could be interpreted in a way that could be called nonreligious.

A separate question, however, is whether 12-step groups' religious underpinning necessarily poses a problem. While religion has at times been an opium of the people, it has also been (during the Civil Rights movement, for instance, or in Brazil) a force of liberation. There is no need to disparage the religious dimension in itself. There are time-worn attributes of religion that are helpful to people—even necessary to some—and clearly have positive mental health effects. Moreover, AA and other 12-step groups make it clear that members can either bypass the religious aspects or interpret them loosely, while strongly emphasizing the spiritual that includes but transcends religion.

7. Critics are often eager to cite statistics that self-help programs usually

have success rates with problems like alcoholism no better than many other programs. This is in a literal sense true: studies indicate groups like AA have about the same percentage of success in reforming alcoholics as several other types of treatment. However, this view misses some key differences. First of all, self-help reaches vastly larger numbers of people than other programs, and at no significant cost. While success rates of several programs may hover around 25 percent, 25 percent of one million is greater than 25 percent of one hundred. And self-help programs are free, unbureaucratic, and self-multiplying.

In addition, measures of success based only on comparative rates of abstinence don't tell the whole story. Self-help groups do more than keep people from addictive behavior. They also contribute to a changed lifestyle, concern for and commitment to helping others, de-isolation and group fellowship, a strong personal sense of worth, a sense of meaningfulness and purpose, a sense of sharing, and participation in community.

8. Self-help has often been said to divert participants from political action—or at least do nothing to encourage it—by psychologizing and individualizing their problems. There is some reason to give credence to this case. For instance, Alcoholics Anonymous wants to help the alcoholic but does not concern itself with reducing the advertising or sale of alcoholic beverages, nor with reducing the social stress that may contribute to alcoholism. Also, AA and other 12-step groups oppose an advocacy stance and present themselves as expressly nonpolitical.

Alcoholics Anonymous has neverthe-less been highly influential in affecting thinking regarding alcoholism and other addictions, has helped to decriminalize alcoholism, has influenced opinion regarding methods of treatment for addictions, and has contributed to expanding the cultural ethos against addiction and mood-altering hedonism as a mode of coping—all this within their framework of "attraction, not promotion."

In addition, it is important to recognize that many self-help groups *have* actively engaged in political actions. The Sisterhood of Black Single Mothers, Disabled in Action, Self-Help for the Hard of Hearing, Centers for Independent Living, Gray Panthers, and various women's health groups, for instance, have all directed focused legislative actions. A prime example is the Association for Retarded Citizens. Chapters of A.R.C. were started in the early 1950s as parents' self-help groups. Parents got together because doctors were telling them they should institutionalize their children born with Down's Syndrome, spina bifida, or other handicaps.

At first, the parents shared mutual concerns: I can't face my neighbors. I feel guilty. Then they started to look at the options for keeping their handicapped children at home. They created and paid for educational programs until the early 1970s, when their lobbying efforts resulted in legislation guaranteeing every child with a handicap a free, appropriate education in the least restrictive environment.

More recently, political action through self-help groups was stepped up when former Iowa governor Harold Hughes, a well-known recovering alcoholic, announced his plans to build a nationwide political organization of recovering alcoholics to lobby Congress, monitor legislation, and act as an ombudsman for recovering people. "We are victims of a disease that kills. We are unashamed, we are recovering and will be heard.... Within five years, not a politician will run for office in any state or any city in this land who doesn't hold a position on the issues of importance that relate to us," he said.

## LIMITATIONS OF SELF-HELP

The recent criticisms of self-help do raise some issues that deserve thoughtful attention. Most self-help groups are based on what might be called identity issues—similarity of circumstance that lead members to join to surmount their difficulties, establish a positive identity, and oppose institutions that disparage them. Examples of an active advocacy stance include people with a disabling condition, gays and lesbians, women, and include many others. The institutional criticisms espoused by these groups do reflect social change—sometimes directly, sometimes indirectly—and the groups have also played a role in institutional changes and changes in how they are portrayed in society. However, the emphasis on psychological identity constrains against social change. Thus the codependency movement, while potentially an ally of the women's movement and a supporter of social change, is powerfully focused on individual psychological change, with social implications left undeveloped and increasingly vague.

An addiction-centered perspective also presents a limitation of self-help groups. For while our society is surely plagued by addictive and addictive-like behavior on many fronts, there are societal factors underlying addiction that need to be addressed as well—poverty, racial tension, sexism, to name only the most immediately obvious. Dealing with one's own addiction through self-help groups *could* be the first step in politicization about the social factors contributing to an addiction, but few self-help groups have gone in this direction. The result is a great tool for dealing with addiction that isn't used for much else.

Finally, the emphasis on empowerment, characteristic not only of self-help but also other consumer-based movements, can be misleading and self-deceiving. Individuals who are encouraged to believe they can deal with their health problems exclusively with self-care and self-help groups may reflect a false empowerment.

Self-help is far from a solution to all problems for all people. Many limitations and contradictions of self-help are addressed above. But nothing could cause us to overlook the concrete, fresh, populist efforts of millions of ordinary people to invent innovative approaches to meet their felt needs. In a sense, people are searching for a new politics, which in the long run will have to be responsive to and integrated with an emphasis on societal reconstruction.

## NOTE

1. Twelve-Step groups—which make up perhaps 20 to 30 percent of all self-help groups—are the fastest-growing, most energetic groups in the self-help movement

# NO

Susan Baxter

## THE LAST SELF-HELP ARTICLE
## YOU'LL EVER NEED

Blame the primordial ooze. If it hadn't woken up one day from its nice warm bed of volcanic rock, looked around at all the *Sturm und Drang* [turmoil], and complained, "I don't like this. Why don't I go out and seek some greater personal fulfillment?", none of this would have happened. But primordial ooze went on to become hydrogen, and, ever since, the Earth has simply teemed with self-improvement schemes. Of course, in those days, transforming oneself didn't involve group hugs and confessions, no one stood up and said, "Hi, I'm Molten Lava and I suffer from dreadful hot flashes." That came later, with civilization.

I first came across the notion of self-help in 1982, with Werner Erhardt's "est" promising self-awareness ("Know myself? If I knew my self I'd run away," said Goethe), fulfillment, and how to get everything you wanted, or "noblesse without the oblige" as one writer called it. Tired of the evangelical zeal adherents displayed (and the nonsense they spouted), I actually met with a bunch of esties (esters?) with a tape recorder cunningly hidden in my bag and a misguided notion of writing the Ultimate Exposé as visions of Pulitzers danced in my head. (The article never got written, but that's another story.) The conversation was totally unremarkable; all I remember is one chap earnestly telling me that, with est, I would learn how to separate from "my act"—look at "my act," stand back and change "my act." I couldn't help myself. "Then can I take it on the road?" I inquired. Which was when I discovered that those who embark on the road to inner peace have absolutely no sense of humor.

Much has changed in 10 years; alas, the "humor thing" has not, and today's self-helpers are just as dreary today as they were then. Self-help has grown to include every permutation of pop-psychology possible, from positive thinking to family systems (est, incidentally, is now the kinder, gentler "Forum"); as well as encompassing mainstream medicine with every disease, disorder, condition, or illness ever known (or imagined). Even the buzzwords have changed: Now, to err is dysfunctional; to forgive, co-dependent.

Self-help is warmer and fuzzier than it used to be, says one critic, but the focus is still *self, self, self....*

Self-help began truly proliferating in the 1980s with what humorist Fran Lebowitz called "a rate of speed traditionally associated with the more unpleasant amoebic disorders"—going from some 300 groups in 1963 to more than 500,000 in 1992. The reason, say the authors of *Self-Help Concepts and Applications* (from Charles Press; 1992), lies in our stars—namely, Oprah, Geraldo, Phil, and Ann Landers; also *New Woman, Cosmopolitan,* and other magazines; plus prime-time TV dramas, which refer, with increasing frequency, to self-help groups. These bastions of popular culture no doubt appreciate that self-help fills a need in a fragmented society, where many traditional sources of support—such as the extended family—no longer exist. They also realize that misery is, well, endlessly fascinating.

I had pretty much decided to ignore self-help after the est debacle, but soon it became difficult. Not only was the language permeating everything I read, from articles on the economy and politics to features in women's magazines; but no less an authority than former Surgeon General C. Everett Koop organized a workshop on self-help and proclaimed that "the future of health care in these troubled times requires cooperation between organized medicine and self-help groups." Koop also said that "a partnership between professional traditional care and the self-help movement can provide a superior service."

\* \* \*

Various self-help groups became politically active, lobbying governments for funding and recognition. I started to get peeved. Then people came out of the woodwork with bizarre phrases like "dysfunctional family" (redundant?)

and "I'm feeling my feelings." Finally, when a (former) friend insisted to me that I was abused as a child (because my parents had expressed disapproval when I declared—at 16, after appearing in two school plays—that I was going to study acting), I had had enough. What next? The vet suggesting my cat read *Nurturing Your Inner Kitten*? A 12-step program for conquering chronic nail-biting? A self-help group for adult children (an oxymoron?) of absent-minded parents? Orwell, I feared, had been right—with the demise of language would come chaos.

Soon, whoever you were, whatever you had, might have, there was a group you could join, and just in case you didn't know there was a name for some of these things, much less support groups, "disease-of-the-week" movies told you in graphic detail. "It matters little whether the threat comes from some modern technology, from heart surgery or hemodialysis, whether it's a threat based on a reaction to stress, or whether it is due to an addiction, to violent behavior, or to trauma," says Leonard D. Borman, Ph.D., former executive director of The Self-Help Center in Illinois and master of the run-on sentence. (Pardon? Cancer equals heart transplant equals hives equals PMS equals an unfortunate tendency to shop till you drop?)

We are obsessed with the recognition, praise, and, if necessary, the manufacture of victims these days, writes Robert Hughes in *Time*. The range of victims has expanded to include "every permutation of the halt, the blind, and the short, or, to put it correctly, the vertically challenged."(!) As one who is vertically challenged, naturally I know that tall people are out to oppress short ones (hey, you try looking through a peephole designed for the Jolly Green Giant), but I would be too polite to say so. But when everyone is equally a victim—of their physiology, their background, their race, their sex, their quirks—then personal responsibility goes out the door. "Whatever our folly, venality, or outright thuggishness, we are not to be blamed," suggests Hughes, since we are all victims.

It may not be perfect, say proponents huffily, but self-help provides bang for the buck. For people with a common problem, groups provide support, information, an opportunity to network, and a focus on emotional, social, and spiritual dimensions—something traditional medicine does not often provide. I have no quibble with self-help groups for serious, life-threatening, chronic illness, where state of mind can improve the prognosis. A host of studies demonstrate that this holistic approach has, for a fraction of the cost, immense value.

For example, David Spiegel, a Stanford University psychiatrist, tired of the touchy-feely claims of therapy, decided to prove, once and for all, that emotional support was useless. He went back to a 1984 study in which 50 of 86 women undergoing conventional cancer therapy also attended a support group, where he found, to his astonishment, that those receiving emotional support not only felt less depressed and in less pain—they lived nearly twice as long (an average of 37 months versus 19) as the women not attending the group. "Believe me," he told Health magazine in 1992, "If we'd seen these results with a new drug it would be in every cancer hospital in the country."

Where the self-help argument breaks down is in extending this model to include everything, from fairly benign (although admittedly unpleasant) conditions such as migraine, PMS, or irritable bowel, to otherwise healthy people going through a normal life passage such as menopause or the death of a parent. Even more problematic is the vast, uncharted sea of the "worried well" into which the John Bradshaw & Co. domain of 12 steps, addiction, and recovery would fall. (If this were an ancient map, at this point it would read: "Here Be Dragons.")

As a migraine, er, survivor (self-help disapproves of words like "victim" or "sufferer")—actually as one who survives migraines on a fairly regular basis—I would seriously question the efficacy of self-help in the benign-illness context. Pain or discomfort, while "real," is nevertheless more than simple physiology, and is irrevocably tied with mood, stress levels, fatigue, even expectation (as Melzack and Wall and countless pain clinics have proved). Oliver Sachs (of Awakenings fame) in his book Migraine, writes that not only will an expected migraine rise nobly to the occasion, but migraines can actually come in handy at times! With some skepticism, I tested Sachs' point—and I'll be gosh-darned if it didn't work. The more I focus on migraine, define myself as a person with migraines, expect migraines, the more it backfires. Which of course makes me wonder: How many migraines did I get simply because I thought I would? Or because I was over-extended and it gave me an acceptable excuse to go lie down?

I can't see how self-help would be anything but counterproductive with migraines, unless short-term and informational—i.e., to exchange tips, find out what other people do to prevent/shorten a migraine, get moral support, and complain about all those people who've never had a migraine and tell one airily to take an aspirin. ("I personally think we developed language because of our deep need to complain," said Lily Tomlin.) But self-help's emphasis on experiential learning and tendency to reject professional input makes me a little nervous. Call me paranoid, but I would prefer to have someone leading a group that knew what they were doing, not just a fellow-traveler who could pass on whatever nonsense they liked.

\* \* \*

Now if migraine, which is relatively cut-and-dried, is prone to psychological mismanagement, what about something with less obvious symptoms, like PMS or chronic fatigue, where membership in the club can be as nebulous as feeling anxious or exhausted? It stands to reason that if you can get a migraine when you expect one, you can also get premenstrual symptoms. Where does one draw the line between life and disease?

We may no longer live lives of quiet desperation, but we do live in nervous times, and quite a lot of people are feeling threatened by quite a lot of problems: pollution, acid rain, HDL (or LDL, who can remember?) cholesterol. Emissions from ubiquitous, humming machines like microwaves and computer monitors. Crime. Unemployment. A dizzying rate of change, and, most ominous of all, the chilling workplace message: Perform or perish. Adapt or "become redundant."

"All of a sudden someone comes along and says it isn't really what you know anymore, it's how quickly you can *learn*," says Carol Kinsey Goman, Ph.D., once a clinical psychologist and now a consultant and keynote speaker on the "human side of organizational change. Today it's impossible to lay out your career or your life in those predetermined paths that were so set [before]." Add to that the fact that most of us are working harder and earning less, and one has to concede that things really are getting more stressful. Get used to it. "Stress control has got to become a way in the '90s," says Goman flatly.

Ably preying on what *Newsweek* calls our "self-doubt and self-deprecation" are the pundits of gloom and purveyors of the quick fix. And whatever the problem, there's somebody out there ready and willing to sell us something to cure it. Woman alone? Worried about crime? Get a car phone so you can call for help faster. Feeling a little tubby compared to all those sleek people in advertisements? Try this powdered-meal substitute. Not happy? Having problems with relationships, anxiety? Have we got a book/tape/group/seminar for you!

And the largest consumers of these claims, be they cosmetics or cosmetic surgery? *Women.* "Women are brought up to believe that they are inadequate and insufficient and that to be complete [they must] seek fulfillment outside themselves," said Ari Kiev. Women flock to self-help in droves, to improve everything from their sex lives and their relationships to their careers. Why? Because, writes Carol Tavris in her brilliant analysis of the second sex, *The Mismeasure of Woman,* "Despite women's gains... the fundamental belief in the *normalcy of men and the corresponding abnormality of women* has remained virtually untouched" (italics mine). Everything from women's management style (cooperative) to their behavior in relationships (conciliatory) is suspect, wrong. So, there are countless books, groups, seminars directing attention to every alleged female flaw—whether it's "fear of independence, fear of codependency, fear of success, fear of failure, or fear of fear."

If a woman—or a man—is lucky enough, through some combination of adequate nurturing, okay genes, reasonable health, enough money, encouragement, and opportunity, to be all right, thank you very much; the latest pop-psychology self-help fad has generously widened its admission criteria so that virtually anyone can join in the rousing chorus of "Nobody knows the trouble I've seen." Because there is, by all accounts, not one "functional" family in the universe. David Rieff, in a controversial 1991 *Harper's* article, "Victims All? Recovery, codependency, and the art of blaming somebody else" writes: "It is hard to see how, given the way (recovery guru) Dr. Whitfield (*Healing the Child Within*) has defined childhood trauma, any reader could feel exempt. Questions range from relatively benign queries like 'Do you seek approval and affirmation?' through the more ominous 'Do you respond with anxiety to authority figures and angry people?' (here one wants to ask, 'With or without a firearm in their hands?') to the... old standby, 'Do you find it difficult to express your emotions?' " It turns out that the whole thing is rigged anyway, says Rieff, since even one answer of "occasionally" means that the respondent needs his or her inner child attended to.

I don't really want to pick on the recovery movement per se, however much I agree with Rieff and, more recently, Wendy Kaminer's well-written indictment of recovery, *I'm Dysfunctional, You're Dysfunctional*. For one thing, the "True Confessions" style of people like Melody Beattie make them sitting ducks—albeit rich, famous ducks. (Beattie cites her own background as proof that 12 steps work. Reading some of those stories one suspects that Thorazine would too.)

Neither do I want to belittle the accounts of those who have experienced genuine childhood trauma such as physical or sexual abuse. But this total focus on experiential proof added to the lack of professional involvement gives me the heeby-jeebies.

"There's no screening in terms of who attends [these groups]," says registered clinical counsellor Jessica Easton, M.A. "Let's say someone had just got out of a psychiatric unit and was on heavy medication. They could attend a 12-step program, they could attend Context, they could attend any group and react quite strongly—or get to a point where they might not be able to function." Furthermore, there is an enormous potential for abuse in this sort of uncontrolled free-for-all pop-psych messing with your head. Easton and a colleague held a free public meeting last December for victims—are you ready for this?—of self-help groups! One of the things they did, said Easton, was distribute a sheet delineating "client's rights."

"I would say that 50 percent of the people sitting there didn't even know they had rights," Easton says indignantly. With many groups, she points out, the assumption or premise is that "process is everything." And woe betide the person who questions it. They can be ridiculed, belittled, damaged.

\* \* \*

Why hasn't anyone—the American Psychological Association, to name the most likely candidate—initiated some sort of public-education program, some process to help people not become victims of self-help, as well as give legitimate groups some backup, such as a *Good Housekeeping* Seal of Approval? The APA spokesman I talked to rather sheepishly admitted that "there is no official position" on self-help; that some 10 years ago there had been a "task force," but that there was some "difficulty in finding a consensus" and a position was "never adopted." Gerald Rosen, Ph.D., a Seattle clinical psychologist who had headed the 1978 Task Force, said he is critical of the APA's "failure to set a standard or provide a direction" for the profession.

The Task Force wasn't *against* self-help; they wrote that self-help has "tremendous potential to help individuals understand themselves and others and to promote human welfare." But they also warned that the "promotional claims and titles that accompany these programs are increasingly exaggerated and sensationalized," promising total cures and professing to eliminate the need for any outside professional help. They recommended that the APA take some steps, for instance publish an informational pamphlet on self-help.

Psychology shares some of self-help's aims. Humanistic psychology has long concentrated on improving the human condition—a lofty, if ambiguous, aim. (Improving it for whom? By whose standards?) Neither have individual clinicians been immune to the self-help trends, from Rational-Emotive Therapy to Bradshaw. But at least they recognize the pitfalls. "I encourage people to use self-help," says Rosen, "but I encourage them to use it with accurate expectancies."

Humanism's notion of developing human potential is one thing; but when everything, including life itself (which, let's face it, is enough to give anyone a migraine) is dangerous and threatening and everyone's a victim, then the solution has become part of the problem.

Some years ago I reviewed a book about adoption, in which the writer painstakingly and painfully described the price she had had to pay for being adopted: an alienated adolescence, "knowing as a child that she felt "different"; insecurities, fears, and moments of anxiety as an adult. I could have sworn, on reading this book that I was adopted. As a child I frequently thought I must be a foundling. I was, like most teenagers, alienated. As an adult, I even felt anxious or fearful at times. Aha!

Suppose that book (as so many now) had instead ascribed those all-too-common feelings to codependency, addiction, or a dysfunctional family? What if the topic were not finding one's birth mother but one's inner child? I could have believed it. I could then spend the rest of my life with a handy label that would explain everything that ever went wrong. I could find a rationale for every failing, every insecurity, every mistake. I could corner people at parties! I could be a bore! I could write a book... get rich! *Hmmmmm.*

It's tempting—to believe that there is one answer and one person, like the Wizard of Oz, who has the formula. (Believe those who are seeking the truth, said Andre Gide, but doubt those who find it.) Unfortunately, wizards are only too often muddled individuals hiding behind a lot of smoke and mirrors; their only genius a knack for pointing out the obvious, which, if we'd only stopped to think for a moment, we could have figured out. Twelve steps (or five or 20) are only one way of reducing complexity in a world we all occasionally feel a little overwhelmed by. But, like it or not, life (unlike surgery—which "robodocs" can do—or drywalling) just can't be reduced to a series of cosmic or karmic how-to's.

But the parable has a long and honorable tradition in our collective unconscious, be it religion, myth, science, or advertising (like The Parable of the Lost Traveler's Checks). It's powerfully didactic. As you journey through life, says the parable, there will be problems; here's how they are solved. The assumption is that (1) there is a problem, and (2) every problem can be solved. Since Darwin and Freud we've steered away from divine intervention and religious determinism, only to replace it with the same old dogma couched in less apocalyptic terms. But the subtext remains perennial: determinism. We are powerless, doomed to live out the dictates of our nature, our childhood, original sin, unless we find salvation through a higher power, holistic medicine, positive thinking, psychoanalysis, est... or something else.

There's something very bleak with this endless fascination with what's wrong, what's lacking. "Self-help usually focuses on that negative quadrant of your life," says Goman, "the thing that isn't working. And the more you define yourself by that narrow little piece that's out of whack, the greater the chances that you're going to stay out of whack." But then maybe there's something restful in being "out of whack" in a world that demands high-powered efficiency, endless flexibility, and, for most of us, a wish for a 29-hour day. It's a lot easier to bleat that it's not my fault.

*Newsweek* used to run a long letter to the editor every week, a forum for individuals to air their views on every-thing from baseball to taxes. I remember vividly a piece written by a woman who wrote that she had been physically abused as a child. She was now a mother, and seriously resented the implication that abusers have to grow up to become abusers themselves. This woman argued that she was far less likely to be abusive with her children because she knew what it felt like (similar to the piece in *Psychology Today* written from prison last issue). She had, quite bluntly, chosen to exercise her free will by breaking free of the pattern.

The truth is that we *do* have free will, provided, like this woman, we choose to exercise it. We can take the lessons of the past and learn from them, not be controlled by them. Use them as a springboard for growth, not as an excuse. We can be overwhelmed by what we lack—or work from a position of strength—maybe even try to help those worse-off than ourselves.

"Low grumbles, high grumbles, and meta-grumbles" was what humanist Abe Maslow (originator of the phrase "self-actualization") called this pessimistic tendency we have to focus on our deficits, deficiencies, and problems. Why not, he asked, radically, "shake free of this cultural relativism, which stresses passivity, plasticity, and shapelessness?" Why not, instead, realize our potential by concentrating on autonomy and growth. Why not think about the "maturation of inner forces?"

Or, as Disney put it, why not look on the bright side?

# CHALLENGE QUESTIONS
## Are Self-Help Groups Helpful?

1. Would you attend a self-help group? Why, or why not?

2. What do you believe has caused the proliferation of self-help groups? Is this increase in self-help groups good or bad? Why?

3. What characteristics or features do you feel are necessary for an effective self-help group?

4. Baxter supports certain types of self-help groups (i.e., for people with terminal illnesses). What types of issues do you see as suited to a self-help group format? Why?

# ISSUE 14

## Is Abstinence the Best Treatment for Drug Addiction?

**YES: Ray Hoskins,** from *Rational Madness: The Paradox of Addiction* (TAB Books, 1989)

**NO: Michael S. Levy,** from "Individualized Care for the Treatment of Alcoholism," *Journal of Substance Abuse Treatment* (vol. 7, 1990)

### ISSUE SUMMARY

**YES:** Ray Hoskins, an alcoholism and drug abuse counselor, supports abstinance for all individuals who are recovering from addictions, especially alcohol addiction.

**NO:** Michael S. Levy, a psychotherapist and a faculty member of the Center for Addiction Studies at the Cambridge Hospital and the Harvard Medical School in Cambridge, Massachusetts, argues that abstinence may not be the best treatment for all addicts and that treatment for addiction is best tailored to each individual's specific needs.

Counselors and members of Alcoholics Anonymous (AA), one of the most well known addiction treatment organizations, usually have no doubt in their minds about the best treatment for addiction. AA views addiction as a disease that the addict can do nothing about, so abstinence—the complete halting of the problem behavior—is therefore the only effective treatment. Alcoholics, AA would argue, have a permanent disease that can only be handled by abstaining from taking the very first drink for the rest of their lives. Otherwise, drinking becomes uncontrollable.

The problem is that many alcoholics, as well as people with other drug addictions, dislike AA and its 12-step recovery program, along with its goal of complete abstinence, for many reasons. Some reject AA's philosophy of treatment. Others reject the types of meetings that AA leaders conduct. Whatever the reason, many people with addictions have trouble adopting the AA program. As an alternative, some therapists support individualized treatment, including teaching addicts to control their problem behaviors instead of stopping them. For example, some psychologists advocate controlled drinking for some types of alcoholics. This strategy permits some drinking but attempts to control it with mental and behavioral constraints. Is this treatment approach possible? Can it be effective?

In the selections that follow, Ray Hoskins answers these questions negatively. He argues that once a behavior has progressed to the addiction level, it cannot be controlled. Addicted individuals, according to Hoskins, must recognize that their lives are unmanageable and will continue to be unmanageable unless they abstain from the problem behavior. If therapists suggest that addicts can control their addictions, they are contributing to the illusion of control that most addicts have anyway. In this sense, any encouragement to "control" an addiction can only lead to greater problems. Hoskins suggests that addicts should ask themselves which of their addictive behaviors are necessary for survival and that they should abstain from those that are not.

Michael S. Levy, on the other hand, asserts that abstinence is not necessary for all persons with drug addictions and that controlled drinking can be the treatment of choice for some problem drinkers. Levy emphasizes the importance of individualized treatment for people experiencing addiction difficulties. He presents a number of case histories of persons with problem drinking behavior to illustrate the vital role of individualized treatment. Levy advocates allowing individuals to discover, through trials, whether or not controlled drinking is a solution for them.

## POINT

- Problems with alcohol are treated successfully only by total abstinence from alcohol.

- Considering alcoholism a disease is helpful to those with alcohol problems.

- "Addictive" drinking and drug-taking behavior is out of the person's control.

- Treatment for alcoholism and drug addiction should focus on abstinence.

## COUNTERPOINT

- Some individuals with alcohol problems are able to drink moderate amounts.

- The disease model of alcoholism can turn some alcoholics away from treatment.

- Addicts should discover for themselves whether or not they can moderate their problem behaviors.

- Psychological and sociocultural factors need consideration in treating addicts.

# YES

**Ray Hoskins**

## ABSTINENCE

*Abstinence and the ability to have a happy life are not the same thing. As one man said, "Abstinence is like standing up at the starting line. The race hasn't started yet, but at least you are standing up rather than lying down."*

—Earnie Larsen

Each of us can best begin recovery by beginning abstinence from all power-level addictions and from all unnecessary security and sensation-level addictive behaviors. This will provide the stability needed to chip away at the rest of life. It will also prevent the failure which occurs when one merely drops one addiction and switches to other addictions in one's menu. In using the self-help group language, it is also helpful to recognize that one's life is unmanageable and will be that way as long as one does not abstain.

### WHY IS THIS NECESSARY?

As one of my clients pointed out, he couldn't think of any other way to know whether he had recovered than to quit. Yet addicts usually go through years of trying to control their addictions rather than practicing abstinence. This points out some controversies about whether addictions can be controlled, or whether an addict must be abstinent from his addictions. In spite of years of research and experience to the contrary, there are still those who believe it isn't necessary to abstain from addictions in order to recover. Unfortunately, some of them are health professionals.

### ABSTINENCE VERSUS CONTROL

Throughout the history of the addiction sciences, there has been this ongoing debate about whether abstinence or control should be the goal of treatment and recovery. Recent evidence comes down hard on the side of abstinence. For example, some professionals have consistently tried to teach alcoholics to control their drinking. At this stage of the research and of our clinical experience, this attempt is irresponsible, and seems to reflect the control addictions of the professionals rather than the clinical realities of alcoholism.

Whenever we encourage an addict to control his addiction, we are setting him up to progress from a sensation addiction to a power addiction. We need to avoid this at all costs.

Once an addictive behavior has progressed to the addiction level, it can't be controlled. If it can, then it isn't an addiction. In most cases, if the person attempts to control it, he will only succeed in making sure the behavior progresses to the addiction and then disease levels. In addition, such attempts are power-based and interfere with the goal of making serenity, rather than power, the top goal of recovery.

Mind you, I am not saying that persons with solely enhancement or infrequent addictive behavior patterns must abstain from those behaviors. I am referring to those persons whose addictive behaviors have reached at least the regular addictive behavior stage. All these people might benefit from abstinence, but for the persons using addictive behavior as a regular coping option, this is critical.

There are differences between truly occasional use of enhancement or addictive behavior and the regular use of such behavior to cope with life. For example, people who have not progressed to addictions to alcohol, drugs, food, or sex do not control those behaviors. They don't have the desire to abuse them! A "social drinker" doesn't want twenty-five beers in a night, at least not more often than on one, crazy night. The fact that you have ever felt a need to control a behavior in and of itself is the best indicator that you have an addiction going or developing.

## PREFERENCES AND ABSTINENCE

In his *Handbook To Higher Consciousness*, Ken Keyes gives some very sound ad-vice. He advises that if an addictive behavior is not necessary for survival, abstain from it. In the case of substances, it is never necessary to drink alcohol to survive. Therefore, alcoholics should quit drinking. They should do so for several reasons, one of which is that their drinking will keep them from enjoying more important things in life. Keyes also talks about upgrading addictions which are necessary for survival, such as eating, having relationships, and loving sex to "preferences."

... [A]ddictions are the attempts of a person to stay happy by coping with external realities by focusing on emotional states. It reflects a core belief that we can feel the way we want to feel, regardless of our problems or the level of responsibility for our behavior. In this manner, it is self-spoiling. It is also self-deluding.

Because of this, the addict in recovery should treat himself in much the same manner that a parent should treat a spoiled child whom he is trying to retrain. He should ask which of his addictive behaviors are necessary for survival, and plan on changing those behaviors from addictions to preferences. Sometimes this will be difficult. He should also decide to abstain from those addictive behaviors which are not necessary for survival, and from those parts of necessary addictive behaviors, such as eating massive amounts of sweets within food addiction, which are detrimental to him. His ability to upgrade addictions to preferences will depend greatly on whether his primary pleasure within the addiction is a security, sensation, or power-centered pleasure. He needs to look at this closely.

[For] example:

| Security | Sensation | Power |
|----------|-----------|-------|
| *work* | *cocaine* | *sex* |

There are three addictions in this complex. Using the first rule of which addictions are necessary for survival, only work qualifies. The client will have to upgrade his work addiction to a preference to recover. In both of the other addictions, he needs to learn abstinence from the addictive behavior. If this does not occur, the progression will continue.

Security addictions can usually be changed to preferences. We can, for example, change from feeling a desperate need for love to preferring to be loved by certain people. We can prefer to have money, but not commit suicide if we don't. We can stop drinking to fit in with a crowd, and base the decision to drink or not to drink on other factors. We can decide to eat to survive, not survive to eat.

Mild sensation addictions can sometimes be upgraded to preferences. Sex addiction, as long as it is in the security or sensation level of progression, can be changed to a preference by most people. Eating for sensation can sometimes be changed in the same way. *As a general rule, the recommendation is to upgrade those addictions which are centered on behaviors necessary for survival to preferences, while learning to abstain from those which are not.*

This is a fine line, which should not be applied to chemical addictions. Chemicals, especially most addictive chemicals, are almost never necessary for survival.

Once an addiction has become primarily a search for power, the addict's first choice should be abstinence. This is very consistent with clinical experience, that true pedophiles and violent rapists are rarely able to return to limiting themselves to normal sexuality. It is also consistent with the accepted standard that physically addicted (powerless) alcoholics should learn to be abstinent from alcohol. Giving up the behavior is often the only way to escape the struggle a power-level addiction creates. This is true of sadomasochistic, abusive relationships, totally power-centered work addiction (he should change to a different line of work), materialism addicts who constantly abuse credit, and extreme gambling addiction in which the gambler risks becoming powerless in society or becoming injured if he loses.

The only addictions which are truly necessary for an individual's survival regardless of progression are eating and working. Everyone needs to eat, and few people do not need to work at some level to survive.

Overeaters Anonymous and other groups which help the food addict recognize the limits on the need to eat, help the overeater change preferences for which foods to eat. This is an excellent approach, but it is far more difficult for most advanced overeaters to do this than it is for most other addicts to abstain from unnecessary addictions.

Work addiction is also very insidious because the ingrained belief system is supported by almost all of society and recovery depends on a total shift of preferences which is not sanctioned by society.

## PREVENTING FURTHER PROGRESSION

Perhaps the most important reason for learning abstinence from your unneeded addictive behaviors is to prevent further progression from the current stage of the behavior to addiction and disease. In some addictive behaviors, this will almost always happen. Let's review the earlier example:

| Security | Sensation | Power |
|----------|-----------|-------|
| *work* | *cocaine* | *sex* |

In this example there is a good likelihood that the system will shift in the near future unless abstinence from cocaine occurs immediately. The complex will probably soon look like this:

| Security | Sensation | Power |
|----------|-----------|-------|
| *work* | | *sex* |
| | | *cocaine* |

This shift will occur because of the rapidity with which cocaine users become powerless in their relationship with the drug. For this reason, the person encountering this client during the earlier pattern would have been wise to follow my proposed guidelines and recommend abstinence from cocaine while it remained at the sensation level. Further damage would have been prevented if abstinence had occurred.

## OTHER CONSIDERATIONS

In some addictions, abstinence is also necessary for physical reasons. Alcohol and drugs, for example, produce physical dependence and a physical inability to control their use. In order to even begin to think rationally, the person addicted to these substances must spend significant time in abstinence from them.

In food addiction it is impossible to abstain from all food and still survive. It is possible, however, to identify those foods which set off addictive cravings and eating patterns, and to eat other foods instead. Overeaters Anonymous and Weight Watchers are two organizations which are very good at helping people learn to change the foods they eat.

At this time there are, to my knowledge, no self-help groups for the workaddict. This presents a slight problem, but as work addicts usually have other addictions too, they can often simply apply the steps from a self-help program for another addiction to their work addiction.

## IT'S NO FUN ANYMORE

Another point in abstaining from power-level addictions is that the addict can never expect to return successfully to those behaviors, without returning to the addiction. The reasons for this have nothing to do with willpower, or any other such illusion. They have to do with physical and psychological progression. Once we go so far in our addictions, they are simply no fun to practice at a less advanced level.

There have been several movies lately about this phenomena in sexual addiction. The theme of out-of-control sexuality leading to the inability to enjoy less-controlled sexual experiences is common, *and real.* I have had several cases in which a couple experimented with sexual swinging, to have the husband or wife eventually become unable to get excited without others being present. Needless to say, this created some problems with their intimacy.

As an addiction progresses from security to sensation to power levels, the person loses the ability to get any pleasure out of practicing the addiction at the previous level. He builds a psychological, and sometimes physical, tolerance. For example, when my alcoholic clients come in for diagnosis, I ask them how much alcohol it takes for them to achieve the feeling they want. We then compare their answers to blood alcohol levels they produce, and assess the security, sensation, or power levels regarding that addiction.

If a person drinks with friends, and only drinks two drinks to get his effect, he is drinking at security levels, and, if he is telling the truth, is probably not alcoholic. He is not, as common wording has it, "controlling his drinking." He simply desires to drink a small amount and does so. This is true at every level. People do not control drinking. Some people merely want more than others.

If he drinks with friends, and drinks four to six beers to get his effect, he is operating at the sensation and security levels and may or may not be alcoholic.

If he drinks with friends or alone, and drinks eight or more drinks and maintains a level well above the level of .10 blood alcohol content to get the effect he wants, he is drinking at the sensation and power/powerless levels, and needs to quit.

If you notice, the focus is on the amount it takes for the alcoholic to achieve the feeling he wants to achieve, and whether this feeling is security, sensation, or power related. The reason for this is simple. Once a person has progressed in an addiction from security to sensation or to power levels, he will not be able to enjoy addiction at the lower levels again.

If he drank for complete intoxication, there will be minimal satisfaction in drinking for a mild buzz and the addict will increase his drinking eventually to create the desired feelings of intoxication because he gets no pleasure from drinking moderately, in spite of the anticipation that he will.

There are both physical and psychological reasons for this response. Alcoholics seem to have different physical responses to alcohol than nonalcoholics. For example, they have different tolerance levels to alcohol than others have. This tolerance in most cases first climbs quite high, then later, if drinking continues, becomes very low. Another difference seems to be in how pleasurable the alcohol-affected state seems to be. The pleasure from being drunk for an alcoholic is, or at least was, very pleasureful. Both the tolerance and pleasure factors seem to be genetically related, and complement the psychological factors.

If I know a client has more than one addiction, I will explore the other addictions as well because this rule is true in all the addictions. In sex addiction, for example, once a person gets to a point where he can only get completely turned on by dominance, or group sex, or by children, he will not be able to return to casual sex and enjoy it for an extended period, without seeking the type of sex that turns him on the most. He may or may not be able to experience intimate sex in a loving relationship, but that is usually a separate issue from his addictive sexuality.

Just as the alcoholic will experience an intense desire to drink, regardless of the quality of his love relationships, the sex addict will experience an intense desire for casual sex, regardless of the quality of the sexuality within his marriage or primary relationship. In extreme cases, however, it seems that any sexual relationship whatsoever will trigger urges for addictive sexuality, even the sexuality within an intimate relationship.

Work addicts tend to drive themselves to greater and greater levels of achievement in order to achieve those early feelings of power and freedom they had when they began their careers. Since work addiction and addiction to material items are complements, early work addiction has, as its foundation, fantasies of material things and power which are going to make the addict and those close to him happy. Since everyone fails to be happy as the result of the addiction, whether or not the addict achieves his goals, the work addict looks for more powerful positions from which to continue to feed self and family with possessions. He does this in order to make up for the poor emotional quality in the family. He can no longer enjoy the smaller things in life, and doesn't see how the family members are puppets to his addiction.

So you see, all addiction is a gamble, with the stakes going up as the addiction progresses. Once an addict has experienced the intensity of the power-level practice of an addiction, he will not be satisfied with playing for lower stakes.

## ONE-DAY-AT-A-TIME

I need to point out that it is impossible for a power-level addict to commit to abstinence from an addiction for any long period of time. This is not to say he cannot be abstinent for long periods of time, he just can't predict that he can. The ability to be abstinent is a skill, or set of skills, he will have to learn. In the self-help groups, he learns that he can only stay abstinent "one-day-at-a-time." This is actually too long a time span for him to attack. He can only stay abstinent from his addictions in each here-and-now situation. He can stay abstinent now, but he may risk relapse this afternoon.

## MISGUIDED SYMPATHY

Most of us feel sympathy for persons who must be completely abstinent from their addictive behaviors, and sometimes we help them convince themselves this is not necessary. This is extremely misguided, and may be reflective of our own denial of our inability to control our own addictions.

I have known alcoholics who died because they couldn't believe abstinence was necessary. I have also known an abused wife who was killed by a second abusive husband after leaving a first one when she created a new power-level addictive relationship. I have known several people who have filed for bankruptcy more than once because they attempted to control their use of credit. In most cases, this sympathy for the power-level addict is misguided. Abstinence from a power-centered addiction provides far more freedom for the recovering person than he would achieve by trying to continue controlling his behavior.

In fact, abstinence from unnecessary security and sensation level addictions can also offer more freedom than trying to hang on to them. We just can't know this until we upgrade them to preferences and then find we no longer prefer them.

The only addiction in which I feel sympathy for those who must stay abstinent is the sexual addicts who can only be excited by violent dimensions in their sexuality. My sympathy is for their inability to enjoy normal, loving sexuality, and our lack of a method to help them, rather than for their having to give up raping people.

While abstinence from sex is uncomfortable, sex which must entail coercion or violence to be enjoyable is simply not acceptable in civilized society. And abstinence is better than humiliating or killing others and being incarcerated or killed. For this reason, as well as many others, the more power-level addictions addicts have, the more help they need in their recovery. They need to make new friends and learn about reality. They can't do it alone.

These guidelines are hard for some addicts to accept, but usually no addict will be in a situation in which he has no historical addictions to upgrade to preferences. Those will remain sources of pleasure during his recovery, and he will be able to discover more meaningful coping methods.

## PEOPLE DO CHANGE!

Unless we begin recovering from our addictions, we will gradually spend more and more of our time in our combined addictions, until we find another way to cope. As I have said, some of our addictions will have to be completely abandoned. Others can be "upgraded," in Keyes' terminology, to preferences. There are several factors which are relevant to the decision to abandon or upgrade an addiction.

People do move away from an addictive lifestyle. Depending on the addictive configuration, the addict will be able to slowly adopt less addictive coping, once the hangover phenomena overcome the ability to lie to self about the behavior. Once this occurs, he has "hit bottom," and is ready to begin learning other coping means.

When we are practicing addictions, we are practicing a most obvious self-delusion. We tell ourselves we receive pleasure when we don't. If we have an addiction to any behavior at a power level, we are extremely dedicated to that behavior and the inherent selfishness and dishonesty it represents. We have to shed this skin before we can grow another. The only way to begin this shedding is abstinence from any addictive behavior which is not required for survival.

# NO

Michael S. Levy

## INDIVIDUALIZED CARE FOR THE TREATMENT OF ALCOHOLISM

**Abstract**—*Through a discussion of several case vignettes, the author emphasizes the utilization of an individually tailored treatment approach when working with people experiencing problems related to alcohol consumption. Patients may achieve abstinence without believing in the disease concept of alcoholism, and attending Alcoholics Anonymous meetings need not always be a part of the treatment. Furthermore, for some patients, controlled drinking may be as desirable an outcome as abstinence. The importance of entertaining a multiplicity of perspectives when conducting clinical work with such patients is discussed. . . .*

The idea that alcoholism is a disease dominates thinking in the field of alcoholism treatment (Alcoholics Anonymous, 1939; Caetano, 1987; Crawford, 1987; Gitlow, 1973; Jellinek, 1960; Peters, 1983, 1984; Talbott, 1986). As Gitlow (1973) has documented, "The American Medical Association, American Psychiatric Association, American Public Health Association, American Hospital Association, American Psychological Association, National Association of Social Workers, World Health Organization, and the American College of Physicians have now each and all officially pronounced alcoholism as a disease" (p. 8). The essential features of this concept maintain that while not completely understood, due to biological, inherited factors, some individuals have a unique vulnerability for developing alcoholism, which has little, if anything, to do with psychological or sociological processes. From this viewpoint, stricken individuals are seen as sick and are not personally responsible for their difficulties (Trice & Roman, 1970; Szasz, 1974). Furthermore, the disease has a predictable, recognizable, chronic, progressive course if individuals afflicted by this illness continue to drink.

Others, however, have questioned the idea that alcoholism is a disease (Fingarette, 1988; Kissin, 1983; Marlatt, 1983; Peele, 1985; Shaffer, 1985; Szasz, 1974). They argue that alcoholism is a very complicated disorder with many variables playing a role in the genesis and maintenance of an alcohol problem. Cognitive processes, psychological concerns, attitudes, motivational forces, and sociological dynamics, to name a few, may all be exerting their influence in initiating and maintaining a drinking problem.

From Michael S. Levy, "Individualized Care for the Treatment of Alcoholism," *Journal of Substance Abuse Treatment*, vol. 7 (1990). Copyright © 1990 by Pergamon Press, Ltd., Oxford, England Reprinted by permission. References omitted.

How one understands the etiology of alcoholism will greatly affect the treatment of patients afflicted with this disorder. For example, any treatment goal short of total abstinence from alcohol will not be considered if one subscribes to the disease concept (Smith, Milkman, & Sunderwirth, 1985), and most all alcohol abusers will be strongly encouraged to attend Alcoholics Anonymous (AA) meetings, if not 90 meetings in 90 days. In fact, refusing to attend AA may be viewed as an indication of poor motivation for treatment, a sign that the person is not ready to stop drinking, and evidence that the person is headed for a relapse. Along similar lines, a patient's request to attempt controlled drinking will generally be viewed as a form of denial: The patient simply has not yet been able to acknowledge powerlessness over alcohol consumption. Treatment will then focus on broaching the patient's denial. As Tiebout (1951) states, "The alcoholic must be brought to accept that he is the victim of a disease and that the only way for him to remain healthy is to refrain from taking the first drink; that if he attempts to drink moderately, though he may succeed for a time, sooner or later the disease will be rekindled and he will be in trouble again. The job of the therapist is to recognize this inevitable recurrence and to aid his patient in accepting that fact" (p. 56). However, if one adheres to a more biopsychosocial model of alcoholism, helping patients to moderate or control their drinking might be considered. The importance of possible psychological and sociological variables involved in the drinking problem might also be given more consideration than if one endorses the disease concept paradigm.

In this paper, I will present six individuals who came to me for help in managing their problem with alcohol. I have chosen these particular individuals because my work with them has caused me to question my own beliefs concerning whether or not alcoholism should always be viewed as a disease, and more significantly, my beliefs concerning what constitutes adequate care and treatment of this problem. While there are other individuals from my practice whom I could have discussed, I think these case studies very poignantly illustrate the points I wish to make concerning the importance of individualized treatment when conducting clinical work with people experiencing a problem with alcohol consumption.

## CASE VIGNETTE 1

K is a 31-year-old, divorced female, mother of a 5-year-old daughter. She initially entered treatment due to marital difficulties of at least 4 years' duration. Problems centered around her husband's use of alcohol and cocaine, his extramarital affairs, and the patient's own drinking. The patient stated that several evenings per week, her husband would come home extremely late at night, if at all. While he was out, she would experience much anger, depression, and loneliness; to cope with these feelings, she would begin drinking to "blot them out." They frequently got into bitter arguments and on several occasions, K had been physically abused by her husband. K rarely expressed her feelings to her husband. Her style was to repress her feelings, and when intoxicated, her rage would be expressed. Though very unhappy in her marriage, she was terrified of leaving her husband and, thus, felt very stuck. There was a helpless, fragile quality to K, and I frequently had to struggle against my own wishes to rescue her. She frequently asked me for advice, and when I refused and asked why she needed me to tell her how to lead her life, this led into an exploration of how she had great difficulty in making decisions. K reported that she never felt loved as a child, and it was obvious that her self-concept and related ability to trust herself were poor. K reported drinking heavily in her teenage years and admitted that it was a problem at that time. She was not convinced, however, that her drinking was currently a significant problem, and she maintained that if her marriage improved, she would have no desire to drink so heavily.

During the next 2 months I saw her on a weekly basis. We focused on her trying to better express her feelings and dissatisfaction in the relationship to her husband. We also explored her fear of separating from her husband and being alone. K came from an alcoholic family and expressing feelings was something not generally done in her family of origin. Efforts to engage her husband in treatment were unsuccessful, as he wanted nothing to do with psychotherapy. It also was becoming apparent that K had a severe problem with alcohol. In fact, on one occasion, K arrived for her appointment intoxicated. I consistently gave K the message that her own drinking seemed to be a problem. I told her that while alcohol helped her to cope with her feelings, this was not a reason to drink and in fact, her drinking was probably making everything worse. We spoke about the idea of alcoholism being a disease, especially in light of her own history. Her father has experienced serious problems with alcohol. K eventually spoke with her husband about her belief that they both had a drinking problem, and while refusing to attend AA meetings, they both made the decision to become abstinent. Her husband's sobriety lasted approximately 1 month, and K maintained sobriety for about 2 months. After she broke sobriety, K began drinking heavily again, and within 3 weeks she entered a 28-day inpatient alcoholism program.

Since being discharged from the hospital, now 19 months ago, K has continued to maintain sobriety. She initially was attending two AA meetings per day, and even now, attends several meetings every week. AA, including her participation in step meetings, is a very significant part of her life. In her own words, "without AA and the support I receive from the program, I never would have been able to get sober." K knows she had an illness for which the only remedy is never picking up one drink. I initially followed her on a weekly basis, which was cut down to every other week about 5 months ago. K did divorce her husband, and he continues to drink alcoholically. Therapy has focused on her learning how to sit with her feelings without drinking, a major accomplishment for her. Along with AA, I have helped her with the "hows" of maintaining sobriety, always reinforcing sobriety to the occasional exclusion of other concerns. Other issues have involved both her wish for and her fear of intimacy, and other dynamics surrounding her being an adult child from an alcoholic family.

## CASE VIGNETTE 2

D is a 54-year-old, married male, father of four adult children, who owns his own business. D first came to treatment because he was very concerned about his drinking, which was greatly affecting his relationship with his wife of 30 years. D stated that for the past several years, he generally abstained from alcohol due to pressure from his wife. However, several times each year, he would drink with some friends, only to find himself far away from home, not remembering how he had arrived there, and having lost 1 or more days. This pattern of drinking greatly bothered his wife, and to a lesser extent, D; it had reached the point that either his pattern of drinking would stop, or his wife would leave him. D reported that he first tasted alcohol in his teenage years and he loved the feeling it gave him. Since that time he had rather frequently gotten drunk, although during the past 10 years, his drinking bouts had become much less frequent due to his wife's complaints. D reported that when he would start to drink, he simply could not stop and, inevitably, he drank to excess. He also reported that alcohol problems ran in his family. This included both parents, some grandparents, and one sibling. D was very motivated to work on his problem as he loved his wife very much and did not want to lose this relationship. He described no other difficulties in his life, and he appeared to be a rather psychologically healthy, personable, well-functioning individual whose only significant problem was his excessive drinking. I quickly liked D, as he was gracious, affable, and genial. He sought treatment for his alcohol problem and that was the focus of treatment.

D was quite certain that if he were going to resolve this problem, he simply had to make the decision never to drink, as most every time he drank during the past 10 years, he drank to excess. We spoke about the idea of alcoholism being a disease, how it ran heavily in his family, and how for reasons not entirely understood, some people simply could not drink in safety. D had heard this before, but did not truly believe this. In an attempt to placate me he stated, "I know it's a disease, but it's also a bad habit," which I did not challenge. As D was able to maintain sobriety for several months at a time, we began to look at factors related to his relapses. D stated that these always occurred when he was with some of his friends who liked to drink. Without thinking much about the idea that he would lose control and suffer the consequences of doing this, he would join them. He stated that he drank because he enjoyed it. We discussed his trying to remember that he could not control his drinking *before* he started to drink, as well as his needing to think about past consequences of his drinking, again prior to actually drinking. I also told him that I could fully appreciate that he *wanted to drink* and that this might never change; however, in spite of his desire, he could choose not to drink to avoid the consequences of his drinking and possibly losing his wife. I also encouraged him to avoid socializing with his drinking friends, unless he was with his wife. We discussed the idea of his making use of AA, but he had previously been to a few meetings and stated that he had trouble identifying with the other people there as he did not feel his problem was as severe. He stated that if he couldn't stop, he might at some point have to consider AA. I began seeing D on a weekly basis, but after 1 month, we cut down the frequency of our sessions to every 2 weeks as all was going well. After 2 months, we went to monthly visits, and several months later, we began meeting on an every 2 month basis.

I followed D for 2 years, meeting every 2 months. Our sessions had the ambience of two friends getting together to discuss the happenings since our last contact. We always discussed his sobriety, and frequently touched on politics, real estate, and the state of the economy. He had no periods of drinking, and we finally decided to terminate. D felt that he was able to maintain sobriety because he always remembered that he could not even have one drink. He still preferred to understand his drinking as a bad habit rather than as a disease. Interestingly enough, I saw D at a social function approximately one year after we terminated. He still had not drank.

## CASE VIGNETTE 3

T is a 23-year-old, single male, who first came to treatment at his lawyer's suggestion. A short time before seeing me, T was arrested for an unauthorized entry into a building. T had no recollection of what actually happened as he was grossly intoxicated and in a blackout. He reported that one evening, he and a friend apparently decided to break into a retail store, which is where the police found them after the burglar alarm sounded. T reported that he was an episodic alcohol drinker who first started drinking at age 13. He reported drinking more heavily for the past 2 to 3 years. This consisted of getting drunk usually twice per week, while consuming between one and two quarts of gin at a sitting. He reported previous problems related to alcohol consumption, including financial difficulties, the loss of a girlfriend, and one prior arrest for breaking into a store while intoxicated. He stated that he wanted to stop because approximately 3 years ago, he stopped on his own for about 6 months, only to start drinking again and having it escalate.

T was currently living with his parents and working full-time. He and his parents were also caring for T's 3-year-old daughter from a previous relation-

ship, and he was currently involved in efforts to obtain full custody of her as he believed the mother of his daughter was unable to care for her properly. We discussed the "hows" of achieving abstinence and agreed to meet the following week. We also discussed his beginning to attend AA meetings, but he stated that he did not want to do this for now.

At our next session, T told me that he had not drank, except for having one beer on one day and three beers on another day. He then stated that he preferred to control his drinking rather than to stop entirely. T had never tried to control his drinking in a formal way and we mutually made up a drinking contract. He agreed that he would drink, at most, 2 days per week, and when he drank he would have, at most, three beers. T stated that if he could not do this, he would then have no choice but to consider abstinence. He also agreed that he should not drink at the bar where he typically met his drinking friends. I did not think that T would be successful at controlled drinking. I thought that his history of serious alcohol-related difficulties and the amount he could drink at one time were poor prognostic signs. I also sensed that he came to treatment to aid his legal situation and not to recover from his drinking problem. In spite of my reservations, which I shared with T, we began the controlled drinking contract.

For the next 2½ months, I saw T weekly. He experienced no difficulty holding to the contract and was extremely pleased with himself. In fact on most occasions, he did no even drink the allowed three beers. We frequently discussed the importance of holding faithfully to the contract and not breaking it even once, as violating the drinking rule could be most dangerous and could lead to his drinking eventually escalating again. T had also gotten involved in some outside interests and his self-esteem was greatly enhanced. I also began to realize that T was sincere in wanting to work on his problem with alcohol, and I experienced pleasure in seeing T's self-concept improve.

I followed T for an additional 10 months, generally seeing him every 3 months. His drinking remained totally in control, with little reported effort on his part. When I questioned T as to how he was able to do this, he simply stated, "I was sick of alcohol screwing up my life, I don't want to get drunk anymore, and I like my new identity." We mutually decided to terminate, as both he and I no longer saw the need for him to continue to come for psychotherapy.

## CASE VIGNETTE 4

S is a 36-year-old, currently divorced male, father of two children from his previous marriage. S first came to see me for continued care after being discharged from a 28-day, inpatient alcoholism program. The precipitant to his admission was severe marital stress, including his physical abuse of his wife. This behavior, from his report, was all secondary to his drinking.

S had been drinking since his teenage years, and according to both him and his wife, alcohol had been a problem for him for at least the past 5 years. Prior to his hospital admission, S had been drinking daily: it was at these times when he was abusive towards his wife. His drinking and related abuse of his wife had resulted in a marital separation. When I first began seeing S, he was living apart from his wife, hoping to get back together with her soon. At that time, he was attending about five AA meetings per week, and I saw him on a weekly basis in order to further support his sobriety. His wife had made the decision to live separately from him for at least 3 months in order to see how his recovery from alcoholism progressed. This was very difficult for S. Not only did he want to be with his family, but for the first time his wife was in control of him. After seeing S for about 3 months on an individual basis, I began having conjoint sessions with him and his wife to help them negotiate possibly living together again. They eventually decided to live together, and I continued to see them conjointly. While S did not resume drinking, his wife could not forgive his past abuse of her, and she discovered that she no longer loved him. After 4 months, they decided to separate. I then followed S individually.

During S's first year of recovery, he did no drinking, and his regular attendance at AA gradually stopped. After his year anniversary, to "celebrate," he drank four beers and reported feeling physically ill the next day, which surprised him. We spoke about the dangers of drinking again in that it could escalate, and thus the best means of control would be not to drink at all. He agreed and stated that he simply wanted to drink that once just to see what it was like, as it had been so long since he had drank. S was and is not particularly introspective or insightful, and he could not describe any other reason for his drinking. During the next year, I saw S on an every 2 month basis. S was totally sober during the first 9 months of the year, but did drink on three occasions during the last 3 months of that year without experiencing any difficulties related to his drinking. He generally drank three to six beers on each occasion, and his drinking typically occurred on either holidays or when he was on vacation. Again, the only reason S could give to explain the drinking was that he wanted to drink. S consistently maintained that he knew he had to control his drinking, as without great care it could escalate. He also stated that he never wanted to be drinking the way he was prior to treatment, which was "absolutely crazy." I consistently gave S the message that I thought it would be best not to drink at all.

During his third year of treatment, I continued to see S every 2 months. Perhaps due to my warnings or because S, too, became concerned about his recent drinking, he did not drink for 8 months. He reported that he agreed with me that the best means of control for him was abstinence. However, during the next 4 months, he drank on three occasions. At each of these times, he drank between four and six beers, and he did not get into any difficulties as a result of his drinking. He stated that he drank on two occasions to relieve some life stress he was experiencing. The third occasion was because he was out of town on vacation and he simply wanted to drink. S also began to state that he thought he could drink occasionally (and drink safely), although abstinence would generally be his rule of thumb. During the past 3 years, he had drank on seven occasions, each time it had been in control and he had not experienced any problems secondary to his drinking.

During the next 2 years of treatment, I continued to see S on an every 2 month basis. During this time his pattern was to drink an average of not quite once per month and to drink between three and five beers per occasion, although his range was between one and nine beers. His drinking did not interfere in his life nor did it cause him problems. He did not drink and drive, and his drinking most often occurred while vacationing or celebrating a birthday or holiday. My work with him continues and has been modified from supporting abstinence to helping him control both the frequency and amount of his drinking. S continues to exercise control over his drinking knowing full well his potential for again abusing alcohol. He has no fantasies that he can be a social drinker. After he drinks he makes a conscious decision not to drink for awhile. Over the past 2 years, his pattern of drinking has remained consistent.

## CASE VIGNETTE 5

L is a 30-year-old, married male, father of one child, who came to treatment due to concern about his drinking. L was employed full-time and also was attending school on a part-time basis to earn a bachelor's degree. He described drinking most every day, but was most concerned about his heavy drinking with loss of control, which generally occurred three times per week. While he had experienced no legal, financial, or interpersonal difficulties related to his drinking (even his wife was not particularly bothered about his drinking), he was disturbed about some blackouts he had experienced, and was becoming embarrassed about how he sometimes behaved when intoxicated. When he began treatment, he reported that he had only had one beer during the past 3 weeks. He also stated that his parents were both heavy drinkers. I was immediately taken by L's concern about himself. He came to treatment due to his embarrassment about his drinking rather than due to someone else's concern such as his wife's. He had a high self-regard and did not like how his drinking affected him.

During our initial session, L reported that he was open to either abstinence or controlled drinking, but added that he preferred trying to control his drinking. He thought drinking helped him to relax, and he mentioned considerable job stress. We developed a contract in which he would drink no more than 3 days per week and between one and three beers per drinking occasion. We discussed using meditation to help him to relax, something he had some experience with previously. We also agreed that he would avoid going to drinking parties, or if he went, he would not drink at all.

The next week, L reported that his drinking had gone very well. It had been very easy to drink only 3 days within the prescribed amount. In fact, when he drank, he did not even drink all three drinks. As a result L wondered if he could drink more than three times per week, but limit his drinking to nine drinks per week, which was the actual number of allowed drinks in the original contract. He also agreed that he still would never drink more than three drinks per occasion. I saw no problem with this, and thus, the contract was revised. We scheduled another appointment in 2 weeks.

During our next appointment, L stated that he had no problems holding to the contract. He stated that when he drank, he typically drank either one or two beers, and most importantly, it was not even a struggle. On one occasion, he drank three beers and afterwards, he did not like how he felt, feeling somewhat intoxicated and bloated. We scheduled another appointment 3 weeks later, and during this session, he reported drinking less than nine drinks per week. Fur-

thermore, he said that when he drank he had one or two beers. We scheduled another appointment in 1 month, and in this session L reported more of the same. He described having a new "head set" in which drinking heavily and getting drunk was simply unacceptable and was not part of the image he wanted of himself. He also found it almost amusing to think of how he used to drink to intoxication most of the time.

I continued to see L on a monthly basis for the next 8 months. He stopped counting the number of drinks he had each week, and his drinking became even less. He reported no craving, and consciously thinking about his drinking had receded into the background. L found ways to alleviate his stress other than by drinking. He continues to see me, as I provide a place for him to vent his feelings; he does not want to burden his wife or his friends. Our work has focused almost entirely on his drinking problem, although we have occasionally explored his style of not expressing his anger. I imagine that we will soon terminate.

[Case vignette 6, not reprinted here, describes the experiences of G, who, like T, S, and L, learned in time to control his drinking behavior.—Ed.]

## DISCUSSION

When people initially enter treatment and a drinking problem becomes evident, some soon reach the conclusion that they must stop drinking entirely. They know on some level that drinking safely is not an option for them. K is an example of such an individual. For many years her drinking was out of control and made her feel worse. For such people, the disease concept of alcoholism can be of considerable value. It alleviates the person's guilt about past drinking, it provides a way to understand and explain the person's difficulty with alcohol consumption, and it can help curtail the person's struggle to control alcohol intake. If a person can accept that having a disease is why controlling the amount one drinks is impossible, the battle to control alcohol consumption can be dropped with dignity and respect, and acceptance of total abstinence will be all the easier. Attending AA meetings can be extremely useful as it reinforces this idea. The peer support it provides is simply invaluable as well. Without AA, it is unlikely that K would have been able to attain sobriety.

Other individuals realize that they cannot drink safely. However, they do not want to get involved in AA and do not believe that they have a disease called alcoholism. D knew he could not drink safely: For too many years, whenever he drank, he ran into difficulty. However, D could not accept the notion that he had a disease and always referred to his drinking as a "bad habit." Efforts to understand his difficulty with the disease concept of alcoholism were never fruitful. I did not really think it was important whether D believed that he had a disease called alcoholism, and I did not try to break his "denial" and get him to acknowledge this. Neither did I pressure him to attend AA meetings. We did agree that if his drinking continued, we would need to reassess his need to attend AA. How D understood his problem with alcohol was not important. What was important was that he was no longer drinking and that he was enjoying his abstinence from alcohol.

Other individuals come to treatment for an alcohol problem and want to learn how to control their drinking. They do not accept the idea that they have a "disease" and that they must be totally abstinent from alcohol to cope with their problem. Some of these individuals with all the effort in the world will be unable to successfully drink in moderation in a sustained way. Using the disease concept metaphor, they are in denial, and treatment will eventually have to broach their denial and help them to lead a sober life style. While not specifically the focus of this paper, an interesting question concerns the best way to assist a person in arriving at this decision. Does one confront the person's denial and insist at the outset that safe drinking is a fantasy and a manifestation of denial? Or rather, does one join with the patient and develop a controlled drinking contract? This gives the therapist and patient the opportunity to monitor the situation together with the understanding that if controlled drinking proves impossible, abstinence will then have to be considered. Certainly, I have had many individuals attempt to control their drinking with little success and eventually come to the conclusion that not drinking is the best means of control for them. I have also worked with some people, who after repeated failures at controlling drinking, terminate treatment because they are unwilling to accept the treatment goal of abstinence. My tendency is to engage individuals in a therapeutic relationship while keeping their goals in the forefront, and allowing the process of therapy to unfold. Often their goals change as the therapy progresses. Unless the evidence overwhelmingly suggests that controlled drinking is most unlikely, I believe people should be allowed to discover for themselves whether or not they are able to control their drinking.

There are some patients who seem able to learn how to drink in controlled, non-problematic fashions. The treatments of T, S, L, and G are cases in point. Lengths of time these problem drinkers (or alcoholics) have been able to drink in controlled ways range from 10 months, in the cases of G and L, to over 5 years in the case of S. Clearly these individuals had been experiencing problems with alcohol and could be diagnosed as being alcoholic. All were experiencing harm in their lives due to alcohol consumption. All had also demonstrated loss of control, a cardinal feature of gamma alcoholism, as defined by Jellinek (1960). While we cannot know for certain, if I had attempted to broach these individuals' denial of their alcoholism and had demanded total abstinence, they might have terminated treatment with me and not received the help they needed. At a minimum, they would not have learned that alcohol consumption was something that they could control.

Therapeutic work with these patients paid considerable attention to psychological and sociocultural variables which were playing a role in each patient's respective drinking problem. For T, it was extremely important that he stop socializing and drinking with his drinking friends. I do not believe he would have been able to control his drinking had he continued to see these people. During the course of therapy, he began to see how alcohol was responsible for many of his past difficulties as well as his current one. This insight helped him to decrease his drinking. The havoc alcohol caused in S's life and his ability to honestly acknowledge this enabled him to decrease and control his drinking. L was also tired of the deleterious effects alcohol was having on his life. A tense and strong-willed man, L learned that there were other ways to relax, and through simple self-control he was able to tremendously curtail his drinking. In addition, he decreased the amount of socializing he was doing with his drinking friends. G responded well to my giving him the control over his drinking, as opposed to my telling him that he could not drink. When growing up, his life was totally out of control, and thus he developed a wish to be in command of his life. He also had great difficulty in dealing with external forces (his treatment program at the hospital and now me) telling him what he could or could not do. My giving him control over how much he drank seemed to resonate well with his psychological make-up. Helping him to structure his time after work also enhanced his ability to recover from his drinking problem. In all of these individuals, attending to the psychological, environmental, and sociocultural aspects of their lives was critically important in enabling them to gain control over their drinking, something the disease concept of alcoholism does not view as particularly relevant.

This is not the first time it has been demonstrated that some alcoholics can learn how to control their alcohol intake. Numerous studies have documented the finding that some previous alcohol abusers can return to asymptomatic drinking (Bailey & Stewart, 1967; Cahalan, 1970; Kendell, 1965; Nordstrom & Berglund, 1987; Reinert & Bowan, 1968; Sobell & Sobell, 1976; Vaillant, 1983). Some of these studies have also conducted follow-up for periods of time much longer than is demonstrated by these four case studies, ranging from 1 year to 3 decades.

In a review of 22 studies specifically designed to help problem drinkers control their drinking, Miller and Hester (1980) observed that only one study failed to provide support for this approach and in the other 21 studies, successful outcome rates ranged from 25% to 90%, with an average success rate of 65% for those studies that followed subjects for 12 months or longer. Such data causes one to question the absolute validity of the disease concept of alcoholism with its implicit assumption that one drink will inevitably lead to a full-blown relapse. Even Vaillant (1983), a strong advocate of the disease concept of alcoholism, has observed that 15% to 20% of men diagnosed as being alcoholic are able to resume social drinking.

A point of further inquiry concerns factors related to a person's ability to control drinking. Nordstrom and Berglund (1987) have found that personality traits, social stability, and age-related variables are all complexly intertwined to enabling previously alcohol-dependent individuals to resume social drinking. Vaillant (1983) found that if young problem drinkers alter their peer group before physical dependence develops, they are often able to reverse their alcohol abuse pattern and chronic progressive alcoholism does not develop. He also observed that high social stability and absence of sociopathy may bear a relationship to a return to asymptomatic drinking.

Despite these findings, the disease concept of alcoholism dominates thinking in this field, and total abstinence from alcohol remains the only goal for alcoholics coming for treatment. Nace (1987), in his otherwise thorough and excellent book concerning the treatment of alcoholism, mentions controlled drinking only twice in his entire book and doesn't even discuss it as a possible

outcome. Gallant (1987) states that it is inappropriate and irresponsible to offer controlled drinking as a therapeutic goal for alcoholics coming for treatment. Rather than meeting patients where they are and prescribing treatment on an individual basis, intervention is conducted to ensure "conceptual conformity" (Shaffer, 1985, p. 65). A heuristic device (Zinberg & Bean, 1981) is being followed as truth, to the detriment of some patients.

As Shaffer (1986) and Gambino and Shaffer (1979) have stated, the addictions field is in a preparadigmatic state, with no one paradigm concerning the etiology and treatment of drug dependencies as yet having ultimate authority. Self-medication, disease, sociological, motivational, and biopsychosocial theories of addiction are all competing with each other. Many clinicians, however, act *as if* if it is scientific fact that alcoholism is a disease, refusing to consider other paradigms. I believe that treatment providers must continually entertain the many different perspectives concerning the etiology and treatment of alcohol problems when working with alcohol-dependent individuals and must choose the one or ones that best suit a particular patient. Resonating with patients' own view of their difficulties, at least initially, can be critical to the task of engaging them in the painful endeavor of looking at themselves. As the therapeutic process advances, patients' perceptions of their problems may change. These changes should, in turn, elicit modifications in clinical orientation. There are many different paths into recovery (Vaillant, 1983), and there is no one universal treatment strategy that will work with everyone experiencing problems related to alcohol consumption. If someone comes to treatment and believes that he or she has the disease of alcoholism, I would not suggest challenging this notion. As Shaffer has stated, "Many individuals respond to the diagnosis of a disease: It reduces their guilt and provides an unambiguous course to recovery" (Shaffer, 1985, p. 74). Along similar lines, it could prove beneficial, if not essential, to educate some patients about the disease concept of alcoholism and help them to accept this concept and attempt abstinence. However, one should be very sensitive to a particular patient's resistance to the disease concept and AA, and not necessarily assume that a refusal to acknowledge having a disease and to attend meetings is a sign of poor motivation to treatment. There are people who cannot tolerate being labeled as having a disease as this can make them feel abnormal or defective. They may still be interested in becoming abstinent.

On the other hand, there are people experiencing problems with alcohol consumption who do not want to become abstinent and do not want to be told that they cannot drink. As this paper and other data have demonstrated, not all people having problems with alcohol must become abstinent for a recovery to occur. Current understanding of problem drinking does not indicate that controlled drinking is, in itself, better or worse than abstinence as an outcome (Pattison, 1976). Consequently, if a person wishes to attempt controlled drinking, I would not globally rule this out, but instead, would try a treatment approach with this goal in mind. I am neither for nor against abstinence as a treatment goal, nor am I for or against controlled drinking as a desired outcome. Rather I see myself as assisting people with their problem with alcohol, be it by becoming abstinent or by learning how to control alcohol intake.

The etiology of an alcohol abuse problem is multiply determined and extremely complex. The treatment of this disorder is equally complicated. It is highly unlikely that there will ever be one way of understanding and treating this illness that will fit with everyone experiencing problems related to this substance. Treatment must be individually tailored to the patient. We must never allow ourselves to be blinded by or solely guided by the disease concept or by any one model of alcoholism, at least not at this stage of development in the field.

# CHALLENGE QUESTIONS

## Is Abstinence the Best Treatment for Drug Addiction?

1. Do you believe that controlled drinking is a possibility for alcoholics? Support your position.

2. If you were a psychologist, how would you approach the treatment of problem drinkers?

3. What is your definition of an addiction? What do you see as the etiology, or origin, of drug addictions?

# ISSUE 15

# Is Electroconvulsive Therapy Safe?

**YES: Raymond R. Crowe,** from "Electroconvulsive Therapy: A Current Perspective," *The New England Journal of Medicine* (July 19, 1984)

**NO: Leonard Roy Frank,** from "Electroshock: Death, Brain Damage, Memory Loss, and Brainwashing," *The Journal of Mind and Behavior* (Summer/Autumn 1990)

## ISSUE SUMMARY

**YES:** Psychiatrist Raymond R. Crowe argues that not only is ECT safe and effective, but it also acts quickly after many other treatments have failed.

**NO:** Leonard Roy Frank, who has been an outspoken advocate against psychiatric shock therapy since his involuntary commitment to the Twin Pines Psychiatric Hospital in Belmont, California, asserts that ECT only seems effective because of the brain damage it causes and that many practitioners of ECT underestimate its risks.

Electroconvulsive therapy (ECT) has been controversial since it was first introduced in 1938. Despite continued questions, approximately 100,000 people in the United States are treated with ECT each year. ECT is used for a variety of problems, including depression, schizophrenia, and obsessive-compulsive disorder. During ECT treatments, electrical current is applied to the patient's brain for one-half to two seconds, which produces a seizure. The number of seizures induced during a course of treatment varies from 6 to 35, depending on the disorder and the severity of the symptoms.

The controversy surrounding ECT originates from both its side effects and its questionable effectiveness. Common side effects include memory loss, confusion, disorientation, apathy, dizziness, and headaches. While most of these seem to subside several hours after treatment, critics of ECT argue that some of these effects—especially memory loss—are permanent and compromise ECT's effectiveness. Proponents of ECT claim that this is an outmoded view. They argue that changes in technology have reduced the side effects and risks formerly associated with the procedure and that outcome research has indicated its effectiveness as a treatment strategy.

Raymond R. Crowe argues that ECT is often the most effective treatment available. In treating depression, for example, ECT is especially useful to individuals who do not respond to medication. He cites evidence that 75 to 85 percent of depressed patients respond positively to this type of treatment.

He also claims that the mortality rate for ECT is very low and that ECT is considered one of the safest medical procedures requiring general anesthesia. Part of the reason why ECT is now considered a relatively safe treatment is the introduction of new procedures—side effects have been dramatically reduced. Memory loss remains the most common complaint, but this can be at least partially a function of depression itself. Crowe reports that the majority of ECT patients proclaim the helpfulness of ECT and that most would undergo it again if it were recommended.

Leonard Roy Frank contends that ECT is just as harmful today as it was when it was first introduced. He describes his own experience with ECT and the long-term effects of this experience. He claims that the use of ECT is increasing due to the financial gains it provides the people who administer it. He further claims that the "effectiveness" of ECT comes from brain damage that is induced by the seizures. Frank explains that following ECT, patients have symptoms similar to those found in persons with head injuries. Psychiatrists simply redefine these symptoms as signs of improvement. Frank also cites evidence indicating that the death rate from ECT is much higher than that claimed by Crowe. In addition, other adverse effects are much more serious and occur more frequently than is typically reported by ECT practitioners. He concludes that ECT is analogous to brainwashing because both ECT and brainwashing produce changes in one's perception of reality.

| POINT | COUNTERPOINT |
|---|---|
| • Electroconvulsive therapy is often more effective than drugs in treating depression. | • ECT's "effectiveness" is actually brain damage that is caused by the procedure. |
| • Electroconvulsive therapy is among the safest of all medical procedures that require general anesthesia. | • Evidence suggests that those who administer ECT underestimate its dangers. |
| • Complaints of memory loss among depressed patients are the result of the depression. | • Memory loss is a common complaint after ECT, regardless of the diagnosis. |
| • Recent modifications in treatment techniques have reduced the occurrence of side effects. | • Although modifications have been made, the underlying destructive potential remains the same. |
| • The majority of ECT patients feel they were helped by the procedure. | • ECT changes an individual's perception of reality. |

# YES

Raymond R. Crowe

## ELECTROCONVULSIVE THERAPY: A CURRENT PERSPECTIVE

Electroconvulsive therapy has become a national issue. Attacks on it have appeared in movies and television documentaries, as well as in the popular and professional press. These criticisms have resulted in legislation restricting its use in several states and, more recently, in an attempt to ban its use altogether in Berkeley, California. Because of growing public concern, physicians are likely to be consulted by the public about the treatment; thus, it is surprising that a current review of the subject is not available in a major general medical journal. A considerable body of research has been carried out on electroconvulsive therapy and several comprehensive reviews have been published, but they appear in books and specialty journals that may not be readily available to the nonpsychiatrist. The purpose of this article is to review the current status of this type of treatment for the nonspecialist.

Electroconvulsive therapy induces a grand mal seizure by means of an electric current applied across scalp electrodes. In current practice a series of 8 to 12 treatments is given at a rate of 2 to 3 treatments per week. Although the mechanism of action is unknown, most investigators agree that the seizure rather than the electricity produces the therapeutic benefit.

### INDICATIONS AND EFFECTIVENESS

The primary indication for electroconvulsive therapy is severe depression, with this diagnosis accounting for 77 per cent of cases in which the treatment is used in this country. Since electroconvulsive therapy is often more effective than drugs, it is indicated in depressions that are refractory to medication, and since it acts more rapidly, it is indicated in cases involving a serious risk of suicide.

In the early 1960s two large trials of treatment for depression included a comparison of electroconvulsive therapy with placebo. In the American study, electroconvulsive therapy resulted in "marked improvement" in 76 per cent of 63 depressed patients, as compared with a 46 per cent response rate among 39 controls given placebo. The difference between electroconvulsive therapy and placebo was even larger in patients who were manic–depressive

From Raymond R. Crowe, "Electroconvulsive Therapy: A Current Perspective," *The New England Journal of Medicine,* vol. 311, no. 3 (July 19, 1984), pp. 163–166. Copyright © 1984 by The Massachusetts Medical Society. Reprinted by permission. References omitted.

or had involutional depression: 78 to 85 per cent of such depressions responded to electroconvulsive therapy, and 25 to 37 per cent responded to placebo. This difference contrasts with the usually milder and more chronic "neurotic" depressions, 78 per cent of which responded to either treatment. In the British investigation 84 per cent of 58 patients treated with electroconvulsive therapy improved, and 71 per cent were rated as having "no or only slight symptoms." In contrast, the respective rates for 51 controls receiving placebo were 45 and 39 per cent.

Although these large studies were conducted in different countries by different investigators using different diagnostic criteria, the agreement in results is striking, and the findings are consistent with those of other studies comparing electroconvulsive therapy with a placebo. In short, the evidence suggests that 75 to 85 per cent of depressed patients will respond to this type of treatment, as compared with a placebo response rate of 25 to 45 per cent. Moreover, acute endogenous depressions are likely to show the largest effects from the treatment.

The effectiveness of electroconvulsive therapy in depression is further supported by 10 trials employing a sham-treatment group. Nine were double-blind and the same number used random assignment to treatment groups and objective outcome ratings. Nine of the 10 studies found electroconvulsive therapy to be superior to sham treatment at a statistically significant level. Two of the studies deserve further comment. The only study with negative results used low-energy stimulation, which may be less effective than stimulation with higher levels of electrical energy. Another study found electroconvulsive therapy to be superior to sham treatments at the

end of the treatment course, but one month later no difference was evident. However, many of the patients in both groups received antidepressant drugs after the trial; therefore, the question this study raises is whether electroconvulsive therapy is superior to conventional antidepressant therapy.

The effectiveness of electroconvulsive therapy as compared with standard antidepressants can be judged from the results of the American and British trials of antidepressant therapy cited above. Both studies administered two classes of antidepressant medication (tricyclic antidepressants and monoamine oxidase inhibitors) in therapeutic doses over an adequate trial period. The American study was an eight-week trial of imipramine (200 to 250 mg), phenelzine (60 to 75 mg), isocarboxazid (40 to 50 mg), and electroconvulsive therapy (nine or more treatments). Marked improvement was observed in 49 per cent of the 73 patients receiving imipramine, in 50 per cent of the 38 receiving phenelzine, and in 28 per cent of the 68 receiving isocarboxazid, as compared with 76 per cent of the group treated with electroconvulsive therapy. The difference between the latter and every other treatment group was statistically significant at the 0.05 confidence level, by a Yates chi-square analysis.

In the British study 58 patients received a minimum of four weeks of imipramine treatment in doses adjusted up to 200 mg, 50 received up to 60 mg of phenelzine, and 58 received four to eight electroconvulsive treatments. The percentage of patients with "no or only slight symptoms" was 52 per cent in the imipramine group and 30 per cent in the phenelzine group, as compared with 71 per cent of those receiving electroconvulsive therapy. The difference between imipramine and electroconvulsive treatment was just short of statistical significance (P = 0.056) but the difference between phenelzine and electroconvulsive therapy was significant (P < 0.001).

Differences in the response rates between active treatments are more difficult to demonstrate than treatment–placebo differences, and it is not surprising that some studies have failed to show a difference between electroconvulsive therapy and either tricyclic antidepressants or monoamine oxidase inhibitors, although others have found such a difference. Assuming that the true response rates are 75 per cent for electroconvulsive therapy and 50 per cent for drugs, a power analysis reveals that at least 43 patients in each treatment group would be necessary to achieve a 50 per cent probability of detecting the difference at the 0.05 level of significance. Indeed, all four studies with sample sizes exceeding this minimum have shown a statistically significant superiority of electroconvulsive therapy over drug. Perhaps more telling, however, is the fact that no study has found drugs to be more effective than electroconvulsive treatment.

Thus, electroconvulsive therapy is clearly as effective as antidepressant medication; moreover, it has two advantages over drugs: its rapid onset of action and its effectiveness when drugs have failed. In a recent double-blind trial comparing electroconvulsive therapy and imipramine (150 mg), 11 patients received sham imipramine and electroconvulsive therapy, and 13 received imipramine and sham electroconvulsive therapy. Both groups responded well after four weeks, but the response to electroconvulsive therapy was significantly greater during the first three weeks. This rapid response has been noted by others as well. The effectiveness of electroconvulsive therapy in cases in which drugs have failed is illustrated by an investigation of 437 depressed patients who were treated with 200 to 350 mg of imipramine per day; when the 190 patients who did not respond after one month received electroconvulsive therapy, a 72 per cent improvement rate was observed.

Schizophrenia accounts for only 17 per cent of cases treated with electroconvulsive therapy. Common indications include unresponsiveness to drugs in an illness of less than 18 months' duration, the presence of a secondary depression, and a superimposed catatonic state. Manic excitement responds well to electroconvulsive therapy but is the indication in only 3 per cent of patients receiving this therapy, since it has largely been replaced by medication in the treatment of mania. Finally, catatonic stupor is a rare condition in which electroconvulsive therapy is often effective even when drug therapy fails. . . .

## Mortality

The mortality rate from 3438 courses of electroconvulsive therapy administered in Denmark during 1972–1973 was 4.5 deaths per 100,000 treatments, or 2.9 deaths per 10,000 patients treated. Complications included six instances of endotracheal intubation due to secretions, several cases of laryngospasm, and a tooth fracture. The largest reported series of deaths included 62 from the years 1947 to 1952. The cause was cardiovascular in 55 per cent of the cases, pulmonary in 31 per cent, and cerebrovascular in 6 per cent, with miscellaneous causes accounting for the remaining 8 per cent. Although the mortality statistics are from Scandinavia, the treatment technique was comparable to current American practice; therefore, the findings should also be representative of experience in the United States. If they are, these figures place electroconvulsive therapy among the safest of all medical procedures requiring general anesthesia.

## Adverse Effects

Adverse effects can be divided into those occurring during treatment, those appearing on recovery from each treatment, and those persisting after the course of treatments is over.

Adverse effects occurring during treatment may result either from the seizure or from the drugs used to modify it. Examples of the former include hypotension, hypertension, and bradyarrhythmias and tachyarrhythmias. Although frequent, they are rarely serious. Fractures, the most frequent complication of unmodified electroconvulsive therapy, have practically been eliminated by the use of muscle-paralyzing agents. Prolonged seizures are rare and easily terminated with intravenous diazepam. Adverse effects secondary to medication include laryngospasm and prolonged apnea due to pseudocholinesterase deficiency.

In the immediate post-treatment period, all patients experience transient postictal confusion. The next most frequently reported effects are memory disturbance and headache, which were mentioned by 64 and 48 per cent, respectively, of patients interviewed about previous electroconvulsive therapy. Less frequent effects after treatment are nausea and muscle pain.

The most frequently reported long-term effect of electroconvulsive therapy is memory disturbance, which has led to concern that the treatment may cause permanent brain damage. The apparent simplicity of investigating this question is deceptive. Patients with depression often perform at an impaired level on cognitive testing, and their performance improves with electroconvulsive therapy, masking any cognitive impairment that may have resulted from the treatment. Conversely, patients who have a relapse or do not improve may perform poorly on follow-up testing, leading to an erroneous assumption of persistent deficits secondary to electroconvulsive therapy. Thus, the importance of an appropriate control group cannot be overstressed, and in this respect, much of the earlier research is inadequate. Fortunately, renewed concerns over possible brain damage have led to a number of properly controlled studies, so that the question can be answered more firmly today than it could a few years ago.

In a recent follow-up study 55 per cent of patients who had received bilateral electroconvulsive therapy reported memory loss three years later. However, memory complaints are common in depression, and many patients who report memory disturbance after electroconvulsive therapy are clinically depressed; thus, it may be misleading to attribute these complaints entirely to the treatment. Nevertheless, considerable evidence indicates that electroconvulsive therapy does affect memory. First of all, complaints after treatment differ from those voiced before treatment and are therefore not entirely due to depression. Secondly, the nature of the memory disturbance differs as well. Depressed patients have poor registration and normal retention, but after electroconvulsive therapy they have normal registration and poor retention. Finally, reports of memory disturbance are more frequent after bilateral than after unilateral electroconvulsive therapy.

Reports of memory disturbance can be verified objectively. Memory tests conducted seven months after a course of bilateral electroconvulsive therapy indicate that memory of events immediately before and during the course of treatments remains impaired, memory of events up to two years before treatment shows minimal impairment, and more remote memory returns to normal. On the other hand, anterograde memory tested six months after electroconvulsive therapy demonstrates no impairment, as compared with the performance of controls with affective disorders.

In contrast to retrograde memory, other cognitive functions return to normal after electroconvulsive therapy. Weeks et al. conducted a prospective study of 51 depressed patients who received electroconvulsive therapy, 51 depressed patients receiving other treatments, and 51 normal controls. The groups were assessed before and after treatment and again after four and seven months, with a battery of 19 cognitive tests. Before treatment the group receiving electroconvulsive therapy scored below the patient-controls on 9 of the 19 tests; no test score deteriorated with treatment, and after four months performance on only one test separated the two groups. By seven months the electroconvulsive-therapy group outperformed the patient-controls on one test, but both patient groups performed at a level somewhat below that of the normal controls on several tests, presumably because of persistent depression in some patients. The Northwick Park trial also found that by six months groups that had received electroconvulsive therapy or sham therapy did not differ on cognitive testing.

How are these findings to be reconciled with the frequent reports of memory disturbance by patients treated with electroconvulsive therapy? First of all, continuing depression undoubtedly accounts for some of the complaints, although it cannot explain all of them. Secondly, continuing retrograde amnesia for events around the time of treatment may sensitize the patient to the normal process of forgetting. These two explanations are supported by the finding that patients who have undergone electroconvulsive therapy perform as well on objective memory tests as patients with depression who have not undergone such therapy. Finally, it is possible that anterograde memory may be impaired after treatment in a small number of patients. One study enrolled patients on the basis of subjective memory impairment that had persisted after electroconvulsive therapy, and administered a battery of 19 cognitive tests on them. The patients scored significantly below controls on three tests of verbal and nonverbal anterograde memory, after the confounding effects of medication and residual depression had been eliminated. However, because of the way in which these patients were identified, it is difficult to attribute their memory impairment to electroconvulsive therapy. Moreover, as already noted, the same investigators prospectively administered an identical battery of tests to carefully matched groups of patients with affective disorders receiving electroconvulsive therapy or other treatments and found no difference on any memory functions seven months after treatment.

## MODIFICATIONS

The fear and adverse effects associated with unmodified electroconvulsive therapy have led to a number of modifications in treatment technique, with the aim of reducing morbidity without sacrificing effectiveness.

First of all, pharmacologic modifications have been used, including a short-acting anesthetic such as methohexitol for general anesthesia, oxygen to prevent hypoxia, atropine to reduce secretions and bradyarrhythmias, and succinylcholine to attenuate the convulsion.

Secondly, unilateral electrode placement on the nondominant hemisphere has been found to reduce the volume of brain tissue exposed to electricity and to spare the language functions located in the dominant hemisphere. A large number of studies comparing unilateral with bilateral electrode placement have reported less memory impairment with the former, but the findings with respect to treatment effectiveness are less clear. The majority of studies have found the two forms of treatment to be equally effective, but a minority have found unilateral placement less effective.

Finally, brief-stimulus therapy has been used. This form of treatment uses a stimulus consisting of a train of brief electrical pulses rather than a continuous sinusoidal wave form. The brief stimulus is capable of inducing a seizure with half the electrical energy of a sine-wave stimulus, and often less. The hypothesis that a brief stimulus causes less cognitive impairment has been difficult to substantiate statistically, although two recent studies have found a trend in that direction. However, the therapeutic efficacy of this therapy has generally equalled that of sine-wave treatment.

## PATIENT ACCEPTANCE

Perhaps the ultimate judge of a treatment should be the person who receives it. How do patients who have received a course of electroconvulsive therapy regard the experience? A recent survey found that 40 per cent remembered approaching the treatment with some degree of anxiety, but in retrospect 82 per cent considered it no more anxiety-provoking than a dental appointment. The most unpleasant aspects were premedication, waiting for treatment, waking up, and recovery—each considered unpleasant by 15 to 20 per cent of patients. Seventy-eight per cent felt they were helped by electroconvulsive therapy, and 80 per cent said they would not be reluctant to have it again.

## CONCLUSION

Electroconvulsive therapy is a safe and effective treatment for severe depression. Its advantages are its rapid onset of action and its effectiveness when other treatments have failed. Recent follow-up investigations have found no evidence of damage to the central nervous system. The most troublesome adverse effect is a transient amnestic syndrome in some patients, which clears but leaves a mild deficit in retrograde memory. The frequency of this disorder can be reduced by treatment modifications, but its occurrence cannot be eliminated altogether. Although the majority of patients with amnestic symptoms do not find them bothersome, some do, and patients should be apprised of the common adverse effects, as well as the benefits, of electroconvulsive therapy.

# NO

## Leonard Roy Frank

## ELECTROSHOCK: DEATH, BRAIN DAMAGE, MEMORY LOSS, AND BRAINWASHING

Since its introduction in 1938, electroshock, or electroconvulsive therapy (ECT), has been one of psychiatry's most controversial procedures. Approximately 100,000 people in the United States undergo ECT yearly, and recent media reports indicate a resurgence of its use. Proponents claim that changes in the technology of ECT administration have greatly reduced the fears and risks formerly associated with the procedure. I charge, however, that ECT as routinely used today is at least as harmful overall as it was before these changes were instituted. I recount my own experience with combined insulin coma-electroshock during the early 1960s.... I report on who is now being electroshocked, at what cost, where, and for what reasons.... I examine assertions and evidence concerning ECT's effectiveness and ECT-related deaths, brain damage, and memory loss. Finally, I... [draw] a parallel between electroshock and brainwashing.

In October 1962, at the age of 30, I had a run-in with psychiatry and got the worst of it. According to my hospital records (Frank, 1976), the "medical examiners," in recommending that I be committed, wrote the following: "Reportedly has been showing progressive personality changes over past 2 or so years. Grew withdrawn and asocial, couldn't or wouldn't work, & spent most of his time reading or doing nothing. Grew a beard, ate only vegetarian food and lived life of a beatnik—to a certain extent" (p. 63). I was labeled "paranoid schizophrenic, severe and chronic," denied my freedom for nine months and assaulted with a variety of drugs and 50 insulin-coma and 35 electroshock "treatments."

Each shock treatment was for me a Hiroshima. The shocking destroyed large parts of my memory, including the two-year period preceding the last shock. Not a day passes that images from that period of confinement do not float into consciousness. Nor does the night provide escape, for my dreams bear them as well. I am back there again in the "treatment room"; coming out

From Leonard Roy Frank, "Electroshock: Death, Brain Damage, Memory Loss, and Brainwashing," *The Journal of Mind and Behavior*, vol. 11, nos. 3 and 4 (Summer/Autumn 1990), pp. 489–504, 506. Copyright © 1990 by The Institute of Mind and Behavior, P.O. Box 522, Village Station, New York, NY 10014. Reprinted by permission. The original article includes 58 references and is also available from the author; address: 2300 Webster Street, San Francisco, CA 94115.

of that last insulin coma (the only one I remember); strapped down, a tube in my nose, a hypodermic needle in my arm; sweating, starving, suffocating, struggling to move; a group of strangers around the bed grabbing at me; thinking—where am I, what the hell is happening to me?

Well into the shock series, which took place at Twin Pines Hospital in Belmont, California, a few miles south of San Francisco, the treating psychiatrist wrote to my father:

> In evaluating Leonard's progress to date, I think it is important to point out there is some slight improvement but he still has all his delusional beliefs regarding his beard, dietary regime and religious observances that he had prior to treatment. We hope that in continuing the treatments we will be able to modify some of these beliefs so that he can make a reasonable adjustment to life. (p. 77)

During the comatose phase of one of my treatments, my beard was removed—as "a therapeutic device to provoke anxiety and make some change in his body image," the consulting psychiatrist had written in his report recommending this procedure. He continued, "Consultation should be obtained from the TP [Twin Pines Hospital] attorney as to the civil rights issue—but I doubt that these are crucial. The therapeutic effort is worth it—inasmuch that he can always grow another" (p. 76). Earlier, several psychiatrists had tried unsuccessfully to persuade me to shave off my beard. "Leonard seems to attach a great deal of religious significance to the beard," the treating psychiatrist had noted at the time. He had even brought in a local

rabbi to change my thinking (p. 75), but to no avail. I have no recollection of any of this: it is all from my medical records....

One day, about a week after my last treatment, I was sitting in the "day room," which was adjacent to the shock-treatment wing of the hospital building. It was just before lunch and near the end of the treatment session (which lasts about five hours) for those being insulin-shocked. The thick metal door separating the two areas had been left slightly ajar. Suddenly, from behind the door, I heard the scream of a young man whom I had recently come to know and who was then starting an insulin course. It was a scream like nothing I had ever heard before, an all-out scream. Hurriedly, one of the nurses closed the door. The screams, now less audible, continued a while longer. I do not remember my own screams; his, I remember.

> [The insulin-coma patient] is prevented from seeing all at once the actions and treatment of those patients further along in their therapy.... As much as possible, he is saved the trauma of sudden introduction to the sight of patients in different stages of coma—a sight which is not very pleasant to an unaccustomed eye. (Gralnick, 1944, p. 184)

During the years since my institutionalization, I have often asked myself how psychiatrists, or anyone else for that matter, could justify shocking a human being. Soon after I began researching my book *The History of Shock Treatment* (1978) I discovered Gordon's (1948) review of the literature in which he compiled 50 theories purporting to explain the "healing" mechanism of the various forms of shock therapy then in use, including insulin, Metrazol, and electroshock. Here are some excerpts:

> Because prefrontal lobotomy improves the mentally ill by destruction, the improvement obtained by all the shock therapies must also involve some destructive processes....
>
> They help by way of a circulatory shake up....
>
> It decreases cerebral function....
>
> The treatments bring the patient and physician in closer contact....
>
> Helpless and dependent, the patient sees in the physician a mother....
>
> Threat of death mobilizes all the vital instincts and forces a reestablishment of contacts with reality....
>
> The treatment is considered by patients as punishment for sins and gives feelings of relief....
>
> Victory over death and joy of rebirth produce the results....
>
> The resulting amnesia is healing....
>
> Erotization is the therapeutic factor....
>
> The personality is brought down to a lower level and adjustment is obtained more easily in a primitive vegetative existence than in a highly developed personality. Imbecility replaces insanity. (pp. 199–401)

One of the more interesting explanations I found was proposed by Manfred Sakel, the Austrian psychiatrist who in 1933 introduced insulin coma as a treatment for schizophrenia. According to Sakel (cited in Ray, 1942, p. 250),

> with chronic schizophrenics, as with confirmed criminals, we can't hope for reform. Here the faulty pattern of functioning is irrevocably entrenched. Hence we must use more drastic measures to silence the dysfunctioning cells and so liberate the activity of the normal cells. This time we must *kill* the too vocal dysfunctioning cells. But can we do this without killing normal cells also? Can we *select* the cells

we wish to destroy? I think we can. (italics in original)

Electroshock may be considered one of the most controversial treatments in psychiatry. As I document below, the last decade has witnessed a resurgence of ECT's popularity, accompanied by assertions from proponents concerning its effectiveness and safety—assertions which deny or obscure basic facts about the historical origins of ECT, the economic reasons behind its current popularity, as well as its potential for destroying the memories and lives of those subjected to it....

## ELECTROSHOCK FACTS AND FIGURES

Since 1938 between 10 and 15 million people worldwide have undergone electroshock. While no precise figure is available, it is estimated that about 100,000 people in the United States are electroshocked annually (Fink, cited in Rymer, 1989, p. 68). Moreover, the numbers appear to be increasing. Recent media accounts report a resurgence of ECT interest and use. One reason for this is the well-publicized enthusiasm of such proponents as Max Fink, editor-in-chief of *Convulsive Therapy*, the leading journal in the field. Fink was recently cited as saying that "[ECT should be given to] all patients whose condition is severe enough to require hospitalization" (Edelson, 1988, p. 3).

A survey of the American Psychiatric Association (APA) membership focusing on ECT (APA, 1978) showed that 22% fell into the "User" category. Users were defined as psychiatrists who had "personally treated patients with ECT," or "recommended to residents under their supervision that ECT be used on patients," during the last six months (p. 5). If valid today, this figure indicates that approximately 7,700 APA members are electroshock Users.

A survey of all 184 member hospitals of the National Association of Private Psychiatric Hospitals (Levy and Albrecht, 1985) elicited the following information on electroshock practices from the 153 respondents (83%) who answered a 19-item questionnaire sent to them in 1982. Fifty-eight percent of the respondents used electroshock (3% did not use electroshock because they considered it to be "inappropriate treatment for any illness"). The hospitals using ECT found it appropriate for a variety of diagnoses: 100% for "major depressive disorder," 58% for "schizophrenia," and 13% for "obsessive-compulsive disorder." Twenty-six percent of the ECT-using hospitals reported no contraindications in the use of the procedure. Darnton (1989) reported that the number of private free-standing psychiatric hospitals grew from 184 in 1980 to 450 in 1988. In addition, nearly 2,000 general hospitals offer inpatient psychiatric services (p. 67). While the use of ECT in state hospitals has fallen off sharply over the last 20 years, the psychiatric wards of general hospitals have increased their reliance on ECT in the treatment of their adult inpatients (Thompson, 1986).

In cases of depression, an ECT series ranges from six to 12 seizures—in those of schizophrenia, from 15 to 35 seizures—given three times a week, and usually entails four weeks of hospitalization. In 72% of the cases, according to the APA (1978, p. 8) survey cited above, electroshock costs are paid for by insurance companies. This fact led one psychiatrist to comment, "Finding that the patient has insurance seemed like the most common indication for giving electroshock" (Viscott, 1972, p. 356). The overall cost for a series of electroshock in a private hospital ranges from $10,000 to $25,000. With room rates averaging $500 to $600 a day, and bed occupancy generally falling, some hospitals have obtained considerable financial advantage from their use of ECT. A regular ECT User can expect yearly earnings of at least $200,000, about twice the median income of other psychiatrists. *Electroshock is a $2–3 billion-a-year industry.*

More than two-thirds of electroshock subjects are women, and a growing number are elderly. In California, one of the states that requires Users to report quarterly the number and age categories of electroshock subjects, "the percentage 65 and over" being electroshocked increased gradually from 29% to 43% between 1977 and 1983 (Warren, 1986, p. 51). More recently, Drop and Welch (1989) reported that 60% of the ECT subjects in a recent two-year period at the Massachusetts General Hospital in Boston were over 60 years and 10% were in their eighties (p. 88). There are published reports of persons over 100 years old (Alexopoulos, Young, and Abrams, 1989) and as young as 34 1/2 months (Bender, 1955) who have been electroshocked. In the latter case, the child had been referred in 1947 to the children's ward of New York's Bellevue Hospital "because of distressing anxiety that frequently reached a state of panic.... The child was mute and autistic." The morning after admission he received the first of a series of 20 electroshocks and was discharged one month later. "The discharge note indicated a 'moderate improvement,' since he was eating and sleeping better, was more friendly with the other children, and he was toilet trained" (pp. 418–419).

Children continue to be electroshocked. Black, Wilcox, and Stewart (1985) reported on "the successful use of ECT in a prepubertal boy with severe depression." Sandy, 11 years old, received 12 unilateral ECTs at the University of Iowa Hospitals and Clinics in Iowa City. He "improved remarkably" and "was discharged in good condition. Followup over the next 8 years revealed five more hospitalizations for depression" (p. 98)....

In the early 1970s electroshock survivors—together with other former psychiatric inmates/"patients"—began forming organizations aimed at regulating or abolishing electroshock and other psychiatric practices which they believed were harmful. In 1975 one group, the Network Against Psychiatric Assault (San Francisco/Berkeley), was instrumental in the passage of legislation that regulated the use of electroshock in California. Since then more than 30 states have passed similar legislation.

In 1982 the Coalition to Stop Electroshock led a successful referendum campaign to outlaw ECT in Berkeley, California. Although the courts overturned the ban six weeks after it went into effect, this was the first time in American history that the use of any established medical procedure had been prohibited by popular vote.

The Committee for Truth in Psychiatry (CTIP), all of whose members are electroshock survivors, was formed in 1984 to support the Food and Drug Administration (FDA) in its original (1979) classification of the ECT device in the high-risk category of medical devices, Class III, which earmarks a device or its related procedure for a safety investigation. To prevent an investigation of ECT, the APA had petitioned the FDA in 1982 for reclassification of the ECT device to Class II, which signifies low risk. After many years of indecision, the FDA proposed in 1990 to make this reclassification—but has not yet done so....

## CLAIMS OF ELECTROSHOCK EFFECTIVENESS

Virtually all the psychiatrists who evaluate, write about and do research on electroshock are themselves Users. This partially explains why claims regarding ECTs effectiveness abound in the professional literature—while the risks associated with the procedure are consistently understated or overlooked. User estimates of ECT's effectiveness in the treatment of the affective disorders (i.e., depression, mania, and manic-depression) usually range from 75% to 90%. Two important questions, however, need to be addressed: What is meant by effectiveness and how long does it last?

Breggin (1979, p. 135; 1981, pp. 252–253) has proposed a "brain-disabling hypothesis" to explain the workings of electroshock. The hypothesis suggests that ECT "effectiveness" stems from the brain damage ECT causes. As happens in cases of serious head injury, ECT produces amnesia, denial, euphoria, apathy, wide and unpredictable mood swings, helplessness and submissiveness. Each one of these effects may appear to offset the problems which justified the use of ECT in the first place. Amnesia victims, having forgotten their problems, tend to complain less. Denial serves a similar purpose: because of their embarrassment, ECT subjects tend to discount or deny unresolved personal problems as well as ECT-caused intellectual deficits.

With euphoria, the subject's depression seems to lift. With apathy, the subject's "agitation" (if that had been perceived as part of the original problem) seems to diminish. Dependency and submissiveness tend to make what may have been a resistive, hostile subject more cooperative and friendly. In hailing the wonders of electroshock, psychiatrists often simply redefine the symptoms of psychiatrogenic brain damage as signs of improvement and/or recovery.

Electroshock advocates themselves unwittingly provide support for the brain-disabling hypothesis. Fink, Kahn, and Green (1958) offered a good example when describing a set of criteria for rating improvement in ECT subjects: "When a depressed patient, who had been withdrawn, crying, and had expressed suicidal thoughts, no longer is seclusive, and is jovial, friendly and euphoric, denies his problems and sees his previous thoughts of suicide as 'silly,' a rating of 'much improved' is made" (p. 117)....

On the question of duration of benefit from ECT, Weiner (1984)—in one of the most important review articles on ECT published during the last decade—was unable to cite a single study purporting to show long-term, or even medium-term, benefits from ECT. Opton (1985) drew this conclusion from the Weiner review: "In this comprehensive review of the literature, after fifty years of research on ECT, no methodologically sound study was found that reported beneficial effects of ECT lasting as long as four weeks" (p. 2). Pinel (1984), in his peer commentary on the Weiner article, accepted Weiner's conclusion that "the risks of ECT-related brain damage are slight" and then added, "it is difficult to justify any risks at all until ECT has been shown unambiguously to produce sig-

nificant long-term therapeutic benefits" (p. 31)....

The underlying assumption of this approach ["maintenance" ECT] is that affective disorders are for the most part chronic and irreversible. There is a popular saying among psychiatrists, "Once a schizophrenic, always a schizophrenic." While not a maxim, "Once a depressive, always a depressive," is nevertheless a core belief among many ECT Users. It "explains" so much for them. From this perspective, there are hardly any ECT failures, only patients with recurring depressive episodes who require ongoing psychiatric treatment, intensive and maintenance by turns.

Proponents also claim, but cannot demonstrate, that ECT is effective in cases of depression where there is a risk of suicide. They often cite a study by Avery and Winokur (1976) to support their position. But this study makes no such claim, as we can see from the authors' own conclusion: "In the present study, treatment [ECT and antidepressants] was not shown to affect the suicide rate" (p. 1033). Nevertheless, Allen (1978), in the very first paragraph of his article on ECT observed, "Avery and Winokur showed that suicide mortality in patients afflicted with psychotic depression was lower in patients treated with ECT than in those who were not" (p. 47).

## DEATH FROM ELECTROSHOCK

Proponents claim that electroshock-caused death is rare. Alexopoulos et al. (1989) cited studies published in 1979 and 1985 indicating that the death rate from ECT was between 1 and 3 per 10,000 persons treated (0.01%–0.03%)— considerably lower than estimates for the early years of ECT and, according to the authors, "probably related to the introduction of anesthesia and muscular relaxants" (p. 80). On the other hand, Kalinowsky (1967), who reported a death rate of up to 1 per 1,000 for the period before the premedicative drugs were being routinely used, had "the definite impression that the anesthesia techniques increased the number of fatalities" (p. 1282). Crowe (1984a, p. 164) cited a study conducted during 1972–1973 in Denmark which reported a rate of 2.9 deaths per 10,000 cases (0.029%).

Can any of these figures be relied upon? In researching my book on shock treatment (Frank, 1978, p. 153–156), I found reports of 384 electroshock-related deaths published between 1941 and 1977 in English-language sources, among which were a number of reports and studies with much higher death rates than those cited above. For example: three deaths in 150 cases—2% (Lowinger and Huddleson, 1945); four deaths in 276 cases—1.4% (Gralnick, 1946); five deaths in 356 cases—1.4% (Martin, 1949); two deaths in 18 cases—11.1% (Weil, 1950); three deaths in 700 cases—0.4% (Gaitz, Pokorny, and Mills, 1956); three deaths in 90 cases—3.3% (Kurland, Hanlon, Esquibel, Krantz, and Sheets, 1959); three deaths in 1,000 cases—0.3% (McCartney, 1961); two deaths in 183 cases—1.1% (Freeman and Kendell, 1980).

In the broadest and most informative study on ECT-related deaths, Impastato (1957) reported 254 deaths: 214 from published accounts and 40 previously unpublished. Most of the fatalities had received unmodified ECT. He estimated an overall death rate of 1 per 1,000 (0.1%) and 1 per 200 (0.5%) in persons over 60 years of age. Impastato was able to determine the cause of death in 235 cases. There were 100 "cardiovascular deaths" (43%),

66 "cerebral deaths" (28%), 43 "respiratory deaths" (18%), and 26 deaths from other causes (11%) (p. 34).

Impastato's estimate of an ECT death rate among elderly persons five times higher than the overall death rate—coupled with his finding that cardiovascular failure was responsible for 43% of the deaths—should be very troubling in light of the growing tendency toward shocking the elderly. To justify this practice, Users usually point to the serious risks of cardiac complications and death involved in treating the elderly depressed—particularly those with heart disease—with antidepressant drugs. In current standard psychiatric practice, these drugs constitute basically the only alternative to electroshock.

Whether ECT or antidepressants offer less risk of fatality for these persons remains an open question, but Users assume ECT is less risky....

The Impastato findings have embarrassed the electroshock camp. As a result, this essential research has been largely neglected in the literature on electroshock since then. Thus, in three key review books authored or co-authored by Kalinowsky (Kalinowky, 1959; Kalinowsky and Hippius, 1969; Kalinowsky and Hoch, 1961), the Impastato study was nowhere mentioned, although Impastato's other works were frequently cited. Kalinowsky is not alone in this regard. Crowe's (1984a) ECT-review article—because it was published in the influential *New England Journal of Medicine*—must be considered among the most important of the 1980s. Citing a paper by Maclay (1953), Crowe wrote that "the largest reported series of deaths included 62 from the years 1947–1952" (p. 164), but Crowe neither referred to the Impastato study in his ECT mortality section nor cited it among his 80 references....

## BRAIN DAMAGE FROM ELECTROSHOCK

One does not need a medical degree to recognize the destructive potential of passing 100 to 150 volts of electricity through the human brain. The same amount of current used to produce a seizure in ECT, if applied to the chest, would be fatal (Task Force, 1977, p. 1).

Fifteen years before the Impastato study (1957) which reported 66 "cerebral deaths," and four years after the introduction of ECT, Alpers and Hughes (1942) commented on their findings in an autopsy performed on a woman who had died following electroshock:

> The foregoing case is the first reported instance, so far as we know, of hemorrhages in the brain attributable to electrical convulsion treatment.... [T]he importance of the case lies in that it offers a clear demonstration of the fact that electrical convulsion treatment is followed at times by structural damage of the brain. (p. 177)

Hoch (1948), a well-known ECT proponent, likening electroshock to lobotomy, claimed that the brain damage each produced was beneficial:

> This brings us for a moment to a discussion of the brain damage produced by electroshock.... Is a certain amount of brain damage not necessary in this type of treatment? Frontal lobotomy indicates that improvement takes place by a definite damage of certain parts of the brain. (pp. 48–439)

Psychiatrist and neurophysiologist Pribram commented in a 1974 interview:

> I'd much rather have a small lobotomy than a series of electroconvulsive shocks.... I just know what the brain looks like after a series of shocks—and it's not very pleasant to look at. (p. 9)

The American Psychiatric Association's (1978) ECT survey, cited earlier, reported that 41% of the psychiatrist-respondents agreed with the statement, "It is likely that ECT produces slight or subtle brain damage." Only 26% disagreed. In their review of the literature, Templer and Veleber (1982) concluded "that ECT caused and can cause permanent brain pathology" (p. 65). Sament (1983), a neurologist, published his views on ECT's brain-damaging effects in a letter to the editor of a professional journal:

> I have seen many patients after ECT, and I have no doubt that ECT produces effects identical to those of a head injury. After multiple sessions of ECT, a patient has symptoms identical to those of a retired, punch-drunk boxer.
>
> After one session of ECT the symptoms are the same as those of a concussion (including retrograde and anterograde amnesia). After a few sessions of ECT the symptoms are those of a moderate cerebral contusion, and further enthusiastic use of ECT may result in the patient functioning at a subhuman level. (p. 11)

Sackeim (1986) also describes in a straightforward manner the effects of ECT:

> The ECT-induced seizure, like spontaneous generalized seizures in epileptics and most acute brain injury and head trauma, results in a variable period of disorientation. Patients may not know their names, their ages, etc. When the disorientation is prolonged, it is generally referred to as an organic brain syndrome. (p. 482)...

Despite evidence of ECT-caused brain damage, most fully documented by Breggin (1979), proponents continue to claim that ECT does not cause brain damage. . . .

In a recent 216-page document, *The Practice of ECT: Recommendations for Treatment, Training and Privileging,* the Task Force on ECT (APA, 1989) dismissed the critical issue of electroshock-caused brain damage with two sentences. The first, "Cerebral complications are notably rare" (p. 63), is false. The second, which concluded the Task Force's recommendations for information to be provided in the formal consent document for ECT—"In light of the available evidence, 'brain damage' need not be included as a potential risk" (p. 77)—is falsely premised. From this latter statement we see that the report's authors not only denied the possibility of ECT-caused brain damage, but found the very notion of such damage so *unthinkable* that they placed the term in quotation marks.

## MEMORY LOSS FROM ELECTROSHOCK

The most serious and common effect of electroshock as reported by survivors is memory loss. The loss stretching backward in time from the treatment period is called retrograde amnesia and may cover many months or years. The memory loss from the treatment period forward in time is called anterograde amnesia and usually covers several months, often including the treatment period itself. The amnesia may be global or patchy; some memories return, others are permanently lost. These losses affect one's entire personality and are often experienced as a diminution of self. They not only impair one's ability to function in everyday affairs but also higher realms of spiritual and creative activity.

Herskovitz (cited in Philadelphia Psychiatric Society, 1943) reported finding memory defects among 174 people treated with ECT at the Norristown State Hospital, Pennsylvania, "to be rather general and often prominent. Therefore, patients whose occupation requires intellectual ability are selected for treatment with caution" (p. 798). In 1973, at the age of 49 Marilyn Rice (cited as Natalie Parker, a pseudonym, in Roueché, 1974) underwent a series of eight ECTs at the Psychiatric Institute of Washington. Soon afterwards, ECT-caused disability forced her into early retirement from her job as an economist. She described her return to work following electroshock:

> I came home from the office after that first day back feeling panicky. I didn't know where to turn. I was terrified. All my beloved knowledge, everything I had learned in my field during twenty years or more was gone. I'd lost the body of knowledge that constituted my professional skill. . . . I'd lost my experience, my knowing. But it was worse than that. I felt I'd lost myself. (pp. 95–96)

Andre (1988) described her memory losses following a series of 15 ECTs at New York Hospital in New York City in 1984 when she was 24 years old:

> My behavior was greatly changed; in a brain-damaged stupor, I smiled, cooperated, agreed that I had been a very sick girl and thanked the doctor for curing me. I was released from the hospital like a child just born. I knew where I lived, but I didn't recognize the person I lived with. I didn't know where I had gotten the unfamiliar clothes in the closet. I didn't know if I had any money or where it was. I didn't know the people calling me on the phone. . . . Very, very gradually—

because you can't know what you don't remember—I realized that three years of my life were missing. Four years after shock, they are still missing. (p. 2)...

Abrams (1988a) summarized his chapter on memory functioning after ECT as follows: "A remarkable amount has been learned in the past decade about the effects of ECT on memory, and the day is now past when the physician administering bilateral ECT can blithely assure his patient that 'the memory-loss will only be temporary'" (p. 153). Abrams favors unilateral ECT, claiming that it causes little or no "memory disturbance" and that "whatever dysmnesia does occur will be transient and probably undetectable 6 months later" (p. 154).

Over the years, ECT Users have tried to discount the significance of amnesia reports from electroshock survivors. Kalinowsky and Hoch (1952) gave an early explanation: "All patients who remain unimproved after ECT are inclined to complain bitterly of their memory difficulties" (p. 139). Implicit in this remark is the suggestion to Users that an ECT series should continue until the subject's memory "complaints" cease. In the same vein, the APA's 1978 report on ECT lent its weight to the notion that ECT "might lead many individuals... to have persistent illusion of memory impairment" (p. 68).

More recently, Users have been arguing that the culprit responsible for memory problems is more likely to be the depression, not the electroshock (Crowe, 1984a). They assert that memory loss is a component of depression. Where the ECT subject is elderly, Users are likely to regard reports of memory loss as a normal sign of the aging process and, in the more severe cases, as symptomatic

of senility. It is interesting to note that the Janis (1950) study—which concluded that ECT caused persistent amnesia (p. 372)—included very few depressed persons (only 3 of 30 subjects). More significantly on this point, the control group of 19 "depressed patients" who had not undergone ECT in the Squire (1983) study... "reported no memory problems at all at follow-up" (p. 6)....

## ELECTROSHOCK AND BRAINWASHING

The term "brainwashing" came into the language during the early 1950s. It originally identified the technique of intensive indoctrination developed by the Chinese for use on political dissidents following the Communist takeover on the mainland and on American prisoners of war during the Korean War. The method involves the systematic application of sleep and food deprivation, prolonged interrogation, brow-beating, and physical punishment to force captives to renounce their beliefs. Once "brainwashed," they are reprogrammed to accept the beliefs of their captors.

While electroshock is not overtly used against political dissidents, it is used against cultural dissidents, social misfits and the unhappy, whom psychiatrists diagnose as "mentally ill" in order to justify ECT as a medical intervention. Indeed, electroshock is a classic example of brainwashing in the most meaningful sense of the term. Brainwashing means washing the brain of its contents. Electroshock destroys memories and ideas by destroying the brain cells in which memories and ideas are stored. A more accurate name for what is now called electroconvulsive therapy (ECT) would be electroconvulsive brainwashing (ECB)....

While electroshock cannot, of course, be used to reshape reality, it—like brainwashing—can and has been used to reshape the subject's perception of reality. Warren (1988) reported on interviews with ten married women 26–40 years old, from the San Francisco Bay Area who had undergone ECT between 1957 and 1961. The salient feature of ECT for these women was memory loss: "Troubling life-events and relationships commonly forgotten by these women included the existence of their husbands and children, their own names, and their psychiatrists" (p. 292). Some of the husbands, Warren reported, "used their wives' memory loss to establish their own definitions of past situations in the marital relationship." Other relatives found they "could freely re-define past situations without challenge" (p. 294). Warren comments: "When the recollections of one [marital] partner are to some degree erased, the dynamic reconstruction of reality shifts a little, or a lot" (p. 297).

Those who define reality usually control it. What had shifted here was power—away from the electroshock survivor. Without referring to brainwashing as such, Warren shows that electroshock and brainwashing serve similar ends. Electroconvulsive brainwashing is psychiatry's cleansing ritual; its method for controlling painful, unhappy memories and false or unpopular beliefs by destroying them.

## CONCLUSION

Mystification and conditioning have undoubtedly played an important role in shaping the public's tolerant attitude toward electroshock. But it is not only the uninformed and misinformed public that has stood by silently during the electroshock era. There has hardly been a voice of protest from the informed elite—even when one of its own has been victimized.

While undergoing a series of involuntary electroshocks at the famed Mayo Clinic in 1961, Ernest Hemingway told visitor A. E. Hotchner, "Well, what is the sense of ruining my head and erasing my memory, which is my capital, and putting me out of business? It was a brilliant cure but we lost the patient. It's a bum turn, Hotch, terrible..." (cited in Hotchner, 1967, p. 308). A few days after his release from the Mayo Clinic following a second course of ECT, Hemingway killed himself with a shotgun. With all that has been written about him since his death, no recognized figure from the world of literature, academia, law, religion or science has spoken out against those responsible for this tragedy. As might have been expected, the psychiatric profession has also been silent. Not only did the psychiatrist who electroshocked Hemingway escape the censure of his colleagues, but a few years later they elected him president of the American Psychiatric Association....

ECT User Robert Peck titled his book *The Miracle of Shock Treatment* (1974). Antonin Artaud (cited in Sontag, 1976), the French actor and playwright, who was electroshocked in the early 1940s, wrote afterwards: "Anyone who has gone through the electric shock... never again rises out of its darkness and his life has been lowered a notch" (p. 530). In which perspective—or at what point between these two perspectives—is the truth to be found? This is no trivia question. For some, it will be the gravest question they will ever have to answer.

# CHALLENGE QUESTIONS
## Is Electroconvulsive Therapy Safe?

1. If you or a close family member were severely depressed and had not responded to other treatments, would you support the use of ECT? Are the benefits worth the risks of treatment?

2. How can you evaluate and make sense of the widely varying claims and the supporting evidence cited in reference to this issue? Crowe is a medical professional, while Frank is a former mental health patient. Does this affect your interpretation of the data in any way? Why, or why not?

3. Is ECT a form of brainwashing? Why, or why not?

4. Frank states that signs of "effectiveness" are really symptoms of brain damage. Do you agree with this position? What evidence supports your position?

5. Frank quotes a psychiatrist as saying that the most common reason for administering ECT is the patient's having health insurance to cover its cost. Why might this be the case? Describe how economic considerations might be weighed into recommendations for treatment.

# PART 6

# Social Psychology

*Social psychologists usually study the more "social" aspects of behavior. These include the influences of society upon the individual as well as the influences of one individual upon another. One particularly controversial example of the former is the question of whether or not pornography is harmful. One especially relevant instance of the latter is the question of whether or not marriage is psychologically beneficial. Both of these questions are addressed in this section.*

- Is Pornography Harmful?

- Is Marriage Psychologically Beneficial?

# ISSUE 16

## Is Pornography Harmful?

**YES: Victor Cline,** from "A Psychologist's View of Pornography," in D. E. Wildmon, ed., *The Case Against Pornography* (Victor Books, 1986)

**NO: F. M. Christensen,** from *Pornography: The Other Side* (Greenwood Press, 1990)

### ISSUE SUMMARY

**YES:** Victor Cline, a professor emeritus of psychology and a copresident of the seminar group Marriage and Family Enrichment, argues that pornography poses a great harm to viewers because it degrades women and desensitizes males to sexual violence.

**NO:** Professor of philosophy F. M. Christensen contends that there is little evidence that pornography is harmful and that pornography is only a scapegoat for other societal problems.

There is no denying that the amount of sexually explicit materials in our society has increased. Whereas movie directors and magazine photographers once feared photographing kisses and plunging necklines, they now do not hesitate to photograph simulated intercourse and nudity. Some consider this type of material pornography. Likewise, there is general agreement that the production of hard-core pornography has also increased. How does this affect our society? Does the proliferation of pornographic materials hurt people, particularly women and children?

In 1985, the U.S. Attorney General's Commission on Pornography, commonly referred to as the Meese commission, was appointed to answer these questions. In the course of the commission's work, many psychological studies were examined and many psychologists were consulted. Although the members of the commission did not agree unanimously on all the issues, they did conclude that pornography is harmful. Interestingly, a "shadow commission"—a citizen group that followed the commission to report on its theory and practice—immediately criticized this conclusion, claiming that it was politically motivated and that it ignored many important psychological investigations of the issues.

In the following selections, Vincent Cline sides with and even adds to the Meese commission's findings. Cline argues that media portrayals of male aggression against women can have very harmful effects on women. He points to research documenting the potential harm of aggressive erotic materials to the male psyche, including studies on the effects of repeated exposure to sexual and violent materials. He believes that these studies show that viewing explicit sexual or violent material can decrease the inner controls that normally prevent violent behavior and increase the likelihood that an individual will act out what was viewed.

F. M. Christensen, in contrast, considers the various charges against pornography and concludes that there is little evidence confirming that it has ill effects. In refuting the charge that viewing pornography leads to wrongful behavior, Christensen argues that we assign too much power to the media. The media do not control our desires and actions, he asserts, but, as a form of media, pornography has nevertheless become a scapegoat for society's ills. Christensen concludes that society's problems related to sex and violence have their origins elsewhere.

| POINT | COUNTERPOINT |
| --- | --- |
| • There is plenty of evidence that pornography is harmful. | • A careful interpretation of the evidence does not show any harm from pornography. |
| • Pornography creates a climate in which a rapist believes he is giving into "natural urges." | • Sexual entertainment has little effect on a person's perceptions of reality. |
| • After repeated exposure to nonaggressive pornography, men show more callousness toward women. | • Pornography has become a scapegoat for the conflicts between men and women. |
| • Pornography can be a threat to marriages and families. | • Pornography can help preserve marriages. |

# YES

Victor Cline

# A PSYCHOLOGIST'S VIEW OF PORNOGRAPHY

### VIOLENT CRIME ON INCREASE

The United States is by far the most violent country in the world compared with all of the other advanced societies. For example, the U.S. rape rate is many times higher than that of the United Kingdom. We have more homicides annually on just the island of Manhattan than those reported in all of England, Scotland, and troubled Ireland combined. Our homicide rate is ten times that of the Scandinavian countries. At the present time crimes of violence in the U.S. are increasing at four to five times the rate of population growth.

Behavioral scientists recognize that there are many causes for any violent act, and it behooves us to investigate and understand those key triggers or contributors—if we care at all about the kind of society we want for ourselves and our children. Many lines of evidence have pointed to media influences such as commercial cinema and television as being especially suspect; as presenting inappropriate models and instigations of violent and antisocial behavior, especially for our young.

### MENTAL HEALTH STUDY BLAMES TV VIOLENCE

In reviewing all of the scientific evidence relating to the effect TV violence has on behavior, the National Institute of Mental Health in 1984 issued a ten-year-report that concluded that there is in deed "overwhelming evidence of a causal relationship between violence on television and later aggressive behavior."

Some long-term studies and cross national studies also indicate that this learned aggressive behavior is stable over time—the victims stay aggressive. It is by no means just a transient kind of effect.

The reviewers of the research at the National Institute of Mental Health also note the role that TV (and by implication, commercial cinema) play as sex educators for our children. TV contributes significantly to sex role socialization as well as shaping attitudes and values about human sexuality. Various studies suggest that in TV presentations sex is commonly linked with violence. Erotic relationships are seldom seen as warm, loving, or stable. When sex is depicted it is almost always illicit. It is rather rare to suggest or depict sexual relations between a man and a woman married and who love each other. This agrees with similar results from my own research on the content of commercial cinema conducted several years ago.

## RAPE RATE GROWS 700 PERCENT

Aggression against women is increasingly becoming a serious social problem. This can be seen in the escalation of wife battering, sexual molestation of female children, and sexual assaults on adult females.

Examining empirical data on the incidence of this type of thing is risky. This is because nearly all statistics on rape, for example, tend to underreport its actual occurrence. Many women for reasons of shame, humiliation, embarrassment, or seeking to avoid further trauma do not report these experiences. Data from many sources indicates that police get reports on one in four attempted or actual rapes. And of those reported less than 5 percent result in prosecution and conviction. Since 1933 the increase in the rape rate in the U.S. is in excess of 700 percent (this is in relation to population growth—in actual numbers the increase is much greater).

This means that the chances of a woman being sexually attacked are seven times greater now than in 1933. This clearly indicates major changes in male attitudes about sexual aggressiveness toward women. Obviously, more men

today have a lower esteem of women. Why should this be in an age such as ours when women are being heard and winning rights?

## PORNOGRAPHY DEGRADES WOMEN

Feminists such as Susan Brownmiller, Diana Russell, Laura Lederer, and Kathleen Barry point to the fact that our culture influences men to regard women as things—to be used. They note, for example, that nearly all pornography is created by males for a primarily male audience. Most of it is hostile to women. There is much woman hatred in it. It is devoid of foreplay, tenderness, caring, to say nothing of love and romance. They see its main purpose to humiliate and degrade the female body for the purpose of commercial entertainment, erotic stimulation, and pleasure for the male viewer. This is perceived as creating a cultural climate in which a rapist feels he is merely giving in to a normal urge and a woman is encouraged to believe that sexual masochism is healthy liberated fun.

Susan Brownmiller states, "Pornography, like rape, is a male invention designed to dehumanize women."

Many of the men's magazines such as *Hustler* are filled with antifemale messages both overt and covert. The victims in most "hard R" slasher movies are women—it is they who are most often sexually assaulted, tortured, and degraded. The feminist's concern is that these films sexually stimulate men while at the same time pairing this erotic arousal with images of violent assaults on women. The possibility of conditioning a potential male viewer into deviancy certainly has to be considered here.

## MEN CONDITIONED TO SEXUAL DEVIATION

In a laboratory experiment using classical conditioning procedures at the Naudsley Hospital in London, England, Dr. Stanley Rachman conditioned a number of young males into being fetishists—a mild form of sexual deviation. A number of studies by such investigators as Davison, Bandura, Evans, Hackson, and McGuire suggest that deviant sexual fantasies through a process of masturbatory conditioning are related in many instances to later acted-out deviant sexual behavior. What happens here is that deviant sexual fantasies in the man's mind are paired with direct sexual stimulation and orgasm via masturbation. In this way the deviant fantasies acquire strong sexually arousing properties—which help sustain the sexual interest in the deviant behavior. Thus reinforced sexual imagery and thoughts (accompanied via masturbation) are a link in the acquisition and maintenance of new deviant sexual arousal and behavior. In the light of this, media portrayals of sex modeling male aggression against women logically can have a harmful effect on certain viewers. These portrayals, it would be concluded, facilitate deviant conditioning by providing new malignant fantasy material as well as increasing motivation for masturbatory experiences—leading to changes in the man's sexual attitudes, appetites, and behavior.

For example: A Los Angeles firm is currently marketing an 8mm motion picture film, available through the mails to anybody wishing it, which depicts two girl scouts in their uniforms selling cookies from door to door. At one residence they are invited in by a mature, sexually aggressive male who proceeds to subject them to a variety of unusual and extremely explicit sexual acts—all shown in great detail. This film is what is usually referred to as "hard-core" pornography. If the research of Rachman, McGuire, and others has any meaning at all, it suggests that such a film could potentially condition some male viewers, via masturbatory conditioning, into fantasies and later behavior involving aggressive sex with female minors.

Also, we might mention, that sex therapists have for years used carefully selected erotic material to recondition men with sexual deviations and help them out of their problems. In other words, the conditioning can go both ways using erotic materials. If all sexual deviations are learned, as psychologist Albert Bandura suggests, then one would assume that most deviations occur through "accidental conditioning"—which is exactly what many feminists have concerns about—especially as they see how they are treated in male-oriented media presentations.

At the present time in most urban areas of the U.S., there have arisen groups of women with concerns about what the media are doing to them—and especially about the social/sexual enculturation of males. Women Against Violence in Pornography and Media, based in San Francisco, is one example of this kind of group. Initially, their concerns were intuitive, moralistic, and emotional. They picketed various establishments—movie houses, adult bookstores, etc., selling or marketing highly sexist and antifemale materials—material that might tend to engender hate toward women. This includes the so-called "snuff films" in which women were supposedly murdered on-camera for the voyeuristic entertainment of male viewers.

However, in the last five years there has been a flood of well-done behavioral studies by researchers that appear to scientifically legitimize the concerns of these groups. These studies have repeatedly given documentation of potential harms to viewers of aggressive erotic materials, especially males.

These findings have been given very little attention by the popular press and are known only to a few scientists who are privy to the journals that these articles are showing up in. Thus, most ordinary citizens, journalists, as well as professionals in other disciplines, are not aware of these studies. For example, one of the editors of the *Utah Daily Chronicle* on March 1, 1985, in an editorial column discussing the cable TV bills before our state legislature, wrote, "Research has shown there is no demonstrable relationship between watching TV and increased aggressiveness... [and] regardless of what Utah legislators may believe, there is no scientific correlation between obscenity and antisocial conduct."

Both of these statements are totally incorrect. I am sure they were written as a result of ignorance, not as a conscious attempt at deception. In fact, quite ironically, on the day this editorial appeared, the Department of Psychology was sponsoring a widely publicized seminar featuring one of the nation's leading authorities on television effects, Dr. Raoul Huesmann, who discussed a pioneering 22-year study on the long-term negative effects of TV violence viewing.

## WORLD'S MOST VIOLENT ADVANCED SOCIETY

I will not further belabor the issue of media violence and its potential negative effects on viewers. The evidence is really quite overwhelming on this issue. But let me briefly summarize what the literature suggests:

(1) We are the most violent advanced society in the world.

(2) We have the highest rates of media violence (in our entertainments) of any nation.

(3) There are something like 20 years of behavioral studies linking exposure to media violence with violent behavior. These include both laboratory and field studies. And while there are many contributions to any particular violent act, I do not think that any fair reviewer of the literature can deny that the media are one important contributor to the violence problems in our society.

In my judgment repeated violence viewing also desensitizes the observer to the pathology in the film or material witnessed. It becomes with repeated viewing more acceptable and tolerable. We lose the capacity to empathize with the victim. Man's inhumanity to man (or woman) becomes a spectator sport. We develop and cultivate an appetite for it, no different than in early Rome, where people watched gladiatorial contests in which men fought to their deaths, dismembering their opponents' bodies. In other contests, others fought wild animals bare-handed, eventually to be eaten alive. Again, a spectator sport. We become to some extent debased, even dehumanized, if you wish, by participating in these kinds of experiences. And, of course, approximations of what happened in the Roman arena nightly occur in some movie houses and on some TV screens—especially the cable variety where explicit violence is broadcast unedited. And usually—women are the victims.

## INCREASING ASSAULTS
## IN MARRIAGE

Let us now move to the issue of linking aggressive pornography to increased aggressive behavior in marriage. It can be physical abuse, psychological abuse, or both. I see many couples in marital counseling. Violence between spouses is a common problem. Of course many women have learned to fight back. And this leads to an ever-escalating exchange of anger and hostility. Divorce usually doesn't solve the problem. If you don't know how to handle anger and aggressive feelings in one relationship, switching partners doesn't necessarily solve that problem for you in the next relationship.

There have been many experiments on aggressive pornography and its effects on consumers conducted by such capable investigators as Edward Donnerstein and Leonard Berkowitz at the University of Wisconsin; Neil Malamuth and James Check at the University of Manitoba; Dolf Zillman and Jennings Bryant at Indiana University; and Seymour Feshbach and his associates at UCLA.

## SEXUAL AROUSAL,
## AGGRESSION LINKED

There has been a convergence of evidence from many sources suggesting that sexual arousal and aggression are linked or are mutually enhancing. Thus materials that are sexually exciting can stimulate aggressive behavior and, contrariwise, portrayals of aggression in books, magazines, and films can raise some people's levels of sexual arousal.

Thus it is not by accident that some four-letter words are frequently used in the context of an epithet or as part of a verbal attack on another.

Many theorists have noted the intimate relationship between sex and aggression—including Sigmund Freud, or more recently, Robert Stoler at UCLA who suggests that frequently it is hostility that generates and enhances sexual excitement.

A large number of research studies consistently and repetitiously keep coming to one conclusion—those subjects who are sexually aroused by strong erotic stimuli show significantly greater aggression than nonaroused controls.

The typical experiment will sexually arouse with pornographic stimuli a group of experimental subjects who will then be given an opportunity to punish a confederate with electric shock. Their aggressiveness will be compared to a neutral group who will have seen only a bland nonsexual film or reading material.

If the film combines both erotic *and* aggressive elements, this usually produces even higher levels of aggressiveness (as measured by the subjects' willingness to shock their partners at even higher and apparently more painful levels of shock intensity). If the erotic material is very mild—like pin-ups and cheesecake type photos—then it appears to have reverse effect on aggression—tending to dampen it.

In the situation of reading about or witnessing a filmed presentation of rape, if the female victim is seen as in great pain this can also have a dampening effect on aggressive arousal. It serves as an inhibitor. But if the portrayal showing the woman as finally succumbing to and enjoying the act (as is typical of most pornography), then the situation is reversed for males (but not females). It becomes very arousing. For men, the fantasy of a woman becoming sexually excited as a result of a sexual assault reverses any inhibitions that might have been initially mobilized by the coercive nature of the act and seeing the woman initially in pain.

This message—that pain and humiliation can be "fun"—encourages in men the relaxation of inhibitions against rape.

Doctors Gager and Schurr in their studies on the causes of rape note that a common theme in pornography is that women enjoy being raped and sexually violated. Sexual sadism is presented as a source of sexual pleasure for women. The Gager and Schurr studies note: "The pattern rarely changes in the porno culture.... After a few preliminary skirmishes, women invite or demand further violation, begging male masters to rape them into submission, torture, and violence. In this fantasy land, females wallow in physical abuse and degradation. It is a pattern of horror which we have seen in our examination of sex cases translated again and again into actual assaults."

## UNIVERSITY STUDY SHOWS EFFECTS OF MOVIES

Going outside the laboratory, Neal Malamuth at the University of Manitoba sent hundreds of students to movies playing in the community. He wanted to see what the effects would be of their being exposed to films portraying sexual violence as having positive consequences. The movies they went to see were not pornography, but everyday "sex and violence" of the R-rated variety. The films included *Swept Away* (about a violent male aggressor and a woman who learns to crave sexual sadism; they find love on a deserted island). A second film, *The*

*Getaway*, tells about a woman who falls in love with the man who raped her in front of her husband, then both taunt the husband until he commits suicide.

A second group of students was assigned to see two control films, *A Man and a Woman*, and *Hooper*, both showing tender romance and nonexplicit sex. Within a week of seeing the films, Malamuth administered an attitude survey to all students who had participated in the experiment. The students did not know that the survey had anything to do with the films which they seen. Embedded within the survey were questions relating to acceptance of interpersonal violence and acceptance of such rape myths as "women enjoy being raped." Examples of questions asked also included: "Many women have an unconscious wish to be raped and may unconsciously set up a situation in which they are likely to be attacked."

The results of the survey indicated that exposure to the films portraying sexual violence significantly increased male subjects' acceptance of interpersonal violence against women. For females, the trend was in the opposite direction.

Dr. Malamuth concluded: "The present findings constitute the first demonstration in a nonlaboratory setting... of relatively long-term effects of movies that fuse sexuality and violence." And, of course, these were not hard-core pornography but rather R-rated type, edited films that have appeared on national commercial TV and unedited films shown on cable TV.

As I review the literature on media effects, it appears that in the areas of both sex and violence materials depicting these kinds of behaviors do several things: (1) they stimulate and arouse aggressive and sexual feeling—especially in males; (2) they show or instruct in detail *how* to do the acts—much of it antisocial; (3) when seen frequently enough have a desensitization effect which reduces feelings of conscience, guilt, inhibitions, or inner controls, the act is in a sense legitimized by its repetitive exposure; and finally, (4) there is increased likelihood that the individual will act out what he has witnessed.

Seymour Feshbach's research at UCLA has a direct bearing on this issue. After exposing a group of male college students to a sadomasochistic rape story taken from *Penthouse* magazine—telling of a woman's pleasure at being sexually mistreated—he asked these men if they would like to emulate what the rapist did to the woman. Seventeen percent said they would. When asked the same question but with the added assurance they would not get caught—51 percent indicated a likelihood of raping. This finding has been replicated in a number of other studies—though the percentages vary somewhat from research to research.

Doctors Edward Donnerstein and Neil Malamuth, in reviewing a large number of both field and laboratory experiments, found that exposure to media materials that mix both sex and violence causes six things to happen: (1) it sexually excites and arouses (especially) the male viewer; (2) it increases both his aggressive *attitudes* and *behavior*; (3) it stimulates the production of aggressive rape fantasies; (4) it increases men's acceptance of so-called rape myths (such as: "women ask for it"); (5) it produces a lessened sensitivity about rape (and increased callousness); and (6) it leads to men admitting an increased possibility of themselves raping someone—especially if they think they can get away with it.

## PORNOGRAPHY REDUCES COMPASSION

What about exposure to nonaggressive erotic materials? Do these have any kind of effects on the consumer? Doctors Dolf Zillman and Jennings Bryant at Indiana University studied 160 male and female undergraduates who were divided into groups where they were exposed to: (1) massive amounts of pornography over a period of six weeks; (2) a moderate amount of pornography over that time period; and (3) no exposure over the same time period. Among their many findings were that being exposed to a lot of pornography led to a desensitization effect. The more they saw, the less offensive and objectionable it became to them. They also tended to see rape as a more trivial offense. They had an increasing loss of compassion for women as rape victims (even though no aggressive pornography was shown them).

Massive exposure to nonaggressive pornography clearly promoted sexual callousness in males toward women generally. This was measured by a scale where men agreed with such items as: "Pickups should expect to put out." Or, "If they are old enough to bleed, they are old enough to butcher" (referring to women).

The thrust of this presentation is to suggest that there is an abundance of scientific evidence suggesting social harms from some types of media exposure as has been previously discussed. The studies we have discussed are only illustrative. Many others have not been mentioned due to time limitations. Extensive documentation and lengthy bibliographies on this subject matter are available from the speaker on request.

## CAN WE CONTROL
## PORNOGRAPHY?

We now come to the really hot issue—the bottom line. Does a community have a constitutional right through democratically enacted laws to censor or limit the public broadcast of these kinds of materials—because of their malignant nature? The recent controversy about the First Amendment of the Constitution? Where does or where can one draw the line? How bad or pathological does material have to be before it can be limited? Or should our position be: anything goes regardless of the consequences? Free speech is free speech.

Seymour Feshbach, the UCLA psychologist, states: "As psychologists, we would support community efforts to restrict violence in erotica to adults who are fully cognizant of the nature of the material and who choose knowingly to buy it. We are opposed to advertisements that have appeared in some popular magazines depicting sadomasochism; a recent fashion layout in *Vogue*, for instance, featured a man brutally slapping an attractive woman. We also oppose the practice of some therapists who try to help their patients overcome sexual inhibitions by showing them films of rape or by encouraging them to indulge in rape fantasies. Psychologists, in our judgment, ought not to support, implicitly or explicitly, the use and dissemination of violent erotic materials."

In reference to the First Amendment to our Constitution, we must recognize that today there are many kinds of democratically enacted prohibitions of speech and expression. These, of course, can be amended or repealed anytime we wish. Examples include libel, slander, perjury, conspiracy, false advertising, excitement to violence or speech that might create a "clear and present danger" such as yelling "Fire!" in a crowded theater. Still other examples include TV cigarette advertisements and also obscenity. In fact most of the people who went to jail in the Watergate scandal did so because of what they said—or for words they spoke (e.g., perjury and conspiracy).

In certain public broadcast mediums such as TV and radio, even obscene language can be proscribed without running afoul of the First Amendment.

At present, cable TV is the most controversial area about what is appropriate or inappropriate for broadcast. Currently there are virtually no restrictions on what can be aired. There are some channels in the U.S. broadcasting the roughest kind of hard-core pornography. There are others, including some in Utah, that are regularly broadcasting soft-core pornography mixed with violence. Last spring one of the local cable networks broadcast some 15 times *Eyes of a Stranger*. This film shows in explicit detail a young woman and her boyfriend being attacked by a sadist. He chops the boyfriend's head off, then proceeded to tear the girl's clothes off, strangle her, then rapes the dead body. The film continues with a series of attacks, rapes, and killings of other females. In my judgment this kind of programming, some of it in primetime, represents antisocial and irresponsible behavior on the part of the cable station owners.

Of course, there are many other similar type films which are being regularly broadcast. This is not an isolated incident. But along with this are films of great merit and quality which represent a major contribution to our cultural life as well as entertainment.

At present close to 30 percent of homes in the U.S. have cable. Industry analysts project that by 1985 this will be up to 50 percent and by the end of the decade 80–90 percent. This means that within a few years most all of us will have cable. This is not hard to understand when you consider that very shortly the cable networks will be able to outbid the regular networks for choice sporting events, fights, new Broadway musicals, etc. Even now all the latest movies come to cable before they reach regular commercial TV.

At present there is a double standard in television. The FCC (Federal Communications Commission) has control over the broadcast of appropriate materials by the regular commercial TV channels. They cannot air obscene or other objectionable material without threat of losing their licenses. Cable TV has no restrictions whatever. And, of course, cable firms are taking advantage of this. And there are some adults in our community who are delighted. Others are appalled and have concerns, especially about exposing their children to this kind of programming.

As with most controversial issues, there are no simple solutions which will please everybody. But somewhere a line must be drawn—if we care about the quality of life in our community. We have a right to protect ourselves in our own self-interest.

## MEDIA SAVAGERY GROWS

George Elliot has commented: "If one is for civilization, for being civilized . . . , then one must be willing to take a middle way and pay the price for responsibility. To be civilized, to accept authority, to rule with order, costs deep in the soul, and not the least of what it costs is likely to be some of the sensuality of the irresponsible." Some have argued, as Elliot notes, that since guilt reduces pleasure in sex, the obvious solution is to abolish all sexual taboos and liberate pornography, which in turn would supposedly free the human spirit—and the body.

This is a cheery optimistic view, not unlike the sweet hopefulness of the old-fashioned anarchist who thought that all we had to do in order to attain happiness was to get rid of governments so that we might all express our essentially good nature unrestrained. But sexual anarchism, or the aggressive impulse turned loose, like political anarchism before it, is a "lovely" but fraudulent daydream. Perhaps, before civilization, savages were noble, but if there is anything we have learned in this century, it is that those who regress from civilization become ignoble beyond all toleration. They may aspire to innocent savagery, but what they achieve too often is brutality and loss of their essential humanity.

The issue of how we should deal with the savagery which continues to escalate in our media presentations is just as much your problem as mine. I have shared with you some of the consequences of its presence on our culture. But the solution has to be a shared one—if we really believe in democracy.

# NO

# F. M. Christensen

# ALLEGED ILL EFFECTS FROM USE

[T]he belief that pornography is evil in itself is simply wrong. This leaves open the important question of whether it has effects on the user's attitudes or behavior that are harmful to anyone. Charges that this is so are continually being made, so... we will explore [a few aspects of] that issue [here]....

One particularly profound problem involves the issue of human agency. Now, some people are logically inconsistent in regard to this issue. In response to the suggestion that a violent criminal was made that way by a traumatic childhood, they invoke a notion of absolute free will: "His circumstances are not to blame; he *chose* to let them affect him!" But let the subject be something as comparatively minor as exposure to words or pictures, and suddenly the same people insist on a causal influence. The perennial debate over freedom of the will can hardly be discussed here. But one thing is perfectly clear from all the evidence: heredity and environment have a powerful influence on human behavior. The only room for rational debate is over whether that influence is total (deterministic) or not—and, once more, over just how much effect different types of causal factor exert....

## THE DOMINO THEORY OF CHARACTER

The first of the claims we will discuss is usually expressed in vague generalities; it is basically the charge that use of pornography tends to produce all sorts of wrongful behavior. From the rhetoric some of its proponents employ, one would swear they believe sexual thoughts that are not strictly confined will create a desire to rush out and break windows or steal cars. It is as if they retained the primitive belief that individuals are motivated by only two basic desires—to do good or to do evil—rather than by a complex panoply of needs and emotions. In the minds of some, this idea seems to rest on the conviction that one sort of corruption just naturally leads to others. Few, if any, scientists take such ideas seriously today; "degeneracy theory," with its concept that physical, psychological, and moral defects are all bound together, was popular in the last century but died with the rise of psychology and scientific medicine. In the rest of the population, unfortunately, notions like this one linger on.

The more specific suggestion is sometimes made that "losing self-control" in regard to sex—as allegedly might be precipitated by the use of pornography—produces a general lack of self-discipline, hence a tendency toward selfish libertinism or worse. This sort of thinking has a long history. In Victorian times, married couples were advised to limit the frequency of their sexual activities strictly lest they lead to a weakening of the will and of general character. And the myth that sexual excess brought about the decline and fall of Rome has been around for centuries, having come down to us with those old suspicions about bodily pleasure. (Never mind the gladiators and slavery and brutal imperialism; sexual pleasure was Rome's real failing.) Part of what is involved in the thinking, evidently, is an inability to distinguish between the very specific matter of sexual "permissiveness" and the rejection of *all* restraints on behavior. Alternatively, it is a confusion between a strong interest in sex and a failure to care about any other sources of happiness, or else a tendency to be concerned only with one's own happiness or with the pleasures of the moment. Such tendencies are certainly bad; for example, a person or nation fixated on momentary satisfactions will lack the discipline to plan for and protect future happiness. But there is no reason to suppose that sexual desires are any more apt to have such consequences than are other strong desires.

... [I]t is revealing to point out the inconsistency between these concerns and the lack of fears associated with other needs and pleasures, say, those involving food, love, religious devotion, or the arts. How many are alarmed that our lack of eating taboos—so common in other cultures—will lead to a general obsession with the happiness of the moment? Perhaps we should ban the Wednesday food section in the newspaper, with its seductive pictures and emphasis on the pleasure of eating over its utilitarian function. How many suppose that getting great enjoyment from music or dance will lead to a general lack of self-discipline, or to a disregard for the welfare of others (say, of those who perform them)? The rhetoric about the perils of "pleasure-seeking" is remarkably selective in regard to which pleasures it notices. The real source of this belief, it seems clear, is the sexual anxiety with which so many are raised; it produces the fear that something terrible will happen if one should ever "let go."

The most important response to such charges, however, is that those who make them do not have a shred of genuine evidence. They have been accepted and repeated endlessly, like so many other cultural beliefs, without critical examination. In earlier times, when racism was more socially acceptable than it is now, mixing of the races was often alleged to have brought about the decline of Rome and other civilizations—on the basis of the same worthless *post hoc* reasoning.... Certain commentators have claimed to have evidence from one or two studies that reported finding a statistical association between exposure to sexual materials and juvenile delinquency in the United States. It could well be true that in this society, there has been a tendency for those who lack the traditional sexual attitudes to reject other social standards as well. The former is easily explained as a result of the latter, however: those who have been less well socialized into or have rebelled against the system as a whole will naturally be among the ones whose sexual behavior is less constrained. Alternatively, those whose needs have led them to break one social taboo will feel less threatened by other societal rules....

Of course, that a belief is held for bad reasons does not mean there are no good reasons for it. Nonetheless, it can be said without hesitation that the evidence available is strongly against the "domino theory" of character. One has only to consider the cross-cultural picture to begin to realize this, say, the promiscuous children and youth of Mangaia or the Trobriand Islands or the Muria villages, who grow up into hard-working adults who have internalized all of their society's moral standards. More generally, there is no indication that sexually positive cultures have greater amounts of antisocial behavior. In fact, one cross-cultural survey found significantly more personal crime in groups where premarital sex is strongly punished than in others. (The fact that the crime rate in permissive northern Europe is much lower than that in the United States may already be known to the reader—but beware of *post hoc* thinking.) The belief that gratifying sexual feelings tends somehow to turn into a general state of moral corruption, or even to damage one's capacity for self-discipline, is sheer superstition....

## PERSONAL RELATIONSHIPS

A second variety of claim that pornography has ill effects is that its use tends to damage personal relationships between men and women. This charge takes several different forms, including some that are bizarre (e.g., the idea that many men prefer it to real women and hence will avoid relationships with them if given that option). The simplest of these allegations, however, just points out that numerous women are upset by their partners' interest in pornography, so that it becomes a source of conflict. Part of the problem here is jealousy: the mere biologically normal fact that the partner is attracted to other persons is threatening to some, even when it is all fantasy. But that is evidently not the main difficulty. Few men feel upset over their partners' interest in love stories, say, in soap operas, with their romantic hunks and adulterous love affairs. The real problem seems to be the woman's aversion to nudity and sexual openness.

That being so, this argument presupposes that pornography is hurtful rather than proving it. For it could equally well be said that it is the woman's prudishness, rather than the man's interest in pornography, that is "the real" source of the trouble; which it is would have to be argued for rather than just assumed. Mention to the feminists and religionists who employ this objection that women's liberation or religious devotion has broken up many relationships, and they will make the same basic point.... [M]oreover, it seems clear which one is the real culprit. In earlier years, the attitude that explicit sex is offensive to women led men to go off by themselves to watch "stag films"; what could have been an enjoyable shared experience became a source of alienation. Although female interest in such things might never approach that of males, the ones who divide the sexes are those who say, "My desires are noble and yours are nasty," not those who believe in the equal worth and dignity of the needs of both.

One special argument of this kind alleges that pornography harms relationships by its overemphasis on sex, and also by its underemphasis on companionship or romantic love. It is said to "teach men" to value the former too much and the latter too little. With its culture-bound and egocentric notions of how much emphasis is too much or too little, this claim ignores the possibility of keeping the sexes in harmony by teaching women to want sex in the same way. Its biggest error, however, lies in assigning to media depictions far more power to influence basic desires than is at all justified. As usual, those who make this claim express no similar beliefs about the persuasive powers of the constant barrage of love songs and love stories in all the entertainment media. If such exposure were really so effective, one would think, we would all be incurable love-junkies by now. In any case, there is certainly no lack of publicity promoting love and companionship in our society. Moreover, male sexuality is not detectably different in cultures without appreciable amounts of pornography; indeed, it is evidently very much the same the world over.

What really underlies this claim is an old problem: the unfortunate fact that, on average, men's and women's needs in regard to love/commitment and sex are not well matched. Unable—or perhaps just unwilling—to believe men could ultimately have such different needs than they themselves do, some women suppose it must be the different amount of stress on sex or love among men that does it. One common response is simply to deny that men are really different. For example, these women say men just *think* they have a strong need for sex because advertisers keep telling them they do. Others grant the reality of male sexual responses but do not want to believe they are natural. (Among feminists, this is just part of the wider conviction that there are *no* innate differences between the sexes except anatomical ones.) Yet those who make both claims insist it is men who have been most affected by culture in this regard. Over and again, without offering any argument as to which is cause and which effect, they assert that men would not be so interested in sex, or so attracted to female bodies, if only there were not so much emphasis on those things in this society. Besides projecting their own responses onto male nature—responses that are themselves largely culture-conditioned—the women (and sometimes men) who make such claims are somehow blind to all the societal efforts to suppress male sexuality and promote female needs.

What is true is that a double standard is still taught to adolescents in our culture. But it is glaringly false to say that it encourages males to be sexual; it merely discourages them less. Consider the common charge that "this society" teaches young males they have to "score" to be real men, for example. In fact, you will not find this preached by any of the major socializing institutions, not by church, government, school, family, *or* the media. Even that small segment of the latter that celebrates sex overtly cannot really be said to do this—and it is standardly maligned and even banned by the society at large. The one place where such a thing is taught is in the peer groups of some young men as they themselves rebel against society's teaching on the subject, trying to justify their own needs and feelings. However all this may be, the point remains that pornography is not the cause of male sexuality. It has again become a scapegoat in connection with male-female conflicts whose real causes lie in biology, or at least much deeper in the socialization of men—or of women....

Some have claimed there is scientific evidence that standard pornography causes misperception of other people's sexual desires. In a certain type of experiment, volunteers are exposed to a presentation of some kind and then asked questions about their beliefs or attitudes. (A subterfuge is used to keep them from realizing the true purpose of the test.) In one version of this test, subjects who have been shown sexual materials indicated they regarded women (as well as men) as somewhat more sexually liberal than did subjects who had not been shown the materials. In itself, this is no evidence of misperception; the former might have been closer to the truth than the latter. In any case, the result is not in the least remarkable. A recent or extended experience of *any* kind looms large in one's consciousness. Hence just about any book or movie, *or* real person that one has recently met, would have a similar influence on one's other judgments, temporarily. For a more striking example, one who has just seen a scary movie is much more likely to look under the bed before retiring at night. The effect soon fades, however; it is swamped by that of subsequently encountered books or movies or real people. And most of the latter tend to promote the culture's current party line on sex, just as they do on other subjects. Except in unusual circumstances, the conclusion remains: sexual entertainment will have little effect on perceptions of reality.

A variant of this objection says that the ecstatic pleasure often portrayed in pornography will tend to make the readers or viewers disappointed with their own sexual experience and, hence, with their partners or their partners' performance. (Although it is women who standardly complain about the latter, this new claim is usually framed in terms of male dissatisfaction.) It is not always clear whether those who present the argument believe ordinary tepid sex is really all that is possible—the half-hour orgasms of Mangaian women argue otherwise—or whether for some reason they just think it unwise to aspire to greater enjoyment. In any case, few people would be misled even by genuine exaggeration, which is an extremely common part of life. Does the hysterical euphoria of the consumers in commercials for hamburgers and soft drinks make anyone seriously expect them to taste different? Once again, the only reason for possibly being misled in the special case of sex is societally imposed ignorance. And it is people who use arguments like this one who often want to keep young people in that vulnerable state....

Most of the... claims about pornography's "effects" assume that too much stress on sex is dangerous to an intimate relationship. That can certainly be true, but the proper balance of emphasis between sex and other needs in that context is one that requires sensitive exploration, not dogma. In fact, those who give these fallacious arguments typically overlook the opposite problem. Surveys and clinical experience have long revealed that a high percentage of couples have unsatisfying sex lives. That is a major destroyer of relationships in itself. There are many reasons for this, but a serious one continues to be the sexual inhibition this society inculcates, with its *negative* stress on sex. Conversely,... countless women have discovered that sex could be a joy rather than a burden, and they have done so precisely by learning to become more sexually assertive and more adventurous in bed.

What is especially relevant to our purposes about the latter fact is that pornography has often aided in the process. Large numbers of people have reported that it has helped their sex lives and hence their relationships. In one survey of couples who went to sex movies together, for example, 42 percent made that claim. In her beautiful little book on female sexuality, *For Yourself*, Dr. Lonnie Barbach tells how women have overcome difficulty in getting sexually aroused, or in having orgasms, by learning to use fantasy and pornography. Indeed, it has become standard practice for therapists to use sex films to treat the sexual disabilities of individuals and couples. The ways in which they help are very revealing in light of what has just been discussed: they aid in overcoming inhibition, enhance arousal in preparation for sex, and introduce ideas and techniques that bring freshness to a stale routine. So far from harming intimate personal relationships, pornography can have the very opposite effect.

## MARRIAGE AND THE FAMILY

A third general charge of social harm from pornography has been put forth, mostly by traditionalists. Its use is seen as a threat, not to love and personal relationships as such, but to marriage and the family. The basic claim is that by celebrating sex for its own sake, pornography entices people to leave or refrain from entering committed relationships—"Why be married if you can get sex without it?"—or else leads to their breakup by encouraging extramarital adventures that result in jealous conflicts. This is a serious charge indeed. The legalistic concern some have with marriage ceremonies is highly questionable; but the family, in its role of raising children, is of crucial importance. And divorce, with its adverse effects on children, has become increasingly common in recent decades. Such a large and complex topic can hardly be explored adequately here, but we can address two relevant questions: Is a positive attitude toward sex for its own sake necessarily a threat to marriage? And is pornography an appreciable factor in promoting that sort of attitude, hence itself such a threat?

The answer to the first question seems to be negative. For one thing, there have been many cultures with a stable family life and also an accepting attitude toward nonmarital sex. In fact, prior to the rise of the world religions and the empires that spread them, socially sanctioned premarital sex may well have been the cross-cultural norm. It has even been suggested that such behavior contributes to later marital stability by providing young people with experience on which to base a wiser choice of mate. In any case, it does not speak very well of marriage to suggest that, given a choice, people will reject it. As a matter of fact, most do have a strong inclination toward pair-bonding. Since they do not marry just for sex in the first place (and *shouldn't* do so), liberal sexual attitudes are not likely to dissuade them; only the timing is apt to be affected. In addition, there are many good reasons for not forcing young people to rush into marriage by making it the only way they can get sex.

As for the case of *extra*marital sex, where it has been socially sanctioned and controlled, it too has not been a serious threat to the stability of the family. It is true that jealousy is a powerful emotion. But it is also true that humans are far from being strictly monogamous in their feelings. Although our culture has

NO F. M. Christensen / 315

traditionally taken jealousy as morally justified and condemned extramarital desires, others have done just the reverse: they have sought to mitigate the conflict between the two emotions by controlling the former more than the latter. And the anthropological reports indicate that they succeed rather well. It just may be, for all we know, that their system works better than ours in this respect. In fact, it can be argued that our unbending attitude toward sexual exclusivity contributes to marital breakup by creating unrealistic expectations. The offending party may not want such a break but feel it is necessary to satisfy other desires; and the offended one may fear loss of face in not avenging the act, or else think there must be something wrong with one of them or with the marriage for such a thing to have happened.

However all this may be, it is not the immediate question here. For us the issue is whether pornography is in any of the ways suggested a threat to the family in our culture. In spite of what many assume, it is far from obvious that it is. Indeed, it may be more likely to act as a "safety valve" for preventing marital breakup by providing a substitute way to satisfy nonmonogamous desires. Many cultures of the world have had special festival times and special locations in which the usual sexual taboos could be broken. (For just one example, consider the temple "prostitution" of the ancient Near East, in which all men and women took part.) The seeming value of such institutions in maintaining both monogamy and mental health has been noted by many students of the subject. The fact that such large numbers of strictly monogamous couples in the present time have come to use sexual entertainment together hints that it can serve the same purpose. Given the strong biological urge to have more than one sex partner, this may be an extremely important consideration.

Furthermore, pornography can help to preserve marriages by means of the positive effects listed earlier. As for the chance that it can also have the opposite effect, it might be suggested that romantic love stories present more of a danger to long-term pairing by awakening desires that many a marriage gone stale cannot satisfy. After all, falling in love with someone else is more likely to produce the wish for divorce than is a one-night stand. In any case, factors other than sexual fantasies have been vastly more influential in creating marital instability. The data indicate that such things as the following have been responsible for increasing divorce rates: greater independence for women (most female advocates of long-term commitment do not assail *this* causal factor), changes in laws and attitudes regarding divorce, unemployment and other financial troubles, and the greater mobility of the population, which has led to a loss of controls by the extended family and the community.

To really answer the question before us, however, we must consider the possible dynamics. Exactly how might pornography produce the allegedly destabilizing desires? Those who make the charge sometimes talk as if it is just a matter of arousing feelings that would not otherwise exist. But that is *their* fantasy, for biology can quite adequately do so. It does not take "outside agitators" like pornography to produce lust and wandering eyes. There is one thing, however, that pornography certainly can do, and that is to thwart attempts to suppress such feelings. Efforts to promote one moral point of view are indeed apt to be hampered when people are allowed to become aware of other views as genuine alternatives. This is just to say, however, that freedom and knowledge are an obstacle to attempts at thought control. "How're you gonna keep 'em down on the farm, after they've seen Paris?" asks an old song. It was not only the pill, but the loosening of restraints on sexual content in the media, that launched the reassessment of traditional sexual attitudes that occurred in the 1960s.

So there is a much broader point here that is very important. It is clear that formal and informal education—learning more about the world—tend to make people more tolerant and liberal in their views. For just one apparent example, surveys have revealed that half the readers of sex magazines are college educated, in contrast to a third of the readers of magazines in general. Ideologues, however, do not like such tolerance; what they are opposed to at bottom is the right of other people to make up their own minds. (From Moscow to Washington, they answer, "Don't *let* 'em see Paris.") But it cannot easily be argued that keeping people in ignorance of different ideas is best for them. As Carl Sagan pointed out in *Cosmos*, science has flourished at those times and places in history where there

have been the greatest social openness and freedom. So it is for good reasons that we have our tradition of freedom of expression: aside from the great value of liberty itself, we have a better chance of discovering truth in a "free marketplace of ideas" than in conditions where only certain beliefs and attitudes may be extolled.

In particular, our best hope of working out the most viable social arrangement concerning sex and the family is to allow an open dialogue in which all human needs are given consideration. It is just as wrong to censor portrayals of alternative sexual lifestyles as it is to suppress those of different political or religious systems. In all likelihood, given the large range of human differences that exists, the best system in the present regard is a pluralistic one that allows individuals to discover the different modes of living that maximize their fulfillment. To rigidly impose the same kinds of relationships upon everyone (on homosexual and heterosexual, pair-bonder and non-pair-bonder and so forth) surely does not serve the best interests of individual people. And the common assumption that it is best for society as a whole is the product, not of a careful study of alternatives, but of the very prejudice that censors consideration of alternatives. Socially enforced error is self-perpetuating.

# CHALLENGE QUESTIONS

## Is Pornography Harmful?

1. How do you explain the increase of sexually explicit materials in our society? How does this affect our society?

2. Do you believe that today's more liberal attitudes toward sex have an effect on the incidence of rape, including date rape? Why, or why not?

3. Should policymakers pass legislation controlling or even banning pornography and other sexually explicit materials? Support your position.

4. Cline reports that viewing nonaggressive pornography can lead men to be more callous toward women. Do you agree? Do you think that other circumstances can lead to such attitudes? If so, what?

# ISSUE 17

# Is Marriage Psychologically Beneficial?

**YES: Bryce J. Christensen,** from "The Costly Retreat from Marriage," *The Public Interest* (Spring 1988)

**NO: Liz Hodgkinson,** from *Unholy Matrimony: The Case for Abolishing Marriage* (Columbus Books, 1988)

## ISSUE SUMMARY

**YES:** Bryce J. Christensen, director of the Rockford Institute Center on the Family in America, argues that there is voluminous evidence linking good mental health with marriage.

**NO:** Freelance writer Liz Hodgkinson contends that marriage is generally stifling and that it often leads to violence or depression.

The institution of marriage is often taken for granted. Not all people get married, to be sure, but most tend to see marriage as a natural part of life. Most young people envision themselves getting married at one time or another, and many people consider marriage a prerequisite to having children. Although more and more single parents are raising children successfully, most people still consider it necessary to be married before having babies and rearing children.

The valuing of marriage and its dominance in our culture do not in any way guarantee its success. With the divorce rate hovering at roughly 50 percent, it would be foolish to assume that everyone who marries enjoys wedded bliss. Still, those who do remain married seem to have a ready support system, and social and clinical psychologists have shown quite conclusively that people with significant support systems—which can consist of friends, family, caring coworkers, and so on—tend to be more physically and mentally healthy than people without support systems. Does marriage, despite its high probability of dissolution, function as a beneficial support system?

Bryce J. Christensen answers this question affirmatively. He not only believes that marriage is psychologically beneficial, but he also considers marriage a significant weapon in the battle against rising health care costs. Quite simply, he says, marriage is good for your health. Obviously, this belief does not come from any particular physical or medical advantages of marriage per se. But, Christensen argues, married people are less likely to experience depression, severe anxiety, and any number of psychologically related illnesses, such as headaches and high blood pressure, than are single people.

Liz Hodgkinson, however, insists that "marriage is in a bad way." She contends that marriage has primarily negative effects on a person's mental health, partly because married people are subject to all sorts of unreasonable expectations and stresses. For example, married people are required to spend the majority of their time together, share parental and housework chores, invade each other's privacy, and generally develop specialized roles that foster dependency and, ultimately, helplessness. The inevitable result, according to Hodgkinson, is anger, which is either turned outward (as in the case of wife battering) or turned inward (as in the case of depression).

| POINT | COUNTERPOINT |
|---|---|
| • Marriage has many psychological benefits. | • Most marriages end up either in divorce or as some sort of stifling relationship. |
| • Marriage is a ready-made support system. | • Just because people are married does not ensure that they are supportive of one another. |
| • Many research studies indicate numerous positive effects of marriage. | • People, including scientists, are culturally biased to see marriage in the most positive light. |
| • Marriage promotes physical as well as psychological health. | • It has been found that 70 percent of all serious crimes take place in the homes of married couples. |

# YES

Bryce J. Christensen

# THE COSTLY RETREAT FROM MARRIAGE

The costs of providing medical care in America, it is frequently noted, have skyrocketed in the recent past, and promise to continue doing so in the future. There is, of course, at least a partial solution to this problem, one involving little or no expenditure of either public or personal funds. This solution calls for an increased emphasis upon preventive medicine: exercising and dieting today help to avert heart disease tomorrow; not smoking now increases the likelihood of avoiding lung cancer later.

My purpose in writing this essay is to suggest something else that Americans can do on their own to improve their health, something that government ought to do more to encourage—Americans can get married and stay married. Quite simply, marriage, no less than jogging and lowering cholesterol intake, is good for your health. Although it is obviously up to individual Americans to decide whether to marry, stay single, or divorce, it is nevertheless past time for policymakers to acknowledge the profound health benefits of marriage: the nation's runaway medical costs could be partially controlled were government to implement policies that did more to foster and encourage longer-lasting, child-producing marriages.

The new evidence linking health to marriage and family life is voluminous. Writing... in *Social Science and Medicine*, Catherine K. Riessman and Naomi Gerstel observe that "one of the most consistent observations in health research is that married [people] enjoy better health than those of other marital statuses." Drs. Riessman and Gerstel note that compared with married men and women, the divorced, single, and separated suffer much higher rates of disease morbidity, disability, mental neuroses, and mortality. "This pattern has been found for every age group (20 years and over), for both men and women, and for both whites and non-whites." According to James Lynch of the University of Maryland Medical School, the health advantage enjoyed by the married over the unmarried has actually grown in recent decades.

Only a small fraction of the statistical health gap separating the married from the single and divorced can be accounted for by the common-sense observation that sick people either don't get married or don't make satisfac-

From Bryce J. Christensen, "The Costly Retreat from Marriage," *The Public Interest*, no. 91 (Spring 1988), pp. 59–66. Copyright © 1988 by National Affairs, Inc. Reprinted by permission of *The Public Interest* and the author.

tory marriage partners. According to Dr. Lynch, married people are healthier largely because marriage per se "influences the general life-style of the individual." In a study published... in the *Journal of Health and Social Behavior*, Debra Umberson of the University of Michigan finds that mortality rates are "consistently higher" for the unmarried than for the married, because marriage exerts a "deterrent effect on health-compromising behaviors" such as excessive drinking, drug use, risk-taking and disorderly living. By providing a system of "meaning, obligation, [and] constraint," family relationships markedly reduce the likelihood of unhealthy practices. Interestingly, Dr. Umberson's research also underscores the difference between the widowed and the divorced. Although both groups have poorer health habits than the married, the habits of the divorced are far worse than those of the widowed.

In his research into the effects of marriage on health, Harold Morowitz of Yale University concludes that "being divorced and a non-smoker is slightly less dangerous than smoking a pack or more a day and staying married," adding facetiously that "if a man's marriage is driving him to heavy smoking he has a delicate statistical decision to make."

## HAPPILY AND HEALTHILY WED

The advantage that the married enjoy over the unmarried in death rates due to cancer and heart disease is astonishing. The lung-cancer rate for divorced men is twice that for married men, while the rates for some forms of cancer (genital, buccal, and pharyngeal) are three to four times as high among the divorced. The pattern among divorced women, while

not quite so stark, is similar. Among both men and women, the single and divorced die from hypertensive heart disease at rates between two-and-a-half and three-and-a-half times those found among the married. Dr. Lynch reports that even when their diseases are not fatal, divorced and single people stay in the hospital longer than do married men and women suffering from the same illnesses. This pattern of longer hospital stays is costing America "uncounted billions of dollars" every year.

Just as impressive are the mental-health benefits bestowed by marriage. According to Peggy A. Thoits of Indiana University, "married persons have significantly lower anxiety and depression scores than unmarried persons, regardless of gender." Dr. Thoits notes that married individuals appear to enjoy better mental health even when they have experienced more potentially traumatic experiences than the unmarried. Surprisingly, even the mentally ill sometimes find psychological benefits in marriage. The British medical journal, the *Lancet*, ... reported that in some cases marriages between the mentally ill prove "stable and may even show improved function.... The support provided by a shared mental disability may have a beneficial effect."

Some feminists have claimed that marriage benefits only men; but available health statistics show otherwise. While men do realize a somewhat greater health advantage from marriage than women, both sexes are clearly healthier if married than if unmarried. The latest findings only partially confirm Emile Durkheim's famous hypothesis that marriage is more important for the mental health of men than for that of women, while raising children is more important for women than for men. According to Dr.

Umberson's 1987 study, "marriage and parenting relationships work together to deter health-compromising behaviors" for both men and women. In fact, for at least one disease—breast cancer—marriage protects women's health in particular, by increasing the likelihood that they will bear two or more children: a recent study at the University of Bergen in Norway found a correlation between the number of children a woman has borne and her likelihood of developing breast cancer, with the childless and the mothers of only one most vulnerable.

Nor is it just husbands and wives whose health is affected by marriage. In a study published... in the *New England Journal of Medicine*, researchers at the National Center for Health Statistics found that unmarried women, compared with married women, run "a substantially higher risk of having infants with very low or moderately low birth weights." Because birth weight is one of the best predictors of infant mortality, many more illegitimate than legitimate babies die. The NCHS researchers believe that marriage exerts no "direct causal influence on the outcome of pregnancy," but that a life course that includes marriage is likely to be healthier than one that does not. (For example, unmarried mothers are more likely to smoke than married mothers.)

Though divorce is less threatening to a child's health than is illegitimacy, it still takes its toll. The *Canadian Journal of Psychiatry* reports that divorce increases the likelihood of mental disturbances among children, with over a third of children still "troubled and distressed at the five year mark" (after their parents' divorce). According to John McDermott of the University of Hawaii, "divorce is now the single largest cause of child-hood depression." Dr. Lynch believes that parental divorce not only causes mental neuroses among children, but also contributes to "various physical diseases, including cardiac disorders," later in their lives. The *Journal of the Royal Society of Medicine* reports that members of single-parent families also complain more frequently of less serious maladies, including "headaches, backaches, tummy aches, listlessness,... depression, [and] a host of other ailments," than do those in two-parent households. Finnish health authorities at the University of Tampere find that children from nonintact families are much more likely to require medical attention for psychosomatic symptoms than children from intact families. The ailments, real and imagined, of children from single-parent homes may well persist, creating sizable public costs in the decades ahead.

## THE FLIGHT FROM MARRIAGE

The latest health findings should foster concern about falling marriage rates. In recent years, as the national media have glamorized the freedom and excitement of the single "life-style," an unprecedented number of young people have decided that marriage should be avoided—or at least postponed. Since 1970 the American marriage rate has fallen 30 percent, while the divorce rate has climbed 50 percent. By 1983 the average age at first marriage had risen to 24.5 for women and to 26.8 for men. If current trends continue, one American in seven will never wed. But the statistics already cited suggest that the fern bar and health spa may serve as mere way stations for singles headed for the hospital—or the cemetery.

During the 1970s, Americans witnessed what Lenore Weitzman has called "the divorce revolution." Within a decade, legislators in almost every state replaced traditional divorce laws with new "no-fault" statutes that made it much easier to dissolve a marriage. Cultural attitudes changed, as divorce shed its stigma as a "calamity" or "tragedy" and came to enjoy widespread acceptance as a simple "uncoupling," or even a laudable act of "courage," a valuable "growth opportunity." Although the divorce rate has shown signs of leveling off, it is still 50 percent higher than it was in 1970. Demographers estimate that 44 percent of all marriages formed in 1983 will end in divorce. Weitzman has documented the harmful, if unintended, economic consequences of the divorce revolution for both women and children.

Epidemiologists are now accruing data on the harm done to health by the divorce epidemic. A 1984 study by the National Center for Health Services concluded that divorced women were not only less healthy than married women, but also more likely to rely on public assistance in securing medical care. This finding is especially striking because "the divorced population is somewhat younger than the married."...

Clearly, public-health officials have reason to worry about what demographer Robert Schoen has described as America's "retreat from marriage." The medical costs created by this social trend will surely strain government programs such as Medicare and Medicaid. Indirect effects ought also to be taken into account. The social retreat from marriage not only drives up the nation's future medical bills, but also reduces the number of future taxpayers available to pay those bills. In explaining why our national fertility rate has languished below replacement level for more than a decade, Ben Wattenberg points to the trend toward fewer, later, and less stable marriages. Although illegitimacy rates have risen significantly since 1950, unmarried women still bear far fewer children than do married women. While the birthrate for married women aged 18–44 stands at 92.0 per 1,000 women (an historic low), the birth rate for unmarried women in the same age group remains much lower (33.4 per 1,000). Fewer babies now mean a much smaller tax base in thirty or forty years. Wattenberg believes that the "birth dearth" could cause Social Security to fail early in the next century, if—as is widely predicted—the Social Security trust fund is combined with the Medicare trust fund.

As low fertility erodes the tax base, it simultaneously imposes higher public costs for institutionalization of the elderly. Recent surveys show that taxpayers bear the burden of institutionalizing the elderly far less frequently when they are married and have three or more children than when they are single or divorced, or when they have few or no children. Looking at statistics from 1976, Stephen Crystal concludes that "the more children an older person has had, the smaller the odds of institutional placement." Historians have noted a similar pattern in the early years of this century. A 1910 Massachusetts survey found that almost 60 percent of the aged poor then living in almshouses or benevolent homes had no living adult children; a Pennsylvania survey in 1919 found that almost two-thirds of those living in almshouses had no living children; comparable statistics were reported in a 1929 National Civic Federation Survey conducted nationwide. Clearly, if fewer

American marriages ended in divorce and fewer American families were small, nursing-home care would not consume 41 percent of all Medicaid expenditures.

Worse, however, is in store. Writing in the *American Journal of Public Health,* researchers from Vanderbilt University predict that the increased future costs of providing nursing-home care for aging Americans without children able or willing to care for them in their homes will be troublesome. The anticipated increase of $6 billion (in 1982 dollars) in nursing-home expenses by the year 2012, they warn, will "exacerbate... intergenerational conflict."

## POLICY IMPLICATIONS

Public-health officials are already beginning to rediscover the importance of marital and family relationships in their fight to contain ballooning health costs. Richard Morse of Kansas State University sees "some movement, at present, to deny welfare or Medicaid to those individuals whose families cannot prove they are unable to perform that responsibility." Alexa K. Stuifbergen of the University of Texas at Austin likewise believes that "policymakers are increasingly looking to the family as a hedge against the rising cost of health care services."

This rediscovery of family responsibility could mark a positive first step in reshaping public-health policy. Unless, however, it is matched by some policies that help intact marriages, the rediscovery of family responsibility could create economic injustices: it could push intact families to the end of the line of those eligible for federal benefits, while keeping them near the front of the line of those responsible for paying for those benefits.

One possible approach would be to restructure Medicare rates so that married recipients pay a lower monthly premium than the unmarried. But it is politically unthinkable and ethically questionable for government to favor the married over the unmarried directly: millions of older Americans are unmarried because of the death of a spouse; many others either had no opportunity to marry or divorced only for the most serious of reasons, after making every effort at reconciliation.

Yet policymakers could benefit most young marriages by framing a tax policy that offers greater advantages to households with children present. First, tax reformers could raise the personal federal income-tax exemption for dependent children from $2,000 to $4,000. (Even at $4,000 the personal exemption would remain hundreds of dollars below its 1948 value, when adjusted for inflation.) Second, the income ceiling for the Earned Income Tax Credit could be raised—to perhaps $25,000 or $27,500— and the benefits could be scaled to the number of children in the home (while still restricting the credit to no more than the total payroll taxes paid by the recipient). Third, the current child-care tax credit could be universalized, allowing households with a stay-at-home mother to share the benefits now received by dual-income homes.

Admittedly, such a child-centered approach would help unwed and divorced mothers, but not childless couples and older married couples with no children at home. Yet the young married couple remains the most fertile unit and would therefore receive most of the benefits. Although married American women now bear fewer children than in past decades, only about one married couple in twenty is both childless and infertile. Even a cohabiting couple is only half as likely as a married couple to have a child in its household. Moreover, improving the economic status of the nation's children is a worthy policy objective in itself, quite apart from the gain for marriage. The two objectives of helping children and encouraging marriage could actually prove mutually reinforcing: married couples might well choose to have more children if some of the economic hardship of childrearing were eliminated, while children arguably provide the strongest cement for a marital union. It is no accident that the divorce rate dropped during the baby boom of the 1950s.

Many of the forces fueling America's retreat from marriage are ultimately cultural, hence not under the direct control of policymakers in a liberal democracy. Nonetheless, policymakers must cope with the rising medical costs created by the flight from marriage. In discharging this responsibility, simple prudence suggests the need for approaches that will reduce these medical costs by encouraging marriage. At the same time, justice dictates that those who build successful marriages and families be relieved of at least some of the public burdens created by those who repudiate marriage. Child-based tax benefits could help achieve these objectives without unfairly penalizing those who are unmarried for reasons beyond their control.

# NO

## Liz Hodgkinson

## MARRIAGE TODAY

Modern marriage is in a bad way. Although couples may agree to love, honour and share all worldly goods at the outset, few of them stick to these vows for any length of time. Many couples end up hating and resenting each other, even resorting, in extreme cases, to violence and murder.

The condition of being married and having to live in close and intimate contact, day after day, year after year, with just one adult member of the opposite sex, encourages very strong dependencies to develop. Married people expect, and are expected, to share general interests and political persuasions, to take an active involvement in each other's work and hobbies, and to go on holiday together. Such cosy togetherness is constantly encouraged by society. Many of us get married, or form partnerships, assuming that this familiarity will make us happy, content and fulfilled. Indeed, in modern Western marriages it is almost impossible for partners to get away from each other for any length of time. Married people are expected to sleep together, in the same bed, and to live as much of their lives as is humanly possible as a unit rather than as individuals. The idea of joint mortgages and joint bank accounts, hardly heard of twenty years ago, is regarded as a good idea, and the concept of joint finances underlines the way in which we like modern couples to operate.

In the old days, and also in marriages in traditional societies, men and women did not, and do not, spend so much time together. In many traditional societies today (Muslim ones, for example), it is usual for husbands and wives to entertain separately, to eat separately and to have completely separate tasks. It has been said that this separation occurs in societies where women are kept down, but in her book *Sex and Destiny* Germaine Greer makes the wise point that it at least allows the wives a bit of a breather on occasion, time away from the spouse. It has long been received wisdom that Western marriages allow more freedom to the wife, who does not always have to be at her husband's beck and call. If this is deemed to be good, why should it be so desirable for two disparate human beings, of different sexes and possibly of quite dissimilar characters, to share everything they do?

Nowadays, we insist on shared parenthood, shared housework—even shared secrets (openness of feelings, thoughts and emotions). Men and women sometimes also dress alike, particularly if they are sporty types.

Advertisements aimed at retired or soon-to-retire people reveal an assumption that, once the couple are no longer in paid employment, they will want to spend every single minute in each other's company. No wonder people who stay married for a long time end up looking alike. (There is some scientific credence for this: according to the psychologist Robert Zajonc of the University of Michigan it happens because married people mirror each other's expressions and behaviour, meeting scowls with scowls and smiles with smiles.)

Modern marriage can be stifling, because it makes it so difficult for partners to spend any time away from each other. And however much a couple may be in love when they first meet, however strong the initial 'urge to merge', in time they will most probably want to reassert their individuality. But if they start out with the idea of being mutually dependent, unable to stand on their own feet, they may actually in time be incapable of doing even the simplest tasks alone. What the psychologists call 'learned helplessness' is common in marriage, and the condition is liable to worsen as the years go by. Many women who have been adventurous and independent while single discover that, once they have been married a few years, they are nervous about changing a light-bulb, booking into a hotel alone, or making decisions about even a minor purchase. Men who have been coping excellently as bachelors suddenly forget how to cook, to sew on buttons, change bed linen or how to send trousers to the dry-cleaners.

But the more a couple merge as the years go by, the more we see this as a good thing. Kitty Muggeridge, wife of the journalist Malcolm, once admitted in an interview that over the many years of their marriage they had become one person'. We also have a sneaking admiration for couples who involve themselves in suicide pacts, as did the writer Arthur Koestler and his wife Cynthia, who decided she could not live without him. 'Greater love hath no woman [or man] than this,' we reflect. Yet the fact is that people do not really become more alike over the years. If anything, their differences become more apparent as the years go by. And in those marriages where they seem to have merged, what has really happened is that one partner has allowed his or her personality to become *submerged* by the greater force of the other. Where couples do appear to become 'one flesh' it will not be a case of two separate, strong individuals making a whole that is greater than the sum of the parts: instead, one person will have effectively died, become a cipher, an incomplete human being. In many cases—although not all—it is the wife who allows her personality and individuality to be sucked dry and taken over by the stronger (or more aggressive) personality of the husband.

Nowadays, we seem desperate to tidy people up into couples, so that they will move in society as a team, a unit. We forget that humans are not really designed to be parcelled up in this way. One of the main reasons why marriage tends to bring out so many violent emotions in people is because they are resisting—often without being fully aware of it—being imprisoned for life with just one other person. It is now very common for married women to become clinically depressed. Depression is really anger turned inwards. Husbands tend to turn their anger outwards, and become aggressive, demanding and bad-tempered, blaming everybody apart from themselves for what has upset them. Often, neither partner realizes that he or she is silently rebelling against the straitjacket of marriage, the institution that was supposed to make them so wonderfully happy. Many partners try to escape by having affairs—but all realize that, once married, they are in a cage from which they can never really escape. At most, they go for short sorties, but their wings have been clipped. Even people who divorce usually get married again quite soon. We are so indoctrinated into marriage that few of us can envisage a life without total symbiotic union with another human being.

Again, in the days of the extended family, there was always somebody of one's own sex to talk to, and with whom burdens could be shared. Nowadays, most women have only their husbands to talk to, most men only their wives. There is a general idea that, once married, a couple should be left alone, to sink or swim together. In-laws do not want to 'interfere', and they would rather not know if anything is going wrong. No wonder there are so many marital problems, infidelities and divorces. The institution has become stifling, yet it is constantly presented as the only way to live, the only way to relate to another human being, the only way to love. If you love somebody, so the current wisdom goes, you must want to bind them to you, permanently if possible. This bondage is usually, euphemistically, called 'commitment'.

There is little freedom in the context of marriage. Togetherness is encouraged both on an everyday social level, on which husbands and wives who do not function as couples are deemed to be a problem, and now, increasingly, in a business context: spouses are often expected to attend office parties and similar occasions, and even, if the employer is a sizeable corporation, to go along on business conferences attended by their partners (a big business is growing up in the arrangement of 'spouses' programmes' at such junkets). And for all our talk of sexual freedom, we do not, as a society, condone sexual intercourse outside marriage. It is acceptable for single people to have as many partners as they like—or at least, it was all right before the advent of AIDS—but once married, men and women are expected to be able to channel their sexual urges into their marital partnership. Society very severely castigates anybody who strays, or rather, is caught straying.

Our current fantasy is that marriage partners should be able to satisfy each other sexually, and that neither should look around for somebody more exciting, newer, younger, unless divorce or widowhood has intervened. This concept of so-called 'serial monogamy', now generally accepted, entails getting rid of the current partner before embarking on a liaison with another.

But society still reserves its severest criticism for those who are caught having affairs with other people while they are still married. This is 'cheating', or 'being unfaithful', and those in high public office or with an otherwise high profile cannot normally escape the indignation of press-generated public opinion. For public servants, the penalty for being found out is a duty to resign immediately from their high position, and there is a general understanding that such people will have to atone in some way for what they have done, because they have broken the rules....

The number of well-known men in public life who have had to atone, often for years on end, for having sexual liaisons outside their marriages, is legion: Gary Hart, the 1988 American presidential candidate; John Profumo, who has spent many years working among the deprived of London's East End since his adultery with Christine Keeler was discovered in 1963; and Lord Lambton, who went to live abroad after he too was discovered, in the early 1970s, to be having an affair with a prostitute. It is less often the case that women in high office have to step down because they are having a secret affair, but then very few women are ever in high office. Throughout history, however, the penalties for women 'caught in adultery' have been severe. One can only wonder at the level of shock and horror that would result if it were to be discovered that Mrs Thatcher or the Queen, for instance, had secretly been having affairs while in positions of authority and trust.

Marriage carries with it the notion that sexual fidelity, 'belonging' to each other, is important. This notion has never been more highly upheld than it is now, in the late twentieth century. In the eighteenth century, when marriage was regarded more lightly, both husbands and wives often had lovers and mistresses, and not always in great secrecy. In medieval times, marriage and love were almost completely separated. One married for duty and fell in love for pleasure—but rarely did one fall in love with a marriage partner. If one was lucky, fondness and respect might develop over the years spent together.

Now, as the song has it, love and marriage go together like a horse and carriage. Once we marry, we are expected to be in love with that person forever. But if we fall in love with somebody else, it is all right for us to get divorced and marry that person. However, woe betide any man and woman who choose to live together just as friends, or as brother and sister. They would be regarded as distinctly odd. A conviction prevails that it is part of nature's plan for us to be permanently united, sexually, financially and emotionally, with just one other person. Many of us believe this is what God ordained for us.

The case of the millionaire novelist Jeffrey Archer in 1987 confirmed our entrenched views of the married state. Archer felt that he had to clear his name when newspapers alleged that he had paid money to Monica Coghlan, a prostitute, to prevent her revealing the nature of their relationship. In the event, it will be remembered, Archer cleared his name, thus making himself £500,000 the richer (he gave the money to a variety of deserving causes).

Archer's case had a curious effect on the British public, and encouraged many people to analyse exactly what they thought marriage was all about. Each day throughout the hearing his wife, Mary, at that time a Cambridge don, was loyally by his side, quietly and smartly dressed. Both found themselves bathed in a plethora of publicity.

The facts of their marriage, so far as they have been made public, are these: Jeffrey and Mary Archer married in 1966, when she was 21 and he was 27. Both were Oxford graduates, heading for glittering careers. It says much for their perception of the importance of the ceremony that they had their wedding videoed, and kept a video-recording of it, part of which has subsequently been seen by millions on BBC television. Jeffrey Archer, a compact, ever-smiling confident young man, went on to become a Conservative MP and was also a keen runner. He resigned his seat when a bad business deal bankrupted him, but rapidly restored his fortunes by writing bestselling fiction.

Mary, meanwhile, though she stayed in the background, was not just a wife and mother. She continued a career of her own, as a scientist and university lecturer. As time went on, the Archers prospered mightily, had two sons and became pillars of the Church. Mary was shown on television playing the organ and singing in the choir. Jeffrey was depicted as a devoted father, and shortly after the court case had his first play successfully premièred in London.

But the main focus for the media throughout the period of the libel hearing was on the Archers' marriage. How far could they be considered the ideal modern couple? It appeared that they had everything—money, looks, a family, wonderful homes, domestic staff—and, wonder of wonders, total devotion to each other after 21 years together. Mary has a career, is good-looking, well-dressed, neat, confident. Both, indeed, are very confident. They obliged for the cameras by being photographed hand in hand, arm in arm, the archetypal modern couple, both earning, both successful, both high-profile, and both with very nice things to say about each other. 'Mary is completely honest,' said Jeffrey in his most sincere manner. 'She is the most honest person I know.'

So the story became 'How to stay married, Archer-style'. Mary and Jeffrey became instant experts on marriage and their views were sought in interview after interview. When asked how she made her marriage 'work', Mary Archer replied that she didn't rate strict sexual fidelity that highly, but thought it was important for couples to be loyal, and able to stand by each other. That state-ment alone made many journalists reach for their word processors. 'Do you agree that sexual fidelity is not a top priority for marriage?' asked the *Daily Express* of its readers. The columnist Helen Mason wrote in *The Daily Telegraph* that Mary Archer was 'stuck in the 'sixties' to give low priority to sexual fidelity. 'We have seen the alternative to sexual fidelity and it does not work,' Mason wrote. 'Rejection of concepts such as jealousy and possessiveness sound very noble, but in fact, cleaving unto the other only, as we all promised to do, has a sound practical value.'

Helen Mason went on to say what she thought that 'sound practical value' was, and as one might expect, fear of AIDS came top of the list. Security and trust were also mentioned.

Mary Archer was also widely castigated for saying publicly that she did not think it was possible to be 'in love' after 21 years of marriage, though she declared that she was able to love her husband dearly. This called forth the wrath of newspaper columnists, in particular Lynda Lee-Potter of the *Daily Mail*, who said she was not sure Mrs Archer was right in saying that it was impossible to be in love after many years. She asked her readers to disprove this with their own stories and, of course, they obliged in droves, saying that their husbands/wives brought them flowers, presents, declared their love, that they never spent a minute apart and missed each other deeply and inconsolably if one was absent for any length of time. What passed for being 'in love' was, of course, over-attachment and dependence, and not real love. Though we may very much enjoy spending time in the other's company, surely true love means being able to let the other person go, never wanting to bind him or her to you. Wanting to bind a person to you comes from fear, not love.

We try to maintain the fantasy that being in love is a good thing, and that passion and excitement in marriage are also a good thing. In saying that she did not believe it was possible to be in love after many years, and that strict sexual fidelity was not of prime importance, Mary Archer was simply being honest—one of her greatest qualities, as we heard from her husband himself. But honesty would now seem to be a rare commodity where marriage is concerned.

All of us conspire to keep alive the fiction that marriage works, that closeness and commitment are of paramount importance. If we were to admit what marriage is *really* like, it would be revealed as an emperor without clothes, a cloying, confining and repressive union which has the power to imprison at least one, if not both, partners. Modern marriage is, I believe, largely a pretence—a hollow state that we all pretend to like because most of us cannot envisage any other way to live. Society now moves in couples and will exclude us, we believe, if we dare to move alone. The fiction is that, so long as we have a partner, all will be well. Even if that partner causes us more anguish than happiness, it is still better, we believe, to have somebody to whom we are joined by law than to be alone.

The 'ideal' for marriage is in fact a continuing honeymoon. At this stage, although the partners may be sexy and passionate with each other, they are not allowed to be sexy with anybody else. They are also supposed to have the other's interests at heart all the time, to stay in love, to prove this with presents and acknowledgement of anniversaries, and to become mutually dependent on each other. They are not supposed to want to look elsewhere for intellectual, emotional, sexual or any other kind of personal satisfaction, but are supposed to find all they are looking for in this other partner. We seem to feel that men and women are, by themselves, incomplete and can only be 'completed' by attaching themselves permanently to a member of the opposite sex.

Even gays and lesbians are now aping the married state, and are increasingly forming lifelong liaisons of a marital type. Some homosexual couples are even getting 'married' or, rather, having their unions blessed in church. The whole world, it seems, must get married. Anybody who does not do so is considered slightly odd, somewhat eccentric, or even unlovable, and is likely to be put under pressure by his or her peers to form such a liaison.

Married people are supposed to support each other and be devoted to one another. They are not supposed to grow apart or develop their own personalities. People do, of course, all the time, but as a society we do our best to encourage the idea that, once married, a couple are welded together for all time.

The supposition is that total togetherness is a highly desirable, indeed enviable, condition. Autonomy is out.

From time to time, reports and surveys about marriage appear in the newspapers. The surveys always prove that there is still overwhelming support for the institution, and as a subject marriage fascinates everybody, not least because there is such a huge disparity between the fantasy and the reality.

There is also a widespread belief that marriage is now treated too lightly by many couples. In one survey about 75 per cent of adults interviewed felt that the institution ought to be regarded with more seriousness. The leading virtues in a married couple were listed as faithfulness, mutual respect and understanding. Sex and good housekeeping also appeared on the list, but much further down. Unsatisfactory sex was not considered a good reason for divorce, whereas sexual infidelity was. A happy sexual relationship was considered important by about 50 per cent of those questioned.

By and large, the British public showed themselves conservative in their attitudes: 76 per cent believed that women with small children should stay at home and look after them, and 19 per cent felt that women with teenagers should do the same.

An opinion poll survey carried out for the *The People* in October 1985 purported to reveal the 'intimate secrets' of 1000 married men and women. One 'intimate' secret revealed was that people now expect an awful lot from marriage. We are no longer content to co-exist with somebody towards whom we feel lukewarm or indifferent; we feel we have the right to be madly in love, and that marriage should make us happy, fulfilled and secure. If a marriage does not live up to these expectations, couples will not hesitate to head towards the divorce courts. No longer will people tolerate—as their forebears did—a miserable marriage, or one where there is no compatibility.

The newspaper spelled out, in order, the nine most important ingredients of a happy marriage, as revealed by its survey. These were give and take; treating each other as equals; liking each other as friends; staying in love; staying faithful; good sex; having individual interests; financial security; and children.

These all sound reasonable, but what do they really mean?

'*Give and take*' seems to be what does *not* happen in the average marriage, however much the partners hope it will. Whenever an old married couple celebrating a golden wedding is asked the secret of a successful marriage, the answer is always 'give and take'. To give and take really means to be tolerant, to have the best interests of the other person at heart. How many people do that? More often than not, individual wishes prevail and a power struggle develops, with one partner trying to dominate the other while the dominated partner struggles to assert individuality.

Very often it is the man who takes and the woman who gives. At least, that is how the wife usually sees it. The husband more often sees it the other way round. He sees himself (if the marriage follows the traditional pattern of breadwinning husband and dependent wife, as fewer and fewer do) as giving everything, providing everything, and getting precious little in return.

The main problem in modern marriage is that the majority of people are desperately hungry for love. They want constant assurances that they are loved and wanted and held in respect. When the husband comes home and finds his meal is not on the table, he becomes angry because this means he is not loved enough. When the wife discovers he has forgotten her birthday yet again, she is angry because this means he is not thinking of her. People demand respect and love from others when they have little for themselves. But you cannot demand respect. You cannot even demand give and take.

Genuine give and take in marriage can be hard to find. What often happens is that there is a trade-off: I will have sex with you tonight if you buy me that new dress tomorrow; I will have your boss to dinner if you take me to the ballet. These are crass examples, of course, but they serve to illustrate the principle. Give and take, in the average marriage, usually means bargaining positions and power struggles, in which both sides tend to end up feeling miserable and cheated. So much is expected of the other person—generally more than he or she is able to give, and we are deeply disappointed when our partners fail to come up to the mark. Yet why *should* somebody else be expected to fulfil our fantasies?

'*Treating each other as equals*', the second 'ingredient' of a successful marriage according to the survey, is fundamentally impossible in the context of marriage. Embedded in the marriage laws themselves is the concept that men and women are *not* the same and *not* equal. The only way in which a man and woman can stay equal is not to marry, but to remain single. Marriage, by its very nature, is an arrangement which renders the two parties unequal. It is only in the twentieth century that a married woman has even been considered a person at all. In the past, she was little more than one of her husband's goods and chattels. Her property, if she had any as a single woman, became his, while his remained his, on marriage. (Personal possessions such as clothes and jewellery did not constitute property.) We may imagine things have improved, but in reality little has changed.

As the law does not see married men and women as equals, so it is impossible for them to regard each other as equals. A woman is usually expected to join her husband wherever he goes, to support him emotionally, to believe that everything he does is right. Even today, a wife cannot be compelled to give evidence against her husband in court.

Many wives will stand by their husbands even when they have been accused of cheating, consorting with prostitutes, lying, even murder. This happens because, in the majority of marriages, the woman becomes more dependent and attached than the man—and often truly imagines she cannot live without him.

If you want an equal relationship, do not get married: once married, you simply will not be allowed by society or by the law to remain equal.

'*Liking each other as friends*' was the third ingredient suggested by the survey.

Yes, this is really the ideal. But again, it is impossible in the average marriage. Why? Simply because you are forced to be so close, so emotionally involved, so financially entangled, that friendship becomes impossible. Many wives of famous men, when interviewed, will say, 'My husband is my best friend.' By that, they often mean that this man is their *only* friend: they have in fact forsaken everybody else and are often physically isolated, to the extent that friendship is almost impossible after marriage. Many married women simply do not go to the theatre, the pub, or any place of entertainment unless the spouse is there as well. They become actually incapable, in time, of doing anything on their own. And if their husbands work very long hours they find themselves virtual prisoners in their homes, passing whole days and evenings without seeing or speaking to anyone else.

'*Staying in love*' was the next requirement listed by the survey. The idea of being perpetually in love, in the romantic sense, is actually impossible for more than a very short space of time, as Mary Archer so rightly declared in her interview. If being 'in love' continues, it becomes an obsession, almost an illness. We like to promote the idea of being in love because we believe this emotion elevates us as human beings. It is a fine emotion to be able to love, but not to be in love. That is a selfish, high-arousal state of short duration, and it should be acknowledged as such.

'Staying faithful' was requirement no. 5. Most married people put a high value on sexual fidelity, because they would far rather their partner never so much as looked at another man or woman. The feeling comes from insecurity. Fidelity in marriage is now (and has always been) extremely rare. Though there are no reliable figures, newspaper surveys tend to reveal that at least 30 per cent of wives have affairs (of those who will admit to them) and the number is probably even higher for men. The problem is that it is absolutely impossible to feel both highly passionate and highly sexed and remain faithful to one person. Men and women who are sexy will almost certainly have affairs at some time in their marriage.

'Good sex' came next in the survey's conclusions, but although this is now seen as a vital ingredient of a happy marriage, it would not have been thus viewed in the past. Whenever people look to their marriage partners to fulfil their sexual fantasies, they are bound to be disappointed. Even the wildest, most ecstatic sex life dulls with repetition, as we all know, and the only real way to obtain 'good sex' (for those who see it as important) is to have a variety of partners—which does not quite square with the other requirements mentioned in the survey. In asking for fidelity, good sex and a good friendship, people ask for the moon. They are quite simply expecting far too much.

'Having individual interests', on the other hand, really is important. Contrary to what people like to believe, most married people do not become more like one another as the years go by. For partners to try to pretend they have identical interests is only a recipe for disaster. Yet many have the idea that they must share everything: they go on holidays together even when one hates the place or type of holiday chosen, and one partner will try to bamboozle the other into pursuing the interests or activities that appeal to him or her. Maintaining individual interests is a far preferable idea, though very few couples seem to manage it.

'Financial security' was also mentioned on the shopping list of 'ingredients' for a happy marriage. Most of us would like financial security, but we are fools if we expect marriage to provide it. Girls have traditionally dreamed of marrying rich men. Those who did often discovered there was a high price to pay for access to the riches. The Bible tells us that it is harder for a rich man to enter the kingdom of heaven than for a camel to go through the eye of a needle. The reason for this saying, which is not very popular in an age when financial success is seen as the only sort worth having, is that material riches often make people believe they have more power and influence, and are more important, than is really the case. Rich husbands often treat their wives badly, as they see them as yet another possession, as something else they can buy. There is no greater inequality in marriage than financial inequality, and one's partner's possession of wealth does not make for any kind of security for the one who has nothing. The only financial security any individual can be sure of is that provided by himself or herself. Any other assumption is dangerous and can lead to rows and disappointments.

Is financial security attained when your spouse provides for you with insurance policies and pension schemes? Not necessarily; money can always be lost, as leading financiers have often found to their cost. At least the *People* readers had the sense to put financial security in marriage near the bottom of the list.

'*Children*', which appeared ninth and last in priority in the results of the survey, are a contentious subject. Readers were wise to put them at the bottom of their list. As we marry for 'happiness', so we have, or say we have, children for the same reason. But all the surveys show that couples without children are at least as happy as those with, and tend to stay together longer. Children do not and cannot bring happiness; neither can they cement a disintegrating marriage, although their presence might ensure that couples stay together longer than they might otherwise have done when things have gone wrong. Children are very often seen as part of the kit, something one 'goes in for' after marrying—and sometimes before or outside wedlock. As Princess Anne bluntly put it: 'Children are an occupational hazard of being a wife.' In the old days, people married mainly in order to have children, to continue the line, to have more hands to work the land, or to provide heirs or marriageable daughters. Now, those reasons for having children have largely gone, and most people do not know why they have them. We are told by infertile couples that they 'desperately' long for children, but we rarely ask them why. Children are supposed to crown a couple's happiness, but we can see all around us glaring evidence that this is rarely the effect they have.

Children can be a joy, it is true, but are they an ingredient of a happy marriage? I

doubt it. It seems to me that children, particularly nowadays, cause more problems than they solve. Certainly they can never act as adhesive, to bring couples closer together, as some erroneously imagine....

\* \* \*

Of all the crimes that are brought to court in any one year, a high proportion of them will be domestic. In fact, it is said that about 70 per cent of all serious crimes committed take place in the matrimonial home. Not all husbands and wives are driven to violence or murder, of course, but many are sorely tempted, and many experience moments when they feel that life would be easier and more pleasant if the spouse were permanently out of the way.

These feelings arise because we invest so much in marriage—in 'making it work'; naturally we are deeply disappointed, even enraged, when all our efforts seem to come to nothing, or are unappreciated. A husband may slave at his job for fifteen hours a day to give his wife 'everything' only to find that while he has been out building up his business she has been carrying on with her hairdresser, the lodger, an old schoolfriend or a neighbour.

A woman may consider that she has 'devoted' the best years of her life to being a good and faithful wife, giving up her own career, cooking her husband nice meals and trying to be passionate in bed, only to discover that on his late nights 'at the office' he has been having an affair with his secretary or a high-powered career woman he has met. Such discoveries usually lead to highly emotional scenes—quarrels, recriminations, anger, jealousy, resentment and lasting hostility.

It appears that modern marriage brings out far more negative than positive emotions. What is usually seen as 'love' between two people who are married is often not love at all—it is a degraded, vice-ridden form of the emotion. Those who truly love somebody else will simply let them be free to develop their own personalities, to do as they wish—even if that includes being physically unfaithful.

People are horrified when they find evidence of a spouse's affairs; the discovery makes them afraid. All through the marriage, they have thought they owned the other person and controlled his or her life: the affair is evidence that they do not. We try to cling to other people when we have little self-respect and self-confidence. We vainly hope that the other person will give us what we lack—forgetting that the other person is, like ourselves, a fallible, weak human being who is probably unable to cope with such demands.

Those who are strong, and who value themselves, will be able to see the person they have chosen to live with as a friend, as somebody who is entitled to live a life of his or her own and with whom they can be civilized and respectful at all times. Very few modern marriages fall into this category. The 'commitment' we expect from a marriage partner is similar to a commitment to jail: it prevents our being free individuals. We are serving a sentence, supposedly for life.

Of course, not all marriages follow this pattern. But the majority will have elements of this negativity in them. We have come to feel it is right to be so bound up with another human being that every single thing he or she does, every twitch of the face, every fleeting expression, intimately affects us. Many wives live in constant fear of their husbands' anger, just as many husbands are terrified if their wives become depressed, or 'frigid', because these emotions mean that there is a cut-off, that communication lines are no longer open.

Modern marriage is in a parlous state, as any marriage guidance counsellor or divorce lawyer will confirm. It stifles individuality, encourages us to tell lies, to practise deceit, and to be manipulative, cunning and child-like, all because we live in fear that this (usually) rather ordinary and unremarkable individual whom we have married will do something that rocks the boat—be cross, not speak, throw things around, generally make life unpleasant, or go off with somebody else.

A moment's reflection will show that it is ridiculous that so many people should allow their lives to be ruined, even prematurely ended, as in the cases described earlier, just because they cannot see how to co-exist with somebody to whom they said, 'I do' a few years previously.

The discredited Indian guru Bhagwan Shree Rajneesh said that one reason why he never married was because 'all wives and husbands come to hate each other in time'; judging by the evidence available, this is largely true.

Marriage guidance counsellors, sex therapists, advice columnists and many others have pondered the matter of how to make marriage work better and with less acrimony and distrust between the partners. The newspapers, television and radio carry lengthy debates about what constitutes a happy, perfect marriage.

Usually, the only way we can envisage marriage working is if it 'goes back' to how we think it used to be, with bread-winning husband, dependent wife and total fidelity. It is commonly assumed by traditionalists that the main reasons why today's marriages are not working is because women these days want to be financially independent, have careers and maintain their individuality. If they were content to put their families first, goes the argument, all would be well. It is extremely unlikely that marriages of the past which did follow this pattern were happy—or even that women of previous centuries were as loving and giving as they were made out to be. Even a cursory reading of novels by famous Victorian writers will give an impression of marriage that differs substantially from the fantasy we fondly carry in our heads....

Men and women, fed by romantic fantasies and illusions, both yearn for marriage to be some kind of safe haven, where they will be protected from the harsh outside world. People yearn for this in marriage as they used to pray for it in their religion.

Christian hymns abound with injunctions to the Lord to keep us safe from all the perils and dangers of the world. 'Safe in the arms of Jesus' has been translated in our modern times to being safe in the arms of a loving spouse.

It is a current cliché to say that we have substituted love in marriage for the love that used to be reserved for God. Modern marriage is in a parlous state because we want and expect so much of each other, yet never stop to consider whether our marital partner is actually capable of providing what we want. There is no way to make marriages work better while we bring to them false hopes and expectations.

Any attempt to bind people closer together, by law or by custom, is bound to fail. People become violent and hateful towards each other when they are deeply disappointed. We buy a dream—and all too often end up with a nightmare.

In her almost painfully honest book *Deceived with Kindness*, Angelica Garnett, daughter of Vanessa Bell and Duncan Grant, describes her marriage to 'Bunny' Garnett, 26 years her senior:

The story of our marriage could be summed up as the struggle on his side to maintain the unlooked-for realization of a private dream, about which, in spite of an almost wilful blindness, he must have had deep misgivings: and on mine of the slow emancipation from a nightmare, which was none the less painful because I thought of it as almost entirely my own fault.... Had I not married him, he would have been a perfect friend, one in whom I could have safely confided and who would always have given me good advice.

'At bottom,' she continues, 'my love for him was simply a delusion—a dream which I had not the strength to sacrifice... I saw myself being swept along by a dangerous current, but was unable to lift a finger to prevent it... I knew inwardly that I was doing the wrong thing.'

Angelica concludes that what she had found was not life, but a backwater. Sadly her experience is not an isolated one. When I look at the marriages of most of my friends and acquaintances, I can see all too clearly that they are living a nightmare, one which, frequently, they have the courage neither to admit nor to escape from; they are living with the consequences of a ghastly mistake.

Marriage, at least in its present form, fails all of us. How much better relationships between the sexes would be if we truly could be friends, as Angelica Garnett realized she could have been with Bunny, and did not feel this overpowering need to tie ourselves together in Gordian knots....

\*  \*  \*

The institution of marriage carries a heavy historical burden. It seems, from this brief historical survey, that it was ordained in order that communities could consolidate and strengthen their position. All the historical arguments in favour of marriage now seem to have disappeared yet, strangely, we still cling to it.

Today, large numbers of people have no religious belief, yet still we adhere to the basic Christian idea of marriage—which has to a significant degree permeated the rest of the world. Even civil weddings held in registry offices have a veneer of religiosity. It is now becoming common for those undertaking their second, or even third, marriages to have them 'blessed' in church by a priest, which would have been unthinkable even as recently as the 1950s.

It seems we are left with the empty shell of an institution which has no real purpose in the modern world. People can function and exist just as well without marriage as with it. The only reason it has survived for as long as it has seems to be that the inspiration of romantic fantasy has prolonged an otherwise superannuated institution.

At one time it was virtually a necessity for men and women to marry, and thenceforth to raise families in an established household which could defend itself against human enemies and physical disasters. There was safety and strength in numbers. Now that the state has taken over most of the former functions of the family and we no longer need older sons to inherit and to defend territory, there seems little justification for continuing marriage as an institution.

# CHALLENGE QUESTIONS
## Is Marriage Psychologically Beneficial?

1. Have you ever been married, or do you intend to get married someday? Discuss whether or not reading these two articles has affected your thinking about marriage, and why.

2. If marriage is beneficial, it may be because it provides a ready-made support system. Why are support systems in general considered psychologically beneficial? Try to find research to support your comments.

3. If some marriages are "stifling," to use Hodgkinson's term, and other marriages are beneficial, explain how these types of marriage might differ.

4. What are the causes of family abuse? Use resource materials on the issue to formulate your answer.

# PART 7

# Research Methods

*Research methods allow psychologists to investigate their ideas and subject matter. How psychologists perform their research is often a subject of controversy. For example, sometimes animals are used to test experimental procedures before they are applied to humans. Is this right? Should animals be experimented upon—and sometimes sacrificed—in the service of humans? The question of whether or not psychological research methods can even be used to investigate such controversial topics as ESP and telepathy has also been sharply debated in the field.*

- Should Animals Be Used in Psychological Research?

- Is Parapsychology a Credible Science?

# ISSUE 18

## Should Animals Be Used in Psychological Research?

**YES: John R. Cole,** from "Animal Rights and Wrongs," *The Humanist* (July/August 1990)

**NO: Steven Zak,** from "Ethics and Animals," *The Atlantic Monthly* (March 1989)

### ISSUE SUMMARY

**YES:** John R. Cole, an anthropologist and the assistant director of the Massachusetts Water Resources Research Center, argues that although animal research has declined in recent years due to newly developed alternatives, some animal research is still necessary and beneficial to society.

**NO:** Attorney Steven Zak asserts that animals have the right to not be treated like instruments for the betterment of humankind and that legal barriers should be erected to prevent animal exploitation.

Until recently, humans were thought to be distinctly different from lower animals. Only humans were thought of as having self-consciousness, rationality, and language. Today, however, these distinctions appear to have become blurred by modern research. Many scientists, for example, believe that chimpanzees use language symbols and that many animals have some type of consciousness.

This apparent lack of hard-and-fast distinctions between humans and other animals have many implications, one of which concerns the use of animals in experimental research. For hundreds of years animals have been used by humans as tools of research. In fact, research ethics has demanded that most experimental treatments be tested on animals before they are tested on humans. Another view, however, has come to the fore. Because there is no clear distinction between lower and higher animals, this new view asserts that the lower animals should be accorded the same basic rights as humans. Animal experimentation, from this perspective, cannot be taken for granted; it must be justified on the same moral and ethical grounds as research on humans. This perspective has recently gained considerable momentum as supporters have become politically organized.

In the following selections, John R. Cole argues that animal rights groups are too extremist in their positions. One can promote animal protection against abuse without also banning animal research. Cole contends that scientists have the right to improve the life of humans through research. Animal research has been instrumental in the development of vaccines, antibiotics, antidepressants, tranquilizers, insulin, cancer treatments, and most surgical procedures, just to name a few. Cole notes that few animal rights activists refuse to undergo medical procedures that were developed through animal research. Moreover, changing cultural attitudes and the development of experimental alternatives (such as tissue cultures and computer models) have reduced the amount of animal research being performed.

Steven Zak discusses the activities and beliefs of several animal rights activist groups, such as True Friends, the Animal Liberation Front, and the Royal Society for the Prevention of Cruelty to Animals. He states that "the animal rights advocates' position is that animal research is an ethical travesty that justifies extraordinary, and even illegal, measures." Animal rights efforts have been a catalyst for needed reforms in animal rights laws, but Zak holds that these reforms do not go far enough in protecting the rights of animals. Opponents of animal rights argue that animals do not live by moral rules and therefore are not entitled to the same rights as humans. Zak contends that living beings do not have to be qualitatively the same to be worthy of equal respect.

| POINT | COUNTERPOINT |
|---|---|
| • To claim that animals have the same rights as people is an elitist stance. | • Animals have rights, and these should be protected by the Constitution. |
| • Animal research has achieved major benefits for both humans and animals. | • The interests of human beings should not overwhelm the interests of animals. |
| • Animal research is declining, but it is still necessary and justified for some uses. | • Animal research is an ethical travesty that justifies extraordinary and even illegal measures to prevent it. |
| • Less invasive animal research procedures have been developed and are being used in animal research. | • If researchers were not allowed to use animals in research, more alternative research methods would be explored. |
| • Laws and research guidelines that protect animals are followed during research. | • Animal protection laws should be replaced by a rights act that would prohibit the use of any animals to their detriment. |

# YES

**John R. Cole**

# ANIMAL RIGHTS AND WRONGS

According to Chris DeRose, head of Last Chance for Animals: "A life is a life. If the death of one rat cured all diseases it wouldn't make any difference to me. In the scheme of life we're equal."

According to Cardinal John O'Connor, speaking on Earth Day 1990 (and endorsing some environmental concerns other than the "non-truth" of over-population as a problem): "The earth exists for the human person, not vice versa." (O'Connor was taking his cue from Genesis 1:29, which issues the following command: "Fill the earth, and subdue it, and rule over... all the living creatures that move on the earth.")

Finally, in the words of a leading national science figure whose position re-quires diplomatic anonymity: "The animal rights issue is anti-intellectualism, know-nothingism. It's the single biggest threat to American science education today."

These comments may represent easily attacked extremes but, unfortu-nately, they are not straw-man arguments. Neither the animal rights move-ment, its more militant animal *liberationist* wing, nor its critics are monolithic, although both sides sometimes portray each other (or themselves) as if they were. To argue that science and commerce require the use of animals is not an argument for animal abuse. To advocate animal protection, one need not go so far as to argue that other animals have the "right" to exploit each other but that humans somehow do not without standing accused of speciesism. (What about *kingdomism*? Animalia can be hard to distinguish from Plantae—hence the recognition of Fungi, Monera, and Protista as kingdoms. Some of these have at least something like rudimentary nervous systems, and they are built from the same basic kinds of cells as monkeys, rats, and people. Since plants, fungi, protista, and monera are more numerous than animals, are experiments with them acceptable? And in this scheme of things, where do we put viruses?)

Turn the argument around one hundred and eighty degrees. Since humans are animals, should not people have certain rights, too? The primitive hunter who felt a kinship with his prey and apologized for killing when necessary but went ahead and did it anyway was, I suggest, displaying more natural humanism than today's extremist advocate of absolute animal rights. So, too,

From John R. Cole, "Animal Rights and Wrongs," *The Humanist*, vol. 50, no. 4 (July/August 1990). Copyright © 1990 by The American Humanist Association. Reprinted by permission.

are the scientists concerned with improving the lot of our own and fellow species through their research.

To decide what is acceptable and what is not requires values clarification. What is the value of life, and how is that value determined? When, if ever, are animal—and human—experiments ethical and worth the sacrifice? (Sacrifice *is* the term used by experimenters.)

* * *

To claim that animals have the same rights as people (perhaps more) is an oddly elitist stance which would shock almost anyone in the Third World. Who other than a few masochistic fundamentalists can argue in good conscience that suffering is desirable in itself? One would think any argument insisting that animals should not suffer unduly in the laboratory could be extended to say that humans and other animals should not suffer unduly *outside* the lab, either. Telling a Tanzanian farmer stricken with malaria or schistosomiasis or polio to "lie back and enjoy it" is as inhuman and arrogant (if not more so) as applying that callous phrase to rape victims. It would make no sense whatever to most people if you told them that they or their children could not be cured of disease because it would require experimenting on monkeys or rats or fertilized duck eggs. Anyone not comfortably ensconced in a well-fed, upper- or upper-middle-class sanctuary in Western culture would find it especially absurd. I may be mistaken, but I would guess that virtually everyone arguing for a total ban on animal experimentation has already had their shots (or is not living in a vulnerable area) and goes to a doctor who has dissected monkey and human cadavers whose real tissues do not look (and cannot feel)

like a computer-screen simulation. Put another way, what training or research would *not* be acceptable to the parents of a child needing serious medical or surgical treatment? Who decides?

Animal research has developed vaccines (for such diseases as typhoid, diphtheria, and polio, to name but a few), antibiotics, local anesthetics, steroids and hormone treatments, insulin, antihypertensives, diuretics and Beta blockers, leukemia and cancer therapies, tranquilizers, antidepressants, and most surgical procedures, from transplants to suturing to blood typing. Even an abbreviated and strictly medical list like this is impressive. It can be argued that some of these are only partially due to animal experimentation or that some, in retrospect, could have been developed using other techniques such as *in vitro* tissue cultures, but the picture is not a simple litany of horrors.

* * *

It is often argued by animal rights activists that all species are unique, so that animal experiments are not really applicable to humans. This is really a "scientific" creationist argument and simply untrue. Even though humans and other animals are not biologically or genetically identical, they are similar enough that many aspects of animal research are applicable to humans. While there was already a strong linkage between smoking and lung disease, for example, the case was not made airtight until countless rats were sacrificed to prove it. One can regret that the rats suffered at all and hope that they were sacrificed humanely, but it is hard to get around the fact that *potentially* unnecessary experiments were necessary, after all.

After sixty years of growth, the number of animals used in research—at least in America—has declined sharply in recent years. One reason is the increased concern for animal welfare on the part of researchers; another is the drastically increased costs of animal research; and yet a third is the growing availability of alternatives such as *in vitro* tissue cultures and computer modeling. Animal welfare reformers, ethicists, and changing cultural attitudes all deserve some of the credit for this change; so, too, do the scientists who have developed experimental alternatives and mastered many of the earlier trial-and-error experiences of biology moving beyond its rudimentary stage of development. There has also been a shift away from the use of such procedures as the Draize test for rabbit eye sensitivity to cosmetics as noninvasive tests become available. Thus, one major use of animals that has widely been considered frivolous is being phased out.

We know now that some earlier lines of experimentation were dead ends, but hindsight is always clearer. Similarly, every high-school science class in the country does not have to replicate every well-established experiment, and the National Association of Biology Teachers has established fairly thorough guidelines for classroom instruction in the United States and Canada.

However, selective replication of experiments is needed in order to test variants of earlier hypotheses or new procedures. The major aspects of animal experimentation are controlled by federal and state laws, National Institutes of Health and other guidelines monitored by peer review committees, humane societies such as the International Primate Protection League, and disciplinary codes of ethics in medicine and the sciences. Universities and animal research laboratories are required by law to have review committees to approve research proposals and to monitor experiments and the treatment of animals. They are legally required to include neutral public representatives, not just science insiders. This does not mean that everything is now perfect or that tension and disagreement will soon go away or even *should* go away. Even though it needs to be strengthened and clarified, I suggest that this matrix of protection and sensitivity to the issues involved is too often ignored or dismissed by animal rights activists who imply that there is only one side to the story and that all experimenters are sadistic or ignorant or both, plying a brutal trade for mindless profit and glory.

Trauma injury research is traumatic by definition. The University of Pennsylvania experiments which involved inflicting head injuries on baboons and other animals resulted in raids by animal liberationists, who destroyed records and stole and later publicized videotapes of the experiments. These tapes *are* horrifying; on the other hand, a tape of a rally of children and adults supporting this research has had little publicity. People saved by surgical and recuperative techniques developed in these experiments felt that they owed their lives to the controversial scientific research—and to the baboons who died in the process.

Currently, protests have halted a long-term United States Army project in Texas in which goats were shot and then treated by Army physicians and medics. The Army claims that the work was vital training for people who will have to treat battlefield injuries uncommon in everyday life or in medical schools; animal rights activists argue that animals are being harmed for no good reason. They do not seem to oppose *all* military research on the classic pacifist grounds that preparing for war makes it more likely or "thinkable"; the question seems to involve only the animals' right not to be shot, not the question of whether young people sent to war should suffer unduly.

Pound dogs have been collected by the U.S. Surgical Corporation, a Connecticut company, and used to train salesmen in how to sell their new suturing staple technique to surgeons. Does this constitute a waste of thousands of dogs' lives if they are used for sales—not medical—training? At the risk of insulting its clients, the company might respond that practicing doctors in fact get most of their ongoing training from salespeople, and that the dogs were doomed anyway. Is surgical training limited to classrooms? To computer simulations? I personally do not know the answers.

Is there an intellectual justification for the proliferation of laws banning experiments on pound animals, or is it simply another case of American romanticism about pets? Does it devalue life to extract some use from it—as painlessly as possible—at or near death? These questions are not easy to answer, I hope, nor are they meant to be.

When seemingly horrible experiments are actually looked at in context, they may prove to have been very useful to humans and other animals. On the other hand, many experiments are poorly designed and do not achieve their goals, whether or not they employ animals. Can the process be made more humane *and* better scientifically without actual prohibition?

A "good end" certainly does not justify all means of animal experimentation, but it is worth bearing in mind. Seen in the context of their real or potential gains versus their cost in animal life, some experiments look better at second glance. For example, sticking tubes into horses' hearts one hundred and fifty years ago was rather grisly, but it answered basic questions about anatomy. Moreover, catheterization is now a major part of the treatment and relief of many illnesses. Reenacting such experiments today without anesthesia should be judged differently than we judge the original experiment—or current research. An AIDS vaccine might be desirable enough that colonies of monkeys or chimpanzees bred for scientific use should be sacrificed in its development. At the same time, we should, in my opinion, avoid further endangering dwindling populations living in the wild.

We cannot simply equate painlessness with acceptability; rather, we need to recognize that some pain or discomfort (or at least inconvenience) accompanies most experiments, even if long-term suffering is avoided via euthanasia. Now that pain can be considerably controlled, it may be tempting to think that it can be abolished. As anyone who has ever had surgery or even a tooth filling can testify, anesthesia is not perfect, so its mere availability should not be the only factor considered in judging invasive animal research. This does not justify doing things in other than the least painful way possible, but it is a reminder that experimental goals often cannot be reached magically and painlessly. Researchers must now consciously decide that benefits will outweigh drawbacks, rather than falling back on the idea that animals cannot suffer. This realization has already cut down on animal experimentation, even among people who reject the antivivisectionist argument that virtually *no* experiments are conscionable.

On Earth Day, I was approached by a man asking for petition signatures. One petition called for the outlawing of animal breeding and genetic records, and the other aimed at banning leashes and other animal "movement and activity restrictions" such as fences. (I was there disseminating information about research on acid rain causes and effects, I might add.) I refused to sign on the grounds that the petitions were both harmful and silly. "Won't more animals—and people—be killed or injured in traffic if restrictions are forbidden?" I asked. "Are farmers and geneticists better off unaware of genetics and left to folk wisdom, at best?" He accused me of being like Nazi "experimenter" Josef Mengele and told me that acid rain might be the Earth Mother's revenge on humans for mistreating her creatures. (Did Mother Nature build dirty power plants and devastate clean and economical mass transit in favor of automobile sales and poisoned fish?) He had quit college to work on his cause, and he accused me of being an "intellectual" bought and paid for by the university before moving on to a possibly more receptive audience at the adjacent crystal power exhibit. Given his supposedly humane objective, this person was, I submit, simply wrongheaded and counterproductive. The general public is greatly concerned about the slaughter of cute baby seals or giant pandas but not as worried about the welfare of frogs and bats which, arguably, serve more vital functions in the world ecosystem. Virtually no one is militant about protecting flies, mosquitoes, or other slimy, crawly things. The extinction of smallpox is not widely bemoaned. A few people argue that plagues like AIDS are desirable checks on population, but this shows their poor understanding of human demographics—the response to wars, plagues, and so forth has always been an *intensification* of reproduction and other pressures upon the environment. Carried a step further, a few people misinterpret the Gaia hypothesis to suggest that the earth is actually sentient and would like to be rid of its human "infection," but this is a naive application of nineteenth century Spencerism, not modern Gaiaist systems theory.

It is tempting for people who get their meat from plastic packages to ignore the fact that it came from a living cow, sheep, or whatever. Is the person who kills or butchers an animal any less human than the one who eats the packaged result? Or do people who hunt and slaughter their own food have just as much humanity—if not more, since they accurately see the connections between life, suffering, and death? Are people who take polio vaccines consisting of weakened or murdered viruses more humane than the people who painstakingly developed the vaccines, consciously harming some animals (as well as viruses) in the process? There are some absolutists who could answer all of these questions easily. And while many people recognize that the earth is not a human toy to be used and thrown away—that the earth would get along quite well without us and our fantasies of being the pinnacle of perfection and goal of evolution—most people (certainly most scientists) believe that a more feasible and desirable middle way exists for relating to our environment.

* * *

Animal liberationists resent being branded "terrorists" by their critics. As the saying goes, one person's terrorist is another person's freedom fighter, and in any case it should be noted that most people in the movement oppose "terrorizing" people or animals, even though extreme civil disobedience can be threatening. Some do not disavow property damage, however, and some condone destroying laboratories and research records and "liberating" lab animals, even though the latter is hardly humane; the animals are usually unable to live on their own because of the experiments conducted on them or the mere fact of having been raised in captivity.

The absolutist true believer, either animal rights activist or animal experimentation advocate, takes a rather easy path—the first claiming that no harm or perhaps even inconvenience to animals is ever justified, the second that virtually all experiments are conscionable and that "civilians" should stay out of the way. The truth is never so cut-and-dried, however. For example, many people opposed to abortion do not demand that the practice be made illegal for all people no matter what the circumstance, but until recently they have been outshouted by an extremely narrow leadership cadre. The animal rights movement has had a similar history of drowning out its own potentially widely acceptable concerns and constructive viewpoints with a barrage of militant oversimplification.

Many scientists are repelled by arguments equating human rights or civil rights with animal rights because these arguments demean people more than they elevate the status of animals. Understandably, many African-Americans resented the 1960s song "Woman is the Nigger of the World," noting that white women were better off than poor people of color of either gender. Similarly, Third World people today—most of whom have fewer rights and a lower standard of living than American household pets—will be hard pressed to understand the industrial world's growing concern over the rights of animals.

# NO
# Steven Zak

# ETHICS AND ANIMALS

In December of 1986 members of an "animal-liberation" group called True Friends broke into the Sema, Inc., laboratories in Rockville, Maryland, and took four baby chimpanzees from among the facility's 600 primates. The four animals, part of a group of thirty being used in hepatitis research, had been housed individually in "isolettes"—small stainless-steel chambers with sealed glass doors. A videotape produced by True Friends shows other primates that remained behind. Some sit behind glass on wire floors, staring blankly. One rocks endlessly, banging violently against the side of his cage. Another lies dead on his cage's floor.

The "liberation" action attracted widespread media attention to Sema, which is a contractor for the National Institutes of Health [NIH], the federal agency that funds most of the animal research in this country. Subsequently the NIH conducted an investigation into conditions at the lab and concluded that the use of isolettes is justified to prevent the spread of disease among infected animals. For members of True Friends and other animal-rights groups, however, such a scientific justification is irrelevant to what they see as a moral wrong; these activists remain frustrated over conditions at the laboratory. This conflict between the NIH and animal-rights groups mirrors the tension between animal researchers and animal-rights advocates generally. The researchers' position is that their use of animals is necessary to advance human health care and that liberation actions waste precious resources and impede the progress of science and medicine. The animal-rights advocates' position is that animal research is an ethical travesty that justifies extraordinary, and even illegal, measures.

The Sema action is part of a series that numbers some six dozen to date and that began, in 1979, with a raid on the New York University Medical Center, in which members of a group known as the Animal Liberation Front (ALF) took a cat and two guinea pigs. The trend toward civil disobedience is growing. For example, last April members of animal-rights groups demonstrated at research institutions across the country (and in other countries, including Great Britain and Japan), sometimes blocking entrances to them by forming human chains. In the United States more than 130 activists were arrested, for offenses ranging from blocking a doorway and trespassing to burglary.

To judge by everything from talk-show programs to booming membership enrollment in animal-rights groups (U.S. membership in all groups is estimated at 10 million), the American public is increasingly receptive to the animal-rights position. Even some researchers admit that raids by groups like True Friends and the ALF have exposed egregious conditions in particular labs and have been the catalyst for needed reforms in the law. But many members of animal-rights groups feel that the recent reforms do not go nearly far enough. Through dramatic animal-liberation actions and similar tactics, they hope to force what they fear is a complacent public to confront a difficult philosophical issue: whether animals, who are known to have feelings and psychological lives, ought to be treated as mere instruments of science and other human endeavors....

Animal-rights activists feel acute frustration over a number of issues, including hunting and trapping, the destruction of animals' natural habits, and the raising of animals for food. But for now the ALF considers animal research the most powerful symbol of human dominion over and exploitation of animals, and it devotes most of its energies to that issue. The public has been ambivalent, sometimes cheering the ALF on, at other times denouncing the group as "hooligans." However one chooses to characterize the ALF, it and other groups like it hold an uncompromising "rights view" of ethics toward animals. The rights view distinguishes the animal-protection movement of today from that of the past and is the source of the movement's radicalism.

## "THEY ALL HAVE A RIGHT TO LIVE"

Early animal-protection advocates and groups... seldom talked about rights. They condemned cruelty—that is, acts that produce or reveal bad character. In early-nineteenth-century England campaigners against the popular sport of bull-baiting argued that it "fostered every bad and barbarous principle of our nature." Modern activists have abandoned the argument that cruelty is demeaning to human character ("virtue thought") in favor of the idea that the lives of animals have intrinsic value ("rights thought"). Rights thought doesn't necessarily preclude the consideration of virtue, but it mandates that the measure of virtue be the foreseeable consequences to others of one's acts.

"Michele" is thirty-five and works in a bank in the East. She has participated in many of the major ALF actions in the United States. One of the missions involved freeing rats, and she is scornful of the idea that rats aren't worth the effort. "These animals feel pain just like dogs, but abusing them doesn't arouse constituents' ire, so they don't get the same consideration. They all have a right to live their lives. Cuteness should not be a factor."

While most people would agree that animals should not be tortured, there is no consensus about animals' right to live (or, more precisely, their right not to be killed). Even if one can argue, as the British cleric Humphrey Primatt did in 1776, that "pain is pain, whether it be inflicted on man or on beast," it is more difficult to argue that the life of, say, a dog is qualitatively the same as that of a human being. To this, many animal-rights activists would say that every morally relevant characteristic that is lacking in all animals (rationality might be one, according to some ways of defining that term) is also lacking in some "marginal" human beings, such as infants, or the senile, or the severely retarded. Therefore, the activists argue, if marginal human beings have the right to live, it is arbitrary to hold that animals do not. Opponents of this point of view often focus on the differences between animals and "normal" human beings, asserting, for instance, that unlike most human adults, animals do not live by moral rules and therefore are not part of the human "moral community."

The credibility of the animal-rights viewpoint, however, need not stand or fall with the "marginal human beings" argument. Lives don't have to be qualitatively the same to be worthy of equal respect. One's perception that another life has value comes as much from an appreciation of its uniqueness as from the recognition that it has characteristics that are shared by one's own life. (Who would compare the life of a whale to that of a marginal human being?) One can imagine that the lives of various kinds of animals differ radically, even as a result of having dissimilar bodies and environments—that being an octopus feels different from being an orangutan or an oriole. The orangutan cannot be redescribed as the octopus minus, or plus, this or that mental characteristic; conceptually, nothing could be added to or taken from the octopus that would make it the equivalent of the oriole. Likewise, animals are not simply rudimentary human beings, God's false steps, made before He finally got it right with us.

Recognizing differences, however, puts one on tentative moral ground. It is easy to argue that likes ought to be treated alike. Differences bring problems: How do we think about things that are unlike? Against what do we measure and evaluate them? What combinations of likeness and difference lead to what sorts of moral consideration? Such problems may seem unmanageable, and yet in a human context we routinely face ones similar in kind if not quite in degree: our ethics must account for dissimilarities between men and women, citizens and aliens, the autonomous and the helpless, the fully developed and the merely potential, such as children or fetuses. We never solve these problems with finality, but we confront them....

Both advocates and opponents of animal rights also invoke utilitarianism in support of their points of view. Utilitarianism holds that an act or practice is measured by adding up the good and the bad consequences—classically, pleasure and pain—and seeing which come out ahead. There are those who would exclude animals from moral consideration on the grounds that the benefits of exploiting them outweigh the harm. Ironically, though, it was utilitarianism, first formulated by Jeremy Bentham in the eighteenth century, that brought animals squarely into the realm of moral consideration. If an act or practice has good and bad consequences for animals, then these must be entered into the moral arithmetic. And the calculation must be genuinely disinterested. One may not baldly assert that one's own interests count for more. Animal researchers may truly believe that they are impartially weighing all interests when they conclude that human interests overwhelm those of animals. But a skeptical reader will seldom be persuaded that they are in fact doing so....

Even true utilitarianism is incomplete, though, without taking account of rights. For example, suppose a small group of aboriginal tribespeople were captured and bred for experiments that would benefit millions of other people by, say, resulting in more crash-worthy cars. Would the use of such people be morally acceptable? Surely it would not, and that point illustrates an important function of rights thought: to put limits on what can be done to individuals, even for the good of the many. Rights thought dictates that we cannot kill one rights-holder to save another—or even more than one other—whether or not the life of the former is "different" from that of the latter.

Those who seek to justify the exploitation of animals often claim that it comes down to a choice: kill an animal or allow a human being to die. But this claim is misleading, because a choice so posed has already been made. The very act of considering the taking of life X to save life Y reduces X to the status of a mere instrument. Consider the problem in a purely human context. Imagine that if Joe doesn't get a new kidney he will die. Sam, the only known potential donor with a properly matching kidney, himself has only one kidney and has not consented to give it—and his life—up for Joe. Is there really a choice? If the only way to save Joe is to kill Sam, then we would be unable to do so—and no one would say that we chose Sam over Joe. Such a choice would never even be contemplated.

In another kind of situation there *is* a choice. Imagine that Joe and Sam both need a kidney to survive, but we have only one in our kidney bank. It may be that we should give the kidney to Joe, a member of our community, rather than to Sam, who lives in some distant country (though this is far from clear—

maybe flipping a coin would be more fair). Sam (or the loser of the coin flip) could not complain that his rights had been violated, because moral claims to some resource—positive claims—must always be dependent on the availability of that resource. But the right not to be treated as if one were a mere resource or instrument—negative, defensive claims—is most fundamentally what it means to say that one has rights. And this is what members of the ALF have in mind when they declare that animals, like human beings, have rights.

Where, one might wonder, should the line be drawn? Must we treat dragonflies the same as dolphins? Surely not. Distinctions must be made, though to judge definitively which animals must be ruled out as holders of rights may be impossible even in principle. In legal or moral discourse we are virtually never able to draw clear lines. This does not mean that drawing a line anywhere, arbitrarily, is as good as drawing one anywhere else.

The line-drawing metaphor, though, implies classifying entities in a binary way: as either above the line, and so entitled to moral consideration, or not. Binary thinking misses nuances of our moral intuition. Entities without rights may still deserve moral consideration on other grounds: one may think that a dragonfly doesn't quite qualify for rights yet believe that it would be wrong to crush one without good reason. And not all entities with rights need be treated in precisely the same way. This is apparent when one compares animals over whom we have assumed custody with wild animals. The former, I think, have rights to our affirmative aid, while the latter have such rights only in certain circumstances. Similar distinctions can be made among human beings, and also between human beings and particular animals. For example, I recently spent $1,000 on medical care for my dog, and I think he had a right to that care, but I have never given such an amount to a needy person on the street. Rights thought, then, implies neither that moral consideration ought to be extended only to the holders of rights nor that all rights-holders must be treated with a rigid equality. It implies only that rights-holders should never be treated as if they, or their kind, didn't matter.

## ANIMALS, REFRIGERATORS, AND CAN OPENERS

The question of man's relationship with animals goes back at least to Aristotle, who granted that animals have certain senses—hunger, thirst, a sense of touch—but who held that they lack rationality and therefore as "the lower sort [they] are by nature slaves, and ... should be under the rule of a master." Seven centuries later Saint Augustine added the authority of the Church, arguing that "Christ himself [teaches] that to refrain from the killing of animals ... is the height of superstition, for there are no common rights between us and the beasts...." Early in the seventeenth century René Descartes argued that, lacking language, animals cannot have thoughts or souls and thus are machines.

One may be inclined to dismiss such beliefs as archaic oddities, but even today some people act as if animals were unfeeling things. I worked in a research lab for several summers during college, and I remember that it was a natural tendency to lose all empathy with one's animal subjects. My supervisor seemed actually to delight in swinging rats around by their tails and flinging them against a concrete wall as a way of stunning the animals before killing them. Rats and rabbits, to those who injected, weighed, and dissected them, were little different from cultures in a petri dish: they were just things to manipulate and observe. Feelings of what may have been moral revulsion were taken for squeamishness, and for most of my lab mates those feelings subsided with time.

The first animal-welfare law in the United States, passed in New York State in 1828, emphasized the protection of animals useful in agriculture. It also promoted human virtue with a ban on "maliciously and cruelly" beating or torturing horses, sheep, or cattle. Today courts still tend to focus on human character, ruling against human beings only for perpetrating the most shocking and senseless abuse of animals....

Most states leave the regulation of medical research to Washington. In 1966 Congress passed the Laboratory Animal Welfare Act, whose stated purpose was not only to provide humane care for animals but also to protect the owners of dogs and cats from theft by proscribing the use of stolen animals. (Note the vocabulary of property law; animals have long been legally classified as property.) Congress then passed the Animal Welfare Act [AWA] of 1970, which expanded the provisions of the 1966 act to include more species of animals and to regulate more people who handle animals. The AWA was further amended in 1976 and in 1985.

The current version of the AWA mandates that research institutions meet certain minimum requirements for the handling and the housing of animals, and requires the "appropriate" use of pain-killers. But the act does not regulate research or experimentation itself, and allows researchers to withhold anesthetics or tranquilizers "when scientifically necessary." Further, while the act purports to regulate dealers who buy animals at auctions and other markets to sell to laboratories, it does little to protect those animals....

The 1985 amendments to the AWA were an attempt to improve the treatment of animals in laboratories, to improve enforcement, to encourage the consideration of alternative research methods that use fewer or no animals, and to minimize duplication in experiments. One notable change is that for the first time, research institutions using primates must keep them in environments conducive to their psychological well-being; however, some animal-rights activists have expressed skepticism, since the social and psychological needs of primates are complex, and the primary concern of researchers is not the interests of their animal subjects. Last September [1988] a symposium on the psychological well-being of captive primates was held at Harvard University. Some participants contended that we lack data on the needs of the thirty to forty species of primates now used in laboratories. Others suggested that the benefits of companionship and social life are obvious.

The U.S. Department of Agriculture is responsible for promulgating regulations under the AWA and enforcing the law. Under current USDA regulations the cages of primates need only have floor space equal to three times the area occupied by the animal "when standing on four feet"—in the words of the USDA, which has apparently forgotten that primates have hands. The 1985 amendments required the USDA to publish final revised regulations, including regulations on the well-being of primates,

by December of 1986. At this writing the department has yet to comply, and some activists charge that the NIH and the Office of Management and Budget have delayed the publication of the new regulations and attempted to undermine them.

One may believe that virtue thought—which underlies current law—and rights thought should protect animals equally. After all, wouldn't a virtuous person or society respect the interests of animals? But virtue thought allows the law to disregard these interests, because virtue can be measured by at least two yardsticks: by the foreseeable effects of an act on the interests of an animal or by the social utility of the act. The latter standard was applied in a 1983 case in Maryland in which a researcher appealed his conviction for cruelty to animals after he had performed experiments that resulted in monkeys' mutilating their hands. Overturning the conviction, the Maryland Court of Appeals wrote that "there are certain normal human activities to which the infliction of pain to an animal is purely incidental"—thus the actor is not a sadist—and that the state legislature had intended for these activities to be exempt from the law protecting animals.

The law, of course, is not monolithic. Some judges have expressed great sympathy for animals. On the whole, though, the law doesn't recognize animal rights. Under the Uniform Commercial Code, for instance, animals—along with refrigerators and can openers—constitute "goods."

## ALTERNATIVES TO US-VERSUS-THEM

Estimates of the number of animals used each year in laboratories in the

United States range from 17 million to 100 million: 200,000 dogs, 50,000 cats, 60,000 primates, 1.5 million guinea pigs, hamsters, and rabbits, 200,000 wild animals, thousands of farm animals and birds, and millions of rats and mice. The conditions in general—lack of exercise, isolation from other animals, lengthy confinement in tiny cages—are stressful. Many experiments are painful or produce fear, anxiety, or depression. For instance, in 1987 researchers at the Armed Forces Radiobiology Research Institute reported that nine monkeys were subjected to whole-body irradiation; as a result, within two hours six of the monkeys were vomiting and hypersalivating. In a proposed experiment at the University of Washington pregnant monkeys, kept in isolation, will be infected with the simian AIDS virus; their offspring, infected or not, will be separated from the mothers at birth.

Not all animals in laboratories, of course, are subjects of medical research. In the United States each year some 10 million animals are used in testing products and for other commercial purposes. For instance, the United States Surgical Corporation, in Norwalk, Connecticut, uses hundreds of dogs each year to train salesmen in the use of the company's surgical staple gun. In 1981 and 1982 a group called Friends of Animals brought two lawsuits against United States Surgical to halt these practices. The company successfully argued in court that Friends of Animals lacked "standing" to sue, since no member of the organization had been injured by the practice; after some further legal maneuvering by Friends of Animals both suits were dropped. Last November [1988] a New York City animal-rights advocate was arrested as she planted a bomb outside United States Surgical's headquarters.

In 1987, according to the USDA, 130,373 animals were subjected to pain or distress unrelieved by drugs for "the purpose of research or testing." This figure, which represents nearly seven percent of the 1,969,123 animals reported to the USDA that year as having been "used in experimentation," ignores members of species not protected by the AWA (cold-blooded animals, mice, rats, birds, and farm animals). Moreover, there is reason to believe that the USDA's figures are low. For example, according to the USDA, no primates were subjected to distress in the state of Maryland, the home of Sema, in any year from 1980 to 1987, the last year for which data are available.

Steps seemingly favorable to animals have been taken in recent years. In addition to the passage of the 1985 amendments to the AWA, the Public Health Service [PHS], which includes the NIH, has revised its "Policy on Humane Care and Use of Laboratory Animals," and new legislation has given legal force to much of this policy. Under the revised policy, institutions receiving NIH or other PHS funds for animal research must have an "institutional animal care and use committee" consisting of at least five members, including one nonscientist and one person not affiliated with the institution.

Many activists are pessimistic about these changes, however. They argue that the NIH has suspended funds at noncompliant research institutions only in response to political pressure, and assert that the suspensions are intended as a token gesture, to help the NIH regain lost credibility. They note that Sema, which continues to keep primates in isolation cages (as regulations permit), is an NIH contractor whose principal investigators are NIH employees. As to the makeup of the animal-care committees, animal-rights advocates say that researchers control who is appointed to them. In the words of one activist, "The brethren get to choose."

However one interprets these changes, much remains the same. For example, the AWA authorizes the USDA to confiscate animals from laboratories not in compliance with regulations, but only if the animal "is no longer required... to carry out the research, test or experiment"; the PHS policy mandates pain relief "unless the procedure is justified for scientific reasons." Fundamentally, the underlying attitude that animals may appropriately be used and discarded persists.

If the law is ever to reflect the idea that animals have rights, more-drastic steps—such as extending the protection of the Constitution to animals—must be taken. Constitutional protection for animals is not an outlandish proposition. The late U.S. Supreme Court Justice William O. Douglas wrote once, in a dissenting opinion, that the day should come when "all of the forms of life... will stand before the court—the pileated woodpecker as well as the coyote and bear, the lemmings as well as the trout in the streams."

Suppose, just suppose, that the AWA were replaced by an animal-rights act, which would prohibit the use by human beings of any animals to their detriment. What would be the effect on medical research, education, and product testing? Microorganisms; tissue, organ, and cell cultures; physical and chemical systems that mimic biological functions; computer programs and mathematical models that simulate biological interactions; epidemiologic data

bases; and clinical studies have all been used to reduce the number of animals used in experiments, demonstrations, and tests. A 1988 study by the National Research Council, while finding that researchers lack the means to replace all animals in labs, did conclude that current and prospective alternative techniques could reduce the number of animals—particularly mammals—used in research.

Perhaps the report would have been more optimistic if scientists were as zealous about conducting research to find alternatives as they are about animal research. But we should not be misled by discussions of alternatives into thinking that the issue is merely empirical. It is broader than just whether subject A and procedure X can be replaced by surrogates B and Y. We could undergo a shift in world view: instead of imagining that we have a divine mandate to dominate and make use of everything else in the universe, we could have a sense of belonging to the world and of kinship with the other creatures in it. The us-versus-them thinking that weighs animal suffering against human gain could give way to an appreciation that "us" includes "them." That's an alternative too.

Some researchers may insist that scientists should not be constrained in their quest for knowledge, but this is a romantic notion of scientific freedom that never was and should not be. Science is always constrained, by economic and social priorities and by ethics. Sometimes, paradoxically, it is also freed by these constraints, because a barrier in one direction forces it to cut another path, in an area that might have remained unexplored.

Barriers against the exploitation of animals ought to be erected in the law, because law not only enforces morality but defines it. Until the law protects the interests of animals, the animal-rights movement will by definition be radical. And whether or not one approves of breaking the law to remedy its shortcomings, one can expect such activities to continue. "I believe that you should do for others as you would have done for you," one member of the ALF says. "If you were being used in painful experiments, you'd want someone to come to your rescue."

# CHALLENGE QUESTIONS

## Should Animals Be Used in Psychological Research?

1. Can you personally justify the use of animals in medical and psychological research? How and where would you draw the line on the use of animals in other types of research? Is the use of animals justifiable in cosmetics research? Why, or why not?

2. Cole contends that even extremists in the animal rights movement do not reject the medical benefits resulting from animal research. Assuming you were against all instances of animal research, would you turn down medical procedures for yourself or your children because they were developed at the expense of animals? If so, would there be exceptions, such as vaccinations for your children or a life-threatening illness?

3. Cole makes the case that experimentation with animals has produced many important medical and psychological findings. Can you think of other benefits? How can this research be justified in light of the current controversy?

4. Zak asserts that animal research is an ethical travesty that justifies extraordinary and even illegal measures to prevent it. Do you think illegal methods are justified in protecting the rights of animals?

5. Zak claims that animals deserve to have their rights protected by the Constitution. Do you agree with this position? Why, or why not? Should these rights extend to insects and nonanimal species as well? Where would you draw the line in the recognition of such rights?

# ISSUE 19

## Is Parapsychology a Credible Science?

**YES: Ruth Reinsel,** from "Parapsychology: An Empirical Science," in Patrick Grim, ed., *Philosophy of Science and the Occult* (State University of New York Press, 1990)

**NO: Susan Blackmore,** from "The Lure of the Paranormal," *The New Scientist* (September 22, 1990)

### ISSUE SUMMARY

**YES:** Ruth Reinsel, a member of the Parapsychological Association and the American Society for Psychical Research, maintains that the discipline of parapsychology relies on solid scientific investigations.

**NO:** Professor of psychology Susan Blackmore challenges the soundness of parapsychological research and argues that paranormal beliefs come from misjudgments about the causes of events.

Have you ever felt that you had already experienced a situation that you knew you had to be experiencing for the very first time? This feeling is commonly referred to as *déjà vu*. Perhaps you have had a premonition of some important future event from a feeling or a dream. Although experiences such as these are typically considered to be outside the realm of normal science, it is surprising how many people have them. Parapsychology is the discipline that attempts to investigate these and many other experiences, including telepathy, clairvoyance, and extrasensory perception (ESP).

But how do parapsychologists conduct investigations of paranormal phenomena? Many parapsychologists view their discipline as a branch of psychology, with investigations that do not differ in kind from any other psychological specialty. The trouble is that many psychologists disagree. They argue that parapsychological investigations cannot stand the same scientific rigor as other psychological experimentation. There is also considerable debate regarding the existence of paranormal phenomena. Are parapsychologists conducting experiments on phenomena that do not exist? Are such phenomena impossible, and should claims of any related "scientific" findings be viewed with suspicion?

In the selections that follow, Ruth Reinsel argues that parapsychological findings are indeed rigorously scientific. She maintains that parapsychology "relies heavily on objective evidence, quantitative evaluation, and the experimental method." Reinsel also emphasizes that current parapsychology research incorporates strict controls and scientific precautions. Similar to any science, these controls and precautions help researchers rule out possible causes for experimental findings other than paranormal causes.

Susan Blackmore, on the other hand, attacks parapsychological research as unsound. She questions its methods as well as the objectivity of its investigators. Blackmore also argues that what people describe as paranormal phenomena are actually misjudgments of probability. That is, people experience seemingly improbable events and then attribute these improbabilities to paranormal phenomena, such as ESP. According to Blackmore, however, most events of this nature are not as improbable as most people believe and, in fact, are readily explainable with conventional understandings of the world.

| POINT | COUNTERPOINT |
|---|---|
| • Research shows that paranormal phenomena do exist. | • Parapsychology has made no gains in understanding paranormal phenomena. |
| • Parapsychological research is based on conventional scientific methods. | • Parapsychological research is methodologically flawed. |
| • Findings show relations between paranormal phenomena and personality factors. | • Parapsychology is based on illusions and probability biases. |
| • Repeatability of parapsychology experiments is higher than is generally assumed. | • Unbiased researchers have not been able to repeat parapsychology experiments. |

# YES

**Ruth Reinsel**

## PARAPSYCHOLOGY:
## AN EMPIRICAL SCIENCE

Although the historical roots of scientific parapsychology are tangled with nineteenth-century spiritualism, the history of parapsychology is to a large extent the story of its struggle to disassociate itself from the occult. The occult and parapsychology can be distinguished both in the choice of methods and in the choice of subject matter. The occult relies on traditional bodies of arcane lore interpreted with a healthy dose of personal intuition. Because of this combination of tradition and intuition, what are sometimes called the occult "sciences" should more properly be called the occult "arts." Parapsychology, on the other hand, relies heavily on objective evidence, quantitative evaluation, and the experimental method. The occult includes topics of popular appeal but of questionable validity, such as astrology, numerology, and magic. Parapsychology, on the other hand, restricts itself to the study of ways of gaining knowledge or affecting the world around us that do not involve the five normal senses. Since no known process or energy can account for the accumulating mass of parapsychological data on ESP, precognition, and psychokinesis, these abilities are termed "paranormal." This, it is to be hoped, will be only a temporary designation, since it is possible that some explanatory principle remains to be discovered that will satisfactorily reconcile these phenomena with conventional science.

If dated from the founding of the Society for Psychical Research in London in 1882, parapsychology will soon celebrate its first century of development. Philosophers have been intimately connected with the development of parapsychology from its inception—witness the membership rolls of the English and American Societies for Psychical Research, which include William James, Henry Sidgwick, C. J. Ducasse, C. D. Broad, and H. H. Price—and it seems appropriate now for parapsychologists and philosophers together to evaluate the progress that has been made in this area. In what follows I shall present... a survey of methodological difficulties and skeptical objections overcome, and a discussion of current techniques in parapsychological research. No honest appraisal of a century of research in parapsychology can, I think, conclude that parapsychology is anything less than it purports to be: a solidly empirical investigation of certain anomalies in our psychological makeup that we call, for want of a better term, "psychical abilities." ...

## SKEPTICAL OBJECTIONS AND METHODOLOGICAL CONSIDERATIONS

... The early criticisms of laboratory psychical research centered on the following possibilities:

(1) Subjects might have had an opportunity to cheat while left alone with the targets [hidden materials the subjects were attempting to identify].

(2) Some form of normal sensory cuing (such as markings on the targets, or slight variations in the experimenters' facial expression, body language, or tone of voice) might account for the extra-chance scoring levels, with no extrasensory information transfer involved at all.

(3) Non-randomness in the target sequences might coincide with a subject's response bias tendencies, yielding a spuriously above-chance score.

(4) The experimenter(s) might have inaccurately recorded the subject's responses.

(5) Data analysis might have involved inappropriate use of statistical tests.

(6) In order to prove that ESP exists, the experimenter(s) might have deliberately fabricated the evidence.

These methodological criticisms prompted further refinement of experimental techniques. Current parapsychological methodology emphasizes the need to incorporate rigid controls in order to exclude all explanations other than the operation of ESP. The following precautions have become standard methodological procedure in experiments accepted for publication in the reputable journals of the field.

1. Strict procedures are followed to ensure that the subject has no opportunity to cheat. The subject is never left alone with the targets in a clairvoyance experiment, and is not allowed to communicate with the agent in telepathy experiments. Targets are concealed from the subject by a screen or an opaque envelope, or better yet, they are kept in a distant place to which the subject has no access.

2. In order to eliminate sensory cues, targets are handled as little as possible, so that random scratches or markings do not become the basis for the subject's responses. The targets are prepared by an independent assistant who has no contact with the subject. Thus the experimenter who presents the sealed targets to the subject is "blind," that is, has no knowledge of which target is in which envelope, and cannot systematically influence the subject's response in the direction of a higher score.

3. Elaborate procedures are followed to ensure random selection and presentation of targets. Random number tables or other random sources (REG determination, or computer algorithms) are the source for target sequences, and targets or conditions are presented to the subjects in a counterbalanced sequence.

4. Scoring must be double-checked later by an independent scorer blind to the hypothesis of the experiment, and ignorant of the experimental group to which the subject belongs. Alternatively, two observers can make simultaneous but independent records of the subject's responses and later compare them for errors in recording.

5. The question of the appropriateness of the statistics used to evaluate ESP data was submitted to the American Institute of Mathematical Statistics for evaluation. In 1937 the president of that organization issued a public statement that verified the adequacy and integrity of the statistical techniques used by Rhine and his colleagues at the Duke Parapsychology Laboratory (Camp, 1937).

6. The charge of experimenter fraud has often been made against parapsychological data as a kind of last resort, after all other criticisms have been answered or invalidated. Regrettably, however, the charge of experimenter fraud has not been without validity in some few cases, notably those of W. J. L. Levy and S. G. Soal.... Although fraudulent manipulation of data may have occurred on only one occasion in these investigators' research careers, that is sufficient to bring into question all of their published research. Parapsychologists are generally among the first to repudiate those among their ranks who are found guilty of such unethical practices, first because this represents unacceptable procedure in science, but perhaps also since these occurrences cast doubt on the integrity of all other researchers in what is already a highly controversial field. But does the fact that two experimenters have been found guilty of fudging data mean that *all* the published evidence for the existence of ESP is fraudulent? To contend that, over the decades, scores of highly respected researchers with otherwise impeccable reputations have conspired in a gigantic hoax to falsify evidence and deceive the public and their fellow scientists is even less parsimonious than the alternative hypothesis: that ESP exists.

To summarize the crucial elements of methodology: no matter what the form of psi* being investigated, double-blind methods are essential. That is, the assistant who prepares the targets has no contact with the subjects. The experimenter who interacts with the subjects does not know what the targets are on any given trial. Scoring is double-checked by an assistant who is blind to the hypothesis of the experiment, had no contact with the subjects, and does not know to which experimental group or condition the subjects belonged. Finally, it is important in parapsychological research, as in other fields of scientific endeavor, to await independent replication of a finding before drawing any definite conclusions.

In the "hard" physical sciences, the criterion of the repeatable experiment is interpreted to mean that anyone can follow the same experimental procedures and get the same results every time. ESP experiments, on the other hand, tend to be frustratingly inconsistent. A novel procedure will often give highly significant results when it is first introduced, only to seem to "fail" later on, when results decline to chance, or when the effect reverses direction completely. If psi is indeed a natural and lawful phenomenon, it should be consistent and predictable once one can specify the laws and conditions that govern its occurrence. To many scientists, this lack of repeatability in psi experiments is the most powerful argument against the existence of psi.

But this argument may be somewhat too extreme (Rhine, 1959). The repeatability of psi experiments is actually higher than is generally assumed. Certain findings have been demonstrated experimentally over and over again.

---

* [Psi is the group of parapsychological phenomena, including clairvoyance, extrasensory perception, and psychokinesis.—Ed.]

Take, for example, the effect of belief in ESP on scoring levels (the "sheep–goat effect," reviewed by Palmer, 1971); or the positive effects on ESP scoring of high interest and motivation, and the negative effects of withdrawal, apathy, and negativism (Nicol and Humphrey, 1955; Rao, 1962; Scheerer, 1948; Shields, 1962). On the other hand, it is incorrect to assume that the repeatability criterion is met by all fields of scientific endeavor *except* parapsychology. Epstein (1980) points out that the social or "soft" sciences in general (including many fields within psychology) experience difficulties in replicating experiments. Epstein suggests that this problem may be inherent in the nature of the sampling assumptions within the experimental method itself. If repeatability in psychology in general is less than perfect, the problem in ESP experiments is even more pronounced. Psi scores have been shown to be affected by the subject's personality, attitudes, mood and motivation, and the nature of the subject's social interaction with the experimenter and the testing situation. Experiments in which these variables are not taken into account generally show chance results. The high variance in the data caused by the effects of these uncontrolled variables may in many cases obscure the operation of the underlying psi processes.

## CURRENT TECHNIQUES IN PARAPSYCHOLOGY

The combined weight of experiments [of early psychical research]—including the weight of much more recent work with progressively tighter methodological controls—is strongly against a "random-chance" explanation. As it became obvious that merely demonstrating the existence of non-random scoring tendencies in the data would not yield any immediate understanding of the psi process (or processes), interest turned to a search for the conditions under which psi was manifested and for the kinds of personality attributes that correlated with psi success (see, e.g., Carpenter, 1977; Honorton, 1977; Palmer, 1977). As researchers became dissatisfied with repetitious card tests that failed to hold subjects' interest, new instrumentation and more sophisticated experimental methods were introduced.

One of the recent developments in parapsychological research has been the attention given to the importance of an alteration in the normal state of consciousness in order to make the psi signal "heard" above the "noise" of the other sensory stimuli against which it must compete. Honorton (1977) has provided a complete review of all major research dealing with alterations in state of consciousness in the direction of "internal attention states."

Relaxation is one of these states that has been quite extensively investigated as a psi-conducive technique. For example, L. W. Braud and Braud (1977) conducted a clairvoyance experiment where 100 subjects were to attempt to describe art prints in sealed envelopes. Subjects listened to a tape of suggestions selected to promote relaxation, calmness, feelings of coolness in the forehead, and heaviness and warmth in the extremities. The tape was designed to test the theory that a reduction in arousal of the autonomic nervous system would facilitate psi scoring. Apparently the tape was successful, because 36 of the 100 subjects made direct hits (first choice on ranking the possible targets) when asked later to identify, from among several art prints, the one that had been their concealed target ($p = .0055$). In total, 63 of these 100 subjects placed the actual target in the top half of their rankings of the art prints ($p = .0047$).

Earlier research by the same team of Braud and Braud (1974) reports two studies using the same tape of relaxation suggestions in a telepathy (GESP) paradigm. In the first study, 16 subjects listened to the same tape-recorded instructions. Subjects recorded their impressions of the ESP target and then ranked their degree of relaxation on a ten-point scale. Highly relaxed subjects scored significantly better on the free-response GESP task than did less relaxed subjects ($p < .04$; that is, less than 4 chances in 100 of this result occurring by chance alone). In the second study, involving 20 subjects, 10 of the subjects listened to the relaxation tape, while the remaining 10 heard a tension-inducing series of instructions. The relaxation group showed significantly more psi success on the ESP task than did the tension group ($p < .025$). The degree of relaxation was monitored by EMG recording devices (though no feedback was given) and the degree of both objective (EMG) and subjective (self-rated) relaxation correlated significantly with psi success (correlations of .49 and .53 respectively, $p < .05$ in both cases).

In line with the hypothesis that reducing external sensory distractions and redirecting attention internally will facilitate psi, a large number of studies involving the ganzfeld technique have been reviewed by Honorton (1978). The ganzfeld is a mild form of sensory deprivation where the subject sits in a comfortable reclining chair, with eyes covered by screens that exclude patterned visual stimulation (usually ping-pong balls cut in half and taped over the eyes), with the visual field flooded with red light. The subject simultaneously listens to a tape of white noise [a heterogeneous mixture of sound waves extending over a wide frequency range]. Thus patterned stimulus input is totally excluded and the subject can turn his attention inward and report his ongoing mentation into a tape recorder. An agent sits in another room, without contact with the subject, and views a target picture while trying to "send" information about the picture to the subject (percipient). At the conclusion of the session, the percipient is shown several pictures, one of which was the actual target, and he is asked to rate the pictures for the degree of correspondence to his ongoing imagery and associations.

The ganzfeld has proven to be one of the most successful techniques for eliciting psi and has stood up under the test of numerous replications. Seven of the eight studies conducted in Honorton's lab were independently significant, giving a combined significance level of $7.9 \times 10^{-8}$. Honorton demonstrates in his review that of 23 studies from 11 different laboratories (not including his own), 14 studies demonstrated overall significant psi scoring rates. This constitutes a replication rate of 54 percent where only 5-percent-successful replications would be expected if the results were just flukes caused by chance variations of the normal curve.

A major methodological advance over the early work with ESP cards and dice was made when Helmut Schmidt, an electronics engineer by profession, developed a series of automated machines known as random event generators (REGs). These devices are based either on radioactive decay processes (the most completely random processes yet discovered) or on random electronic-noise source. The Schmidt machines operate by generating random binary electrical pulses that serve as targets, in the manner of an electronic coin flipper: a positive pulse is "heads" and a negative voltage is "tails." The Schmidt REGs have several advantages over earlier experimental techniques: (1) they are completely random, so that their target sequences do not suffer from the problem of "pseudorandomness" inherent in printed random number tables or in computer algorithms; (2) they allow for automatic target and response recording, thus excluding the possibility of experimenter error in recording the results; and (3) they provide immediate feedback to the subject on whether his guess was right or wrong, thus allowing for experimental study of the application of operant conditioning learning techniques to ESP (see Tart, 1976).

One of these random event generators was used by Schmidt (1969a) in a clairvoyance test to compare the responses of six subjects to a prearranged random target sequence. Over 15,000 trials, the results of these tests were highly significant, with odds of over a million to one against chance. The Schmidt REGs have also been very useful in studying precognition. The subject makes his response a fraction of a second before the random target is electronically generated; thus many trials can be accumulated over a short period. Schmidt (1969b) used his random event generator to test precognition with three gifted subjects. Over a total of 63,066 responses, the results from these three subjects were highly significant, with odds of 2,000 million to 1 against chance.

In another experiment also using one of the Schmidt REGs, large numbers of subjects were tested in groups. Five hundred trials were run in both precognition and PK [psychokinesis] test modes, and results were significantly above chance in both cases (Schmidt and Pantas, 1972). In Part 2 of this same experiment, a single subject meditated for approximately twenty minutes before making a series of either precognition or PK calls. With 500 trials in each mode, extreme deviations from chance expectation were found in both conditions, and no difference in scoring rate was found between the precognition and PK conditions. This overlap between the PK and precognition abilities has profound theoretical implications: it may be that we do not merely gain "knowledge" of our future, but actively create it.

Along with experiments on dice and electronic random event generators, much recent PK work has used natural or biological systems as targets. Interest has focused on whether the reports of "psychic healing" might not be founded in a PK ability to influence living systems. Thus Smith (1972) had a noted psychic healer (Mr. Estebany) hold a sealed flask of enzyme solution (trypsin), and found significant increases in the rate of enzyme catalysis when the flask was held by the healer, as opposed to the rate in a control (untreated) condition. To control for the effects of temperature on trypsin activity, a sensitive thermistor was placed between Mr. Estebany's hands as he held the trypsin sample; the water bath in which the control sample was placed was kept at the same temperature. Replications of this experiment have been moderately successful (see Edge, 1980); the limited success is attributed to the difficulty the healer has in establishing a caring personal relationship with a flask of enzyme solution. In Smith's experiment, a control condition where identical flasks of enzyme solution were exposed to a high-intensity (1,300 gauss) magnetic field for three hours showed definite results in the same direction as, but stronger than, the effects produced by the healer. It is therefore possible that psychic healing produces its effect by inducing a magnetic field; however, using a magnetometer, Smith found no indication of any unusual magnetic field around Estebany's hands while he was "healing" the enzyme solution.

Grad (1965, 1976) has worked with the same healer who claimed to be able to heal through the laying on of hands. In this work, Grad had available to him the facilities of a biomedical research laboratory with large numbers of experimental animals (mice). For the psychic healer to administer the "treatment," mice were placed into a specially constructed iron cage with a solid bottom and a wire mesh top. The healer held one hand below the cage and the other one covering the top of the cage. At no time did the healer actually touch the mice themselves in any of the experiments. In control conditions, mice were exposed to warm temperatures by placing a heating pad under their cages for an equivalent amount of time

In one experiment, mice were fed an iodine-deficient diet that produced large goiters in two control ("untreated") groups of mice, whereas mice whose cages were held by the healer showed significantly less goiter development. In another experiment, which has been successfully replicated several times, equal-size patches of skin were removed from the backs of 300 mice. Mice whose cages were held by the healer showed a much faster rate of wound healing than did the control animals ($p < .01$).

Mice whose cages were held by skeptical medical students healed the most slowly of all three groups.

This PK explanation of psychic-healing phenomena has also been studied with plants. A state of "need" in the plants was induced by treating the seeds with a one percent sodium chloride solution. Salt treatment damages the seed and tends to inhibit sprouting and subsequent plant growth. However, seeds treated with saline solution that had been previously held by the healer for fifteen minutes showed significantly more subsequent growth than control seeds treated with solution not held by the healer. A chemical analysis of the hand-held saline solution revealed no difference between the hand-held and the control saline solutions in sodium concentrations or pH value.

In another experiment along these lines, Watkins and Watkins (1971) tested the ability of nine reputedly psychic subjects to hasten the resuscitation of anesthetized mice. Five of these subjects claimed to have healing abilities, and eight of the nine scored well on laboratory PK tests. On the average, the experimental mice (those concentrated on by the psychic subjects) awoke in 87 percent of the time taken by the control mice. Eight of the nine psychic subjects were able to induce a significantly shorter duration of anesthesia in their mice, whereas none of the three control subjects could produce this effect ($p < 10^{-5}$).

Another experiment, conducted by Schmeidler (1973), attempted to determine whether the effects of PK could be voluntarily controlled and localized in space. This time, instead of using living systems as targets, a talented psychic attempted to influence temperature-sensitive devices (thermistors) which were sealed into vacuum bottles and connected to an automatic recording device. The subject was asked to raise and lower the temperature of specific thermistors on demand, following a predetermined, counterbalanced sequence. The subject was successful at producing temperature changes in the desired direction over repeated trials. Sixteen trials made up an experimental session, and in seven out of ten sessions the temperature deviations of the sixteen trials were statistically significant. In five of these seven sessions, the probability was less than one in a thousand of chance fluctuations being responsible for the results. Curiously, a drop in the temperature recorded by one thermistor was often accompanied by a rise in air temperature in a different part of the room, as if the heat energy had somehow been transferred from one part of the room to another. The results suggest that PK may operate in accordance with the laws of thermodynamics.

## CONCLUSION

This brief review has only scratched the surface of the issues in collecting and interpreting parapsychological data. There is a great deal of evidence, which it has not been possible to review here in detail, that the psi process bears a lawful relation to personality and attitude, interest and motivation. Psi seems to be related to a host of other psychological variables. Spontaneous cases show that ESP may lie dormant for many years, a small voice that is not heeded above the demands of coping with everyday life, until a moment of overwhelming personal crisis. It is not possible to duplicate in the laboratory the crisis situation and the intense emotional involvement evident in spontaneous cases. Thus ESP experiments offer at best a shadow of the true nature of psi. And yet the scientific method has had great success in unraveling other mysteries of nature. Can it not be fruitfully applied to mysteries of human nature as well?

Of course, any experimental evidence is only as good as the conditions under which it was obtained. This is the reason for the meticulous attention to details of methodology in parapsychological research, given the importance of what we are trying to demonstrate.

If one accepts the evidence as valid, then how is it to be interpreted? At least four different aspects of psi functioning have been identified (clairvoyance, telepathy, precognition, and psychokinesis). But curiously they often seem to occur in the same individuals, and to be influenced by the same conditions. Once the existence of these discrete forms of psi had been demonstrated, it was no longer possible to interpret unequivocally the results of any ESP experiment in terms of only one psychic ability. The evidence in support of precognition using the "psychic-shuffle" technique could be explained, with somewhat less violation of causality in temporal relations, as clairvoyance by the card shuffler, or alternatively as PK effect on the cards or on the mechanical card-shuffling device. Psychokinesis results could be interpreted as involving precognition in the correct call of the die face before it actually came to rest. Telepathy could be seen either as unassisted clairvoyance on the part of the percipient, or conversely as a PK process exerted by the agent on the percipient's brain cells, causing him to "perceive" the correct answer.

These overlapping theoretical explanations of psi phenomena give rise to a feeling that psi phenomena might not actually be discrete classes of events, involving different processes and mechanisms. Instead, psi ability might be a unitary phenomenon. Our thinking about the different aspects of psi may be more a consequence of the different methods we use to elicit them than an indication of any fundamental differences in the nature of the psi process itself.

Those who have tried to theorize about the nature of the psi process have taken many different approaches. At first the search centered on physical conditions and variables. But tests with Faraday cages (Vasiliev, 1963) have ruled out most of the frequencies of the electromagnetic spectrum as "carriers." Psi does not obey the inverse square law; thus one cannot speak of it as a kind of "mental radio." Psi appears to be independent of space and time; therefore no presently known form of physical energy can account for the observed data. Speculation has turned to the esoteric fringe of contemporary physics (Oteri, 1975). Paradoxically, some theorists in quantum mechanics do not seem to feel that ESP violates any physical laws at all!

Building on a quasi-physical approach, Murphy (1945) and Roll (1966a) have speculated on the existence of interpersonal "psi fields." More within a mainstream psychological tradition, Roll (1966b) has proposed that psi information may be mediated by the personal memory structure. Stanford has developed a theory relating to unconscious motivation (1974a,b). W. G. Braud (1975) described a "psi-conducive syndrome" characterized by relaxation and imagery, and Honorton (1977) has emphasized the importance of "internal attention states." These theories are based on a noise-reduction model, which allows the "weak" psi signal more access to processing capacity (Irwin, 1978a,b).

Yet the final word has not yet been uttered in these debates. As the human race begins to explore outer space, this aspect of our inner space still remains a mystery. We search for other forms of intelligent life elsewhere in the galaxy, but we have not yet fulfilled Socrates' command to "Know thyself."

## REFERENCES

Braud, Lendell W., and Braud, William G. "Further Studies of Relaxation as a Psi-Conducive State." *Journal of the American Society for Psychical Research* 68 (1974): 229–245.

Braud, Lendell W., and Braud, William G. "Clairvoyance Tests Following Exposure to a Psi-Conducive Tape Recording." *Journal of Research in Psi Phenomena* 2(1) (1977): 10–21.

Braud, William G. "Psi-Conducive States." *Journal of Communication* 25 (1975): 142–152.

Camp, Burton H. Statement in notes section. *Journal of Parapsychology* 1 (1937): 305.

Carpenter, James C. "Intrasubject and Subject-Agent Effects in ESP Experiments." In *Handbook of Parapsychology*, edited by B. B. Wolman. New York. Van Nostrand Reinhold, 1977.

Edge, Hoyt. "The Effect of the Laying on of Hands on an Enzyme: An Attempted Replication." In *Research in Parapsychology 1979*, edited by W. G. Roll. Metuchen, N.J.: Scarecrow Press, 1980, pp. 137–139.

Epstein, Seymour. "The Stability of Behavior. II. Implications for Psychological Research." *American Psychologist* 35 (1980): 790–806.

Grad, Bernard. "Some Biological Effects of the 'Laying-on-of-Hands': A Review of Experiments with Animals and Plants." *Journal of the American Society for Psychical Research* 59 (1965): 95–127.

Grad, Bernard. "The Biological Effects of the 'Laying-on-of-Hands' on Animals and Plants: Some Implications for Biology." In *Parapsychology: Its Relation to Physics, Biology, Psychology and Psychiatry*, edited by Gertrude R. Schmeidler. Metuchen, N.J.: Scarecrow Press, 1976, pp. 76–89.

Honorton, Charles. "Psi and Internal Attention States." In *Handbook of Parapsychology*, edited by B. B. Wolman. New York: Van Nostrand Reinhold, 1977, pp. 435–472.

Honorton, Charles. "Psi and Internal Attention States: Information Retrieval in the Ganzfeld."

In *Psi and States of Awareness*, edited by B. Shapin and L. Coly. New York: Parapsychology Foundation, 1978, pp. 79–100.

Irwin, Harvey J. "ESP and the Human Information Processing System." *Journal of the American Society for Psychical Research* 72 (1978a): 111–126.

Irwin, Harvey J. "Psi, Attention and Processing Capacity." *Journal of the American Society for Psychical Research* 72 (1978b): 301–314.

Markwick, Betty. "The Soal-Goldney Experiments with Basil Shackleton: New Evidence of Data Manipulation." *Proceedings of the Society for Psychical Research* 56 (1978): 249–277.

Murphy, Gardner. "Field Theory and Survival." *Journal of the American Society for Psychical Research* 39 (1945): 181–209.

Nicol, J. Fraser and Humphrey, Betty M. "The Repeatability Problem in ESP-Personality Research." *Journal of the American Society for Psychical Research* 49 (1955): 125–156.

Oteri, Laura., ed. *Quantum Physics and Parapsychology.* New York: Parapsychology Foundation, 1975.

Palmer, John. "Scoring in ESP Tests as a Function of Belief in ESP. I. The Sheep-Goat Effect." *Journal of the American Society for Psychical Research* 65 (1971): 373–408.

Palmer, John. "Attitudes and Personality Traits in Experimental ESP Research." In *Handbook of Parapsychology*, edited by B. B. Wolman. New York: Van Nostrand Reinhold, 1977, pp. 175–201.

Rao, K. Ramakrishna. "The Preferential Effect in ESP." *Journal of Parapsychology* 26 (1962): 252–259.

Rhine, J. B. "How Does One Decide about ESP?" *American Psychologist* 14 (1959): 606–608.

Rhine, J. B. "Telepathy and Other Untestable Hypotheses." *Journal of Parapsychology* 38 (1974a): 137–153.

Roll, William G. "The Psi Field." *Proceedings of the Parapsychological Association (1957–1964)* 1 (1966a): 32–65.

Roll, William G. "ESP and Memory." *International Journal of Neuropsychiatry* 2 (1966b): 505–521.

Scherer, Wallace B. "Spontaneity as a Factor in ESP." *Journal of Parapsychology* 12 (1948): 126–147.

Schmeidler, Gertrude R. "PK Effects upon Continuously Recorded Temperature." *Journal of the American Society for Psychical Research* 67 (1973): 325–340.

Schmidt, Helmut. "Clairvoyance Test with a Machine." *Journal of Parapsychology* 33 (1969a): 300–307.

Schmidt, Helmut. "Precognition of a Quantum Process." *Journal of Parapsychology* 33 (1969b): 99–109.

Schmidt, Helmut and Pantas, Lee. "Psi Tests with Internally Different Machines." *Journal of Parapsychology* 36 (1972): 222–232.

Shields, Eloise. "Comparison of Children's Guessing Ability (ESP) with Personality Characteristics." *Journal of Parapsychology* 26 (1962): 200–210.

Smith, M. J. "The Influence on Enzyme Growth by the 'Laying-on-of-Hands.' " In *The Dimensions of Healing: A Symposium.* Los Altos, Calif.: Academy of Parapsychology and Medicine, 1972, pp. 110–120. See also *Human Dimensions* 1 (1972): 15–19.

Stanford, Rex G. "An Experimentally Testable Model for Spontaneous Psi Events. I. Extrasensory Events." *Journal of the American Society for Psychical Research* 68 (1974a): 34–57.

Stanford, Rex G. "An Experimentally Testable Model for Spontaneous Psi Events. II. Psychokinetic Events." *Journal of the American Society for Psychical Research* 68 (1974b): 321–356.

Tart, Charles T. *Learning to Use Extrasensory Perception.* Chicago: University of Chicago Press, 1976.

Vasiliev, L. L. *Experiments in Mental Suggestion.* Church Crookham, Hampshire, England: Institute for the Study of Mental Images, 1963.

Watkins, Graham K., and Watkins, Anita M. "Possible PK Influence on the Resuscitation of Anesthetized Mice." *Journal of Parapsychology* 35 (1971): 257–272.

# NO

## Susan Blackmore

# THE LURE OF THE PARANORMAL

Why do so many people believe in the paranormal? The answer to this question, and the recent research exploring it, tell us little about the paranormal itself but much about the way our minds work.

There have been many surveys of belief in the paranormal. The proportion claiming belief varies with the sample and the question asked but is usually well over half. More interesting is the main reason given: that people have had psychic experiences themselves.

There are three obvious explanations for this. First, they might really have experienced the paranormal. If true, we need to rewrite much of science, and soon. Secondly, they might be making it up. For anyone who has had these experiences this does not seem a plausible explanation. Thirdly, they might be misinterpreting perfectly normal events—suffering from what we might call a paranormal illusion.

We often see things that are not there. Stunning visual illusions happen because of the way our visual systems try to make sense of the world. Even when we know how the illusion works, it does not go away. The illusions are the price we have to pay for a perceptual system that does very well in a confusing world. Paranormal experiences may be analogous; the price we have to pay for the way our brains look for connections in chance and probability.

In describing psychic experiences, people typically claim that they dreamed of something that came true or they "knew something was wrong" with their mother, sister or great-grandfather, and it was. In other words, something happened that was far too unlikely to have been "just chance". So it must have been psychic.

Put like that, it is easy to see how a mistake can happen. The conclusion that the event was paranormal depends on a probability judgment and people are notoriously bad at making them. If you think you are an exception try some of the questions in the Box.

Psychologists have long known that people use a variety of heuristics [techniques of learning or problem-solving using experimental, trial-and-error, feedback, and other self-educating methods], not mathematics, to guess prob-

From Susan Blackmore, "The Lure of the Paranormal," *The New Scientist*, vol. 127 (September 22, 1990). Copyright © 1990 by *New Scientist*. Reprinted by permission.

abilities. These heuristics include "representativeness" and "availability"—the ease with which examples can be brought to mind. Such errors might not be so bad except that people also tend to have great confidence in their erroneous judgments, even in the face of contrary evidence. Could it be that all belief in the paranormal comes from misjudgments of probability? Recent evidence suggests that it may be so.

Paranormal phenomena fall into two classes. The first is ESP, or extrasensory perception—the pseudo-sensory aspect of the paranormal. It includes telepathy, clairvoyance and precognition. If this does not seem to be probability in action, consider an example.

The most common form of spontaneous ESP is the dream that comes true. Imagine you dream of your friend Maximillian. In the dream you are at his funeral and his friends and relatives are weeping at his death. The next day you hear that Maximillian died that very night. For most people this seems too much of a coincidence to be just chance.

The problem with chance is that it is very hard to understand. In the case of the dream, could we work out the chances? Trying to do so will show up some of the problems.

How often do you dream of your friend dying? You would probably say you never had that dream before. So let us take a conservative estimate and assume that you have such a dream once in a lifetime. Next we need to know how likely it is that man died the same day as your dream. Or do we?

Thinking this way we are already committing the most obvious but easily overlooked fallacy. It all depends on how much information you have before you start. If you had woken from the dream,

immediately written it down, sent it off to the Society for Psychical Research, and if you had never done that before, then you would be justified in asking "how likely is it that Maximillian will die now?" Naturally the answer would be "very unlikely" and you might need to seek some alternative explanation to "just chance".

But it is far more likely that you noticed the coincidence only when you heard about his death. So this kind of coincidence might have happened to anyone on any day. Now the calculation is different. How often would you expect anyone to dream of a friend dying the night that it happened?

Statistician Christopher Scott has analysed it this way. There are about 55 million people in Britain and they live about 70 years each. If each has one such dream in a lifetime there should be 2000 every night. Also about 2000 people die in each 24 hours. So there will be 4 million coincidences among 55 million people. In other words such an "amazing" coincidence will be expected about once every two weeks. No further explanation is required but try to believe that if it happens to you. As Scott puts it: "You, if you're human at all, will conclude that there's cause and effect there. You can't regard yourself as just one among 55 million."

So most people reject the chance hypothesis and if they can find no "normal" alternative they will turn to the idea of ESP.

But what kind of explanation is that? I would say none at all. Psychical research has been under way for more than 100 years, and parapsychology (its more laboratory based counterpart) for more than 50. Yet they have made virtually no progress in understanding what, if anything, ESP is. There are certainly some impressive experiments. Recent fully automated ganzfeld tests at Princeton are an example.

The idea is to isolate the subject from ordinary sensory input by covering the eyes with halved ping-pong balls and playing white noise through headphones while they relax on a comfortable bed and describe their imagery. Meanwhile a "sender" is looking at a target picture chosen randomly from a set of possible targets. After the half hour or so is over the subject has to try to match up the imagery experienced with each of the pictures and choose which was the target.

Earlier experiments were criticised for all sorts of shortcomings but the recent ones have been automated at every stage of the procedure—and still the subjects seem to pick the right picture more often than expected by chance. (Here we are back to chance again.) There are some who still argue that the results could be spurious and this argument is not likely to be easily resolved. But either way this still does not give us an explanation. If there is an "extrachance" effect here, what is it?

We get nowhere by saying that something happened "by ESP". We have no acceptable theory of what ESP is, what constraints apply to it or when and how we can expect it to operate. After a century of research on ESP, it is still negatively defined. To say that the dream was due to ESP is only to admit our ignorance.

So people who experience amazing coincidences are either subject to some totally mysterious new phenomenon, or they are suffering from an illusion of probability. How could we find out?

Tom Troscianko and I, at the University of Bristol, hypothesised that if the origin of belief in ESP lies in misjudgments of probability, then we would expect believers (usually referred to as "sheep") to be less accurate in their probability judgments than goats (disbelievers). This we tested by giving schoolchildren, university students, medical workers and others, a set of computerised tests (see Box).

In general the goats did better at these tasks, as we predicted, and as is consistent with the idea (but does not prove) that the sheeps' errors are responsible for their belief in ESP. Interestingly, the university students did no better than the schoolchildren which implies that these judgments are not improved by education. Another well-known error lies in "subjective random generation". Put simply, most people have no idea of how random numbers behave. When they are asked to generate a string of random numbers many people avoid repeating the same digit twice—it is as though they think that this would not be random.

At the University of Zurich in Switzerland, Peter Brugger and his colleagues have been exploring the relationship between this error and belief in the paranormal. In keeping with our hypothesis they found that sheep avoided pairs more than goats did—in both real ESP experiments and in tests of random string generation. They suggest that most, if not all, of the major findings in parapsychology can be attributed to errors in random number generation or response bias.

For example, it is claimed that young children do better at ESP tests—the children are more biased. Extroverts apparently do better at ESP—they are more biased than introverts. Brain injury and psychiatric disorder are associated with the paranormal—and also with increased bias. And finally there is the famous decline effect: that ESP scores are found to decrease with longer trials—so does bias.

---

## TEST YOUR MENTAL POWERS ON THESE PROBABILITY PUZZLES

1) A hat contains a large number of pieces of paper with the numbers 1, 2, 3, 4 and 5 on them in equal proportions. Write a list of 30 numbers in the order you think they might be drawn from the hat.

2) A hat contains 10 red and 10 blue Smarties. I pull out 10 and 8 are red. Which am I more likely to get next?

3) A box contains green and yellow buttons in unknown proportions. I take out 10 and 8 are yellow. Which am I more likely to get next?

4) In the last four matches between Mytholmroyd Athletics and Giggleswick United, Mytholmroyd have kicked off first every time, on the toss of a coin. Which is more likely to kick off next time?

5) How many people would you need to have at a party to have an even chance that two of them will have the same birthday (not counting the year of birth)?

These questions are based on those used in the Bristol experiments. The first question asks for a string of random numbers. A truly random string would, on average, contain just under 6 repeats of the same digit. Most people produce far fewer repeats. The answers to the others are blue, yellow, either and 22. Most people give much higher answers for question 5. The reason may be that they are thinking of it in terms of the question: "How many people would you need to have an even chance that one has the same birthday as me?" This egocentric view underlines much of our confusion over probabilities.

---

Of course this could explain the parapsychological findings only if there were inadequacies in the randomisation procedures used. In a perfect ESP experiment the subjects' bias should make no difference. So to refute this idea parapsychologists will have to show that their findings appear just as strongly in the best controlled ESP tests.

The other major kind of paranormal effect is psychokinesis (PK) or "mind over matter". This may seem even further from being a matter of probability, but oddly it is not.

Imagine you are driving along the road in a hurry towards some red traffic lights. You ought to slow down. If they stay red you will be going too fast. "Change, change" you are tempted to mutter, as though this would make any difference. If they do change at that precise moment it is tempting to feel that you have made it happen.

This feeling of being in control can easily overwhelm logic. The most bizarre example I ever experienced was taking part in a ritual to make the sun rise at dawn on Midsummer Day. After hours of chanting and processing, when the sun popped up, dead on schedule, we really felt as though we had made it happen!

This temptation to attribute random events to one's own actions is called the illusion of control. First described by Ellen Langer, it appears in all sorts of behaviours. In a way it is the equivalent of the tendency to want to make sense of coincidences. We learn how to control the world around us by observing coincidences between our own actions and the things that happen. Just as with visual illusions, the processes that help us to learn carry a cost—we sometimes associate things that are actually unconnected.

Could it be that this underlies a belief in having PK powers? The idea is simple. A coincidence happens between an action we make and some external event. We make a connection between them and look for an explanation. If there is no obvious normal one (I wasn't touching the thing, whistling at it, predicting its actions by inference and so on) then it must be paranormal. So I have experienced PK.

We may be disappointed if we look to parapsychology for an explanation of the coincidence. The most recent hope for evidence of PK lies in experiments on random number generators. A computer is typically connected to a source of random numbers. A subject then attempts to bias the output in one direction or another. Dean Radin, at Princeton University, recently analysed all 597 such experiments in the literature. Many of the experiments included a control condition in which no one was trying to influence anything. He found that, "results showed effects conforming to chance expectation in control conditions and unequivocal non-chance effects in experimental conditions" and he took this as evidence of a "consciousness-related anomaly in random physical systems".

Does this point to a possible explanation for people's PK experiences? There are two issues here. One is the size of the effect which, in this database, was so tiny that it is extremely doubtful anyone would notice it in everyday life. In this sense parapsychology fails to provide an explanation. Also this research provides no theory as to how or why the random numbers might behave differently when someone is trying to influence them. It is not even clear why consciousness should be involved.

If the alternative is that people are misjudging probabilities, bow could this be tested? We hypothesised that sheep should be more prone to an illusion of control than goats. This would then lead them more often to think they had exerted PK.

Previous experiments had shown that sheep thought they had more control in a PK task. However, if sheep believe they actually have PK (and we cannot rule out the possibility that they do) then it is quite reasonable for them to think they are in control. So this result is only to be expected. We wanted to know whether the greater illusion of control would also appear in tasks which did not appear to be PK tasks.

At the University of Bristol we asked people to play a computer game where they had to stop a flipping coin on the desired face. They pressed a button and then the coin stopped flipping either a fixed number of times after the press, or a random number of times, although the subjects were not aware of this difference. We predicted that in the random conditions (which amounts to PK) sheep would still think they had more control than goats. This is indeed what we found.

We also found something else much more interesting. We asked the subjects, if they imagined doing the task with their eyes closed, how many hits they would get. The average should be 10 and indeed most of the goats said 10 but less than half the sheep did, with an average of 7.9. We called this the "chance baseline shift".

The implications of this are quite interesting. If someone thinks that by chance they will get 7 hits and they actually get 10, they are going to think they have done very well and look for an explanation. Obviously no reasonable explanation will be found since only chance was operating. So the obvious leap is to the paranormal.

I think all belief in the paranormal may come about this way: as an illusion of causality. It is not stupid to have apparently psychic experiences, any more than it is to see visual illusions. It just reflects the way our minds work. So does the paranormal "really" exist? I have no idea. I can only say that the fact that so many people have psychic experiences is no evidence that it does.

# CHALLENGE QUESTIONS
## Is Parapsychology a Credible Science?

1. Have you ever had an unusual experience that you attributed to paranormal phenomena? If so, how would Blackmore criticize this attribution?

2. Blackmore criticizes the available research on paranormal phenomena. What do you see as the weaknesses of this research? How can the research be improved?

3. Why do you think people sometimes attribute unusual experiences to ESP and other paranormal phenomena?

4. Why do you think many psychologists are unwilling to believe in paranormal phenomena?

# CONTRIBUTORS
# TO THIS VOLUME

## EDITOR

**BRENT SLIFE** is a clinical psychologist and a professor of psychology at Baylor University in Waco, Texas. A fellow of the American Psychological Association, he has authored over 60 articles and books, his most recent being *Time and Psychological Explanation* (State University of New York Press, 1993), which describes the overlooked influence of linear time on mainstream psychology. Recently designated the Outstanding Research Professor at Baylor University, he is also the editor of the *Journal of Theoretical and Philosophical Psychology* and serves in editorial capacities on the *Journal of Mind and Behavior* and *Theory and Psychology.* He received a Ph.D. from Purdue University, where he and Joseph Rubinstein, his coeditor in the previous seven editions of *Taking Sides: Clashing Views on Controversial Psychological Issues,* began the dialogue approach to psychology that is the basis of this volume.

## STAFF

Marguerite L. Egan    Program Manager
Brenda S. Filley    Production Manager
Whit Vye    Designer
Libra Ann Cusack    Typesetting Supervisor
Juliana Arbo    Typesetter
David Brackley    Copy Editor
David Dean    Administrative Editor
Diane Barker    Editorial Assistant
Richard Tietjen    Systems Manager
Shawn Callahan    Graphics

## AUTHORS

**ALAN C. ACOCK** is a professor in and the chair of the Department of Human Development and Family Sciences at Oregon State University in Corvallis, Oregon.

**NANCY E. ADLER** is a professor in the Department of Psychology at the University of California, San Francisco.

**DANIEL R. ANDERSON** is a professor of psychology at the University of Massachusetts–Amherst. He has written numerous articles on the television viewing habits of children.

**MARCIA ANGELL** is a pathologist and a lecturer in the Department of Social Medicine at the Harvard Medical School.

**ELLIOT ARONSON** is a professor of psychology at the University of California, Santa Cruz. He was recently elected to the American Academy of Arts and Sciences.

**ELLEN BASS** is a nationally recognized counselor, lecturer, and professional trainer who works with survivors of child sexual abuse.

**SUSAN BAXTER** is a psychotherapist in the Department of Psychiatry at the Alaska Area Native Medical Service in Anchorage, Alaska.

**SUSAN BLACKMORE** is a professor in the Departments of Psychology at the University of Bristol and at the University of Bath in England.

**PATRICK CARNES** is the primary architect of an inpatient program for sexual dependency at the Golden Valley Health Center in Minneapolis, Minnesota.

**BRYCE J. CHRISTENSEN** is the director of the Rockford Institute Center on the Family in America in Rockford, Illinois.

**F. M. CHRISTENSEN** is a professor in the Department of Philosophy at the University of Alberta in Edmonton, Alberta, Canada.

**VICTOR CLINE** is a professor emeritus of psychology at the University of Utah in Salt Lake City, Utah. His research interests include media effects and person perception issues.

**JOHN R. COLE** is an anthropologist at the University of Massachusetts–Amherst. He has long been an advocate of improved science education and a critic of creation science.

**LEE COLEMAN** is a psychiatrist in Berkeley, California, and a critic of the role of mental health professionals in legal settings. His current research interests focus on false accusations of child sexual abuse.

**ROGER CRISP** has published several articles on practical ethics.

**RAYMOND R. CROWE** is a clinical psychiatrist and a professor in the Department of Psychiatry at the University of Iowa College of Medicine in Iowa City, Iowa.

**HENRY P. DAVID** is the director of the Transnational Family Research Institute in Bethesda, Maryland, and a consultant to the American Psychiatric Association and the World Health Organization.

**LAURA DAVIS** is an expert on healing from child sexual abuse and a nationally recognized workshop leader.

**DAVID H. DEMO** is an associate professor in the Department of Sociology at Virginia Polytechnic Institute and State University in Blacksburg, Virginia. His research focuses on the influences of family structure and family relations on parents and children.

**BERNARD DIXON** is the vice president of the General Section of the British Association for the Advancement of Science and the chair of the Programme Planning Committee of the Edinburgh International Science Festival.

**HERBERT FINGARETTE** is a professor emeritus of philosophy at the University of California, Santa Barbara. He has also served as an alcoholism and addiction consultant to the World Health Organization.

**LEONARD ROY FRANK** is a cofounder of the Network Against Psychiatric Assault (NAPA) in San Francisco and Berkeley, California, and a member of the Concerned Citizens Opposing Electroshock in San Francisco.

**PETER HERMAN** is a professor of psychology at the University of Toronto in Toronto, Ontario, Canada. His research interests include cognitive, social, and emotional issues surrounding food intake.

**LIZ HODGKINSON** is a freelance writer whose book *Sex is Not Compulsory* established her as an expert on the subject of sexual and other relationships.

**RAY HOSKINS** is an alcoholism and drug abuse counselor at Prevention, Intervention, and Treatment Services in Indianapolis, Indiana. He is also a member of the National Association of Alcoholism and Drug Abuse Counselors.

**ARTHUR R. JENSEN** is a professor of educational psychology at the University of California, Berkeley. His research interests focus on psychometrics, behavioral genetics, and theories of intelligence.

**DOREEN KIMURA** is a neuropsychologist and a professor in the Department of Psychology at the University of Western Ontario in London, Ontario, Canada. Her research interests focus on the brain and hormonal bases of human intellectual abilities.

**MARTY KLEIN** is a California-licensed marriage and family therapist. He also serves on the national board of the Society for the Scientific Study of Sex.

**MICHAEL S. LEVY** is the clinical director of behavioral medicine at Southwood Community Hospital in Norfolk, Massachusetts, and an instructor in psychology at the Harvard Medical School in Cambridge, Massachusetts.

**BRENDA N. MAJOR** is a professor of psychology and the director of the Social Psychology Program at the State University of New York at Buffalo. Her current research interests focus on the psychological consequences of prejudice, gender, and self-esteem.

**HARA ESTROFF MARANO** is the executive editor for *Psychology Today*.

**JANET POLIVY** is a professor of psychology and psychiatry in the Erindale College of the University of Toronto in Mississauga, Ontario, Canada, and a research associate in psychiatry at Toronto

General Hospital. Her research interests include dieting and eating behaviors.

**ANTHONY R. PRATKANIS** is an associate professor of psychology at the University of California, Santa Cruz. His testimony on subliminal persuasion at the trial of CBS Records/Judas Priest was instrumental to the defense.

**RUTH REINSEL** is the Clinical Assistant Psychologist in the Department of Anesthesiology and Critical Care Medicine at the Memorial Sloan-Kettering Cancer Center in New York City.

**FRANK RIESSMAN** is a professor of education at Queens College and a professor of sociology in the graduate school at the City University of New York, both in New York City. He is also the director of the National Self-Help Clearinghouse.

**SUSAN H. ROTH** is a professor of psychology at Duke University in Durham, North Carolina. Her clinical and research interests focus on adult survivors of sexual trauma.

**VINCENT M. RUE** is a codirector of the Institute for Pregnancy Loss in Portsmouth, New Hampshire.

**NANCY F. RUSSO** is a professor of psychology and women's studies in the Department of Psychology at Arizona State University in Tempe, Arizona, and a fellow of the American Psychological Association.

**ALBERT SHANKER** is the president of the American Federation of Teachers in Washington, D.C

**ANNE C. SPECKHARD** is a clinician, a researcher, and a consultant practicing in Alexandria, Virginia, who has consulted on several postpartum stress research projects.

**ROBERT J. STERNBERG** is the IBM Professor of Psychology and Education at Yale University and a member of the Educational Testing Service Board of Visitors.

**CAROL TAVRIS** is a social psychologist and author based in Los Angeles, California, and a member of the American Psychological Association.

**GEORGE E. VAILLANT** is the director of Adult Development at Harvard University in Cambridge, Massachusetts, and a recipient of the Jellinck Prize for Alcoholism Research.

**JUDITH S. WALLERSTEIN** is a lecturer in social welfare at the University of California, Berkeley, and the executive director of the Center for the Family in Transition.

**MARIE WINN** has written 12 books for parents and children, including *Children Without Childhood* (Pantheon Books, 1983).

**GAIL E. WYATT** is a professor in the Department of Psychology at the University of California, Los Angeles.

**STEVEN ZAK** is a research attorney for the California Superior Court in the County of Los Angeles. He has written about animals with regard to ethics and the law for numerous publications.

**EDWARD F. ZIGLER** is the Sterling Professor of Psychology, the chair of the psychology section of the Child Study Center, and the director of the Bush Center in Child Development and Social Policy at Yale University in New Haven, Connecticut.

# INDEX